RENEGADES

ANN MATTHEWS

RENEGADES

IRISH REPUBLICAN WOMEN 1900-1922

MERCIER PRESS
IRISH PUBLISHER – IRISH STORY

MERCIER PRESS
Cork
www.mercierpress.ie

Trade enquiries to CMD BookSource,
55a Spruce Avenue, Stillorgan Industrial Park,
Blackrock, County Dublin

© Ann Matthews, 2010

ISBN: 978 1 85635 684 8

10 9 8 7 6 5 4 3 2 1

A CIP record for this title is available from the British Library

To Brendan

Printed and bound in the EU.

CONTENTS

Acknowledgements

This book is based in part on my PhD dissertation 'Women activists in Irish republican politics 1900–1941' which was completed in 2004 under the supervision of Professor Vincent Comerford at NUI Maynooth. Through the period of research and analysis of my findings Professor Comerford gave me unstinting support. Since I completed the PhD, I have carried on researching and discovered new archive material, which led me to re-evaluate some of my earlier work and in this I have been encouraged by Professor Comerford. I am deeply appreciative to him for the time and support he has given me over the years.

I would like to thank the staff of the History Department at NUI Maynooth, who have given me total support in my work over the years. Here I would also like to mention Dr Sinead McEnaney, who is a colleague and friend who over the years has listened to me talk about my work and gave the book its terrific title. Another friend and colleague is Rita Edwards, who encouraged me to keep participating by giving me a forum to speak about my work.

My introduction to women in republican politics took place in the Military Archives at Cathal Brugha Barracks in Dublin, when the late Commandant Peter Young introduced me to the Irish Civil War Captured Documents. He was keen that the story of women should be explored and when I saw the material I was hooked and he effectively introduced me to a life-long journey of research and investigation. I will always remember and appreciate him for that gift. During the long period of this study Commandant Victor Laing and his staff have continued to support me, and their professional interest, encouragement and friendship has sustained me through the years. Their support, both professional and personal is something that I appreciate very much.

Aside from the Military Archive, I used the sources from a wide range of archives. These were the Allen Library, the Cork City Museum, Cork Archives, Dublin City Library Archive, the Garda Archive Dublin, University of Limerick Archive, the National Archive, Dublin, the National Archives in Kew, London, the National Library Dublin, the Russell Library at NUI Maynooth, the College of Physicians, the Quaker Museum and University College Dublin Archive. Without exception, the staff in these repositories were supportive. Here I would like to mention a conundrum that I came across recently regarding the RIC files held in London. I have discovered that permission to use these files lies with the Garda Archive in Dublin, and so thank you to Inspector Patrick McGee of the Garda Archive for his permission to use this material.

I cannot finish without thanking family and good friends who during a time of personal crisis have given me absolute support, which enabled me to pursue my work. They include my brother Séan Matthews and my lifelong friend Rita Donnelly, who is like a sister to me. Other friends who kept me active are Jim and Peggy Cumberton, Tony Donnelly, Margo Dalton, Henry Dent, Breda Halligan, Kathleen Murphy, Moira Maguire, Nora Purcell and Fifi Smith, all in whose friendship I feel blessed.

Ben Halligan, my late husband, died a year after my PhD dissertation was finished. He was an immensely intelligent man who possessed the gift of a wonderful sense of humour, which was wicked and often bordered on the anarchic. He was a talented man who taught me how to use computers and brought me from the dark ages of taking notes with pencil and paper to the wonders of the computer. In addition, I learned a great deal about international military history from him. Here I would like mention my stepdaughter Suzy Halligan, who inherited many of her father's qualities, in particular his determination and courage: she, like him, is an inspiration to me.

Finally, a thank you to my daughter Alison, her husband Tommy and my wonderful grandson Benjamin Emmett, whose love and support I treasure.

ABBREVIATIONS

AARIR	American Association for Recognition of the Irish Republic
ACRI	American Committee for Relief in Ireland
ALD	Allen Library Dublin
BMH	Bureau of Military History
BLPCI	British Labour Party Commission to Ireland
CPIVD	Committee for the Protection of Ireland from Venereal Disease
DORA	Defence of the Realm Act
DWC	Dublin Watch Committee
INAA	Irish National Aid Association
INAAVDF	Irish National Aid Association and Volunteer Dependents' Fund
INE	Inghinidhe na hÉireann
IRA	Irish Republican Army
ISCVD	Irish Society for the Combating of the Spread of Venereal Disease
ITC	Irish Transvaal Committee
ITGWU	Irish Transport & General Workers' Union
IVDF	Irish Volunteer Dependants' Fund
IWC	Irish White Cross
IWFL	Irish Women's Franchise League
IWWU	Irish Women Workers' Union
JAN	Jeunesse Antisémite et Nationaliste
LDC	Ladies Distribution Committee
LGB	Local Government Board (Ireland)
LSDC	Ladies School Dinner Committee
NAI	National Archives Ireland
NDU	North Dublin Union
NLI	National Library of Ireland
PRO	Public Record Office, London
SDU	South Dublin Union
SFF	Sinn Féin Fund
Sinn Féin SC	Sinn Féin Standing Committee
WDIC	Women Delegates to the All Ireland Conference
WNHA	Women's National Health Association

INTRODUCTION

Within the existing body of work on Irish history, there is a lack of real engagement with women's participation within the rise of the nationalist and republican movement from 1900–1921. This is for the most part, due to very effective, though misleading, promotion of two female figures in the iconography of women republicans – Maud Gonne MacBride and Countess de Markievicz.[1] This book explores the role of the numerous women who were active in both the nationalist and republican movements. Their story is explored within the changing cultural and political landscape of Irish politics from the start of the twentieth century to the signing of the Anglo-Irish Treaty in 1921 and the ensuing split in the republican movement in 1922.

From the late nineteenth century, women played a major role in the rapidly growing cultural nationalist movement. Auxiliary ladies committees were formed within several major cultural and political associations, which allowed their members not only to influence the development of the thinking of these associations, but also enabled the women to circumvent the Victorian social mores of the period, in particular the one that deemed it improper for unmarried women to mix freely in the company of men. By 1900, associate ladies committees interlinked at various levels, coming together to found Inghinidhe na hÉireann. The ethos of this organisation was purely cultural, but its importance lies in the fact that it was the first autonomous all-female nationalist organisation.

In 1905, when Arthur Griffith founded the Sinn Féin party, women were beginning to emerge in politics in their own right and this new party encouraged their participation. One of the most

formidable and underestimated women in nationalist history, Jennie
Wyse Power, joined the party and by 1908 she was on its executive
committee. Also in this first decade of the new millennium, women
were exerting their influence in other movements. For example,
Hanna Sheehy Skeffington and Margaret Cousins founded the
Irish Women's Franchise League in 1908. Three years later in
1911, working-class women had an introduction to politics when
Delia Larkin formed the Irish Women Workers' Union. All these
developments led to some interesting developments in the history
of Irish nationalism and republicanism, as these women came
from disparate backgrounds and were often diametrically opposed
in terms of political ideology. The movements collaborated with
great success, most notably in 1913 when they worked together
during the Dublin Lockout, serving food to the children of the
workers, while simultaneously proselytising their specific political
agenda. The collaboration of these women boded well for the Irish
women's political movement, because it appeared to suggest that
these women could transcend their class and political differences
in a common cause.

After 1913, the political scene changed, with the rise of the
Volunteer movement in Ireland and the emergence of Cumann na
mBan, which saw itself as an associate ladies committee operating
within the ambit of the Irish Volunteer movement. When the
Irish National Volunteers split in September 1914, a minority of
the members kept the Irish Volunteer organisation going. This
new group was avowedly militant and committed absolutely to
a separatist nationalist agenda. On Easter Monday 1916, when
the rebel army marched out to challenge the might of the British
Empire, Cumann na mBan and the women associated with the
Irish Citizen Army at Liberty Hall formed an integral part of this
army.

Following the collapse of the rebellion, women continued to
play an important role in the nationalist movement. The Ladies

Distribution Committee, which was set up to help administer the Irish National Aid Association and Volunteer Dependents' Fund, financially supported the widows, children, mothers and sisters of rebels, and this gave the women involved a major role within the growing separatist movement. In addition, it enabled the leading politically oriented women to claim a significant place in the post-1916 republican movement.

Meanwhile, women were once again seeking an active political role. In 1917, Dr Kathleen Lynn led the pro-active pursuit of significant positions for women in the reformed Sinn Féin party. A lobby group known initially as the Women Delegates to the All Ireland Conference of 19 April 1917 was formed and began a campaign to have a clause inserted into the new Sinn Féin constitution to give equal status to women. This was successful and it convinced the political women that a new Ireland held the promise of opportunity.

Cumann na mBan took a different path from the political women and changed their constitution to reflect this separation, embedding the organisation more firmly within the military sphere of republicanism. They inserted a programme of 'Military Activities' into their constitution that effectively subsumed the organisation within the ambit of the Volunteers. From this point on, there was a dual aspect to female participation in republican politics, one military and the other political. In this the women were mirroring the political men of Sinn Féin and the soldiers of the Irish Volunteers.

In January 1919, the successful candidates of the 1918 election convened the Provisional Republican Dáil Éireann and a new phase of the struggle began. In July 1919, the Lord Lieutenant, Lord French, proscribed Sinn Féin, the IRA, Cumann na mBan and the Gaelic League, and consequently they operated underground. During the following two years, as the fighting escalated it drew the whole population into the chaos of war. During this time the

women within the civilian population suffered greatly as they were
subjected to all kinds of abuse by both sides in the conflict. This
was effectively a 'war on women' and it terrorised them almost
beyond endurance. Now in formal positions within the republican
movement, the elite women remained largely ignorant of this
because, like their male counterparts, they were secure in their
position within the new political power structure and had lost
touch with the reality of the lives of the civilian population. This
abuse of women within the general population is explored using
various reports and commissions of investigation into the situation
in Ireland at that time.

By July 1921, the Truce was declared between the British
government and the Dáil. A period of relative peace followed,
giving the IRA and Cumann na mBan time to reassess their
respective organisations. During the period of relative quiet, both
organisations experienced an increase in membership. However,
when the Anglo-Irish Treaty was signed in London in December
1921, the republican political establishment disintegrated as the
bitterness of division and petty personal rivalry emerged in the
chamber of Dáil Éireann. The assembly became the centre of
furious wrangling between those who believed the Treaty was a
good deal and others who believed the negotiation team who signed
it were traitors to the Irish Republic. As the reality of division
became clear, the women within the political elite added to the
already widening chasm. Like the men, the women were split over
whether to support the Treaty and in the end the bitter divisions
on this issue led to a split and the subsequent formation of the
pro-Treaty Cumann na Saoirse and a much reduced Cumann na
mBan.

The role of the women who were active in politics in Ireland
during the early part of the twentieth century is extremely
important, and it is vital that their story is looked at from a
politically inclusive perspective.

BUILDING THE FOUNDATION
1865–1900

During the 1890s in Ireland women began to emerge in a significant way in the escalating nationalist movement and by 1921 were accepted as an integral part of republican politics. While these women did break ground with their determination to gain access to public life, they did not instigate the idea of female participation in Irish politics. Rather, they built on the foundation that was created by the Fenian women and the Ladies' Land League.

Sylke Lehne in her study of the women who formed the Ladies Committee for the Relief of the State Prisoner's in October 1865 has presented a sound case, which is that the women who launched this committee set the precedent that the later generation of Irishwomen followed.[1] In September 1865, the British government began an offensive against the Fenian movement by raiding the premises of the Fenian newspaper, the *Irish People,* and arresting the staff. Following this, there were mass arrests and imprisonments of men from different areas of the country. These arrests left many families without an income and subsequently reduced them to destitution. Mary Jane O'Donovan Rossa and Letitia Luby gathered together the female relatives of the prominent Fenians and formed the Ladies Committee for the Relief of the State Prisoners. The women's first act was to publish an appeal for financial support for the destitute families of the men who had been imprisoned. According to Lehne, both women 'played a major role in the foundation of the committee while O'Donovan Rossa became secretary of the committee and Luby was the treasurer'.[2] The other members of the executive committee were Ellen and Mary O'Leary, Mrs Dowling, Catherine Mulcahy, Isabella Roantree and Jane Stephens.

Mary Jane O'Donovan Rossa (née Irwin) was born in Clonakilty, County Cork, in 1845. She married Jeremiah O'Donovan Rossa on 22 October 1864, becoming his third wife. O'Donovan Rossa at this time had five sons by his earlier marriages. Mary Jane 'gave her services free to the ladies committees until August 1866, when her own circumstances became difficult and she began to draw a salary of £2 a week from the fund'.[3] The committee raised money and supported many families and they tried to support the men in prison. This committee very quickly became an integral part of the Fenian movement and it was still collecting funds in the early part of the twentieth century. Sylke Lehne argued that this group of women laid the foundation on which later nationalist and republican women were able to build. She says, 'the work these women became involved in gave them the self-confidence which became the most important precondition for later women's movements'.[4]

The Ladies' Land League was founded in New York on 15 October 1880 by Fanny and Anna Parnell. The purpose of this committee was to raise money for the Irish National Land League, which had been formed in 1879 to pursue the issue of security of tenure for Irish tenant farmers and of which Charles Stewart Parnell was president. On 31 January 1881, in Dublin, Anna Parnell presided at the inaugural meeting of the Ladies' Irish National Land League. (Subsequently its name was changed to the Ladies' Land League.) Katharine Tynan, who was present at the meeting, recalled in her autobiographical work *Twenty-Five*

Years that when she had suggested the organisation be called the Women's Land League she was told she 'was being too democratic'.[5] Shortly after the Ladies' Land League was formed, a young woman named Jennie O'Toole visited the office of the league intending to join the committee. She recalled her unease at calling without having a proper introduction, but said that 'Anna Parnell put her at her ease'.[6] She described Anna Parnell 'as about twenty-seven, of medium height, with thick golden hair, a slender figure and very attractive with a fair complexion and humorous blue eyes'.[7] O'Toole became very involved with the Ladies' Land League and eventually became the secretary.

In October 1881, the leaders of the Land League were imprisoned and the British government officially suppressed the organisation. The women then took over the work of the Land League. They kept a register of land valuations, rents, and the names of the landlords and their agents. They also kept a register of evicted tenants, provided them with relief and enabled the Land League paper *United Ireland* to remain in publication. The women also organised aid for the prisoners. They set up and funded catering arrangements at jails where the men were incarcerated. However, in the aftermath of the release of the leaders of the Land League in 1882, Charles Stewart Parnell cut off the funds to the Ladies' Land League to make sure of their compliance, and consequently the organisation was dissolved. The league had lasted just nineteen months, but, in a similar way to the Fenian women, it left a lasting impression on many of the young women who came after.

In July 1883, Jennie O'Toole married John Power and at some point took the name Jennie Wyse Power. She remained a staunch supporter of Parnell, to the extent of naming her son Charles Stewart Wyse Power. In the 1890s she became involved with the Gaelic League.

The Gaelic League, founded in 1893, was a non-political organisation, which aimed to foster the Irish language throughout the country and enable people to rediscover an Irish past. This rediscovery was made possible by the translation of ancient Irish manuscripts. The league used this scholarship to create an interest in the Irish language within disparate sections of the population. A system was set up whereby trained teachers taught classes on a voluntary basis. In 1899, the league appointed its first full-time travelling teacher. These teachers, who were paid £1 a week, travelled throughout the country setting up branches of the league. By 1900, the number of travelling teachers had increased dramatically. A travelling teacher, known as a *timire*, serviced each newly established branch. They brought learning through Irish to many rural and urban areas of Ireland by setting up classes in primary schools outside official class hours. In these classes they taught Irish dance, history, folklore and music, and they also organised feiseanna, ceilidhe and aeriochtaí. Some children on reaching adulthood 'joined the social clubs of the Gaelic League'.[8]

The policy of mixed membership attracted both sexes. Contemporary social life was dictated by the rigid social mores of Victorian respectability and now an alternative social life developed which appealed to many, as young people from a wide spectrum of Irish life were drawn to the classes and the clubs' social activities. The clubs attracted bishops, priests, students, teachers, civil servants, post office workers, soldiers, policemen, tradesmen and labourers. Under the auspices of the league, dances, poetry readings and musical evenings were held, which evolved into a pleasant social scene. These clubs also became the means whereby both sexes could meet in a respectable setting, and several relationships developed that endured. Áine Ceannt (née Frances O'Brennan), who was born in 1880 in Dublin, joined the Central branch of the Gaelic League as a young girl and recalled 'engaging in traditional Irish dancing, singing and fiddle playing'.[9] She was also an active member of the piper's band which was attached to the branch. In 1905 she married Éamonn Ceannt, who was a member of the same club. Both signed their names on the marriage register in Irish.[10] Eamon de Valera also met his future wife, Sinéad O'Flanagan, at this club.

Society was still largely Victorian in ethos, although this period was one of transition from the rigid rules of Victorian society to the beginning of a modern society where men and women, regardless of their marital status, could mix freely. The old social system did not allow young single women to mix in the company of men without a chaperone. So for many, particularly the middle classes, the Gaelic League functions engendered a form of social revolution. In particular, the membership of the Gaelic League reflected the significant growth of a lower middle class in Ireland.

This development echoes a similar situation in Britain, where developments in technology due to the second Industrial Revolution and the expansion of the British Empire, had enabled a lower middle class to develop exponentially. Between 1850 and 1900 in Britain, 'the lower middle classes grew from 7 per cent to 20 per cent of the population' and these changes were reflected in Ireland.[11] This came about through the increased need for clerks in banks, railroads and insurance companies. The men who worked in these areas did not wear working clothes and they developed a sense of superiority towards the working classes 'that gave rise to the expression white collar employees and they were therefore respectable'.[12] Due to the growing bureaucracy of the British Empire there was a need for the expansion of the civil service. The need for an educated workforce that would understand the changed industrial technology also led to changes in education. For women, these changes gave them access to clerical positions which had not been available previously, particularly after the invention of the typewriter in the 1880s.

In 1878, the British parliament enacted the Intermediate Education (Ireland) Act, which made provision for scholarships. While this Act made higher education accessible to both sexes, it affected only a very small section of the population. The young women who were able to avail of this education, were already in secondary schools receiving the traditional finishing school education. The new Act encouraged many schools to stream the brighter pupils towards a more academic education. However, the new system did not open doors to education for the majority of children whose parents could not afford to send them to secondary school. Consequently, education remained confined to a relatively small elite from the middle classes in both rural and urban sections of Irish society. In 1884, the first group of nine women received degrees from the Royal University of Ireland. These young women were the first generation to benefit from the new developments. In her work *Before the Revolution*, Senia Pašeta analysed the level of change wrought in Irish society by the Intermediate Education Act of 1878. She found it had little overall impact on the class structure. By 1911, 'just six per cent of the school-going population was enrolled at secondary or superior school while the vast majority of children dropped out before completing their final year'.[13]

The opportunities created by open competition for posts within the civil service had a more significant impact on the lives and ambitions of women and girls from the lower middle classes. New commercial colleges began operating in Dublin, Belfast and Cork. These commercial colleges became training schools for many of the new jobs being created, particularly in the British Post Office. Siobhán Lankford (née Creedon), born in the mid 1890s, was the daughter of a farmer from Clogheen, County Cork. She was a pupil at the Munster Civil Service College on the Grand Parade in Cork city, owned and operated by Philip Murphy, a native of Enniskillen, County Fermanagh.[14] In her autobiography, *The Hope and the Sadness*, Lankford described her fellow students as 'the sons and daughters of farmers, shopkeepers, civil servants, and the RIC, whose families could afford to pay the fees' and she also said that she and her fellow students were 'planning a career in the British Civil Service'.[15]

In 1912, Siobhán sat an exam for a vacancy in the Mallow Post Office and succeeded in getting the position. This enabled her to work and live at home. Opportunities for young women in the post office became an attractive prospect and these positions became keenly sought after. Figures for Britain show that in 1861, women held just 8 per cent of the jobs in government and the post office. By 1901, this had risen to 50 percent. The situation in Britain was reflected in Ireland.

Developments in vocational education in the 1890s allowed young people from less well-off backgrounds to avail of further education after primary school. In 1898, the Local Government (Ireland) Act created the local authority structure for Ireland. The following year the government enacted the Agricultural and Technical Instruction (Ireland) Act. This Act enabled the Board of Agriculture and Technical Instruction to be created and allowed the county and borough councils in Ireland to levy a rate of one penny in the pound for technical education. The Act also enabled the councils to raise money by borrowing for such schools. Eight municipalities responded to the scheme. By 1902–3, there were twenty-seven county schemes and twenty-four urban schemes in existence.

Technical schools operated a skills-based education system. The demand for this type of education was not as great as that for the more academic system of the secondary schools, so two parallel second level systems developed. According to John Coolahan in his work *Irish Education,* the reason for this lay in the attitude of middle-class parents towards education:

> Irish social attitudes tended to disparage manual and practical type education and aspiring middle-class parents preferred the more prestigious academic-type education, which led to greater opportunities for further education and white-collar employment.[16]

In the 1890s, a young woman named Mary Colum, who would go on to be one of the founders of Cumann na mBan, observed her uncle making a similar statement. In her memoir, *Life and the Dream*, Colum recalled his criticism of her because she wanted an academic education:

> Over-education in the middle-classes is the curse of the country. The learned professions are crowded, too many doctors and briefless barristers and nobody able to mend a timepiece or make a good suit of clothes.[17]

None of these innovations in education had a profound affect on the class barrier. Irish society remained very stratified. The majority of the female population from the urban working class and rural labouring class still finished school at primary level. Many of these young people turned to the technical schools for education. The technical schools provided evening classes to allow early school leavers access to further education. Mona Hearn recorded that at the technical school in Kevin Street in Dublin, 'four hundred women availed of classes which ranged from shorthand, typing, bookkeeping, French, German, to cookery and dressmaking'.[18] The 1911 census shows very clearly the reality of available occupations for the Irish female.

TABLE 1: CATEGORIES OF FEMALE OCCUPATION, CENSUS OF POPULATION 1911

Class	Occupation	Numbers
1	Professional Class	37,531
2	Domestic	144,918
3	Commercial	9,918
4	Agricultural	59,198
5	Industrial	178,698

6	Indefinite & non productive class	1,768,079
	Total	2,198,171

Source: 1911 Census of population.

Those women in industrial occupations were urban based and worked in factories, those in domestic occupations were servants, and women in agriculture generally worked as farm servants. The professional classes were divided into four categories: law, medicine, teaching and the arts.[19] The women in the first category were barristers, solicitors and clerks of the courts. In the second category were physicians, surgeons, dentists, general practitioners, apothecaries and medical assistants. The third and fourth categories included university professors, teachers, journalists, authors, artists and scientific women.[20]

The last group, described as an 'indefinite & non-productive class', is problematic. In his work, From Public Defiance to Guerrilla Warfare, Joost Augusteijn, when discussing the social background of the rank and file of the IRA, said that 'the male described in 1911 census as "farmer's son" was making a statement of social status'.[21] The expression 'farmer's son' or 'farmer's daughter' appears to have evolved from the instructions on census forms advising households how to fill in the occupation categories. Farmers were advised to describe their sons and daughters who had finished school and were still living at home (even if they were working on the farms) as 'farmer's son' or 'farmer's daughter'.[22] This would appear to have been absorbed over time by Irish rural peasant communities as a category of social distinction. For example, a study of the Clonbern parish in Galway in the 1911 census shows the parish had a total population of 2,007, which broke down into 397 individual family units. There were 227 males recorded as farmer's sons whose ages ranged from thirteen to fifty-four. Thirty-nine females were recorded as farmer's daughters, who ranged in age from fifteen to seventy-one.[23]

The instructions for filling in the category for all females living at home, who were not engaged in any work apart from domestic work, directed that it should be left blank. 'At home' began to evolve as a term used to describe unmarried women who did not engage in paid work outside the home.

The term 'at home' has its origins in the early nineteenth century, when upper-class women had a specific day or evening each week for receiving visitors – this became known as the 'at home' day. According to the *Oxford English Dictionary*, the term 'at home' was originally used by individuals 'to indicate the specific day and set time on which they were home to receive callers'. As afternoon tea became fashionable within middle-class circles, a woman in a specific social set had a specific day and time when visitors were received. This information was printed on a *carte de visite*. Michael Taaffe, who as born in 1898, described this ritual in his autobiography *Those days are gone away*:

'At Home' days played a large part in the social life of the time. In the corner of the lady's visiting card, the necessary information could always be found engraved in small script. 'At Home, Second Thursday' the legend might run, denoting that on the second Thursday of each month tea and cakes would be available to all with whom the hostess had previously exchanged cards.[24]

By the early twentieth century the term 'at home' had expanded to become an all encompassing description, which ranged from the servant girl between jobs, to those from the higher social classes who were literally at home and dependent on their families. It also included the daughters of small shopkeepers and small farmers who worked for the family (without wages). The term 'at home' remained in use until the late 1940s.

A group of women from this middle-class milieu, who gathered at the 'at home' of artist Sarah Purser, were to play a significant role in cultural nationalism and in the development of Neo Gaelic art. These women were artists Beatrice Elvery, Elizabeth and Lily Yeats, the historian Alice Stopford Green, the Irish language enthusiast Margaret Dobbs, the writer and poet Susan Mitchell and Lady Gregory (whose association with Yeats led to the creation of the Abbey Theatre). All of these women were members of the Church of Ireland community. The biography of Sarah Purser, *The Life and Work of Sarah Purser* by John O'Grady, is an excellent examination of the life and work of this talented woman. Purser was born in 1848, in Kingstown, County Dublin. She was the youngest of eight children. Her parents sent her and her sister to school in Switzerland when Sarah was thirteen. At the age of twenty-four, she had her work exhibited by the Royal Hibernian Academy of Arts (RHA) in Dublin. In 1872, her father's milling business declined and went into debt. Her parents separated and she moved with her mother to Dublin and set up home in Ballsbridge. Left without means, Purser had to find a way of earning her living and supporting her mother. She began offering her paintings for sale. With £30, which she borrowed from her brother, Sarah then travelled to Paris in 1878 to work and study at a studio known as the Académie Julian, which was accessible to women. O'Grady describes the studio as 'an *atelier* belonging to a man named Rodolphe Julian who provided studio facilities and models for young artists'.[25] Purser spent six months in Paris and when she returned to Ireland she began working towards gaining acceptance as a professional painter. According to O'Grady, within seven years she had established herself.

Purser was the trail-blazer for many women of the Irish gentry and upper middle class in Ireland who aspired to a life of artistic merit. In general, many of them had no formal education and their expectations previously had been that they would have to remain dependent on a male relative. Now Purser's career laid down a marker for them and they could aspire to earning an income using their skills, without appearing to have to work for a living. In this way they could retain their social position of genteel respectability. Consequently, it became a fashionable trend, particularly within the ranks of the penurious unmarried women of the Irish aristocracy and gentry, to travel to Paris and London to study art.

In 1886, Purser moved to Harcourt Terrace in Dublin and set up a studio. A distinctive social circle developed around her home and studio, which became a centre for artists. Each month she held her 'at home' and it developed into a select salon where debate ranged from developments in the visual arts to politics and the emergence of Irish Ireland. Invitations to these events were coveted. Purser's studio and home became a hub of cultural nationalism where young artists and writers were imbued with new ideas, defining the emerging strands of a distinctive Irish art. 'In 1903, Purser founded the Túr Gloine (the tower of glass) which specialised in developing distinctly Irish stained glass.'[26]

Purser became a mentor and role model to the women within her social circle such as the Yeats sisters, Beatrice Elvery and the writer Susan Mitchell. These young women were trying to make a living using their skills in the arts. They had been reared and educated to find husbands, but without money and refusing to marry outside their religion or class, they remained unmarried and subsequently found themselves relying on their own resources. Elvery was the exception, marrying at the age of twenty-six when her parents were beginning to worry about her single status. By marrying, she escaped the financial penury of Mitchell and the Yeats sisters. While the women of this group had their religious allegiance in common, a distinct social division existed which was obvious to those who belonged within.

Nora Robertson, who was born Nora Parsons sometime in the late 1880s, was the daughter of Lawrence Parsons from Birr in County Offaly. Lawrence Parsons was a lieutenant colonel in the British army and he was first cousin of the Earl of Rosse whose ancestral home was at Birr Castle. During 1890s, Lawrence Parsons was stationed at various barracks in Ireland, including Fermoy, Limerick, Athlone and Cahir. Robertson's family background and her father's occupation enabled her to observe all the nuances of this social order from the inside. In her autobiography, *The Crowned Harp*, published in 1960, Robertson described the social structure within the Church of Ireland community. Her description implies that this community had an exceptionally esoteric structure. To explain her view, she created a system of classifications to identify the class system within 'the hierarchy of Anglo-Irish social order or Church of Ireland membership because it was not defined, but was deeply implicit to the members of this community'. Robertson explained this social system in terms of four levels, which were:

Peers who were Lord or Deputy Lord Lieutenants, High Sheriffs and Knights of St Patrick. If married adequately their entrenchment was secure and their sons joined the Guards, the 10th Hussars, or the Royal Navy.

Other peers with smaller seats, ditto baronets, solvent country gentry and the young sons of Row A (sons in Green Jackets, Highland Regiments, certain cavalry, gunners, and the Royal Navy). Row A used them for marrying their younger children.

Less solvent country gentry, who could only allow their sons and younger sons £100 a year. They joined the Irish Regiments that were cheap or transferred to the Indian Army. They were recognised and respected by A and B and like them belonged to the Kildare Street Club.

Loyal professional people, gentlemen professional farmers, trade, large retail or small wholesale, they could often afford the more expensive regiments than Row C managed. Such rarely cohabited with Rows A and B but formed useful cannon fodder at Protestant Bazaars and could, if they were really liked, achieve Kildare Street.[27]

Robertson summed up her descriptions saying that 'absurd and irritating as it may seem, this social hierarchy formed and dominated their lives'. She did not mention any of the working class who were of the same faith. This group would have included artisans, servants, labourers and shop workers. She also recalled that there were a number of retired British pensioners from the British Raj (Indian civil service), who were living on pensions and settled in Ireland because it was cheap. Robertson placed her family within Row C because although her father was the first cousin of an earl, he was landless, so within her classification he was a poor relation. She went on to observe that, 'while breeding was essential it still had to by buttressed by money'.[28]

Lady Glenavy (née Beatrice Elvery), whose father owned a shop in Dublin that specialised in waterproof clothing, could be categorised as Row D. In her autobiography, *Today We Will Only Gossip*, she recounts that when her family moved to Carrickmines in County Dublin – an area comprising mainly families of the professional classes – one child in the neighbourhood informed her, 'we are not allowed to play with you because your father has a shop'.[29] These children never mixed with the Elvery children.

These women were a significant part of the cultural nationalist movement. Their contribution to Irish Ireland is significant because their work involved creating a visualisation of the legends and tales of old Ireland, and the development of new concepts of neo-Gaelic Art. Beatrice Elvery said that through her involvement with this movement she developed a romantic and emotional view of Irish politics. She was so influenced by W.B. Yeats and his play *Cathleen ní Houlihan*, and the paintings of Jack Yeats, that she painted a picture 'which was an allegorical hooded figure of Kathleen Ní Houlihan with a child on her knee, presumably Young Ireland stretching out his arms to the future, and behind her a ghostly crowd of martyrs, patriots, saints, and scholars'.[30] Maud Gonne purchased the picture and presented it to St Enda's school. Years later, a young man who attended the school told Beatrice, much to her horror, that the painting had inspired him to want to die for Ireland.

These developments in the arts gave rise to a new fashion. During this period, many of the young male members of the Gaelic League began to wear Gaelic-style kilts. The young women followed this example. Nellie Bushell, a linen weaver who lived in Newmarket Street in Dublin, was one of the people making these Gaelic-style garments. Mary Colum described in detail the outfits they concocted as traditional Irish garb. She described her day wear as:

> An Irish costume in blue green, a brath [cloak] of the same colour with embroideries out of the Book of Kells. These were snakes eating one another's tails. With this went a blue stone necklace, a little silver harp fastening the brath, a sliver Claddagh ring, and a silver snake bracelet that I am afraid was early Victorian rather than early Celtic.[31]

The women wore these clothes when attending Gaelic League functions. Other young women also dressed in this fashion. On one occasion, Mary and her friend Siav Trench (niece of Lord Ashtown) decided to promenade in their day wear through the streets of Dublin. As they passed a fishwoman they were subjected to the observation, 'will yez look at the Irishers trying to look like stained glass windows? What is the country coming to at all? Them Irishers are going daft.'[32] Mary and Siav did not wear their Gaelic clothes in public again. The comment of the fishwoman exemplifies the chasm developing between those involved in the nationalist movement and the general population.

Aspiring female writers found the cultural nationalist environment encouraging and supportive. One of these writers was Alice Milligan, who was born in Omagh in 1866. Sheila Turner Johnson in a short biography of Milligan, *Alice*, described Milligan's family as a prosperous Methodist business family. 'Milligan benefited from the Intermediate Education Act 1878, winning a gold medal and going to study at King's College in London'.[33] By 1887 she was teaching in Derry. During her formative years, Milligan had developed a keen interest in the Gaelic League and was an aspiring poet and prose writer. Sometime in the early 1890s she moved to Dublin to study the Irish language, and she found the Gaelic League activities intellectually stimulating. In Dublin, she made the acquaintance of many prominent figures in the Irish literary movement, such as W.B. Yeats and George Russell (Æ). Milligan was not a woman of independent means, so she frequently returned to her parent's home in Belfast.

In 1895, Milligan participated in launching the Henry Joy McCracken Literary Society in Belfast and was elected vice-president of the association later that year. The society decided to publish its own paper, *The Northern Patriot,* and appointed Milligan and the writer Anna Johnson (pen name Ethna Carbery) as joint editors. Johnson was from Ballymena, County Antrim and was a leading member of the Irish revival circle in Belfast. Their editorship was brief, lasting for just three issues. Undaunted, in January 1896 they launched the paper *The Shan Van Vocht.* The support of the Johnson family made this possible because the two women were permitted to set up their office in a timber yard that belonged to Robert Johnson, Anna's father. The paper became a vehicle that gave voice to the several strands of developing Irish self-identity. The women also published some of the early writings of James Connolly, who founded the Irish Socialist Republican Party (ISRP) in 1896 and brought socialism into the growing melting pot of Irish nationalism.

Meanwhile, the associate ladies committees of several Irish nationalist organisations came together in 1900 and founded Inghinidhe na hÉireann (INE). The formation of this new organisation evolved from a series of protests against an official visit to Ireland by Queen Victoria in April. In preparation for this royal visit, a citizens' committee was created to plan a children's party at the Vice Regal Lodge in the Phoenix Park to honour the queen. The Lady Mayoress of Dublin, Lady Pile, with the help of the Countess of Fingall formed this committee, which grew to a membership of fifty-three women. (At this time in Irish society, women were addressed very formally by their title and consequently it can be difficult to discover their Christian names.) These women set about raising donations from businesses in the city of Dublin to fund the party. The committee decided to invite children from all social and religious backgrounds, including children from middle-class schools, orphanages, workhouses and industrial schools from all parts of Ireland.

The party became a focus of nationalist resentment. The national newspapers were inundated with letters of protest against it, accusing the citizens committee of using the poor children who would attend the party as propaganda to convey the impression that Ireland was a loyal colony of the British Empire. A letter written to the editor of the *Evening Telegraph* by 'Anti Flunky', provides an example of the tone of the protest. In the letter Anti Flunky warns parents against allowing their children to attend the party, saying, 'let them [the parents] bear in mind, however, that in doing so they are leaving their children open in after life to the charge of having been the recipients of outdoor relief'.[34]

Meetings of the Board of Guardians of various workhouses became hothouses of debate and discussion about this issue. The Board of Guardians of the South Dublin Union received a letter from the citizens committee asking the guardians to allow the workhouse children go to 'the Phoenix Park to see the entry of the Queen into the city of Dublin and offered to supply them with cakes and jam for the children's breakfast'.[35] After a heated discussion, a vote was taken and the offer was refused. Mr M. Molloy, who was in attendance at the meeting, proposed an amendment to the first motion 'that while they would refuse the supply of jam, they should allow the children to attend the reception for the Queen at the Phoenix Park'.[36] Mr W. Howard seconded this and it was passed by twenty-five votes to nineteen. Several orphanages also allowed their charges to attend. One of these was the convent school and orphanage in North William Street, Dublin. Children from middle-class schools also attended, although some families refused to allow their children to attend. The party was held on 7 April and according to *The Irish Times* of 9 April, '52,000 children from all parts of the country attended'.

The origin of INE has been somewhat distorted by Maud Gonne MacBride's account. Gonne had not been in Ireland since January 1900 and arrived back in Dublin on 12 April, three days after the party. She had been on a lecture tour of the USA from late January until late March, trying to raise support for the Boers. On her return to Dublin she attended a commemoration for Napper Tandy, one of the leaders of the 1798 rebellion. The commemoration took the form of a procession through the city from St Stephen's Green to the Cornmarket, where Gonne unveiled a plaque at the site of Napper Tandy's former home. The police report of the meeting recorded that:

> All the most advanced and worst Secret Society men, as well as the Transvaal Committee and Socialist Republican Party attended this demonstration. Miss Gonne on this occasion said, 'Queen Victoria was the symbol of greed, tyranny, injustice and selfishness'.[37]

When Queen Victoria left Ireland, a group of women representing various nationalist associate ladies committees decided to hold an alternative party in protest. The group decided to call this new committee the Ladies Committee for the Patriotic Children's

Treat (LCPT) and it had eighty-five women members. The LCPT committee set the date of the protest party for 1 July 1900, almost three months after the royal visit. At this point Gonne was still living in France, but would visit Ireland (with her menagerie of birds and animals) when something big was happening. She would return to Ireland and work in short bursts of intense activity, make rousing public speeches and then leave almost immediately again for Paris. She never spent lengthy periods in Ireland and did not make an exception for this committee. She presided at the second meeting of the LCPT and immediately left Ireland on 14 May, not returning to Dublin until 24 June, a mere six days before the treat was due to take place. The rest of the committee did all the work of organising the event.

In Gonne's absence, the women created an executive committee to organise and execute the work involved in the venture. This committee comprised Jennie Wyse Power, Mrs O'Leary Curtis, Mrs O'Beirne, Miss O'Kennedy, Miss Morgan, Mrs O'Malley and Miss White. This group of women were responsible for the success of the Patriotic Children's Treat. They placed advertisements in the *United Irishman* inviting children who wished to attend the party to put their names on an attendance list at an address in 32 Middle Abbey Street, the meeting rooms of the Irish Transvaal Committee (ITC). They specifically pitched their appeal to children from the poorer areas of the city. The executive committee then organised a working sub-committee. The sub-committee arranged that two of its members would attend the ITC every day between 4 p.m. and 6 p.m. to enable children to put their names on the attendance list. The committee created a weekly rota: Miss Perolz and Miss O'Kennedy attended on Mondays, Miss Griffith and Miss Kennedy on Tuesdays, Miss Brown and Miss Devlin on Wednesdays, Mrs Egan and Mrs O'Beirne on Thursdays, Mrs Power and Miss McQuaide on Fridays, with Miss Mulvey and Miss Clarke attending on Saturdays. The attendance list was essential to enable the committee to ascertain how much money they needed to raise by subscriptions. By 16 June, the committee claimed that 20,000 children had signed the list and on 30 June, the day before the picnic, they claimed to have 25,000 names.[38]

The children who had attended the picnic for Queen Victoria were not welcome at the Patriotic Children's Treat. At a committee meeting on 16 June, Jennie Wyse Power proposed a resolution:

> In view of the testimony of several members of the committee to the fact that all or nearly all the children of the convent national schools North William Street attended the Queen's breakfast, none of the children of these schools should be permitted to attend the Patriotic Children's Treat. A copy of this resolution be forwarded to the Lady Superiors and principal teacher of the school.[39]

The proposal was seconded by Miss McQuaide and passed unanimously by the meeting. This proposal also excluded the children from the South Dublin Union workhouse. In fact, it excluded most of the 52,000 children who had attended the first party, but it was easier to target children in institutions.

The primary objection of the LCPT to the children's picnic with Queen Victoria was that people loyal to the queen had used poor, orphaned and workhouse children for political ends. However, the LCPT used these children in exactly the same way. Their high moral tone expressed in the pages of the *United Irishman* indicates that they were oblivious to this contradiction. These children served the LCPT well in their political tug-of-war. Six days before the picnic Maud Gonne arrived back in Dublin just in time to claim the accolades. The women who actually did all the work were ignored. Interestingly, the two main Dublin papers, *The Irish Times* and *The Freeman's Journal*, ignored the picnic story entirely. Gonne wrote a report for the *United Irishman*, claiming that 30,000 children (the numbers were increasing at the rate of 5,000 a day at this point) attended the picnic and went on to tell the readers:

> As the children marched through the streets to Clonturk Park at Fairview singing God Save Ireland and the Transvaal War Song, with their fresh young voices ... they waved green branches of hope and flags of liberty and have done more for the Irish cause than all ... resolutions which have been passed in many a long year. Yes little ones you have done your part well, you have brought your brightness to cheer us in our struggle with your uncompromising and fearless nationality ... I feel sure you will serve our mother and Queen Ireland as devotedly and unselfishly when you are men and women as you have done as children.[40]

It is doubtful that Queen Victoria noticed the protest because she had left Ireland three months earlier. Both the Patriotic Children's Treat and the children's party were successful because so many children had fun. The Patriotic Children's Treat was not exactly a success as a political protest because the children were mostly unaware they were being patriotic.

In the aftermath of the Patriotic Children's Treat, the LCPT, having perceived the children who attended the treat to be un-educated and ignorant of their Irish history and heritage, decided to do something about it. At the meeting to wind up the LCPT, Jennie Wyse Power proposed a resolution: 'to encourage the boys of Dublin to join the new National Boys Brigade'.[41] This organisation had been in existence since May 1900, one week after the formation of the LCPT. It was set up in the middle of the slum areas of the north city to attract boys from those areas. 'Its purpose was to protest at events celebrating the Queen's visit.'[42] Henry Dixon founded the brigade because he objected to Irish boys being educated with the same curriculum as English children. Dixon hoped to train the boys in the habits of temperance and foster Irish nationality, language and history. Two hundred boys apparently registered at the first meeting. Jennie Wyse Power's suggestion about the boys prompted Mrs O'Leary Curtis to observe that something needed to be organised for little girls. After some discussion, they decided to form a permanent national women's committee. They postponed their first meeting until after the summer holidays and met in early October 1900, with thirteen of the original members of the LCPT in attendance.

In her autobiography, *Servant of the Queen*, Maud Gonne states clearly that she was the primary mover behind the event: 'It was in that year [1900] I at last succeeded in founding Inghinidhe na hÉireann; I called a meeting of all the girls who like myself resented being excluded as women from national organisations.'[43] This inference that she was still a girl is interesting because by this time Maud was a matronly thirty-three.

Subsequent biographers support this version of events to various degrees. However, Maud Gonne did not found the organisation, although she was one of the founding committee.

TABLE 2: THE FOUNDING COMMITTEE OF INGHINIDHE NA hÉIREANN

Title	Name	
Miss Harriet Rose	Byrne	
Miss	Devlin	
Annie	Egan	Vice-President
Alice	Furlong	
Miss Maud	Gonne	President
Anna	Johnson	Vice-President
Miss	Meagher	
Miss	Morgan (no. 2)	

Miss	Morgan (no. 1)	
Mrs	O'Beirne	
Miss Mary	O'Kennedy	Secretary
Mrs	O'Leary Curtis	
Miss Maria	Perolz	
Mrs M.J.	Quinn	
Miss Máire	Quinn	Treasurer
Margaret	Quinn	Secretary
Miss Sarah	White	Treasurer
Jennie	Wyse Power	Vice-President

Source: United Irishman, *April–October 1900, annual report Inghinidhe na hÉireann 1901.*

The women decided to change the name of the committee, renaming it Inghinidhe na hÉireann (Daughters of Erin). They apparently took this name from the existing Daughters of Erin, which was an associate ladies committee of the "98 Club' in Belfast. Having identified a problem, namely the ignorance of the children of the poor about their Irish heritage, the executive of INE set about educating them. The committee were determined that this new organisation would be an autonomous female organisation dedicated to the aspirations of cultural nationalism. The women created an executive committee and elected Maud Gonne president. The other members of the executive committee were Jennie Wyse Power, Annie Egan, and Anna Johnson, all elected vice-presidents, Máire Quinn and Sarah White, elected treasurers, and Mary O'Kennedy and Margaret Quinn, elected secretaries. The organisation used the offices of the ITC at this time.

One rule adopted by INE caused problems for the married women. It required that every member adopt a Gaelic name and that the use of English forms such as Miss or Mrs would cease.

The primary source material for the period 1905–1930 has a preponderance of the title Madame amongst this group of women. This apparently has its origins in INE and it led to an observation by Kathleen Behan that:

> We had a lot of gentry on our side – the nationalist side … and they did not want to use English expressions like Mr and Mrs. On the other hand, if they used the Gaelic versions Mrs MacBride would come out as Bean MacBride, which means MacBride's woman. Moreover, that would not do for them, it was too common. So all these grand ladies were Madame this and Madame that as though they were French. The working classes did not bother with such nonsense. Mrs Furlong or Mrs Behan was good enough for me.[44]

Another rule of INE required that every member had to be of Irish birth. This is interesting to note, because Maud Gonne, who by this time had (based on an invented family biography) taken upon herself the role of the Irish Joan of Arc, saviour of the Irish nation, was not actually eligible to become a member of the organisation. When INE was founded its major significance was that it was the first all-female cultural nationalist organisation. In electing Englishwoman Maud Gonne as president, they gave credence to her claim to the mantle of the Irish Joan of Arc.

2

CLAIMING THE MANTLE OF THE IRISH JOAN OF ARC

Maud Gonne is a dominant figure within the current iconography of women and Irish nationalism. By 1901, as president of INE, Gonne had a wide audience for her many speeches about fighting and dying for Ireland, which gave her a prominent media profile. This image was further bolstered by her autobiography, *Servant of the Queen*, which was published in 1938. This memoir, which is a work of self-aggrandisement and fantasy, subsequently gave rise to an unsustainable iconography that suggests Maud Gonne was one of the foremost leaders in the Irish nationalist movement. Gonne also falsely claimed Irish descent and staked a claim to the mantle of Ireland's Joan of Arc, but never explained what she meant by this. It appears that her claim was essentially a response to her French lover's suggestion that she present herself in this way. Using new research, this chapter challenges the perception of Gonne as a leader of Irish women nationalists, refutes some aspects of her memoir and proffers a more realistic perspective on her role in Irish history.

Maud Gonne published *Servant of the Queen* when she was seventy-two years old, and it is a masterpiece of self-absorption. In the world created by this memoir, she is the most important person, everyone and all events are secondary and she apparently believed that everything she said would be perceived as absolute truth and remain unquestioned.

For almost thirty years, a historiography grew around this work, with writers such as Samuel Levenson, who published *Maud Gonne: A biography of Yeats' Beloved* in 1977, and Nancy Cardozo, in her work *Lucky Eyes and a High Heart*, using it as a guide. More recently Margaret Ward published *Maud Gonne: A Life*, a work located within the developing feminist and women's writings of the 1980s. These three works, written within the genre of romanticism, have inflated the importance of Maud Gonne's memoir and allowed a picture of her importance in Irish history to develop that is now insupportable.

The first challenge to this body of work was in 1979, when Conrad A. Balliett published an article called 'The Lives – and Lies – of Maud Gonne'. Balliett was the first historian to examine Maud Gonne's autobiography within the framework of historical and critical analysis. He summed up *Servant of the Queen* saying, 'it could not be described as an honest book, since Gonne conceals, distorts, alters and rearranges facts, incidents and dates for both personal and political reasons'.[1] The main importance of Balliett's work lies in the fact that it was the first to initiate a breach in the smokescreen that Gonne had created with her autobiography.

Lack of access to Maud Gonne's papers has created problems for writers and historians. For example, when Elizabeth Keane published the excellent biography of Gonne's son, *Seán MacBride: A Life*, in 2007, her inability to access Gonne's papers made it difficult for her to bring any new perspective to Maud Gonne's early life. Consequently, the powerful façade created by Gonne in *Servant of the Queen*, largely endures. However, developing computer technology has now made it possible to access primary source material, and this has opened up a new range of possibilities, making it feasible to explore some of the events discussed by Maud

Gonne within a chronological timeframe and place her role within the growing nationalist movement into perspective.

Maud Gonne was an Englishwoman who spent a short part of her young life in Ireland, where her father Thomas Gonne was an officer with the British army. Captain Thomas Gonne of the 17th Lancers and his wife, Edith Frith Cook, came from families firmly established within the prosperous upper middle-class stratum of English society. They engaged in trade, both domestic and international. Their sons became members of the officer rank in the British army and served in the Indian civil service, the church and the international mercantile community. In general, the daughters of these families received their education from governesses and, if they found an acceptable husband and possessed a sizeable dowry, they were able to marry within their own class. On occasion a woman with a significant dowry could find a husband in a higher social class. Those without dowries filled the ranks of governesses and unpaid lady companions, who lived lives of servitude. It was from this constrained world that the leaders of the nineteenth-century British suffrage movement emerged.

Maud Gonne's mother came from a family of successful merchants who specialised in the import and export of a wide range of textiles. They could trace their family back on one side to William Cook, who was a Yeoman farmer in Norfolk in the 1700s, while the Frith ancestry was traceable back to the twelfth century. Over the centuries Edith's family were farmers, medical men, rectors, military chaplains and officers in the British army and the Indian civil service. The women of these families, when they married, stayed within this social group.

Edith Frith Cook was born on 17 June 1844 at Roydon Hall in East Peckham in Kent, a Tudor mansion purchased by her grandfather in 1837. Her father, William Cook, was married to Margaretta Frith, who died in 1846 at the age of twenty-eight. William Cook died in 1854 and Edith's sister Emma died in 1856.

The orphaned Edith went to live with her grandparents at Roydon Hall. Contrary to Maud Gonne's assertion that Edith's guardians sent her away to school, the 1861 Census of England indicates that she was educated at home by a governess.

On 19 December 1865, Edith married Captain Thomas Gonne. Thomas Gonne came from a family of wine merchants who, since the early eighteenth century, were significant importers of port wine from the Portuguese cities of Lisbon and Porto, and were highly respected within the British ex-patriot community in Porto. Thomas was the third son of Charles Gonne. In November 1855, Thomas Gonne purchased a commission of the rank of coronet in the 2nd Dragoons and he gradually worked his way up the ranks of the officer classes through the system of purchasing rank. In 1862, while he was with the 17th Lancers at Aldershot, he purchased the rank of captain.

Maud Gonne presents the marriage of Thomas and Edith as a romantic story worthy of a Jane Austen novel. However, as in the works of Austen, the issue of a significant dowry was a consideration in the match. Thomas Gonne loved Edith, but he was not a wealthy man and did not have sufficient income to marry a woman without a significant dowry. Therefore, Edith, an only child and an orphan, with her dowry of '£25,344,18 5s as a marriage settlement', was an ideal choice of wife.[2] The capital was her inheritance from her father, and in accordance with his will a trust fund was created to provide an annuity for Edith. While the annual income of £760 3s 2d was not a vast fortune, it was a very comfortable income and it made Edith Frith Cook an excellent match for an officer of Gonne's rank. On 21 December 1866, Edith Frith Gonne gave birth to her first child, Edith Maud.

In 1868, Captain Gonne was appointed brigade major for a five-year term of duty to the staff headquarters of the British army at the Curragh Camp in Kildare.[3] He arrived in Ireland with his wife and child in April, when Maud was fourteen months old, and the family settled into life at the Curragh Camp. In September of that year, Kathleen Mary Gonne was born. A year later Edith Frith Gonne was diagnosed with tuberculosis.[4] In 1870, Edith became pregnant again but due to the diagnosis of tuberculosis, the outlook was not promising. In February 1871, when Edith was about five months pregnant, Captain Gonne was granted 'extended leave of absence for twenty-one days' and the family travelled to London.[5]

The census for April 1871 shows that Edith and the two children stayed with their nurse Mary Ann Meredith at the home of Augusta Tarlton, who was Edith's maternal aunt. In her memoir Maud claimed that they were in London because her father was bringing the family to Italy when her mother died suddenly.[6] However, Captain Gonne had taken a lease on a house at 63 Gloucester Terrace in Paddington, which indicates that there was no plan to travel to Italy. In May 1871, Gonne received further leave of absence until '11 July on private affairs'.[7] On 15 June 1871, two days before her twenty-seventh birthday, Edith Gonne gave birth to her third child at Gloucester Terrace. It was another daughter, who was named Margaretta Rose. Six days later, on 21 June 1871, Edith died from complications due to the tuberculosis. It is more than probable that the pregnancy had a profoundly detrimental effect on her precarious health. She was buried at Tongham in Aldershot. The infant Margaretta Rose survived for just two months and died in August 1871 due to inanition (failure to thrive), at Rocklands in Tunbridge Wells. In September 1871, Captain Gonne returned to Ireland with his children. Maud recalled:

> We went to live in a little wooden hut in Kildare with a veranda round it and a sun porch where Tommy grew flowers and taught me to sow seeds and make cuttings. Soldiers in red coats came and went and a donkey lived in the paddock.[8]

After his wife's death, Thomas Gonne did not spend any significant time with his small children, leaving them to the care of paid minders, which must have had a long-term effect on their psychological health. By February 1873, Captain Gonne had resumed his social life and in the summer of 1873, Maud and Kathleen moved with their nurse Mary Ann Meredith from the Curragh Camp to Howth in County Dublin. According to Maud, her father had rented a house for the summer because, she said, 'he was constantly worried she might become ill like her mother' and she recalled 'that nurse was worried whenever I coughed and pursued me with cod-liver oil and orange juice'.[9] It can be presumed that Thomas Gonne also worried about Kathleen, but throughout her lifetime Maud Gonne had a powerful need to be always at the centre of attention. Her memoir is laden with tales of her constant illness, pending illnesses and a strong fear of contagion.

Captain Gonne received an appointment as garrison instructor at Aldershot in late 1873 and the family left Ireland in November of that year. In early 1874, when Maud was eight years old, her father received a promotion on merit to the rank of major (the system of purchase had been abolished by this time). Two years later, in February 1876, 'he was appointed Military Attaché to Vienna, and he held this post until October 1878'.[10] In that year, Thomas Gonne was promoted to colonel of the 17th Lancers and the regiment was detailed to prepare for embarkation to Natal in South Africa. During this preparation, while Gonne was supervising the training of the non-commissioned officers, one of his officers accidentally shot him in the thigh with a newly issued revolver, 'the ball lodging in the knee'.[11] This injury prevented Gonne from taking up active duty for almost a year. In August 1879, he was deemed fit enough to rejoin his regiment, now in the East Indies, and he resumed command. He remained with the regiment until March 1881. During this period the two children stayed on the French Riviera with Mary Ann Meredith and 'a governess named Miss Austen who was from Cannes'.[12] Thomas Gonne for some reason did not purchase a family home and consequently both his daughters lived an almost nomadic existence. During their formative childhood years they were effectively denied the stability of a secure family life. The only constant adult in their young lives was their nurse, Mary Ann Meredith.

In April 1881, Colonel Gonne was 'appointed Military Attaché to St Petersburg, as an officer on temporary "half pay".'[13] According to army regulations known officially as *The King's Regulations*, an officer was entitled to go on temporary half pay if he was deemed unfit for active duty. The regulations required him to present a medical report, 'giving the cause and probable duration of such unfitness'.[14] Thomas Gonne remained in St Petersburg until 1884 and was replaced by Lieutenant Colonel Chenevix Trench.[15] When Gonne took up his appointment in Russia in April 1881, Maud and Kathleen were fourteen and twelve respectively. Contrary to her assertion that her father never sent them to school, both girls were then pupils at private school called Rosemount School in Torquay, owned and run by a Scots woman named Miss Margaret C. Wilson. Mary Ann Meredith is also recorded as living at the school. In January 1885, Colonel Gonne arrived back in Ireland, 'to take up the post of Assistant Adjutant to the General Dublin District, while still on half pay'.[16]

There has been a lot of confusion (created by Maud) about when exactly the two Gonne sisters returned to Ireland. However, by examining her autobiography in conjunction with primary source material, a clearer picture emerges and the myths surrounding her eighteen months in Ireland, between June 1885 and December 1886, can be uncovered. It is now possible to place a definitive timescale on her return to Ireland, her presentation at Dublin Castle and her claim that she met and impressed the Prince of Wales. Maud said that the sisters 'arrived back in Dublin the day after the departure of one lord lieutenant and the state entry of another'.[17] In June 1885, the three-year term of office of the Lord Lieutenant, Lord Spencer, had ended and he was succeeded by the Earl of Caernarfon. It is more than likely that Maud witnessed either the departure of the former, or the arrival of the latter, but not both. The Gonne family took up residence in the colonel's quarters at the Royal Barracks, a fact omitted in Maud's memoir.

Between the time of her arrival in Ireland in June 1885 and her departure in December 1886, Maud attended three official functions at Dublin Castle. On 27 January 1886, *The Irish Times* reported that 'the Lord Lieutenant, Lord Caernarfon and the countess held their first Drawing Room of the season, and that the guests of honour were Prince Edward of Saxe-Weimar and his wife'. Prince Edward was a member of the extended British royal family and in 1885 he held the position of commander-in-chief of the British army in Ireland. The newspaper went on to describe Thomas Gonne as a colonel of the military establishment and the list of young women presented shows that 'Miss Gonne and Kathleen Gonne were presented and sponsored by Lady Maurice Fitzgerald'.[18] This belies the story told by Maud that Lady Dunraven presented her and that her sister was presented separately, two years later. It must have been difficult for Maud's intense sensibility to have to share her presentation ball with her younger sister.

Maud's story of meeting the Prince of Wales at an evening dance soon after this bears scrutiny. The Prince of Wales was in Dublin in early March 1886, and on 6 March he attended a dinner held in his honour at Dublin Castle. The new Lord Lieutenant, John Gordon, Lord Aberdeen, and his wife, who had arrived Ireland in February 1886, hosted the dinner. A separate evening party was also organised where the prince was to be the guest of honour. *The Irish Times* published the names of everyone who attended this event and this showed that a Colonel and Mrs Gonne attended, a misprint which possibly gave rise to Maud's claim throughout her memoir that people often thought she was Colonel Gonne's wife. However, the Prince of Wales did not attend the party, 'due to an indisposition'.[19] The Gonne's were also at the annual St Patrick's Ball on 17 March, which was presided over by the lord lieutenant. On the following day, *The Irish Times* published the names of everyone who attended. The list, published according to precedence, shows Colonel Thomas Gonne mentioned in the list of colonel's, while Maud and Kathleen were in the list of 'Mademoiselles'. The guest of honour was 'Prince Edward of Saxe-Weimar'.[20] Perhaps, when writing her memoir at the age of seventy-two, Maud confused this man with the Prince of Wales, but it may also be that she was deliberately misleading her audience. If, as seems likely, Maud did not meet the Prince of Wales in Dublin, is there any truth in her later account of seeing the prince in Hamburg? *The Irish Times* reported on 13 August 1886 that the Prince and Princess of Wales, accompanied by the Princesses Louise Victoria and Maud, had left London for Hamburg. It is possible that Maud Gonne did see him and his entourage because she was in Hamburg at that time with her Grand Aunt Mary, the Countess de la Sizeranne.

Maud apparently met her grand Aunt Mary for the first time in 1882 when 'she was fifteen years old'.[21] Seemingly, this meeting was for the duration of one afternoon and it took place in Paris, where her aunt took her on a round of beauty emporiums and then paraded her on the Bois de Boulogne. Grand Aunt Mary was Thomas Gonne's aunt and she was born at the British chaplaincy in Porto in 1817. In *Servant of the Queen,* Maud described her as a former noted beauty who had buried two husbands and whose 'chief hobby was launching professional beauties. It was quite a dilettante hobby, for she had ample means of her own and I do not think she was influenced by pecuniary motives.' Maud recalled that her Aunt Mary:

... did not mind how ugly her man friends were, but women must be beautiful. Her hobby was to discover a beautiful girl and obtain for her the royal prerogative of beauty … she decided at once that I fulfilled the requirements for her hobby … Mary's whole attention was concentrated on noting whether people duly appreciated her latest production.[22]

Today, this would mean she promoted beauty contests, but in late nineteenth-century Europe, and particularly in France, it meant she procured beautiful girls for wealthy male patrons. With this description, Maud placed her grand aunt unequivocally within the world of the demimonde. In the nineteenth century, the term demimonde, which literally meant 'half-world', was the alternative world of 'gentlemen, artists, writers, social rebels, actors and courtesans'.[23] This half world operated parallel to respectable society, where courtesans and men of property and title met and exchanged opinions, sex and money. Many women were supported by wealthy lovers and consequently lived on the fringes of respectable society. The smokescreen for much of this activity in late nineteenth-century Paris was the salon, which was also a feature in the lives of respectable women of high status. The women of the demimonde and those aspiring to this world, advertised themselves daily on the Bois de Boulogne, in private boxes at the theatre, at major race meetings and at several well-known spa towns in France and Germany where wealthy men gathered.

By 1886, Aunt Mary was determined to find Maud a wealthy man and took Maud on a holiday to Hamburg. She booked rooms in one of the most fashionable hotels and set about revamping Maud's wardrobe. Maud recalled, 'we were continually on parade. She overhauled my dresses', and 'always managed to secure a table at the casino or a box at the theatre where they could be most noticed'.[24] One night at the opera, Mary became very angry when Maud 'did not achieve as high a sensation' as another English girl Mary had chaperoned some years earlier. When the Prince of Wales arrived at the hotel, his entourage contained 'many pretty ladies', but Mary told Maud, 'you are better looking than any of them, he will certainly remember you and he will ask us to supper'.[25] However, according to Maud, her father arrived that day, one week earlier than he was expected, and he removed her from the company of her aunt. She returned to Dublin where she resumed her life within the tightly controlled life of the British garrison.

Nora Robertson described life within the sheltered world of the British garrison in her autobiography *The Crowned Harp*. She described the social self-perception of those who lived within the garrison, saying, 'upon class, depended status and any fun that was going. This sense of loyal superiority was recognised and cherished down to the Protestant office cleaner copying her betters.'[26]

The Gonne family remained in Ireland until November 1886, when Thomas Gonne died suddenly at his residence in the Royal Barracks. He had developed a fever on 10 November and died twenty days later at the barracks. The notice in *The Irish Times* said he died from typhoid, but his death certificate states that he died 'after a twenty-day fever of unknown origin'.[27] Maud and her sister Kathleen accompanied their father's remains to England for burial.

At the time of her father's death Maud was just two weeks way from her twentieth birthday and her sister was eighteen. In Ireland, they had always lived within the tight social circle of the officer class of the British garrison and consequently had little knowledge of life in Ireland, except through the prism of the British military elite. Yet, within three years of her father's death, Maud had become a strident anti-British propagandist and had given birth to a child by a married man. She was subsequently ostracised by her family and her social world. Nora Robertson recalled that:

To have questioned this world let alone defied it … would have meant social extinction, but nobody did except once, when the

most beautiful woman of them all, Maud Gonne, daughter of a
Cavalry Colonel 'lost her head' before the Boer War.[28]

Maud's detachment from her extended family and her old life began
sometime in 1887–1888.

In the immediate aftermath of their father's death, Maud and her
sister Kathleen moved between the homes of their uncle, William
Gonne, and their maternal aunt, Augusta Tarlton, in London. They
also spent some time in Ascot in the home of another uncle, Charles
Gonne, who worked for the Bombay Civil Service. Charles and his
wife Elizabeth had two daughters, Catherine (known as Chotie)
and Mary Kimble (known as May), who were born in Bombay
in 1861 and 1864 respectively. Charles Gonne also had three
sons.

The four female cousins became firm friends. According to
Maud, there were many family consultations about plans for herself
and Kathleen. Maud locates these meetings in the spring of 1887
and says that it was during this time that the four cousins discussed
their future careers. Chotie and Kathleen went on to study at the
Slade School of Art and May went on to train as a nurse. In the
discussion about careers Maud said she wanted to be a nurse, but
she was turned down 'because of her lung weakness' and decided
instead to become an actress.[29] She seemed to be unaware that for a
middle-class woman in the nineteenth century 'acting professionally
was virtually synonymous with prostitution and was a transgression
of another magnitude'.[30]

Maud tells another story which has a strong element of
Victorian melodrama. She recalls how she travelled to London
to study drama accompanied by her nurse Mary Ann Meredith.
According to Maud, Meredith withdrew some of her savings to
pay for these classes. Maud claims to have studied under Herman
Vezin, an actor and well-known teacher of drama and elocution,
whom she said had seen her perform at a charity function in Dublin

and had told her she would have a good career on the stage. She was apparently such a success in her acting classes that Vezin gave her – a relative novice – a lead role in one of his stage productions, *Heartsease*.[31] However, Maud's ambition came to nothing because apparently she had a haemorrhage of the lungs which forced her to abandon her fledgling acting career. According to Maud, she then went to stay with her aunt, Mary de la Sizeranne, who lived in Chelsea in London, to recuperate. In 1887, Mary took Maud and Kathleen to Royat in Auvergne in the South of France, so that, according to Maud, she could take a cure. It was here apparently that she met her future lover Lucien Millevoye.

The story told by Maud is that she was sitting with her aunt under the trees on the promenade listening to the band when they were approached by 'a couple of Frenchmen and there were introductions'. After some brief conversation it began to rain; 'the two men accompanied us to our hotel' and as the pending thunder storm broke, Aunt Mary 'asked the men to come in and wait till the storm had passed'.[32] During the rest of her stay, Maud and her admirer met every day and walked together. This man was Lucien Millevoye, a journalist and minor politician. He was a member of the Boulangerist party and his politics were right wing and anti-republican. He was also involved with the 'anti-Semitic elements of French politics' and was anti-English.[33]

Due to her relationship with Millevoye, Maud transgressed the world of respectability and entered fully the surreal world of the French demimonde. She claimed that her political education began in her relationship with Millevoye. She appears to have absorbed Millevoye's hatred of all things English and around this time she developed a vitriolic hatred of the British Empire. She became an anti-English propagandist rather than an Irish nationalist. In her autobiography, she credited Millevoye with encouraging her in the notion that she should become Ireland's Joan of Arc:

Why don't you free Ireland as Joan of Arc freed France? You do
not understand your power ... free your own country, free Ireland
... let us make an alliance I will help you free Ireland. You will
help me regain Alsace Lorraine.[34]

This flattery by an old roué was very effective on Maud's susceptible
personality. So, despite having spent no more than two years of
her young adult life in Ireland, within the confines of the British
garrison and consequently ignorant of life and politics in Ireland,
she decided to devise a plan and launch herself on the Irish
peasantry as a self-proclaimed Irish Joan of Arc, whose declared
mission was to save the Irish peasant from the perfidious British.

The timescale for this event is a little obscure and Maud did not
appear as an avenging angel in the guise of Joan of Arc on the Irish
political landscape until after she met William T. Stead in Russia
in 1888. Maud had travelled to Russia in that year apparently on
behalf of a section of the Boulangerist Party with 'secret documents
for the Czar'.[35] She spent two weeks in St Petersburg where she
met Stead who was a journalist with the *Pall Mall Gazette*. Stead
apparently told her that 'if she wanted to work for Ireland she
should meet Michael Davitt, the ex-Fenian prisoner, founder of
the Land League, and an MP for the Irish Parliamentary Party at
Westminster'.[36] On returning to London, she went to the House
of Commons to meet Davitt, who was disinterested and, frustrated
by his lack of attention, she travelled to Dublin.

Maud surfaced in Ireland in public in November 1888. She
appears to have arrived in Ireland on the invitation of her friend
Ada Jameson. Jameson, who lived at Airfield in Donnybrook, was
the daughter of the wealthy Dublin whiskey distillers. Maud stayed
at the Jameson home and Ada introduced her to the amateur
dramatic community in Dublin. Over the following months, Maud
participated in several amateur productions in Dublin. She took
part in a grand concert of Irish music in aid of the City of Dublin

Hospital, where she gave a recitation from *Romeo and Juliet*, and also took part in a concert held to raise funds on behalf of the Dublin Orthopaedic Hospital.[37] The latter was held under the 'distinguished Patronage of her Serene Highness Princess Edward of Saxe Coburg'.[38] Obviously, Maud had not entirely detached herself from elite society. Some weeks later, she took part in a 'grand bazaar held to raise funds for the completion of the church of St Augustine and John', and gave a recital under the category of 'most distinguished amateur'.[39] In March 1889, she took part in an event held by the Association of Elocutionists in Ireland.

On 18 December 1889, Kathleen Gonne married Captain Thomas David Pilcher in London, and within three weeks, on 11 January 1890, Maud gave birth in Paris to her son Georges by Lucien Millevoye.[40] By this time, it appears that her large extended family had ceased to have any direct connection with her. She said in her memoir that 'there was a family ukase against me'.[41] However, the birth of her child did not hamper her ambition to become Ireland's Joan of Arc.

Gonne did not intellectualise what the nineteenth-century interpretation of Joan of Arc actually meant. In France, the rediscovery of documents relating to the trial of Joan of Arc led to a resurgence of interest in her life and trial. Over the centuries Joan had not been forgotten by the church, she was a heroine to the old French royalist tradition and was celebrated in Orleans from the fifteenth century. From about 1820, a cult developed within the republican left around the story of Joan. The republicans claimed Joan was a precursor of democracy. 'Her rising to save France was portrayed by them as an inspiration for popular patriotism.'[42] Joan subsequently became an icon for all seasons and all politicians, in particular for Maud Gonne who, following Millevoye's suggestion, adopted a girlish romantic view of Joan without examining the politics of the cult. Around this time a series of plays were being written about the life and trial of Joan. In 1890, the French performer, Sarah Bernhardt, became identified with the theatrical interpretation of the life of Joan and Gonne, with her acting ambitions, appears to have absorbed the history of Joan of Arc from the theatre rather than politics.

Between the 1890s and 1904, she tapped into a personal and confused interpretation of the history of Joan of Arc, in order to create the idea of an Irish Joan of Arc. Gonne adapted the idea of Joan of Arc in her own unique fashion and it was through this particular aspiration by Gonne that Joan of Arc became a minor aspect of the symbolism for female nationalists in Ireland.

From the late 1880s, she began to travel occasionally to Ireland with a vague unformulated notion of becoming the defender of the Irish peasant and supporting them in their travails with the English. For example in 1890 she travelled to Falcarragh in Donegal to take part in a protest at the evictions taking place on the estate of Colonel Olphert. Her entrance and exits from Ireland did justice to the theatrical idea of a liberator arriving to free the poor. She projected herself as a beautiful virginal goddess, the saviour of the downtrodden Irishman. Yet in France, she was mistress to a married man and gave birth to two children by him. Ireland became Gonne's stage, while France was her backstage, where she retreated to create and maintain a sense of mystery about her life. This enabled her to keep her two lives separate.

The poet W.B. Yeats, who first met Maud in early 1889, also fell in love with her and developed a life-long obsession. In his *Autobiographies*, he describes her various theatrical arrivals in Dublin:

> In the next few years I saw her always when she passed to and fro between Dublin and Paris, surrounded, no matter how rapid her journey and how brief her stay at either end of it, by cages full of birds, canaries, finches of all kinds, dogs, a parrot, and once a full grown hawk from Donegal. Once when I saw to her railway carriage I noticed how the cages obstructed racks and cushions

and wondered what her fellow travellers would say, but the carriage remained empty.[43]

All these bird's cages and animals had to be conveyed by railway porters and other workers, thus guaranteeing attention. This was in apparent imitation of the actress Sarah Bernhardt, who was so closely associated with the theatrical Joan of Arc and always travelled with a similar type of menagerie.

As well as attempting to save the Irish peasant in her guise as Ireland's Joan of Arc, Gonne was also becoming more deeply involved in Irish political movements. In Ireland after the outbreak of the second Boer War on 11 October 1899, several representatives of various nationalist clubs came together to form the Irish Transvaal Committee (ITC). Its aim was to protest at the British annexation of the Transvaal in South Africa. On 17 October 1899, Maud Gonne presided at the formation of the ITC. In attendance were Anna Johnson, a Miss Ryan from London and twenty-four men whose number included Arthur Griffith and P. White. The two men were elected joint secretaries and Gonne was elected treasurer. The ITC was clearly open to women and Griffith published their remit in the *United Irishman,* which was:

To express sympathy with the Transvaal Republic in its struggle against English aggression.
To discountenance the enlistment of young Irishmen.
To present an Irish National Flag to the Irish Brigade in the Transvaal.[44]

The committee also expressed its desire 'that public meetings should be held at once throughout Ireland for the carrying out of these objects'.[45] Gonne's association with the Irish Transvaal Committee appears to have been opportunistic. She was not apparently familiar with the history of South Africa and appears to have become involved simply because it was an anti-English organisation. She threw herself onto the Transvaal Committee with great gusto, travelling around Ireland expounding its views. In Britain, a group of aristocratic ladies led by Winston Churchill's mother Jennie raised money to purchase hospital ships for the British troops fighting the Boers in South Africa. In an apparent imitation of this, Maud Gonne decided to raise money for an ambulance for the Irish Pro-Boer Brigade. In this manner, the Irish Transvaal Committee became part of her anti-English campaign. Her father's regiment, the 17th Lancers, were sent to South Africa and her involvement may have been due to some kind of misplaced anger against both him and the government. Her vitriolic speeches often led to rowdy demonstrations, giving her publicity on which she appeared to thrive.

She became publicly associated with the Irish Transvaal Committee due to Arthur Griffith's paper the *United Irishman*. From this time on she made many contributions to the paper. Some of these contributions were the writings of her lover, Lucien Millevoye, translated for the paper. Maud Gonne had absorbed Millevoye's anti-Semitic ethos, and her influence on the editorial decisions of the *United Irishman* from late 1899 to August 1900 gave it an anti-Semitic slant. In the edition of the paper on 23 September 1899, under the title 'foreign correspondence', an article subtitled 'the pirate and the Jew' appeared, which said:

> I have often declared that the three evil influences of the century were the Pirate, the Freemason and the Jew ... the swarming Jews of Johannesburg, who have gained for the mining town the nickname Judasburg.[46]

Under the same by-line, the report described a demonstration in Hyde Park in London, which was held in support of Alfred Dreyfus:

It was a sorry gathering, some thirty thousand Jews and Jewesses mostly of phenomenal ugliness and dirt had come out of their East End dens at the summon of their Rabbis. If they hated France, it was also evident that they detested soap and water still more acutely.

Captain Alfred Dreyfus, a French Jewish army officer, was charged in 1894 with spying for Germany and found guilty by an army court martial. This was a trumped-up charge but it took several years before the truth emerged. In seeking out the truth, France divided into two camps known as the Dreyfusards and anti-Dreyfusards. The former included the radical writer Emile Zola, the socialist politician Jean Jaurès and the republican Georges Clemenceau. Clemenceau wrote 800 newspaper articles on the subject. A League for the Defence of the Rights of Man was founded in France, which attracted Protestants, Freemasons, anti-clericalists and Jews. The Dreyfusards believed that the fate of an innocent man was at stake and it was essential that justice should be done if the Third Republic (1870–1940) was to survive and prosper.

The anti-Dreyfusards included elements of the Catholic church (in particular the Assumptionist Order), the army and French anti-Semites. This led to many public demonstrations that often ended in violence. One of the anti-Semitic groups at the forefront of these activities was the Jeunesse Antisémite et Nationaliste (JAN), which had been formed around 1893 in Lyon before the Dreyfus affair erupted. Bertrand Joly, in an essay about this group, described it as an organisation:

... whose anti-Semitism was the sum total of its beliefs ... of a knee jerk variety, stripped of any doctrinal pretensions. The same was true of its nationalism, which was simply a crude chauvinism accepted as self evident, the basis of which did not have to be discussed.[47]

When Dreyfus was granted a second trial, JAN and similar groups became involved in anti-Dreyfus campaigns. JAN organised its first demonstration in November 1896 and Millevoye was one of the main speakers at this meeting. Joly also described JAN as an organisation, which 'specialised in violent speechmaking, which in many cases incited violence'.[48] Gonne was imbibing this political ambience in France. For the *United Irishman* edition of 21 October 1899, acting as the newspaper's foreign correspondent, she wrote:

> The liberation of the traitor Dreyfus immediately after his re-condemnation has been the last stroke to convince Russia that no French institution is now safe from the domination of the agents of the synagogue.[49]

The tone of the *United Irishman* at this point was anti-English and anti-Semitic, while simultaneously being pro-Boer and pro-Irish nationalist.

Maud Gonne also attempted to pass on her political views to the children of INE. When INE began classes for children in late October 1900, they consisted of a half-hour lesson in Irish history after which 'the children were marched to the Rotunda where they assisted at the [Thomas] Davis Commemoration Concert'.[50] These classes attracted children from all sections of Dublin. The teachers at this time were Miss O'Kennedy, Miss O'Brien, Miss Meagher, Miss Thornton, Miss Maria Perolz, Miss Spring, Miss Dillon and Miss Sinéad O'Flanagan. To make the INE classes attractive and encourage a greater response from the children, the executive decided 'to arrange some Christmas entertainment'.[51] To raise funds for this event, the INE executive committee held its first fundraising ceilidh in October, at the Derrybawn Hotel in 73 Lower Mount Street, Dublin. Mrs O'Beirne, who was a member of the INE executive, was the proprietor of the hotel, and 'Maud Gonne was a guest at the hotel at this time'.[52] The *United Irishman* reported that the evening was successful and that Maud Gonne gave the INE's inaugural lecture, 'called "The Goddess Brigid". Several members of the executive committee gave renditions of various Irish melodies and Jennie Wyse Power with a Mr Lawless, performed an Irish jig.'[53] The children's Christmas party was subsequently held in the working man's club in York Street. There were, according to the first INE annual report, '1,200 children at the party who were entertained with magic lantern shows of Irish historical subjects and scenes from the Boer War explained by Miss Gonne'.[54] In March 1901, a number of the children took part in the Gaelic League Leinster Feis, in the Irish language section, where one of the children obtained first prize and another third prize, and all the children showed 'a high standard of proficiency'.[55]

The young women who taught the classes for INE came from a variety of backgrounds and their involvement with the organisation had a significant impact on their lives. Three sisters, Delia, Anna and Maria Perolz, who were at the inauguration of INE, are interesting examples. They were born in Limerick and their parents' marriage was a mixed marriage, their father being Protestant and their mother Catholic. Maria was the eldest, born in 1878. The family moved from Limerick to Cork where their father worked for the *Cork Examiner*. While in Cork, Maria and her sisters attended the Presentation Convent School. Here, Maria's teacher was Sister Bonaventure, who Perolz says, 'made a rebel of me', presumably by introducing her to nationalist politics.[56] The family moved to Dublin sometime in the early 1890s because, according to Maria, her aunt, who was 'married to a detective inspector, objected to my being brought up with a Cork accent and made us come to Dublin where we would meet genteel people'.[57] In Dublin, Maria witnessed the centenary commemorations of the 1798 rebellion and said of the occasion that her heart nearly burst with joy on seeing the flags. She joined the Gaelic League and attended classes at 87 Marlborough Street, where she met Eoin MacNeill, George

Russell, Dr Sigerson and Douglas Hyde. Her teacher was Pat Nally and she said he taught her whatever Irish she knew.

Raising money for INE activities led to a variety of fundraising efforts. Dances and ceilidhs for adults were provided at evening soirees to which other nationalist groups were invited. They also organised *Tableaux Vivants* (a group of people arranged in a silent and motionless representation of a particular story) with Gaelic themes and set up a choir, which was trained by Brendan J. Rogers. The *Tableaux Vivants* were performed at the Antient Concert rooms in South Brunswick Street, Dublin. The members of INE involved in planning and organising these *tableaux* were Sinéad O'Flanagan, Máire Ní Chillín, Alice Milligan, Anna Johnson, Máire Ní Shiublaigh, Susan Varian, Helen Laird, Susan Mitchell and the sisters Ellen and May Young. The repertoire of the choir included battle songs and the mournful legends of the Children of Lir. The charity of St Vincent de Paul asked INE if the children could repeat some of their *tableaux* for their fundraising bazaar. They agreed to participate, but on learning that the event was to be officially opened by Lady Cadogan, the wife of the lord lieutenant, they withdrew because they 'refused to be identified with any undertaking connected however remotely with the representatives of the British government or their supporters in Ireland'.[58]

In June 1901, the INE executive decided to treat the forty children who had the best attendance record and best application to their studies to a trip to Bodenstown for the Wolfe Tone Celebration. The INE first annual report of 1901 recorded that: 'the children carried Irish flags and the Boer flag and loudly booed and hissed every English soldier they passed'.[59] From the initial commemorative celebrations in 1898, the Wolfe Tone Committee had emerged and every year at around the time of Wolfe Tone's birth date, they would organise a celebration at Bodenstown in Kildare. This had become an annual event and one of the prominent public platforms for the growing separatist movement.

The INE drama group began to move from presenting *Tableaux Vivants* to presenting dramas, and a nucleus of players began to emerge within the organisation. They performed works by the playwrights Padraic Colum and W.B. Yeats. In April 1902, under the auspices of the Irish Literary Theatre, Gonne played the lead role in W.B. Yeats' play *Cathleen ní Houlihan*. When the Abbey Theatre opened in December 1904, a number of the INE actors became part of the Abbey players, the most noted being Marie Walker (Máire Ní Shiublaigh) and sisters Sara and Molly Allgood. Molly took the stage name Máire O'Neill. While the founders of the Abbey Theatre were from the upper and middle classes, the thespians were working class. Acting was not deemed a respectable profession and was generally confined to individuals from the lower classes. In the early twentieth century the theatre, particularly for women, still had the whiff of degeneracy about it.

Meanwhile the children's classes continued. Helena Molony described the children who attended the classes as being 'from the slums'.[60] The classes were 'held in the evenings between seven and eight o'clock because the women teaching the classes were all working women'.[61] Some of the classes were taught in English. Helena Molony described the classes, saying that, 'teaching the children was the chief work of Inghinidhe na hÉireann. There were two books to be taught to the children, as soon as we read one, we taught it to them.'[62] This indicates that some of the teachers were, on occasion, just one page ahead of the young students. Maria Perolz, who also taught the children, recalled, 'what I learned on Monday I taught on Thursday'.[63]

The male children who attended the classes and entertainments of INE were asked to pledge that they would never enlist in the British army. One of the major events of Queen Victoria's visit in April 1900 had been 'the formation of an Irish regiment of Foot Guards' to 'commemorate the bravery shown by the Irish regiments in the recent operations in South Africa'.[64] The new regiment was designated the Irish Guards and both the name and its formation drove the anti-royal protesters, and in particular Maud Gonne, to the point of apoplexy.

INE now became drawn into the activities of the ITC and its pro-Boer campaign. Anti-British army propaganda was one of Maud Gonne's favourite activities and within this campaign she introduced another of her recurring themes, that the British army spread venereal disease. Venereal disease was a health problem worldwide, but in Ireland this gave the nationalist crusade a distinctive flavour, specifically linking venereal disease with the British army. The members of INE became involved in this campaign. At this time Sackville Street was well known as a place where soldiers went to pick up prostitutes and Gonne's plan was to harass British soldiers by handing out leaflets to the women who went out with them, warning them of the dangers of contacting disease from the soldiers. The somewhat convoluted idea behind this was that all ranks of the British army had a problem with venereal disease and by preventing Irishwomen from mixing with British army soldiers, young Irishmen would be detered from joining up.

Helena Molony, who was at the forefront of this campaign, said that the GPO side of Sackville Street was the main area of the city where soldiers promenaded. She recalled that 'one side of Sackville Street was confined to Redcoats and young girls would be walking out with them' and 'no respectable man or woman walked on that side of the street after twilight'.[65]

Seán O'Casey held a similar view, recalling:

Hussars in their crimson trousers, Army Service Corp ... Lancers ... Guards and Highlanders with their kilts swinging, all on the hunt for girls, always strolling on the same side of the street, the west side, never on the other where all the respectable people walked who did not like to make contact with the common soldier.[66]

Molony described the scene in more detail:

> Many thousands of innocent young country girls, up in Dublin,
> at domestic service mostly, were dazzled by these handsome and
> brilliant uniforms with polite young men with English accents
> inside them – and dazzled often with disastrous results to
> themselves.[67]

INGINIDE NA HÉIREANN.

IRISH GIRLS!

Ireland has need of the loving service of all her children. Irishwomen do not sufficiently realise the power they have to help or hinder the cause of Ireland's freedom.

If they did we should not see the sad sight of Irish girls walking through the streets with men wearing the uniform of Ireland's oppressor.

No man can serve two masters; no man can honestly serve Ireland and serve England. The Irishman who has chosen to wear the English uniform has chosen to serve the enemy of Ireland, and it is the duty of every Irishwoman, who believes in the freedom of Ireland, to show her disapproval of his conduct by shunning his company.

Irish girls who walk with Irishmen wearing England's uniform, remember you are walking with traitors. Irish girls who walk with English soldiers, remember you are walking with your country's enemies, and with men who are unfit to be the companions of any girl, for it is well known that the English army is the most degraded and immoral army in Europe, chiefly recruited in the slums of English cities, among men of the lowest and most depraved characters. You endanger your purity and honour by associating with such men and you insult your Motherland. Hearken to the words of Father Kavanagh, the Irish Franciscan Patriot Priest, who pronounces it a heinous crime against Ireland, for Irishmen to join the forces of robber England. Do you think it is less a crime for Irish girls to honour these men with their company. Remember the history of your country. Remember the women of Limerick and the glorious patriot women of the great rebellion of '98, and let us, who are their descendants try to be worthy of them. What would those noble women think if they knew their daughters were associating with men belonging to that army, which has so often wrought ruin and havoc in Ireland, and murdered in cold blood thousands of Irishwomen and children. What English soldiers have done in Ireland in the past they would do again if ordered to do so. They would slaughter our kith and kin and murder women and children again as unhesitatingly as they hemmed in the helpless Boer women and children in those horrible concentration camps, where ten thousand little Boer children died from want and suffering.

Irish girls make a vow, not only that you will yourselves refuse to associate with any man who wears an English uniform, but that you will also try and induce your girl companions to do the same.

Women's influence is strong. Let us see, fellow-countrywomen, that we use it to the fullest for the Glory of God and for the honour and freedom of Ireland.

INGINIDE NA HÉIREANN.

C.D. 119/3/1

Inghinidhe na hÉireann leaflet warning young women against mixing with the members of the British army. Source: Helena Molony papers, CD, Bureau of Military History (MA CD 119/3/1).

The members of INE handed out their leaflets, which contained
extracts from army medical bulletins describing venereal disease,

every evening from around 8 p.m. Operating in pairs, young girls 'spaced at about thirty fifty feet apart' moved from the Rotunda Hospital on Parnell Square to the Bank of Ireland on College Green. As they walked, they 'put a leaflet into a girl's hand before she had time to grasp the contents'.[68] Máire Quinn recalled that 'sometimes they went into public houses with the leaflets, and that their main object was to save the young girls from the soldiers' hands'. She also claimed that 'at this time a decent girl could not walk down the GPO side of Sackville Street without being molested, and that girls seen with soldiers were given the name of "soldiers' totty".'[69] Sometimes the girls with the soldiers thought the leaflets were religious tracts and became hostile.

When the soldiers became aware of INE's campaign they became threatening. According to Molony, 'at that time soldiers habitually took their belts to attack anyone hostile to them'. She also said that some of the women had received several anonymous foul letters and that Arthur Griffith's sister, who was a member of the organisation, had received some of them and was so upset that she resigned from the organisation.[70] Sometimes the girls and women of INE brought their brothers or boyfriends with them for protection. It became a form of regular entertainment to go to Sackville Street and bait the soldiers. The witness statements of some of the women suggest that there was some confusion about this campaign and it appears that some of them thought that it was a campaign to simply stop women going out with soldiers. However, Molony said they were not concerned with the social issue, but solely with 'the national political pride' and that young girls had not 'the faintest idea of the moral, social, or political implications of their associations with the "red-coats"'.[71]

Gonne had a significant fixation about the issue of venereal disease and British army, and this campaign was essentially her attempt to draw attention to this issue. There is one aspect of their campaign, which deserves some consideration – the anti-recruiting aspect. Essentially the campaign was suggesting that young Irish men who joined the British army would contract the disease and then spread it within the Irish population via contact with Irish girls. Maud Gonne's thinking appears to have been that this campaign would perhaps deter young men from joining the army and so prevent venereal disease from spreading in the community. The campaign ended when the ITC went into decline at the end of the Boer War.

One point that appeared to be missed by INE was that the women on the arms of the soldiers were Irishwomen. No intellectual or social connection was made with this. They identified the boys as potential recruits for the British army but the young women were of no concern to them. While their protest explicitly blamed the men for spreading the disease, it also implicitly suggested that it was the girls they had sex with who were responsible for the spread of the disease, and it was implied they were all prostitutes.

However, not all the women with the soldiers were prostitutes. The issue of domestic servants and working-class girls mixing with soldiers was distorted by these campaigns. Working-class girls, unlike the middle and upper classes, had the relative freedom to talk to whomever they wished (in particular men) without having to be formally introduced first. Many marriages resulted from girls meeting soldiers on the streets, a prime example being James Connolly, who was still in the British army and in uniform when he met his future wife, Lillie Reynolds, at a tram stop in Dublin.

Mary Hamilton who was married to a senior British army officer and living at the Royal Barracks in Dublin around 1900, supports the view that many Irishwomen considered marrying a soldier. In her autobiography *The Silver Road*, she recounted that when her cook left her employment to be married, she knew she would not have any difficulty replacing her. This was due to the fact, 'that the Royal Barracks was popular with ladies of that profession because they had excellent prospects of finding a soldier husband'.[72] While it is more than likely that some of the women in Sackville Street were prostitutes, INE did not engage with the issue at a deep social level. They never considered trying to develop a welfare campaign that might save women from the streets. In fact, the campaign had a serious lack of sympathy towards these women. Instead, they inferred the women were a source of contamination. At this point INE was still primarily a cultural nationalist association and had not yet developed a social conscience.

The Boer War ended in 1902 and Gonne travelled to Paris to present Kruger (the Boer leader) with an address she claims was signed by 10,000 women from INE. Like many issues involving Maud Gonne, this appears to be fantasy because the organisation never had this kind of membership and was largely a Dublin and Cork-based organisation.

In 1903, aged thirty-six, Maud Gonne married John MacBride, and they had a son Seán MacBride. The marriage was not successful and they parted in an acrimonious separation two years later. By 1906, these personal problems combined with the loss of significant capital on the French Stock Exchange, limited her funds for travelling. Gonne had always made great press and when she began to live a quieter life, the newspapers of the day were at a loss.

However, by 1905 her divorce from John MacBride had placed her on the periphery of Irish nationalist politics as people within the nationalist camp took sides. Her high public profile gave INE a certain notoriety and many of its members drifted away.

By 1908, the organisation had very few members and in Maud Gonne's absence it was taken over by Helena Molony, who launched a paper *Bean na hÉireann*. This paper became a significant conduit for discussion for women and their growing self-identity within nationalist politics in Ireland and it enabled another aspirant to the mantle of the Irish Joan of Arc to emerge.

3

PROSELYTISM AND
NATIONALIST POLITICS

In the aftermath of Maud Gonne MacBride's separation and divorce, and in her prolonged absence from Ireland, Helena Molony became the *de facto* president of INE, and she tried to move the organisation into the wider political arena. Molony, who became a member of INE in 1903, was a professional actor. She was born in Cole's Lane in the slums of Dublin where her father had a small shop. When she was a few years old, her family moved from Cole's Lane, but her father retained the shop for some time. She later recorded that she 'received training as an actress from the actor Dudley Digges, got her first acting role with the Theatre of Ireland' and later moved to the Abbey Theatre. She also claimed that she was a protégé of W.B. Yeats.[1] It is not clear how good an actress she was because she only ever played minor roles. In later life, she never referred to her place of birth. Molony had a strong sense of her superior position within the lower classes of her neighbourhood and she was inclined to obsequiousness when dealing with people she perceived as her social superiors. She also believed herself to be a friend of the great and considered herself a confidante of Countess de Markievicz and Maud Gonne.

Molony launched the paper *Bean na hÉireann* (Woman of Ireland) in November 1908 as the official paper of INE. It was not a feminist paper and was in fact a rather traditional woman's paper that included regular features like romantic short stories, poetry, travel, gardening, fashion notes, beauty tips and a section called 'Woman of the House', which was devoted to recipes and housekeeping tips. The editorial section was devoted to comment and discussion on suffrage, Irish nationalism, social issues and the problems of the 'servant girl'. When the Irish Women's Franchise League (IWFL) was founded on 11 November 1908, a debate was instigated on women's nationalism and the issue of suffrage in the pages of *Bean na hÉireann*.

There had been suffrage activity in Ireland since the nineteenth century, but in 1908 a group of Irish women led by Hanna Sheehy Skeffington and Margaret Cousins founded the IWFL. It was not a political party and was not affiliated with any other society. The IWFL was an independent Irish suffrage society, but was not seeking universal suffrage. Rather it was demanding the vote on the existing franchise, where the vote was confined solely to men of property – in the IWFL's idea of female suffrage only women with property would be allowed to vote. Extending the existing franchise to women 'would obviously only benefit property-owning middle-class women'.[2] The majority of the population of both sexes were still excluded. While Sheehy Skeffington and the IWFL were radicals in their time, it is essential to realise that at this point the campaign had no real appeal to the general population because the suffrage movement did not reach out to all women. In a discussion on the issue of class and suffrage, Myrtle Hill points out that the *Irish Citizen* in its 'suffrage Catechism' in 1913 stated that the demand for the vote was not for every woman 'because every man has not got the vote'.[3] Nonetheless the IWFL worked towards having a 'votes for women' clause inserted in the Home Rule for Ireland bill then under consideration.[4]

Within the pages of *Bean na hÉireann*, a debate on nationalist women and the IWFL surfaced when the paper published a report on a lecture given by a Miss Shannon, on 25 March 1909, to the central branch of Sinn Féin. It was entitled 'Women and the Franchise' and Miss Shannon raised some interesting points about the attitude of nationalist women towards the IWFL. She stated that in her opinion it was inconsistent for the women of Sinn Féin to participate in any organisation that sought suffrage from Westminster. She believed that 'the women within the Irish Ireland movement already had equality with men in the Gaelic League and the Sinn Féin party, through their representation on the executives of these organisations'. She also said that women within the Irish nationalist movement 'did not need the imprimatur of a hostile government' because the movement 'had plenty of scope where women could operate'.[5]

This is a reference to the proactive policy of the Sinn Féin party and the Sinn Féin League to female participation. In 1907, the Sinn Féin party, the Dungannon Clubs and Cumann na nGaedheal, amalgamated to form the Sinn Féin League. The league essentially operated as an umbrella body for nationalist organisations. The main stated object of the league was to regain the sovereign independence of Ireland, and section fourteen of the constitution states that 'no meeting of any branch shall be held in a public house'.[6] This made it easy for women to become involved in the party, because respectable women did not frequent pubs at this time.

Meanwhile, Hanna Sheehy Skeffington responded to the speech made by Miss Shannon at the Sinn Féin meeting and said that:

> Until the Parliamentarian and Sinn Féin women alike possess the vote, the keystone of citizenship, she will count but little with either party, for it is through the medium of the vote alone that either party can achieve any measure of success.[7]

This brought a reaction from an anonymous correspondent named only as 'Sinn Féiner' who was critical of Sheehy Skeffington for advising Irish women to organise and join with 'Englishwomen's' agitation for the vote. This correspondent believed Sheehy Skeffington was wrong to encourage this activity 'because by working in conjunction with the English army of suffragettes they were harming the Irish cause'. The writer asked Sheehy Skeffington to consider a broader view of the issue and not look at it 'from the standpoint of a woman scrambling for her mess of pottage and willing to join her country's conquerors and its worst enemy to gain her end'. The writer went on to say that granting the vote to Irishwomen along with Englishwomen 'would not make Irish people free as it would Englishwomen' but would only act as another link in the chain keeping Ireland tied to England.[8] Sheehy Skeffington replied that 'because Irish women suffered two-fold by being ruled by an alien government, did not mean they could not seek rights of franchise' and she ended her letter with the words, 'I hope we have heard the last of this egregious argument'.[9] This marked the end of the debate.

In 1908, Irish nationalism gained a new recruit when Helena Molony introduced Countess de Markievicz to the ideology of Irish Ireland. According to Molony, by 1908 Constance de Markievicz was bored with her life, and when she approached Arthur Griffith, he advised her to join the Gaelic League. Molony said de Markievicz 'was looking around for a couple of years for some Irish activities', that she was political mentor to the Countess at this time and brought her to a committee meeting of INE.[10] She continued that when they entered the committee room:

> Everyone looked askance at her the first time she came to a meeting of the Inghinidhe, having come straight from the Castle in her evening gown ... she was not treated well because the members of the Inghinidhe said: "Why is she coming here? Doing a bit of Lady Aberdeen's propaganda?" My fellow members, the Misses

Maher and old stagers said: "We don't want her here at all" ...
They treated her by cold-shouldering her – next door to being
rude ... She also found what she had been seeking for a number
of years – a real revolutionary spirit.[11]

Countess de Markievicz was born Constance Gore Booth, in London, the first child of Lady Georgina Mary and Sir Henry William
Gore Booth, fifth Baronet of Lissadell, County Sligo. Her launch
as a débutante on the Irish ascendancy social season at Dublin
Castle took place in 1887. This was the traditional marriage market
for this class. George Moore, in his book *A Drama in Muslin*,
described the presentation of débutantes to the lord lieutenant at
Dublin Castle:

> Now a lingering survival of the terrible Droit de Seigneur
> – diminished and attenuated, but still circulating through our
> modern years ... this ceremony a pale ghost of its former self
> is performed and having received a kiss on either cheek the
> débutantes are free to seek their bridal beds in St Patrick's Hall.[12]

A Drama in Muslin was an exploration through fiction of the plight
of the landed gentry during the Irish land agitation and in particular the young women of that class. In his semi-autobiographical
book *Hail and Farewell*, Moore observed that:

> Eligible bachelors were scarce and many of the girls could only
> look forward to spinsterhood and genteel poverty. The few girls
> who are courted are approached less for themselves than for the
> dowries they could bring to relieve their future husbands' debts and
> mortgaged estates.[13]

Constance Gore Booth and her sisters did not have the promise of
a large dowry, which was a serious obstacle to finding a husband

within their social circle. After the season finished in Dublin, Constance travelled to London to participate in the social season there and was presented at court. She continued to do the season for eight years without finding a husband and this must have been increasingly hard to bear.

By 1892, Constance Gore Booth was still attending the events at Dublin Castle. Social etiquette dictated that all unmarried women must always be accompanied by a chaperone, which must have been humiliating. One of her regular chaperones was Lady Fingall (née Elizabeth Burke) from Galway. Fingall, who was just two years older than Constance, had met the Earl of Fingall in her first season at Dublin Castle in 1883. They had married after a short courtship. In 1892, at the age of twenty-four, Constance recorded in her diary that while attending a ball in Malmsbury, England, which had a programme of twenty-two dances, she received just one invitation to dance.[14] During this time, like so many other women of her class, she followed in the footsteps of Sarah Purser and enrolled at the Slade School of Art in London. She later travelled to Paris to study at the Académie Julian, while living in the *Quartier Latin*.[15] According to Lady Fingall, this trip was made possible when in 1897 Constance received a small legacy from an aunt. By this time, aged twenty-nine and without a significant dowry, the social dictates within her own class made Constance almost un-marriageable.

Sir Henry William Gore Booth died on 13 January 1900. In his will, he left his three daughters £2,500 each. Mabel, who was planning to marry, received her share as her dowry. Both Constance and her other sister Eva, because they had no immediate plans to marry, received their funds in the form of annuities, which were 'charged at an annual yield of four per cent against the income from the Lissadell Estate'.[16] This gave Constance and Eva an income of £100 per annum, paid out to them on a monthly basis.

This income left both sisters below 'the annual income of £250 deemed necessary for middle-class respectability'.[17] However, this small income meant that neither sister would have to live in absolute poverty, although it was relative poverty compared to their expectations as young girls growing up at Lissadell.

In Ireland, the situation of the Gore Booth sisters was very common and since the latter part of the nineteenth century, many unmarried women of the landed classes faced a similar fate. By 1881 the political upheaval of the Land Wars had caused many families severe financial distress and several women of the landed classes descended into real poverty. In late 1881 the situation of these women was so bad that a fund was formed to raise money. This was called the 'Association for the Relief of Ladies in distress through non-payment of rent in Ireland' and it was launched in October 1881 at the height of the Land War.[18]

In 1902 another organisation was formed to support these women called the 'Irish Distressed Ladies Fund'. It had a remit to 'give relief to ladies suffering through non-payment of rent and land depression throughout Ireland'.[19] Queen Alexandra, Edward VII's wife, became the patron of this fund and the executive chairman was Lord Fredrick Fitzgerald. The fund had an address at 4 Kildare Street and in 1903 it distributed over £1,600, with £1,086 paid out as monthly pensions which ranged from £1 to £2. The Irish Distressed Ladies Fund also organised the ladies to use their skills to make all kinds of produce and it opened a shop in Dawson Street to sell the goods produced by the ladies. In 1903 the fund 'paid out £852 14s for needlework'.[20]

In September 1900, at the age of thirty-three and apparently determined not to become a dependent or a distressed lady, Constance Gore Booth married the widower Count Casimir Joseph Dunin de Markievicz. This was just nine months after her father's death. She had met de Markievicz in Paris and had known him since 1899 when he painted her portrait. His first wife had died in that year. On their marriage certificate Count de Markievicz is described as a Polish nobleman aged twenty-eight.

The couple's daughter Maeve was born in November 1901. Two years later, during the winter of 1903, the family arrived in Dublin where they leased a house at Frankfort Avenue in Rathgar. Within a very short time they sent Maeve to live permanently with her maternal grandmother, Lady Georgina Gore Booth. Maeve did not grow up in Lissadell House itself, but lived with her grandmother in a house called Ardeevin.

In a manner similar to the Yeats sisters, Beatrice Elvery and many women of this background, the de Markievicz's turned to their skills as artists to try to boost their income. They became involved in the social circle of George Russell and held their first exhibition with Russell in 1904. In 1906, the United Arts Club became a centre for men and women interested in all disciplines of the arts and the couple became active members of the club. Membership of this club gave them access to a circle of people like the artists Jack Yeats and William Orpen, the writers W.B. Yeats, Padraic Colum and J.M. Synge, and the musician and songwriter Percy French. The United Arts Club also welcomed women and Beatrice Elvery spent a lot of her time there. Through these contacts, Count and Countess de Markievicz developed an interest in drama as a means to raise income. In 1906, there was a split in the Abbey Theatre and the actors who seceded approached the members of the Arts Club to set up a new dramatic society. This led to the formation of the Theatre of Ireland. Count and Countess de Markievicz became members of the provisional committee and participated in writing dramas and acting. It was through this company that Countess de Markievicz met Helena Molony.

Countess de Markievicz ignored her initial rebuff by the committee of INE. As a daughter of the Irish ascendancy, she was a member by birthright of the higher social circle. This always opened doors to her and she accepted this as a right. She used this to impose herself on any organisations that took her fancy. At this time that fancy was Irish nationalism.

By 1909, Countess de Markievicz was active in INE and its paper *Bean na hÉireann*. Under the auspices of the latter, she delivered a lecture to the Students' National Literary Society (SNLS) in Dublin in 1909, urging the young women of Ireland to become involved in the nationalist movement. She adopted a rhetorical style of speech that was zealous and frenetic physical activity became her hallmark. Seán O'Casey described de Markievicz's speeches as passionate and said that they 'always appeared strained, rarely had any sense to them, and always threatened to soar into a stillborn scream'.[21] O'Casey in comparing de Markievicz's style of speechmaking to Maud Gonne's, said the latter was dignified and graceful, and that de Markievicz 'lagged behind her' and 'couldn't hold a candle to her as a speaker'.[22] Helena Molony said of de Markievicz that her 'greatest defect was a childish love of the limelight'.[23]

The lecture to the SNLS was published in pamphlet form by *Bean na hÉireann* later that year. It was a meander through Irish, Russian, Polish and English history from 1798 to 1900. De Markievicz used analogy and simile to tell the audience that the young women of Ireland were not doing enough for Ireland. The tone of the speech is that of a leader addressing the masses. She ended it with the demand:

> I want the Young Ireland women to remember from me … Regard yourself as Irish, believe in yourselves as Irish, as units of a nation distinct from England, your conqueror … determined to maintain your distinctiveness and gain your deliverance … Arm yourselves with weapons to fight your nation's cause … Arm your minds with the histories and memories of your country and her martyrs, her language and knowledge of her arts, and her industries. And if in your day the call should come for your body to arm, do not shirk that

either … may this aspiration towards life and freedom among the women of Ireland bring forth a Joan of Arc to free our nation.[24]

Here she is clearly staking her claim to the mantle of the Irish Joan of Arc, which was an amazing turn of events for a woman who a mere year before, at the age of forty, had just discovered a sense of Irish identity.

Countess de Markievicz also participated in the founding of the new nationalist boy scout organisation, Na Fianna, in 1909. In its early stages Na Fianna used Baden Powell's scout book for training. *Bean na hÉireann* published the notices for the activities of Na Fianna each month. Countess de Markievicz became the public face of this organisation because of her propensity for marching around Dublin dressed in a version of boy scout uniform at the head of a troop of boys.

An interesting aspect of Na Fianna was that in Belfast, unlike Dublin, girls could join the organisation. For example, James Connolly's daughters, Nora and Ina, joined the Betsy Gray branch there. There is no surviving explanation of why girls were allowed to join in Belfast but not in Dublin, although Helena Molony recalled that de Markievicz disliked girls and often exclaimed, 'they always confuse, those dreadful girls'.[25] This attitude would not have encouraged her to allow girls to become members in Dublin. Subsequently, in 1910, a girl scouts organisation called 'Clan na Gael was formed under the auspices of the Hibernian Rifles, an Irish nationalist organisation which had meetings rooms, at 28 North Frederick Street'.[26]

Countess de Markievicz took the boys of Na Fianna on route marches into the Dublin Mountains, near Ballally, where she rented a cottage. It is often implied that when she went there she enjoyed living a simple life, marching with the boys and having shooting practice. However, Molony's description belies this:

The countess stayed in her cottage, the country was very wild around there. It was a very convenient thing, because it was a double cottage [semi-detached]. Mary Mulligan and her mother lived next door, and did for Madame. It was a one-room cottage.[27]

In 1910 Countess de Markievicz and Molony attempted to form a co-operative at Belcamp Park in Coolock, County Dublin, but were unsuccessful.[28] Following this they turned their attention to the activities of the Irish Transport and General Workers' Union (ITGWU) at Liberty Hall.

In 1909, Jim Larkin founded the ITGWU to campaign for better pay and conditions for unskilled workers. The union held a series of public demonstrations to bring the workers' case before the public. The first time Countess de Markievicz saw Larkin was in 1911, when she attended a public meeting in Beresford Place outside Liberty Hall. Writing in the republican paper *Éire* in 1923, de Markievicz described her first introduction to Jim Larkin as an almost evangelical conversion:

> Sitting there listening to Larkin I realised that I was in the presence of some great primeval force rather than a man … It seemed as if his personality caught up, assimilated and threw back to the vast crowd that surrounded him every emotion that swayed them, every pain that they had ever felt made articulate and sanctified. Only the great elemental force that is in all crowds had passed into his nature forever.[29]

She went on to say that, 'from that day I looked upon Larkin as a friend and was out to do any little thing I could do to help him'.[30] Her response to Larkin and trade unionism was acutely emotional and non-rational. Accompanied by Helena Molony, de Markievicz immersed herself in the activities of the union and became involved in its public activities during the period 1910–1911, causing O'Casey to say of her:

> She usually whirled into a meeting and whirled out again, a spluttering Catherine wheel of irresponsibility. ... No part of her melted into the cause of Ireland, nor did she ever set foot on the threshold of Socialism. She looked at the names over the door and then thought she was one of the family. One thing she had in abundance was physical courage: with that she was clothed as with a garment ... She was born that way and her upbringing in which she received the ready 'Ay ay Madame you're right' from the peasants of Sligo stiffened her belief that things just touched were things well done.[31]

In July 1911, during a demonstration against the visit of King Edward, Helena Molony threw a stone at a shop window containing an image of the king. The window was broken and she was arrested and charged. She subsequently received a sentence of a forty-shilling fine or one month in prison. She refused to pay the fine but after a week, much to Molony's chagrin, she was released from prison when someone paid the fine anonymously. To celebrate her release from prison, the Socialist Party of Ireland held a public meeting, which was 'attended by about 500 people'.[32] The platform was a sand lorry. Francis Sheehy Skeffington, de Markievicz, J. McDermott and Helena Molony were four of the speakers. In the course of her speech, Molony suggested that King Edward was a 'descendent of one of the worst scoundrels in Europe'.[33] The police considered this abusive. A constable named Patrick Smyth, on the instruction of his inspector, moved to arrest Molony. This led to an affray that resulted in the arrest of both de Markievicz and Molony.

Constable Smyth's version of the event was that he grabbed de Markievicz by the arm and she threw sand in his face and kicked him twice in the chest, so he arrested her for assault. She denied having kicked him and counter-charged that the constable had caught her by the leg, not the arm. The court found both women guilty of a breach of the peace, but the judge, Mr M. McInerney, decided on this occasion that 'he would not inflict any punishment as they were ladies'.[34] The resulting publicity engendered more public interest in de Markievicz and her activities than in the cause she was espousing.

By 1911 INE was in serious decline and while Molony had worked hard to keep the paper *Bean na hÉireann* in circulation, it nonetheless ceased to function. The organisation was disintegrating but was never formally dissolved and in November 1911 it came together with the IWFL in a campaign to provide school dinners in Dublin.

The School Meals Act 1906 had empowered local authorities to raise money for school meals, but was not extended to Ireland. Thus in 1911 the women came together to organise a campaign to have the Act extended to Ireland and they formed the Ladies School Dinner Committee (LSDC). The secretary of the committee was Helen Laird, who had been one of the original members of INE. She was a teacher at Alexander College in Dublin and for a time was involved with the Fay brothers' drama group. Her stage name was Honor Lavelle. The other members of the committee were Maud Gonne MacBride, Mrs Molloy, Miss O'Connor, Mrs McCall, Mrs Quinn and Mrs Tuohy, who was appointed treasurer. The women had the use of office space at the Sinn Féin headquarters at 6 Harcourt Street.

This was the second time in twelve years that the members of INE had taken an interest in poor children. However, on this occasion it was the physical health of the children that interested them. The poor were becoming useful as a means of propaganda to nationalist women. Maud Gonne, in *Servant of the Queen*, claimed credit for the idea, while C. Desmond Greaves, in his biography of

James Connolly, *The Life and Times of James Connolly,* first published in 1961, claimed that it was Connolly who first drew attention to this issue.[35] It is not clear how the school dinners campaign came about, but it is possible to make a link between this idea and the work of the Women's National Health Association (WNHA).

At this time the WNHA was subjected to much censure by many within the nationalist movement, in particular the women. Lady Ishbel Aberdeen, the wife of the lord lieutenant, founded the WNHA in 1907 and by 1910 it was the main children's charity in the country. This organisation worked towards reducing the high level of tuberculosis in Ireland, by setting up a wide network of programmes for the care of children. One of these programmes was the provision of school meals. Yet the work of Lady Aberdeen came under voracious attack from nationalists. They accused her, among many other things, of patronising the poor of Ireland. An argument was put forward that the British were responsible for bad health and poverty in Ireland. Therefore, the only solution to the problem of poverty in Ireland was independence. Lady Aberdeen was also accused of setting up the WNHA because she hoped to receive a title from Queen Victoria. The tone of the feelings against her can be gleaned from some of the doggerel verse of the period. The following extract is from a long verse attributed to Seán Connolly, an actor at the Abbey theatre:

> The Dame from Dublin Castle that they call the Vicerene
> Came down an' walked among us-aye! without a thrace o fear
> an smiled on us, an nearly shed a tear.
> At the way those microbes had us pestered night and day ...
> Twill take me all my time to make them loyal to the crown ...
> I wonder what will fetch the women – that's the blooming rub ...
> Och I'll chuck the Sanatorium an' start a Babies Club.[36]

Emerging nationalist philosophy dictated that the Irish people should be free to solve their own problems. The poor, and in particular the poor of Dublin, were Irish poor and women like Lady Aberdeen were castigated for becoming involved in philanthropy in Ireland. Because she was a British aristocrat, Lady Aberdeen and her work in Ireland were viewed as patronising and an unwelcome interference in Irish affairs.

In contrast, on 22 November 1911, the secretary of the LSDC, Helen Laird, accompanied by Maud Gonne MacBride, received permission to address the monthly meeting of Dublin Corporation and present a letter of appeal. The typed letter from the committee (which Gonne later published in *Bean na hÉireann* as her own work) stated:

> Gentlemen: We wish to call to your attention the serious condition of the children of the poor attending the national schools of Dublin. School hours are from 9.30 a.m. to 3 p.m., therefore at least six hours elapse between the time the child leaves home and the time he returns. About half the children attending school in the poor districts bring no lunch with them and remain fasting all these hours and many of the children have had little or no breakfast before starting for school in the morning. It is also certain that their health and brains are being seriously affected by this strain and that these children are bound to grow up weaklings and likely to swell the ranks of the unemployed and unemployable.[37]

The LSDC was concerned that these children would grow to adulthood and become a burden on ratepayers by filling the workhouses, hospitals and asylums. The problem, as the women saw it, was that lack of proper nourishment left these children 'deficient in physical health and therefore morally deficient'.[38] The LSDC asked for funds so they could extend the school dinners to other schools in Dublin. Dublin Corporation responded that the matter would receive their best consideration. At the suggestion of Alderman Dr McWalter, the issue was referred to the council's law agent for his advice 'to ascertain if corporation funds could be used for this purpose'.[39] The law agent's advice was that Dublin Corporation had no power to apply its funds to provide school meals.

Meanwhile, the LSDC claimed they were supplying 450 dinners daily to needy children at St Audeon's School in High Street and John's Lane. The meals were Irish stew, or rice and jam (on Fridays). The LSDC did not cook the food. According to Helena Molony, 'a ladies committee who ran the penny dinners in Meath Street supplied the dinners'.[40] This particular committee operated a communal kitchen at 28 Meath Street and had been feeding the poor since 1901. The LSDC bought the cooked food from the communal kitchen and had it carried in large containers to the two schools each day. Volunteers from INE and the IWFL served the food and washed up afterwards. Not all the children received their food free of charge because, as Molony explained, 'all ideas of pauperism were to be kept out of the scheme as every child who could pay, paid their penny to the teachers (and sometimes it was only a halfpenny), but no one was allowed to know who paid and who did not'. It was organised in this way to enable the teacher to use her discretion, regarding those who could not afford to pay. Molony continued:

> These teachers took a great interest in their pupils and know their family circumstances, insist on payment where it was possible and relaxed where necessary, but payments were not made publicly [sic]. It was amazing the amount we got in pennies and half pennies from the children in that very poor district.[41]

The notion of deserving and undeserving poor was inherent in this arrangement. The committee was determined that the children should be able to access the food while still in their school buildings and they were expected to pay towards their meals. It is vital to point out that the LSDC did not inaugurate a new programme of feeding the children of the poor; they simply used the facilities already being provided by other agencies. The women of the LSDC rerouted the food into the schools to ensure a good school attendance. Up to then the children had left the school premises to go to the communal kitchen for dinner and on many occasions failed to return.

None of the women involved in this venture acknowledged that other agencies were working in the area of childcare, despite the fact that many organisations at the time were working to relieve the problem. The Mendacity Institute was another institution providing food to poor families and schoolchildren. The Institute, on Ushers Island on the quays of Dublin, was a charity that had been in existence since 1818. It also provided meals each day for poor adults and children as well as providing overnight accommodation. According to Audrey Woods in *Dublin Outsiders*, the Institute's annual report recorded that 'when the LSDC launched the school dinners the number of children availing of their services declined'.[42]

The LSDC style of philanthropy came coated with a suffrage/nationalist evangelical fervour. It would appear the poor were now to become a nationalist political issue. In ten years, the women had moved from feeding the minds of the poor to a more holistic approach: that a learning mind needs proper nutrition. Countess de Markievicz was apparently on the periphery of this committee but did on occasion help with the work.

ANOTHER WOMAN who became involved with the activities at Liberty Hall through Helena Molony was Dr Kathleen Lynn. Lynn was born in Mulafarry, Mayo, in 1874, to Robert Young Lynn and Katherine Marion Wynne. Robert was the son of Robert Kerrison Lynn who obtained the licence of the Royal College of Surgeons in Ireland in 1830 and was elected a Fellow in 1844. He graduated with a Bachelor of Medicine from Trinity College Dublin in 1832, was appointed physician to the County Sligo Fever Hospital in 1869 and subsequently to the County Gaol. In the 1911 census, Dr Kathleen Lynn was recorded as living in an eight-roomed house at 9 Belgrave Road, Rathmines. The census also shows that she had a lodger named Margaret Cooke from Waterford, who was aged forty-four and had no occupation. Cooke appears to have been a woman of some independent means. There were many such women in Ireland at this time and part of their survival strategy was to take lodgings with other single women (similar to present-day house sharing). Lynn employed a domestic servant named Bridget Cuffe who was forty-five and from Wexford.

In 1912, Helena Molony became ill and de Markievicz took her to see Dr Lynn. This was the first time Lynn and de Markievicz had met. Lynn says of the meeting, 'I did not know Madame de Markievicz, although she was a distant cousin of mine through the Wynnes, my mother's people'.[43] She is referring to Owen Wynne, who was her first cousin twice removed and was married to Fanny Stella Gore Booth who was de Markievicz's aunt. When a woman married below her place in social strata she was relocated lower down the social scale; likewise when she married upwards she was relocated upwards. Lynn's mother had married below herself, so Lynn and de Markievicz had not met before because, as the daughter of a clergyman, Lynn did not have the same social standing as the Wynne and Gore Booth families.

As Helena Molony was recovering from her illness she stayed with Lynn, who described her as 'a very clever and attractive girl with a tremendous power of making friends'. Lynn said that Molony 'converted me to the nationalist movement' and introduced her to the activities at Liberty Hall, the women of the Irish Women Workers' Union and INE.[44]

By 1912 Inghinidhe na hÉireann was a severely fragmented organisation. On the other hand, the IWFL was growing in strength and by 1912 had a membership of 12,000 women, which was unprecedented for an all-female organisation. In numerical terms the issue of suffrage was overtaking the rise of women in nationalism and in 1912, the IWFL launched its paper the *Irish Citizen*.[45]

At this time, the initiation of working-class women into Irish nationalist politics on an organised scale began to evolve as the members of the Irish Women Workers' Union, founded in September 1911, became active. The IWWU was founded by Delia Larkin at Liberty Hall because she believed that the main unions generally ignored the problems experienced by working women. During the Dublin Lockout in 1913, these women would become intimately involved in alleviating distress among the families of workers in the city.

In August 1913, a group of employers in Dublin came together and demanded that their workforce sign a written undertaking that they would not join the union. Larkin called on the workers of the Dublin Tramway Company to refuse to work and on 26 August 1913, an estimated 700 men complied. The tram service was temporarily restored with the support of the Dublin Metropolitan Police (DMP). Larkin was arrested but released after two days, following which he addressed a crowd in Sackville Street. The DMP reacted to this by baton-charging the crowd. This heavy-handedness left two men dead and many more injured, and created an atmosphere of constant combat between the ITGWU and the members of the DMP. By 22 September, 25,000 workers were locked out by their employers. The hostility of the police to any public protest required that the workers devise some means of self-protection. On the 23 November 1913, the Irish Citizen Army was launched. Captain Jack White, an ex-British army officer, accepted responsibility for the work of organising the army.

White was born James Robert White at Whitehall, Brough-shane, County Antrim in 1879. The White family were Church of Ireland and staunch unionists, and they were also of the Anglo-Irish aristocracy. James was educated at Winchester Public School in England and later at the Royal Military Academy, Sandhurst. At the age of eighteen he served with the First Gordon Highlanders in the Boer War in South Africa and he was decorated with a Distinguished Service Medal (DSO). Between 1901 and 1905, he served as aide-de-camp to his father, Sir George Stuart White, who was then governor of Gibraltar, but resigned his army commission in 1907. It is not clear where he was between the years 1907–12, but he was in Dublin in 1913 and became associated with the labour movement.

Jack White organised military drill exercises for the men at the grounds of Croyden Park in Fairview. Under White, they were taught the discipline of drill and organised defences. They drilled with broomsticks and hurleys. R.M. Fox, who wrote a history of the Irish Citizen Army, described the exercises:

> Clutching their broomsticks, they marched to protect their demonstrations and their band instruments from police attack in the city. Their weapons were as crude and primitive as their movement, and their organisation was rudimentary.[46]

For the duration of the Lockout, the Irish Citizen Army had a specific role, which was to protect the workers at public meetings.

Meanwhile, members of the IWWU came together with INE and the IWFL to organise a food kitchen in Liberty Hall to feed the children of the union members. Liberty Hall was a rambling two-storey building with a large central staircase just inside the front door. On this floor, the union placed a theatre and billiard room. The second floor was a series of corridors, where every room had a thickly studded door. These were the administration offices of the ITGWU. The women from the IWWU, the IWFL and INE carried out the work of preparing and serving food for about 3,000 people every day, in the basement kitchens. The members of the IWWU generally prepared the food for distribution to the wives and children of the workers. Nora Connolly O'Brien described the scene in the kitchens:

> Here the Countess reigned supreme ... all meals were prepared under her direction. There were big tubs on the floor and around these were about a half dozen girls peeling potatoes and other vegetables. There were more girls cutting up meat. The Countess kept up a steady march around the boilers as she supervised the cooking ... some of the striking girls were there to act as waitresses.[47]

The observations by Seán O'Casey of the food kitchen and the role of the Countess are also worth recording. O'Casey had worked for some time with de Markievicz before becoming disillusioned with her *modus operandi*. In 'Drums Under the Window', published in 1945, he said of the food hall:

> Whenever a reporter from an English or an Irish journal strayed into the hall and cocked an eye over the scene, there was the Countess in spotless bib and tucker, standing in the stream, a gigantic ladle in her hand ...[48]

While serving the food in Liberty Hall, the members of the IWFL wore their suffrage badges. An article in the *Irish Citizen* observed that:

> As the IWFL women served the poor their food they overheard snatches of conversation in which the words Suffragettes and Votes for Women occur with almost startling frequency, for the members of the IWFL are at work here and the little orange and green button does not escape observation. Here comes a wee

maiden – almost four years of age – who typifies in her small person all the fundamental qualities of her sex.[49]

Pádraig Yeates in *Lockout: Dublin 1913* explored extensively the involvement of these women in the food kitchen at Liberty Hall. His analysis suggests that the poor and hungry children were becoming the centre of a developing politics of poverty. The idea of feeding a child's mind, initiated by INE in 1900, had now become secondary to feeding the body. The ambition of INE to turn poor children into suitable citizens of Irish Ireland was by this time adopted by several women's committees. INE and the IWFL showed they believed they were competent to help in this work when they formed the LSDC in 1911.

By feeding them and their children, the IWFL believed that they could convince working-class women to support them in their quest for enfranchisement. This bears comparison with nineteenth-century religious proselytising campaigns, where different religious charities used food to claim the poor for God. The women of the IWFL were in fact also proselytisers. They courted poor and hungry women and their children for nationalism and their campaign for enfranchisement. In particular, they propagated the notion that the acquisition by middle-class women of the vote would transform the lives of all women, regardless of class.

When the Lockout ended in February 1914, the membership of the Irish Citizen Army began to drift away as the search for work left 'little time for training' and it ceased to be relevant once the Lockout was over.[50] INE retained a presence at Liberty Hall in the guise of Helena Molony, Countess de Markievicz, Maria Perolz, Elizabeth O'Farrell, Julia Grennan and Nellie Gifford. The IWWU carried on the struggle to look after its members and the IWFL returned to the campaign for suffrage and the publication of their paper *Irish Citizen*. The IWFL was at its zenith at this point, but within a year this changed utterly as the rise of Irish nationalism culminated in the founding of the Irish National Volunteers and its auxiliary Cumann na mBan. This drew women away from the suffrage movement.

4

THE SPIRIT OF REVOLUTION
1914–1916

From 1911, the issue of Home Rule dominated the political discourse in Ireland and when the proposed Home Rule Bill was brought to parliament in London in 1912, it led to the rise of a physical force movement. The first organisation founded as an anti-Home Rule organisation in 1912 was the Ulster Volunteer Force (UVF). In response, the Irish scholar Eoin MacNeill wrote a letter to the paper *An Claidheamh Soluis* suggesting that nationalists could form a similar organisation. This led to the formation of the Irish National Volunteers in Dublin, in November 1913.

Discussions on the creation of an organisation for women remained ongoing until April 1914 when a group of nationalist women founded the Irish Women's Council/Cumann na mBan. (In its early stage, members and observers used the English and Irish titles interchangeably.) This organisation was founded to operate as an auxiliary of the Irish National Volunteers in a manner similar to the associate ladies committees of the nineteenth century. The significance of this committee was that it was the first women's nationalist organisation to ally itself solely to a quasi-military organisation.

The emergence of this new organisation led to a series of high profile arguments between women within the nationalist and suffrage camps. These differences emerged in the *Irish Citizen* and on public platforms. Consequently, by late 1914 the women's suffrage movement began to experience a gradual withdrawal of nationalist women from its ranks.

When war was declared in Europe in August 1914, it had a profound effect on the situation in Ireland and when John Redmond, leader of the Irish National Volunteers, offered the services of the organisation to the British government, this led to a rift in the organisation. In the ensuing split, the majority of the Volunteers, numbered at 170,000, supported John Redmond and a remaining group of 11,000 founded the Irish Volunteers.

The situation in Cumann na mBan mirrored this, with the majority of the membership voting to support Redmond. The original organisation was reduced to a rump and they reformed as (the second) Cumann na mBan. This new organisation was now committed to the separatist nationalist agenda, but it continued to operate as an auxiliary organisation supporting the Irish Volunteers. By early 1916, these two organisations were actively preparing for revolution.

The move towards armed militant separatist organisations began with the founding of Ulster Volunteer Force (UVF) in 1912. It emerged from the protests by Irish unionists against the passage of the Home Rule Bill, when H.H. Asquith introduced the bill in the House of Commons in April 1912. Protest rallies took place all over Ulster and in September 1912, the Ulster Unionist Council inaugurated the *Solemn League and Covenant*, which approximately 200,000 men signed. The UVF became operational in January 1913, with membership limited to those men who had signed the covenant. The original membership is estimated at 100,000.

In the south of Ireland, Eoin MacNeill suggested in *An Claidheamh Soluis* that southern nationalists should form a volunteer movement to oppose the UVF and support the Home Rule Bill.

This led to the inauguration of the Irish National Volunteers on 25 November 1913 at the Rotunda meeting rooms in Dublin, 'where a special platform had been created and reserved for the ladies'.[1] In his address to the meeting of the Irish National Volunteers, Laurence Kettle, who was a member of the provisional committee, told the assembly that there would be work for women to do and that there were 'signs that the women of Ireland true to their record are especially enthusiastic for the success of the Volunteers'.[2]

From her vantage point on the ladies' platform Áine Ceannt noted that when Laurence Kettle rose to speak, some members of the Irish Citizen Army who were present objected to him and shots were fired. This action alienated some people at the meeting from the Irish Citizen Army. The objections to Kettle arose because his father, who was a farmer, was involved in a dispute with his workers. Ceannt said that Jack White of the Citizen Army went onto the platform and addressed the meeting, calming the situation. However, the relationship between the Irish National Volunteers and the members of the Citizen Army remained strained.

In April 1914 the Irish Citizen Army was reformed. The army had been founded in October 1913 as a defensive organisation and around March 1914, a decision was taken to reform the army and make it more relevant within the labour movement. A new constitution was written and it was presented for acceptance. It stated in part that:

> The first and last principle of the Irish Citizen Army is the avowal that the ownership of Ireland, moral and material, is vested of right in the people of Ireland.
>
> The Irish Citizen Army shall stand for the absolute unity of Irish nationhood, and shall support the rights and liberties of the democracies of all nations.
>
> One of its objects shall be to sink all differences of birth, property, and creed under the common name of the Irish people.

The Citizen Army shall be open to all who accept the principle
of equal rights and opportunities for the Ireland people [*sic*].[3]

It was intended that the new constitution would reform the Irish
Citizen Army into a more organised conventional army. While
discussing the constitution, and at the behest of Jim Larkin, Countess
de Markievicz and Thomas Healy proposed an amendment to the
constitution, that, 'before being enrolled, every applicant must,
if eligible, be a member of his Trade Union, such Union to be
recognised by the Irish Trades Union Congress'.[4] This was accepted.
By restricting membership of the Irish Citizen Army in this manner,
it had the effect of keeping membership small. Subsequently, a public
meeting was held at Liberty Hall to elect a provisional army council,
which would hold office for six months. Jim Larkin presided at this
meeting and a provisional officer council was elected with Captain
Jack White as chairman and five vice-chairmen: Jim Larkin, P.T.
Daly, Councillor William Partridge, Thomas Foran and Francis
Sheehy Skeffington. Seán O'Casey was elected secretary. Countess
de Markievicz and Richard Brannigan were elected joint treasurers.
An army executive committee was also elected and its members
were T. Healy, M. Mullin, J. Bohan, T.C.P. Morgan, T. Burke, T.
Blair, Mr Poole, J. McGowan, T. Kennedy, P. O'Brien, P.J. Fox, John
Shelly, P. Coady and T. Fogarty. The committee decided to adopt a
uniform and Captain White ordered fifty uniforms 'made from dark
green serge from Arnott's'.[5] Each member was required to buy his
uniform and most of the men purchased it by weekly instalments.
During the summer months, the committee also organised a series
of camps at Croyden House near Fairview, which provided military-
style training.

Meanwhile, ongoing discussions about forming the women's
section of the Irish National Volunteers came to fruition on 2 April
1914, when about 100 women met at Wynn's Hotel in Dublin
to form the Irish Women's Council/Cumann na mBan. Many of

the women present were already involved in various nationalist organisations, while some were part of the suffrage movement. Agnes O'Farrelly who was a Gaelic scholar addressed the meeting in Irish and English, and put the constitution before the meeting for its approval. The constitution stated that the purpose of the new organisation was to:

Advance the cause of Irish liberty.
Organise Irishwomen in furtherance of the object.
Assist in arming and equipping a body of Irishmen for the defence of Ireland.
Form a fund for these purposes to be called 'The Defence of Ireland Fund'.[6]

Elizabeth Somers proposed acceptance of the constitution. Mary Kettle was designated to second the motion. However, a dispute ensued when Kettle accused O'Farrelly of sneering at the Irish Parliamentary Party in her presidential address and she refused to second the motion until the issue was clarified. In response to Kettle's accusation, O'Farrelly said, 'we do not want party politics introduced into this organisation; we stand for Ireland, and that alone'.[7] Apparently, several of the other women present also objected strongly to the introduction of party politics into the organisation. Mary Kettle was mollified and said that on the basis that neither politics nor creed would be introduced into the Irish Women's Council, she would agree to second the motion on acceptance of the constitution.

A second attempt was made to introduce a political discussion into the proceedings when Mrs Dudley Edwards brought up the issue of the current talk of civil war in Ulster. She simply stated that she hoped the women of Dublin and other places through the south of Ireland would, if necessary, offer the shelter of their homes to the nationalist women and children of Belfast and Ulster.

She then attempted to discuss the situation in Ulster, but she was immediately castigated and the subject was dropped. A member of the audience then enquired amidst much laughter, 'if the principle duty of the new organisation would not be to collect subscriptions for the men', to which O'Farrelly replied, 'we will naturally keep in touch with the men's movement, and do our best in helping to equip and arm them'.[8]

The executive of Cumann na mBan was comprised largely from the ranks of middle-class and professional women. In addition, the age profile of some of the first executive committee indicates that this was not a group of young enthusiastic firebrands. Jennie Wyse Power, who was to the forefront in forming the organisation, was the oldest at fifty-four years, Margaret Dobbs was forty-three, Agnes O'Farrelly was forty and Mary Colum and Louise Gavan Duffy were both thirty years old. A brief description of the background of some members of the committee shows how the disparate elements of Irishwomen's politics came together in this organisation.

In 1899, Jennie Wyse Power had opened the Irish Farm and Produce Company in Henry Street, Dublin. It was a combined shop and restaurant and became a noted meeting place for Irish speakers and nationalists. An RIC surveillance report described the restaurant as 'the resort of a number of Sinn Féiners including Michael J. O'Rahilly, Major MacBride and Arthur Griffith'.[9] This police report, dated 1915, was from the surveillance notes on a man named Joseph Kenny from Bray, County Wicklow, who was a civil servant with the Congested Districts Board and who police believed was a member of the Irish Volunteers. It is worthy of note that the RIC special branch was using the term Sinn Féiners as a form of generic term to describe all shades of nationalism.

Agnes O'Farrelly was born in County Cavan in 1874, into a family steeped in a tradition of Gaelic learning. She received a convent education and went on to take an MA from the Royal

University, Dublin. She became involved in the Gaelic League and came to public prominence when she campaigned for women's rights in the universities. She was also a co-founder of the Irish Women's Graduate Association. In 1909, O'Farrelly was appointed to the first governing body of University College Dublin. From 1909 onward she lectured in Modern Irish at the university.

Mary Colum was born Mary Maguire in 1884, in Sligo. She was educated at boarding school run by the Loreto Order in County Monaghan. Having achieved a scholarship, she went on to teacher training college. While studying in Dublin she became involved with the activities of the Gaelic League and she was a member of INE for some years. She married the playwright Padraic Colum in 1912.

Louise Gavan Duffy was born in 1884 in Nice, France. She came to Ireland in 1903 and became involved in the Irish language movement. She was a student at University College Dublin and worked as a teacher in Scoil Íde, the female equivalent of St Enda's school for boys founded by Patrick Pearse. She was also a member of INE.

Margaret Dobbs was born in 1871 in Antrim, into an upper class unionist family. Her father was high sheriff for County Louth. As a teenager, she developed an interest in learning the Irish language. She became a member of the committee that organised a feis in the Glens of Antrim. In 1904, when the Gaelic League established the first Irish summer colleges at Falcarragh in County Donegal, Dobbs was involved in the initiative. These colleges were created to provide adults with elementary and advanced instruction in speaking, reading and writing Irish. The summer college gave the necessary training in Irish to teachers who wished to use it at primary school level. Margaret was an enthusiastic supporter of the concept of an Irish Ireland. Jack McCann, who wrote an article about Dobbs in the local history journal *The Glynns*, commented on her activities and observed 'there is an unfortunate inclination to link the language with Catholics', but 'when Margaret Dobbs was spreading her gospel in the Glens of Antrim she gathered around her a group of ladies from well-known Protestant families'.[10]

Elizabeth Bloxham was appointed national organiser of Cumann na mBan. Describing her own background, Bloxham says she was 'one of the youngest children of a large farming family in the west of Ireland who were Protestant and unionist'. She explained:

> I have no recollection of any political discussion in the family. It was just taken for granted that we joined in singing 'God Save the King' at the end of our concerts and temperance meetings, just as we took it for granted that the local brass band played 'God save Ireland' and 'A Nation once Again'.[11]

Bloxham was born in Westport in Mayo in 1878 and her father was a member of the RIC. She encountered the ideas of Irish Ireland through a friendship with two elderly neighbours who subscribed to the *United Irishman* and allowed her to read the paper. She began to send articles to Arthur Griffith who published some of her work in the *United Irishman* and his later publication *Sinn Féin*.

At some time during this period she became involved in the Irish suffrage movement in the west of Ireland. When she arrived in Dublin in 1908, she went to meet Arthur Griffith and found him to be a 'kindly and humane individual', because he 'went to a great deal of trouble to introduce her to his friends'.[12] At the election of the first executive of Cumann na mBan, Bloxham told Jennie Wyse Power that she had not been present at the founding of any organisation and received the response that election was done by 'simply electing ourselves'.[13] Bloxham believed she was appointed as the national organiser because of her background as a public speaker at literary and suffrage meetings.

Within two days of the founding of the Irish Women's Council/Cumann na mBan the new executive met to create two branches in

Dublin; these were the Central branch and the INE branch. According to Jennie Wyse Power's daughter Nancy, 'this new branch was given the cumbersome title of "the Inghinidhe na hÉireann branch of Cumann na mBan" because it was necessary to draw a distinction between the original organisation and this new branch of Cumann na mBan bearing the same name'.[14] The women also recorded that they received applications for the promotion of branches in Counties Antrim, Donegal, Mayo and Kildare. The women then turned their attention to the launching of a leaflet as part of their contribution to the Defence of Ireland Fund and they set a date for an open public meeting to be held at the Mansion House in Dublin to promote their objective.[15]

Some weeks later, at the end of April 1914, the IWFL held its national fête to celebrate women's lives and it was named Daffodil Day. The event was not confined solely to the membership of the IWFL and the participants came from several women's organisations including Cumann na mBan.[16] The fête was held at the Molesworth Hall in Dublin on 24–25 April 1914. Margaret Cousins explained the reasons behind the idea:

> We women must work to bring greater beauty into the life of humanity, beauty of the soul, of morals, of living conditions. In order to do so we have to bring activity of the spring into our homes and through our spring-cleaning set them for the summer. Correspondingly, in our Suffrage organisation that aims at the spring-cleaning of our national home we have just now to get especially to work to take stock of our winter's ravages ... The IWFL recognise that Easter is the time above all others when nature and beauty can best come to the aid of Suffrage propaganda ... all members must work to ensure the success of the Daffodil fête ... The daffodil will reign supreme because it stands for the colour symbol of our league.[17]

The main activity of Daffodil Day was a *Tableau Vivant* whose theme was 'the great women in history' and the *Irish Citizen* described it as 'the histrionic portion of the fête'.[18] The official name of the *Tableau Vivant* was the 'Feminist Tableau' and there were fifteen presentations. These ranged from Sappho, presented by Mrs Cogley; Florence Nightingale, by Miss Maxwell; Deirdre, by Ella Young; Maeve the warrior queen, by Mrs MacDonagh; and Ann Devlin, by Sydney Gifford. In addition, there were four presentations of Joan of Arc and these were apparently the most successful presentations. The

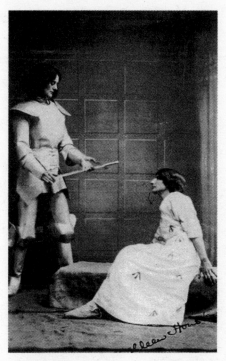

Countess de Markievicz and Kathleen Houston Tableau Vivant *for the IWFL Daffodil Day celebration 1914. Courtesy of the National Museum.*

first was Kathleen Houston, who was presented as Joan of Arc tied to a stake, with the fagots piled round her and a monk holding a cross before her. Constance de Markievicz appeared twice as Joan of Arc and in her first incarnation she was presented in 'full armour' which was described as 'astonishingly realistic', while her second presentation portrayed an apparition of Joan of Arc appearing in a prison cell to offer 'a sword to an arrow clad militant' named as Miss Houston.[19] The fourth Joan was not named.

There are two descriptions of the suit worn by de Markievicz. Apparently, she made the suit of armour herself and, according to Sydney Gifford, it was made from linoleum, but Hanna Sheehy Skeffington claimed it was made of cardboard. Both views concurred: 'the suit was washed over with silver paint and on stage it looked just like a suit of armour'.[20] This picture shows clearly the militaristic element of de Markievicz's sense of where she stood in the cause and her predilection for wearing military uniforms. The *tableau* also combined the militaristic with the religious and the nineteenth-century phenomenon of apparitions of St Joan was also represented.

In 1936, Hanna Sheehy Skeffington recalled in an article in the *Irish Press* that 'de Markievicz flung herself into the part with her usual zest making a magnificent Joan: "When years later I beheld her in action in the College of Surgeons, wearing the uniform of the Irish Citizen Army that earlier vision of Joan flashed upon my mind's eye. They were not so far apart."'[21] The fête finished with a Cinderella Ball and the music, provided by 'The Women's Orchestra', was organised by Eileen McGrane.[22] In the *Irish Citizen*, the purpose of Daffodil Day was explained:

> It was to show the public that we had not lost our power of providing enjoyment and entertainment along the lines that are universally acknowledged to be our sphere … We intend to add depth of motive and lessons from the past for the future to our work, as we flit among the flowers, so that we may share in memory the joy of Wordsworth.[23]

The IWFL appealed to its members throughout Ireland to celebrate the event in their local areas by 'rousing the interest of the public and working with true thoroughness to trumpet for the Suffrage the message of the daffodil'. However, the executive of the IWFL was apparently unaware of the minutiae of small-town life. The celebration of Daffodil Day had not reckoned with the embedded social divisions of Irish country towns and villages. In her autobiography *The Winds of Time*, Lady Gordon (née Edith Leeson), who was born in County Kerry, observed that in the typical Irish town and village 'social precedence had as many classes as there are castes in India'.[24]

In Mallow, County Cork, the Daffodil ball exposed the fallacy of equality. Siobhán Lankford recounts a problem she encountered as a young member of the staff of the Mallow post office. The local IWFL committee planned a Daffodil ball and Siobhán and her co-workers made plans to attend and spent hours discussing their dresses and hairstyles. The invitations arrived at the post office, but only for the men. On enquiring why, they were told that the Daffodil ball committee defined the term 'Ladies' as being 'applied solely only to girls who did not do paid work'. This led Lankford to comment:

> If one worked in the family shop measuring paraffin oil or weighing potatoes one qualified for the title, and for an invitation to this fashionable function, girls who went to work in offices were not eligible.[25]

However, Daffodil Day was generally a very successful and harmonious event for the suffrage movement.

A week after the celebrations on Daffodil Day, relations between IWFL and Cumann na mBan became strained. This came about after Sheehy Skeffington launched a blistering attack on Cumann na mBan at a public meeting in the Mansion House on 2 May 1914. This meeting was organised by Cumann na mBan. Since early April 1914 the *Irish Citizen* had been publishing a series of articles that rigorously berated nationalist women, calling them 'Nationalist Slave women' and a row ensued that descended into name calling on a grand scale.

Agnes O'Farrelly presided at the meeting at the Mansion House and the invited speakers were Professor Eoin MacNeill, Padraic Colum, Alice Stopford Green and Jennie Wyse Power. Hanna Sheehy Skeffington was not invited to speak, but she insisted on doing so. While the *Irish Citizen* and the mainstream newspapers reported on the meeting, none of them had published what she actually said. The *Irish Volunteer* did report the fact that she spoke, but recorded diplomatically that, 'Mrs Sheehy Skeffington had addressed the meeting and many of her remarks did not seem to meet with the approval of the majority at the meeting'.[26] Annoyed by Sheehy Skeffington's action, Agnes O'Farrelly wrote a letter to *The Irish Times* criticising Sheehy Skeffington and making it clear that the latter had forced her way onto the public platform. Without referring to exactly what Sheehy Skeffington said, O'Farrelly once again reiterated the policy of the Irish Women's Council that:

> The basis of the Irish Women's Council was Nationhood first and reforms later. The first liberty we Irishwomen claim is Liberty to organise ourselves on our own lines for any purpose dear to us, without being interfered with or exploited by any person or by any organisation for their own needs.[27]

This letter gave Sheehy Skeffington access to a public forum to disseminate her views and she did not hesitate to grasp the opportunity. In a letter to *The Irish Times* she said:

> It was made abundantly clear by myself, by other speakers and by the chair that I spoke at Saturday's meeting of the Irish Women's Council entirely as a critic of the new organisation. I welcome the opportunity given to me by Miss O'Farrelly's letter to state publicly that I am not connected in any way with the new society. Any society of women, which proposes to act merely as an 'animated collecting box' for men, cannot have the sympathy of any self-respecting woman.[28]

She continued her letter: 'The proposed "Ladies Auxiliary Committee" has apparently no function beyond that of a conduit pipe to pour a stream of gold into the coffers of the male organisation, and to be turned off automatically as soon as it has served this mean and subordinate purpose.'

She finished her letter by saying that she had permission to speak at the meeting because when it was put to a vote the majority decided to hear what she had to say. Sheehy Skeffington also suggested that the Irish Women's Council should seek a place on the executive council of the Irish National Volunteers on an equal footing with the men. The women ignored Sheehy Skeffington's objections and got on with the business of building their new organisation.

Some weeks later, on 23 May 1914, the original INE organisation, which at this time had a membership of fifty-six, held a meeting to discuss its 'relationship with Cumann na mBan'.[29] There are no minutes available for this meeting, but they apparently voted to remain independent and remained closely associated with the Irish Citizen Army and Liberty Hall. Some of the members simply drifted away as the original organisation effectively split, but it was never formally dissolved.

Meanwhile, Seán O'Casey, who believed that Countess de Markievicz was a member of Cumann na mBan, proposed a motion at a meeting of the Irish Citizen Army council to ask for her resignation because she was a member of that organisation and was therefore 'involved with the Irish National Volunteers'.[30] Countess de Markievicz was not a member of Cumann na mBan at this point, but she had attended two of the organisation's public meetings, which more than likely led him to believe she was a member. The motion was defeated and he resigned from the Irish Citizen Army.

Elizabeth Bloxham in her role as national organiser and propagandist for Cumann na mBan was working steadily towards building its membership. She was a domestic science teacher and spent her holidays in 1914 travelling around the country setting up new branches. Setting up a branch required a minimum of fifteen women and Bloxham described the process:

There would be some contact before I would visit these places, a
Volunteer might be in town and ask Mrs Wyse Power to form a
branch. I would always have some place to go and someone would
meet me when I arrived in town. The meeting would be in a room
off some hall perhaps.[31]

Local nationalists always prearranged the meetings and then
Bloxham simply appointed a president and a secretary from the
women and girls present. On one occasion, she travelled to Mary-
borough with Mary Colum and a number of the Irish National
Volunteers to organise a branch of Cumann na mBan and Irish
National Volunteers. The Volunteers were Thomas MacDonagh,
Seán McDermott and Liam Mellows and his brother Barney. The
women organised a branch of Cumann na mBan, while the men
simultaneously organised a company of Irish National Volunteers.
Cumann na mBan and the Irish National Volunteers also set up
branches in London and Scotland. In August 1914, Cumann na
mBan claimed to have forty branches in Ireland and England.[32]

Each new member of Cumann na mBan paid one shilling to join
the organisation. While one shilling does not appear to represent
a lot of money, the average female industrial worker earned about
eleven shillings a week and female farm labourers and domestic and
farm servants earned less, between three or four shillings per week
and so subscriptions to any organisation were generally beyond
their means. Furthermore, as branches met twice a week, domestic
and farm servants were excluded from membership simply because
they did not have sufficient time off to participate in twice-weekly
meetings. These are two of the possible explanations why Cumann
na mBan did not grow in any significant way. In late May 1914,
in an opinion piece in the *Irish Volunteer*, Eoin MacNeill copper-
fastened the notion that Cumann na mBan was an associate ladies
committee and made a link between the new organisation and the
Ladies' Land League when he stated that:

The women of Ireland will have much to do in keeping their place in the van of Irish patriotism! Already ambulance corps and Red Cross associations have taken much of their time in various districts and now embroidering colours and making flags will be an arduous if pleasing task. As in 1882, they will, as a matter of course be wholeheartedly in the movement, and their help and influence will be a valuable asset in the cause.[33]

Another group of women who had trouble when joining the organisation were female post office workers. The British government was very concerned that the Irish National Volunteers and Cumann na mBan might have an alliance with Germany. Consequently, the Special Branch RIC began a systematic campaign of watching civil servants, particularly those who worked for the post office. In Dalkey, County Dublin, the postmistress of the village post office was a Mrs Somers and her daughter Elizabeth held the position of junior clerk. Elizabeth Somers joined Cumann na mBan in 1914. She was observed by the police 'and members of the public collecting money on behalf of the Irish Volunteers' and observed using the post office as a point of distribution for Cumann na mBan leaflets.[34] Mrs Somers subsequently lost her position because 'the authorities were concerned that Elizabeth had access to information passing through the post office'.[35] Elizabeth pleaded with the authorities not to sack her mother because losing her job would leave her penniless, and she promised to move away from home if they would reconsider her mother's position. Mrs Somers was the first civil servant to be sacked for association with separatist nationalist activities. This made post office employees wary of joining Cumann na mBan. Siobhán Lankford, who worked in the post office in Mallow, County Cork, said 'they set up a branch of the Gaelic League in Mallow as a cover for their activities'.[36]

In late April 1914, the Ulster Unionists brought arms into Ireland, at Larne, County Antrim and in response the nationalists sought to get guns for the Irish National Volunteers. They raised £1,500, with Alice Stopford Green donating £500 towards the fund on the condition that she would get this money back when each Volunteer bought his gun. Funds also came from Clan na Gael in the USA, through John Devoy. In June 1914, 900 guns and 29,000 rounds of ammunition arrived at Howth, County Dublin. They had been brought into Ireland on the yacht *Asgard*, which was owned and crewed by Erskine Childers and his wife Molly. The other members of the crew were Mary Spring Rice, who was a member of the Gaelic League and the daughter of Lord Mounteagle, Gordon Shepherd and two unnamed fishermen from County Donegal.

In June 1914 the Wolfe Tone Committee invited the Irish National Volunteers and the Irish Citizen Army to participate at their annual demonstration at Bodenstown. While not yet brothers in arms, the two organisations were brought closer together by this event. Seán O'Casey said of the event:

> It was the first time they had stood side by side ... and took orders from a common commander, and this drawing together was possibly a symbol of a union that would be finally cemented together with the blood of both organisations.[37]

Jim Larkin went to the USA in late 1914 and James Connolly came to the fore as the leader of the ITGWU. When he arrived at Liberty Hall, the presence of women was well established. In her statement to the Bureau of Military History, Helena Molony said that her paper *Bean na hÉireann* was so widely read that James Connolly when he was still in America had enquired about her from William O'Brien, a founder member of the Irish Transport and General Workers' Union. This suggests that her presence within the rising nationalist and labour movements had attracted the attention of Connolly before he arrived in Ireland. However,

Connolly was actually responding to a letter he had received from Molony. In July 1909 she wrote to him, introducing herself, and Connolly asked William O'Brien who she was. He told O'Brien he had received a letter from a Miss H. Molony of *Bean na hÉireann* and asked him, 'Do you know the lady in question?'[38] When Connolly took over at Liberty Hall in late 1914, the women of the IWWU and INE were well established within the network of socialist nationalism.

Under the influence of James Connolly the Irish Citizen Army took on a militant socialist nationalist stance in the debate about Irish Ireland. Within this ambit, equality of the sexes was an integral part of the army, but it was an implicit rather than a written dictate. Socialism encompassed the ideology of equality between class and sex. Connolly was the dominant voice of this ideology in Ireland and brought together in his writings the rhetorical ideal of a socialist nationalist Ireland. This Ireland would be a nation founded on the idea of a classless society, where each was equal, despite class, sex and creed. Female participation in the socialist movement and the Irish Citizen Army was most often a by-product of affiliation to trade union activities from 1911 to 1913. The most well-known women involved were Julia Grennan, Nellie Gifford, Kathleen Lynn, Countess de Markievicz, Helena Molony, Elizabeth O'Farrell and Maria Perolz.

In 1914 the Home Rule Bill passed through the House of Commons. While it waited for the formal assent of King George VI, war broke out in Europe and the bill was shelved for the duration of the war, which it was generally believed would only last until Christmas 1914. The British army recruitment campaign was launched in Ireland in August 1914. Two months later, there was a concerted drive to organise a system of Voluntary Aid Detachments (VAD) by the Joint War Committee.[39] The Joint War Committee had been created by the British Red Cross Society and the Order of St John to avoid any duplication of war work.

The VAD was a unit organised to give support to the military and the civilian population at local and national levels in any emergency that might arise. The VAD were organised separately into male and female detachments. The men learned first aid and were instructed in duties connected with transport and military camps. The women were trained in first aid and home nursing, and underwent tuition in hygiene and cookery. They also received some training in infirmary nursing. In war, these units came together to give a wide range of first aid services to civilians and injured military personnel. Every VAD unit was required to register with the Joint War Committee.

At this time in Ireland there were several organisations involved in running first aid classes as part of their regular activities. These organisations were the Irish Volunteer Aid Association, the St John's Ambulance, the Ulster Volunteers, the Women's National Health Association and the United Irishwomen. Lady Aberdeen, the wife of the lord lieutenant, referred to these activities 'as a form of generic Red Cross work'.[40] She organised a public meeting to bring together interested parties and representatives from the aforementioned women's organisations attended. Lady Aberdeen observed that there were also 'individual members of Cumann na mBan present, though they were not there in the capacity of representation', but simply to see what was going on.[41]

Due to the influence of Lady Aberdeen, the Department of Agriculture and Technical Instruction (DATI) was nominated to become the umbrella body for all organised instruction in emergency first aid. The DATI also funded the classes and became the examining and awarding body for those who successfully completed the first aid course. The organisations present, including Cumann na mBan, undertook to become involved in the programme. Cumann na mBan organised their classes at 6 Harcourt Street, which was the headquarters of Sinn Féin. In other areas of Ireland, individual members of the organisation joined their local DATI classes.

Elizabeth Somers, who attended the first aid classes, said the other women in attendance were Mrs Walker, a National Health Insurance Inspector, Lady O'Connell (Ballybrack), Professor Agnes O'Farrelly, Alice Stopford Green, the Hon. Mary Spring Rice and Miss Chenevieux Trench. Somers claimed that there were 'scores of similar women on the membership roll'.[42]

At the outbreak of the war, John Redmond, leader of the Irish Parliamentary Party, offered the services of the Irish National Volunteers to the British government and he toured the country to enlist men for the British army. The original provisional Irish National Volunteer committee repudiated Redmond and his executive nominees. An emergency convention was held on the 25 October 1914 to reaffirm the Irish National Volunteers' manifesto and resist all attempts at conscription. The ensuing split left the Irish National Volunteers with 11,000 members and they renamed themselves the Irish Volunteers. The remaining 170,000 men formed the National Volunteers under John Redmond.

In October 1914, the executive of the Irish Women's Council/ Cumann na mBan issued a manifesto, essentially repudiating John Redmond, and sent it to all branches of the organisation for approval. However, its effect was to create a split. The rejection of the manifesto by the Naas branch is an example of how branches generally received it. At a meeting called to discuss the manifesto, a proposal was put forward that:

> The branch should secede from the Cumann na mBan, because we cannot endorse its sentiments regarding Mr Redmond, and that furthermore we form ourselves into a Women's Auxiliary Corps attached to the fourth Battalion of the Kildare Regiment.[43]

The proposal was carried eight to three. A second resolution was proposed, which was that 'they endorse their absolute confidence in Mr Redmond and the Irish Party'. This was also approved by eight votes to three.[44] The majority of the branches rejected the manifesto, which subsequently reduced the Irish Women's Council/Cumann na mBan to a rump. According to Kathleen Clarke in her autobiography *Revolutionary Woman*, a convention was called in November 1914 which was a stormy meeting. The meeting was presided over by Margaret Dobbs and Elizabeth Bloxham.[45] A resolution was put forward by the Ard Padraic branch from Limerick, calling for the organisation to pledge itself 'to neutrality between the two sections of the Volunteers', with Mary MacSwiney from Cork and Madge Daly from Limerick leading the convention against the resolution. A vote to support Redmond was put forward and was lost eighty-eight votes to twenty-eight, causing Clarke to comment 'so now Cumann na mBan was split too'.[46] Several of the members at the meeting resigned.

It is difficult to discover how many branches actually existed before this split. There are problems with the figures given by Cumann na mBan on membership at this time. The Central branch had a membership of around eighty and the INE branch had about thirty members. As these were the only two branches in Dublin at this point, these numbers cannot be considered impressive. Their first manifesto of August 1914 claimed that 'the organisation had forty branches'.[47] To date, the primary sources for the period April to August 1914 have yielded just sixteen branches. Counties Antrim, Clare, Cork, Galway, Laois and Mayo had one branch each, and Counties Donegal, Dublin, Kildare, Limerick and Tipperary each had two branches. There was also one branch in both Glasgow and London.

In the aftermath of this division the rump declared their allegiance to the Irish Volunteers and reformed as the (second) Cumann na mBan, committed solely to the ideals of separatist nationalism. From this time the dual language title ceased to exist. A new executive was elected and a new manifesto drawn up, which stated in its preamble that Cumann na mBan:

Came into being to adv   cause of Irish liberty and to
organise Irishwomen in furtherance of that object. We feel
bound to make the pronouncement that to urge or encourage
Irish Volunteers to enlist in the British army cannot, under any
circumstances, be regarded as consistent with the work we set
ourselves to do.[48]

The new organisation became completely immersed in the growing
nationalist separatist movement and continued to function as
an auxiliary to the Irish Volunteers, raising funds for arms and
ammunition by holding flag days, céilithe and concerts.

In August 1915, the coming together of the militant organisations was clarified in the public mind at the funeral of the old
Fenian leader O'Donovan Rossa. The Irish Citizen Army, the
Irish Volunteers and Clan na Gael, all took part in the funeral
procession through the city in uniform. Clan na Gael was formed
in Dublin in 1910 under the auspices of the Hibernian Rifles,
for girls aged between eight and sixteen years. 'It operated as a
parallel organisation to Na Fianna.'[49]

At the funeral, the executive of the second Cumann na mBan
was represented by Mrs Eoin MacNeill, Mrs Wyse Power, Miss Siav
Trench, Miss Walsh and Elizabeth Bloxham. Among the branches
that sent contingents were 'the Central branch, the Inghinidhe na
hÉireann branch, the Cathleen Ní Houlihan branch and branches
from Cork, Limerick, Belfast and Liverpool'.[50] Hanna Sheehy
Skeffington apparently put aside her differences with Cumann na
mBan to walk with them in the funeral procession through the city
to Glasnevin Cemetery. Bloxham later recalled how, as the women
approached the graveyard at Glasnevin, Thomas MacDonagh
made a space for herself and Sheehy Skeffington 'so they could
hear Patrick Pearse deliver his oration'.[51] Bloxham described her
reaction to the oration:

As he spoke, a biblical phrase through my head, and 'he lifted up his voice and said unto them'. Such uplift of voice and spirit I never heard before or since. It swept through the listeners so that for the time we were with him. I am no sentimentalist but the tears stood in my eyes, I knew that we need no longer continue to look to the past for our great men for there was one in our midst who was aflame with the same passionate devotion as the heroes of old.[52]

At their annual convention on 31 October 1915, the second Cumann na mBan changed its constitution and created a new executive comprising a

CUMANN NA mBAN UNIFORM.
N.B. The skirt should be cut much shorter than it appears in above. It should be at least 7 ins. from the ground to be of really practical use.

Official designer drawing of Cumann na mBan uniform.

president, vice-president, secretary and treasurer. Jennie Wyse Power was unanimously elected president. The organisation also adopted a uniform. This was optional and consisted of 'a coat and skirt of Volunteer tweed, the skirt was to be at least seven inches off the ground, and a hat of the same material'.[53] The jacket was to 'have four pockets and a tweed or leather belt' and they were instructed to acquire a haversack with a first aid kit. Those members who were unable to afford a uniform, were instructed to wear a grey or green felt hat, which could be bought in the Boy Scout shop. The membership was also informed that they 'were honour bound to give preference to Irish manufactured goods'.[54]

Possession of a uniform depended on a member's ability to pay for a tailored uniform, unless they had the skills to make it themselves. Consequently, the few uniforms that existed by 1916 varied in quality. Commenting on the quality of uniforms, Kathleen O'Doherty, a

find out if the rifle is loaded, and if so remove cartridges. She then follows in the rear of stretcher. Several different types of rifle are now in use, and members of Stretcher Squads should be familiar with all, if possible.[60]

Generally, the membership of the Cumann na mBan took part in regular military training exercises such as drilling and Morse code. Rifle practice was optional and the decision on whether it should be organised was the responsibility of each branch. However, learning the skills of the cleaning and care of rifles was mandatory, especially for those women who were involved in ambulance training. Revolvers were considered the most suitable weapons for self-defence for members of the ambulance corps and the women were also instructed in the use of '22 miniatures or a converted rifle for target practice'.[61]

One branch that set up training in rifle practice was the Belfast branch. This branch had twenty members who were very active and a report in the *Irish Volunteer* states that they 'engaged in drilling, for the most part, in the open air' and on 5 December they planned on 'marching to the Divis Mountain to shoot at a considerably longer range'. Over Christmas 1915, the branch organised a joint 'Xmas Shooting Competition, with the local Irish Volunteers'. This took the form of a sealed handicap and it took place over four nights at their drill hall at Willowbank. The branch secretary informed Cumann na mBan headquarters that 'keen interest was shown by the competitors, and some fine shooting was made. Friendly rivalry between the Cumann na mBan and the Volunteers gave an additional zest to the competition.'[62]

The winner of the first prize was a Miss Kelly, the first to score 92 per cent. Second prize and third prize went to a Miss Corr and Thomas Mac hUain, respectively.

The men and women from the Scottish branches of these organisations became involved in moving weapons from Scotland to Dublin. For several months before the rebellion, twenty-eight men of the Glasgow Volunteers and two women of the Ann Devlin branch of Cumann na mBan travelled constantly from Glasgow to Dublin with guns and ammunition. Two of these women were Margaret Skinnider, who was the branch captain, and a member who is named only as Miss O'Neill. Lizzie Morrin, another member, was a dressmaker and she made waistcoats and jackets with hidden pockets for carrying guns and ammunition unobtrusively. Skinnider carried 'detonators for bombs in her hat with the wires wrapped around her beneath her coat'.[63]

The second Cumann na mBan kept the flag day as its main fund-raising scheme and in 1915–1916 they supplemented this with a collecting card and by holding dances, concerts and raffles. The collecting card was simply a subscription card on which an individual signed their name and the amount of their subscription.

They always raised money under the auspices of the Defence of Ireland Fund. The paper flag that they sold on flag days was made of green paper with an image of a rifle on it. When the women of Cumann na mBan attended the Wolfe Tone Commemoration in June 1915, they carried a new flag of green, white and orange on which they had embroidered a rifle. According to the *Irish Volunteer*, when they unfurled this flag at Sallins railway station they received a rousing cheer from the men of the Volunteers. By late 1915 the image had become the official insignia of the organisation and they created an official badge. The badges were made from silver and cheap metal and members could purchase them from their respective local branch of Cumann na mBan.

The most popular forms of fundraising were the dances (céilithe) and concerts, because they engendered cohesion within the growing separatist nationalist movement, especially in urban areas, while simultaneously raising money. The *Irish Volunteer* published reports from Cumann na mBan on these events. In Limerick, the local branch held its 'first dance of the season on

6 November 1915 and raised £10'. The paper reported that there were about sixty couples present and that 'a most pleasing feature of the ballroom was the picturesque effect lent by the number of ladies who wore Irish Costumes'.[64]

In Dublin, the Central branch advertised their Christmas concert and apparently secured some of the best artistes. The newspaper report said that the concert was to be very large scale and 'like everything else this vigorous branch handles, it will be a success, and if people wish to have their patriotic emotions aroused this will doubtlessly be a rare treat'.[65] The women had also organised a post-concert dance, to 'give everyone the opportunity of that communion of spirit which one feels such need for under the influence of soul-stirring music and song'.[66] However, due to the plethora of events organised all over Dublin and in the national sphere, the women postponed this event until the New Year.

Apart from these social occasions, they also held several raffles to raise money. On occasion they held a lottery for guns. In Belfast, on 25 January 1915, the branch held a Whist Drive and they also raffled a rifle to raise money for the Defence of Ireland Fund. They made enough money from these ventures to buy an ambulance outfit. Subsequently the person who won the rifle 'returned it to the women of Cumann na mBan for their own use'.[67]

In early 1916, rumours began circulating within the Irish Volunteers, the Irish Citizen Army and Cumann na mBan that some kind of action was expected. By this time the organisation had thirty-nine branches throughout the country and three in Britain.

TABLE 3: LOCATION OF FORTY-TWO BRANCHES OF CUMANN NA MBAN

Area	1916
Ulster	4
Munster	16

Leinster	15
Connaught	4
England & Scotland	3
Total	**42**

Source: Irish Volunteer, *April 1916.*

While the rank and file did not know of the impending rebellion, they were aware that something was imminent because of the constant route marches that took place during the spring of 1916. This impression was disseminated by rumour and given credence in James Connolly's paper the *Irish Worker*, which carried an advertisement for a concert in Liberty Hall on 6 February 1916 and described it as the 'most exciting event of 1916, except the revolution'.[68]

Seamus Robinson, an Irish Volunteer from Scotland, said of this time, 'there was a general impression in our garrison from the time we left Scotland that a fight was bound to come'.[69] He was living in Dublin at the Larkfield Mill in Kimmage with a group of Volunteers from England and Scotland. These men had arrived in Ireland between the end of the 1915 and February 1916 in the aftermath of the introduction of conscription in Britain. On arrival in Dublin they settled at the Larkfield Mill, which was also the headquarters of the Dublin 4th Battalion Irish Volunteers.

Countess Plunkett, who was the wife of Count George Noble Plunkett, held this property under a lease. It consisted of twenty acres of land, four cottages, a shooting range, the disused Larkfield Mill and a significant-sized barn. Also on the property was a substantial house for the mill manager, known as Larkfield House. From late 1915 to Easter 1916, when the countess was in America, the count, with four of his adult children (Joseph, George, Jack and Geraldine), lived in the house. Located in this series of buildings was the Larkfield Chemical Company Limited, which manufactured carbolic acid. Thomas Dillon (Geraldine Plunkett's fiancé) and Rory O'Connor set up the company. Seamus Robinson estimated that there were ninety men living at Larkfield and they slept in the barn.

TABLE 4: ORIGINS OF THE MEN OF THE KIMMAGE GARRISON

Address	Number
Glasgow	18
Tullamore	2
Manchester	14
Dublin	2
London	54
Total	90

Source: Seamus Robinson (UCDAD, Eithne Coyle papers, p61/13 (11-13)).

The men at Kimmage spent their time preparing for the rebellion by making buckshot for cartridges and homemade bombs using billycans. They used the shooting range on the premises, which was also used by the 4th Battalion Irish Volunteers, and this was located on a lower floor of the mill. Robinson described a visit made by Patrick Pearse to Larkfield during Holy Week, where he said that Pearse gave the men a lecture on street fighting and defence of buildings. One piece of information Pearse imparted was 'there would be a full dress parade held on Easter Sunday and he hinted at the possibility of interference by police or the military'.[70] However, the parade was cancelled on Sunday morning and the men spent the day in confusion because they did not know the reason for the cancellation and were not aware of any alternative plans.

During this period, the ongoing preparation of the food supply and medical necessities fell to the women. According to several accounts the women had a sense that something big was about to happen. Eilís Ní Riain recalled that the members of Cumann na mBan were ordered to mobilise for a route march on Sunday 23 April and 'were instructed not to wear uniforms or brooches and to carry sufficient rations for twenty-four hours', which indicated to them that 'something very special was about to happen'.[71] Ní Riain conveys the impression that the whole movement was on tenterhooks. She said that several of the Catholic churches in Dublin were filled on Saturday night by members of the various organisations all 'waiting for confession and on Sunday morning the number at Holy Communion was most impressive'.[72] Maria Perolz, commenting on the large numbers of Volunteers attending the church at Whitefriar Street in Dublin, told Kathleen Lynn that she believed 'Fr Devlin of Whitefriar St must have known about the Rising because there were so many people cleaning up their consciences by going to confession'.[73]

Helena Molony, in her description of the activity in Liberty Hall during Holy Week, recalled that 'there were large quantities of provisions ordered in, to make rations for the men. We bought the supplies: meat, bread, butter, tea and sugar and we cooked it in Liberty Hall'.[74] The women also rolled bandages for first aid kits. Across the river at the Irish Volunteer headquarters in Dawson Street, the women of Cumann na mBan were performing similar tasks. During Holy Week, some women of Cumann na mBan were sent throughout the country to senior figures in the movement, with dispatches bearing the plans for Easter Sunday. To protect the plans from discovery, the rank and file members had been trained over a period of months to be on call. The loyalty and preparedness of the men and women was tested by means of unscheduled route marches. So any time of night or day, members could be called upon to take part in a route march.

The Irish Citizen Army roll book for early 1916 shows that the organisation had 334 registered members; of this number just one was a female: Countess de Markievicz. The roll book is comprehensive and contains the names and address of the members as well as their official army number. It shows beyond doubt that 'the women involved at Liberty Hall were not officially members of the Irish Citizen Army at this time'.[75]

The executive committee of Cumann na mBan planned what they described as an 'Arms Ballot' for Holy Wednesday, 19 April 1916, with 'Eoin MacNeill (who kindly consented), drawing the winning numbers'.[76] Entry for the draw was £1 and it was open to all Irish Volunteer companies, as well as the branches of the Cumann na mBan, 'on the understanding that the arms would be given to the local Volunteers'. The first prize was twenty guns, with subsequent prizes of ten guns, the number of these depending on how much money was collected. This raffle took place just days before the rebellion and there is no report on what happened to these guns.

During Holy Week, Countess de Markievicz moved into Jennie Wyse Power's home at Henry Street, which was above her restaurant. De Markievicz had spent much of the week assembling a uniform and had several formal portrait photographs taken by the Keogh Brothers at their studio in Dorset Street. On Good Friday, Kitty O'Doherty went to visit de Markievicz at Liberty Hall and she recalled:

I was very fond of her and still am ... I thought I was accustomed to her eccentricities. She said, 'I want to show you something. I could not fight in skirts though I am wearing one now.' She had on a short skirt of green material and she just undid one big hook. She stood up in breeches and puttees ... She repeated, 'I could not fight in skirts'. She was very proud of herself. I do not think it was a cast off of Mallin's, this was perfect fitting. She looked marvellous. She had a Sam Browne belt. She wanted to show it to me.[77]

The portrait photographs show a jacket buttoned from left to right, which indicates that it was man's jacket and probably was not specially made for her.

Nancy Wyse Power's recollection of the same incident is that on Good Friday, at her mother's home in Henry Street, 'de Markievicz took a childish delight' in showing her outfit off and added that 'ladies in trousers were less common then'.[78]

On Holy Thursday, the German ship, the *Aud*, which was carrying guns into Kerry, was discovered and Sir Roger Casement was arrested. The captain scuttled the ship off the coast near Cork Harbour the following day. Eoin MacNeill, the chief of staff of the Irish Volunteers, placed an advertisement in the *Sunday Independent* cancelling the route marches for Easter Sunday.

Despite this the proclamation was printed in Liberty Hall on Easter Sunday and that night the decision to go ahead with the rebellion on Monday was taken by the leaders of the new rebel army. Maria Perolz, Elizabeth O'Farrell, Julia Grennan, Maeve Cavanagh and Nancy Wyse Power were called to Liberty Hall at 2 a.m. to begin the task of delivering the new dispatches throughout the country. Grennan travelled to Dundalk and Carrickmacross, while O'Farrell travelled to Galway city, Athenry and Spiddal. Perolz was sent to Tralee and Maeve Cavanagh was sent to Waterford. Nancy Wyse Power was sent to Borris in County Carlow and Kilkenny city. It appears these women were sent with the dispatches because they all lived in the city and were easy to find in a hurry. Kathleen Lynn also recalled:

On Holy Saturday, Connolly told me to come early on Sunday to Liberty Hall to stand by … We may have been giving last touches to dressings etc. and making up sandwiches for the men. We might have been there somewhere around 10 o'clock .We just hung around trying to busy ourselves. I know that Pearse was there and all the leaders were there, coming and going. Connolly was a bit worried and uncertain how things were going to turn out; he and the Citizen Army were determined to go out to fight.[79]

On Sunday, James Connolly ordered Kathleen Lynn to spend the night at the home of Jennie Wyse Power so that she would have a good night's rest. Countess de Markievicz moved out and decided to stay at the home of William O'Brien at Belvedere Place. Winifred Carney had been staying there during Holy Week and de Markievicz simply accompanied her to the house and announced to O'Brien that she intended to stay overnight. He said that as 'Madame' was removing the ammunition from her automatic she 'startled us all by sending a bullet through the door of the room in which we were'.[80] He was the first person to experience her sensitive trigger finger. Over at Henry Street, Kathleen Lynn said she did not sleep because she 'kept thinking of what was coming off'.[81] The plan was that all of the women of Cumann na mBan and those with the Irish Citizen Army would be confined to the areas of first aid, cooking and carrying dispatches.

When Cumann na mBan was founded in 1914 as a ladies auxiliary committee for the Irish Volunteers amidst much celebration and rancour, they cannot have visualised that within a mere two years some of them would be at the centre of a revolution that would utterly change the existing Irish political landscape.

<h1>5</h1>

REVOLUTION AND REPERCUSSION

At Easter 1916, the Irish Volunteers, the Irish Citizen Army and Cumann na mBan came together to pursue their goal for a new Irish republic. However, they continued to acknowledge openly the lack of *esprit de corps* between their respective organisations. When they were thrown together in the chaos of the rebellion, they had no choice but to co-operate, as on Easter Monday, 24 April 1916, they marched out as a united rebel army to challenge the British Empire. In doing so they began a fight, which despite being doomed to failure, infused a grim reality into the romantic dream of Irish Ireland.

ON EASTER Monday at the Larkfield Mill in Kimmage, the men of the Kimmage garrison were assembled at 11.15 a.m. and marched by their officer George Plunkett to Dolphin's Barn, and from here travelled by tram into the city. It was only when they arrived at Liberty Hall that they discovered the rebellion was about to begin. Margaret Skinnider from the Ann Devlin branch of Cumann na mBan (Glasgow) met them at Liberty Hall and told Seamus Robinson 'it's on'.[1] This was the first confirmation they had that the rebellion was to begin that day.

Around noon Easter Monday, 24 April 1916, a combination

of the members of the Irish Volunteers, the Irish Citizen Army and the Hibernian Rifles marched out from Liberty Hall under the leadership of Patrick H. Pearse to take over the GPO for the rebel army headquarters. Cumann na mBan were not represented in this group because they were mobilised at other locations in the city. On the south side of the city, the members of the INE branch under their captain Rose McNamara had been ordered to mobilise at the Weavers Hall at Cork Street for 10 a.m. Twenty-five members of Cumann na mBan turned out. The women marched to Emerald Square where they formed up. They marched behind a section of the 4th Dublin Battalion Irish Volunteers under the command of Commandant Éamonn Ceannt, to a distillery building at Marrowbone Lane.[2] On the north side of the city, 'the women were ordered to mobilise at Palmerston Place, which was in the vicinity of the Broadstone railway station'.[3]

Each garrison had a specific building designated as its head-quarters, which the garrisons had initially to capture. The GPO garrison covered the whole of Sackville Street not just the GPO building. The term Boland's Mills garrison applied to a range of buildings, both private and industrial, spread over several streets and included a stretch of the south-east railway line and the Grand Canal Basin. The commandant of Boland's Mills garrison was Eamon de Valera, who set up his headquarters, not in the mill as current historiography indicates, but in the South Dublin Union dispensary that was located in Barrow Street.[4] De Valera is often castigated for his refusal to have women at his garrison, but he was not unique. There were no women with the garrisons at the South Dublin Union or Mendicity Institute. In her personal recollection of 1916, Josephine Wall of Cumann na mBan said that de Valera did use the women's services for carrying dispatches and that they worked for him, 'during the whole week until Patrick H. Pearse and his comrades in arms eventually surrendered'.[5]

As the designated GPO garrison marched towards Sackville

Street from Eden Quay, Seamus Robinson and five other men were ordered to take over the building on the corner of Sackville Street and Bachelors Walk. These six men had between them a motley collection of guns and ammunition. According to Robinson, they had a service rifle (owned by a Citizen Army man), two shotguns, two small arms, plus 'a fair supply of home made (billycan) grenades'.[6] This supply of guns and ammunition was an indication of the arms situation of the complete rebel army.

Elizabeth O'Farrell and Julia Grennan returned to Dublin having delivered their dispatches and made their way to the GPO. Winifred Carney, who had spent the previous days typing all the dispatches sent out from Liberty Hall, had her typewriter carried to the GPO from where she continued typing dispatches. Carney was a trade union activist from Belfast and had worked with Connolly when he was based there. She had travelled to Dublin on 14 April 1916, to assist in the final preparations for the rebellion. The women involved with the Irish Citizen Army were mobilised to go with the St Stephen's Green and the City Hall garrisons. With Cumann na mBan mobilised elsewhere, Winifred Carney was the sole woman to march with the men to the GPO.[7]

When Cumann na mBan were mobilised at Easter 1916 they were ordered to bring rations for twenty-four hours and not to wear uniforms or brooches. The primary sources indicate that during the six-day rebellion there were in fact just two females in military style uniform. They were Countess de Markievicz and Margaret Skinnider. At this time, de Markievicz was not a member of Cumann na mBan and she had assembled a self-styled military uniform for the occasion. Skinnider, who was from Glasgow, was also wearing a self-styled uniform and she spent the early days of the rebellion cycling a bike around the city, changing in and out of her uniform, until she was shot while attempting to attack a British position.

One of the tasks given to women was to carry dispatches between the various garrisons. This came about because when the rebels seized the GPO, they cut most of the telegraph and telephone wires and consequently contact was almost impossible.[8] Getting information from one place to another was difficult and slow. The use of couriers was the only means the rebels had of knowing what was happening in the city or country. The responsibility for carrying and retaining some semblance of communication became a large part of the workload of the women. They were also involved in moving arms and food supplies from one outpost to another. Although the female rebels were organised into three sections, carrying dispatches was perceived as the elite job. Leslie Price, who was a courier, recalled 'we were told not to go into the kitchens or do washing up or anything, nor first aid. We had our own special function.'[9]

One of these couriers was May McLoughlin, who was a fifteen-year-old member of the Clan na Gael girl scouts. She had been at Three Rock Mountain near Dundrum for the weekend with other members of the scouts, in the charge of their captain, May Kelly. The group did not know about the rebellion until they tried getting a train into the city. They decided to walk into the city and arrived at St Stephen's Green, where William Partridge allowed them into the park. They were placed under the charge of Countess de Markievicz. The younger children were collected by their parents, but McLoughlin stayed behind and became a messenger. Still in her scout uniform, she was asked to walk to Drumcondra and collect ammunition for Joe O'Reilly, one of the men in the park. Having accomplished this errand, she then decided to report to the GPO.

The first casualty of the rebellion was Constable James Brien, who was a member of the Dublin Metropolitan Police (DMP). He was on duty at the entrance gate to Dublin Castle and was shot and fatally wounded during the initial assault by the rebels. Failing to take the Castle the rebels retreated into City Hall, situated beside the entrance to Dublin Castle.

Kathleen Lynn and Countess de Markievicz left Liberty Hall in the latter's car and arrived at City Hall just after noon. They saw:

> ... the dead body of a big policeman lying on the ground – it seemed to be in front of the Castle gate. Just then, Sir Thomas Myles came up evidently going into the castle and I still remember the look of horror on his face when he saw the body. I do not think he noticed me. He rushed in. I heard afterwards that it was to get first aid equipment.[10]

The gate at City Hall was locked and Lynn had to climb over it to gain entry. Seán Connolly of the Irish Citizen Army was the leader of this garrison and he became the first casualty on the rebel side. When Lynn gained entry, Connolly suggested they go onto the roof to defend it in case they were attacked from there. Lynn, accompanied by Jinny Shanahan and about six men, went to the roof, bringing some of her medical equipment with her. Within minutes Connolly was fatally wounded by sniper fire. Lynn, describing this incident, said:

> It was a beautiful day, the sun was hot, and we were not long there when we noticed Seán Connolly coming towards us walking upright although he had been advised to crouch and take cover as much as possible. We suddenly saw him fall mortally wounded by a sniper's bullet from the Castle, first aid was useless and he died almost immediately, that I think was in the early afternoon, Jinny Shanahan whispered an act of contrition in his ear.[11]

Meanwhile, across the city, Michael Mallin led a group of men and women from the Irish Citizen Army into St Stephen's Green park. The group of women who marched to St Stephen's Green, under the leadership of Madeleine Ffrench Mullen, set up a first aid post and an open-air kitchen. Countess de Markievicz arrived later and, according to her, Michael Mallin asked her to stay with him and promoted her to second in command. Apart from de Markievicz's own claim, there is no evidence to support this.

Helena Molony said that before the rebels left Liberty Hall, James Connolly gave revolvers to the girls and women and instructed them to use them as 'a last resort', which makes it clear that they were given the guns for defence, not aggression and that the women involved with the Irish Citizen Army were trained in the use of guns.[12] Connolly also assigned work to all members of the army and he confined all of the women without exception to work in first aid and catering. 'Countess de Markievicz was appointed a Lieutenant and Dr Lynn was appointed Captain and medical officer'.[13] Their designated role was to drive around the various garrisons and check for anyone in need of medical aid. When de Markievicz left Dr Lynn at City Hall, she was ignoring her designated role as chauffeur.

Nora O'Daly, who was a member of the Fairview branch of Cumann na mBan which was attached to the 2nd Dublin Battalion Irish Volunteers, arrived at St Stephen's Green late on Monday evening. She was disappointed to find the men and women of the Irish Citizen Army in control. According to O'Daly, when she arrived at the park she was met by de Markievicz who told her:

> If they cared, they could throw in our lot with theirs … this we eventually did, as no other course seemed open to us and after all, we were fighting for the same cause. I admit for one that I was disappointed at having to make this decision.[14]

Nora O'Daly's middle-class sensibilities made it difficult for her to talk to men and women she had not been properly introduced to, especially if they were working class. She added 'here all were strangers (except de Markievicz) and somehow one cannot feel the same confidence in people previously unknown'. She remained unhappy until she met Ffrench Mullen and all her doubts 'and anxieties were dissipated in a moment when I caught sight of this plucky lady'.[15] O'Daly was very critical of the trenches in the park, considering the whole situation a death trap:

> While quite willing to die for the freedom of Ireland I saw no reason for doing so if I could help it before I had accomplished the purpose which had brought me hither, namely to render all the assistance possible to the wounded and to save life wherever possible ... The sight of bloodshed had always been repugnant to me, although the sight of blood has no affect whatever on my nerves.[16]

When the evacuation of the park to the College of Surgeons took place, the women were ordered to move in twos and threes and run as fast as possible. O'Daly, in her dash to the College of Surgeons, was amazed to see people out sightseeing and overheard the remark, 'look at them running with no hats on them', which irritated O'Daly intensely and she asked 'could this happen anywhere but Dublin?'[17] During this period, every woman in society, regardless of her class, wore her hat when out of her house because 'it was then a badge of respectability'.[18] To be seen without a hat was a sign of slovenliness or, worse, low class. That this remark jarred with her in a moment when she might be shot dead, indicates how strongly this symbol of respectability was bred into women.

From the Shelbourne Hotel, situated on the north-east corner of St Stephen's Green, the staff and guests observed the events in the park. In 1951, Elizabeth Bowen published a history of the hotel and interviewed staff about their memories of 1916. They recalled a scene involving Countess de Markievicz:

> She emerged from the Green and marched up and down, gun on shoulder, in full and rewarding view of the Shelbourne windows

… The fact that the British troops were moving into position all round the Green ready to shoot from houses from all along the confluent streets, did not apparently for some time deter her. It is the stern opinion of some of the hotel staff that 'the countess took unfair advantage of her sex'.[19]

Sometime after 12.30 p.m. on Easter Monday, Geraldine Fitzgerald, a district nurse returning from duty, observed the shooting of a policeman in St Stephen's Green. Fitzgerald, who was aged twenty-six and from Birr in County Offaly, had trained in the Royal City of Dublin Hospital and in 1916 was based at the St Patrick's Jubilee Nurse's home at 101 St Stephen's Green South in Dublin. She recorded in her diary that as she approached the park she was 'astonished to see Sinn Féiners in the park digging trenches while others were ready with rifles to fire on anyone in military or police uniform who passed that way'.[20] She said that inside the nurse's home they 'were just seated to have their soup when they heard the most awful firing from outside the house' and 'they jumped up immediately and rushed to the front of the house to see what was happening'. They 'saw all the men with their rifles fixed towards Harcourt Street' and:

… a lady in a green uniform the same as the men were wearing (breeches, slouch hat with green feathers etc.), the feathers were the only feminine feature in her appearance, holding a revolver in one hand and a cigarette in the other was standing on the footpath giving orders to the men. We recognised her as the Countess de Markievicz – such a specimen of womanhood. We had only been looking out a few minutes when we saw a policeman walking down the footpath … he had only gone a short way when we heard a shot and then saw him fall forward on his face. The Countess ran triumphantly into the Green saying 'I got him' and some of the rebels shook her by the hand and seemed to congratulate her.[21]

This was Constable Michael Lahiff, an unarmed member of the Dublin Metropolitan Police (DMP). Fitzgerald continued:

> We rushed for bandages etc. and all four of us walked across the road in front of the trenches where the rebel's had their rifles ready to fire. We were quite prepared to be shot at any moment but we got the poor man to safety. He was shot in the lung, close to the heart and was bleeding profusely. A doctor arrived at the same time as we did … he bandaged the poor fellow but we could not stop his life blood ebbing away. He was alive and conscious.[22]

This shooting took place outside the Unitarian Church on St Stephen's Green West and the entrance to the park referred to by Fitzgerald was located directly opposite the nurse's home.

ONE OF the most common threads in the personal accounts of Irish Volunteers who fought that week was the shortage of food. The garrison at the GPO had plenty of food because the men had commandeered food from Findlaters provisions shop in Sackville Street and left a receipt signed on behalf of the Provisional Government. There were several hotels in Sackville Street and the rebels obviously took advantage of their stores, as May McLoughlin recalled that the GPO had plenty of food and when she 'was ordered to go to the kitchen and rest she saw for the first time in her life a whole salmon cooked laid in a dish'.[23]

Other garrisons around the city had problems obtaining food. At St Stephen's Green there was no food supply. Mary Hyland left the park and approached a milkman on his rounds and ordered him at the point of a bayonet to hand over one of his cans of milk, and Lily Kempson held up a bread cart with a revolver. Nellie Gifford also acquired sacks of bread and, when this food ran out, the women looted food from local shops. When the garrison moved to the College of Surgeons, the situation deteriorated. May McLoughlin travelled from the college to the GPO and explained to James Connolly that the garrison at St Stephen's Green was short of food and ammunition. He gave her £80 to bring to Michael Mallin, who refused to accept it and explained to McLoughlin that the money was 'no use to him because he needed food and ammunition not money'.[24]

The section of the 4th Battalion Irish Volunteers who occupied the Marrowbone Lane distillery were accompanied by an attachment of women from the INE branch of Cumann na mBan. Lily O'Brennan found herself isolated from her branch of Cumann na mBan (Central branch) and decided to join this group. O'Brennan, unlike O'Daly, was not so tetchy at having to work with women she did not know. She said 'none of them knew me nor did I know them, though the majority were inhabitants of Dolphin's Barn where I was now living'.[25] Lily lived in Dolphin's Barn with her married sister Áine Ceannt and her husband Éamonn, their son David and a maid. The membership of the INE branch was comprised of working-class girls and women, and on a social level O'Brennan would never have mixed with these women. Lily retained her sense of self-imposed disconnection from them and recollected, 'being in a way an alien amongst them I thought the best thing I could offer to do was to keep a diary, so any bits of news were passed to me'.[26] Irish nationalism still had a long way to go in breaking down social barriers.

At this garrison, on the first day, the scarcity of food reduced everyone to consuming dry bread and black tea. O'Brennan said, 'we relished all the more if milk and butter were spared for our glorious fighting men'.[27] On Tuesday the Volunteers commandeered a baker's cart and took milk from a passing milkman's cart. On Wednesday the men acquired 'nineteen chickens and cooked them for dinner, using bayonets to lift the chickens out of the pots'. On Thursday they acquired three calves, 'one was butchered by a Volunteer named Bob Holland and on Friday the women fried veal cutlets and gave the men a good feed'.[28]

At the Four Courts, Ned Daly was in command. There were over fourteen members of Cumann na mBan at this garrison. Eilís Ní Riain, who was based in Church Street, recalled that for the first few days they helped in the kitchen where the Volunteers kept them supplied with food commandeered from various shops. They commandeered 'ham, tomatoes, tea and sugar and I think, milk'. Ní Riain recalled that for the first time in her life she 'sampled some tomatoes and sugarless tea'.[29] After two days, some of the women were assigned to the first aid station based at the Father Mathew Hall, which was part of the Capuchin Friary at Church Street.

A series of barricades were constructed between the hall and the Four Courts. The Irish Volunteers also commandeered stretcher beds for the first aid station. Members of Cumann na mBan working in the first aid station were supplied with a white armlet marked with a red cross to designate their status. This was the internationally recognised Red Cross armband, and some of the women were also wearing a white apron with the Red Cross insignia on the front bib. They were often confused with the Red Cross VAD nurses who were also working in the city. This is a possible explanation as to why the women were allowed relative freedom to move around the city during that week. In examining many of the witness statements of the Bureau of Military History it becomes clear that the rebels were unaware of, or did not understand, the mission statement of the International Red Cross, which was:

The International Committee of the Red Cross (ICRC) is an impartial, neutral and independent organisation whose exclusively humanitarian mission is to protect the lives and dignity of victims of war and internal violence and to provide them with assistance.[30]

The *Irish Volunteer*, in 1915, did publish the mission statement of the International Committee of the Red Cross, but this information does

not appear to have been passed on to the membership of Cumann na mBan at their first aid classes. This is illustrated by Áine Heron's account of how, when she arrived at the Four Courts garrison with her first aid equipment, she also had a flag with a Red Cross which she planned to fly from the dome of the rotunda to denote this section of the building a Red Cross hospital. Apparently Frank Fahy, a member of the Irish Volunteers, warned her that 'he doubted the enemy would respect it because they had little respect for the Red Cross when it is ours'.[31] Elsewhere, other rebel women were busy setting up first aid stations in decidedly non-neutral rebel positions and hanging the Red Cross flag.

The British soldiers, who were trained to recognise Red Cross personnel and, having in many cases experienced their work in Belgium and France, were willing to allow women wearing the Red Cross uniform to pass freely though checkpoints and over barricades without any interference. The members of Cumann na mBan took advantage of this to move around the city carrying dispatches and ammunition. For example, when ammunition was running out at the garrison in St Stephen's Green, two women and a girl travelled from the GPO with the ammunition strapped to their bodies under their clothes. They were Elizabeth O'Farrell, Julia Grennan and May McLoughlin, who was wearing a Clan na Gael scout uniform. When they reached Dame Street they discovered the street was packed with armed British soldiers. They allowed McLoughlin to pass through but refused to allow O'Farrell and Grennan to pass. According to O'Farrell, she had to plead with the soldiers to be allowed to pass and one soldier eventually gave permission, and, as he shepherded them along Exchequer Street, he put his arms around both of them. O'Farrell recalled how she found the soldier's 'good nature embarrassing, because almost beneath his hands were wedges of ammunition'.[32] The two women reached the College of Surgeons safely and passed over the ammunition, but the Volunteers there then demanded food. McLoughlin went back again to the

GPO where she met Hanna Sheehy Skeffington, who was seeking the whereabouts of her husband Francis. She volunteered to help McLoughlin, 'and carried a big sack of food from the GPO'.[33]

Meanwhile, the official International Red Cross VADs had swung into action and by Tuesday morning were setting up emergency medical clinics in public buildings and private houses to attend to the wounded. On several occasions the Red Cross nurses, now known colloquially as VAD nurses, carried several of the injured and dying from the streets and saved several lives.

For the first few days of the fighting the wounds treated by the women of Cumann na mBan were of a minor nature, but as time went on 'the number of more seriously wounded patients increased and they carried them on stretchers into the first aid hall at Church Street, and dressed their wounds'.[34] Eilís Ní Riain recalled that on one of the days she 'removed Ned Daly's shoes and socks, bathed his feet and gave him fresh socks with plenty of boric powder and he told her he felt very comfortable after it'.[35]

The men and women in the rebel garrisons also experienced intense emotional stress. To keep fear at bay many turned to prayer; the rosary became a form of communal outlet for their fears. Religion was a vital component in the lives of Irish people at that time. Everyone was defined by his or her religious allegiance. Nationalist women were no different from the general population in this respect, as they were products of a society that was predominantly socially conservative and Catholic, and the rosary represented immediate access to any spiritual need. One prayer from the nineteenth century is a good example of this:

O queen of paradise, mother, and maiden, mirror of graces, of angels and saints, I place the custody of my soul in your hands. O Mary don't refuse me and I'll be safe.[36]

Devotion to the Mother of God in all her manifestations was an

integral part of daily life. Regardless of how difficult a situation, men and women resorted to prayer and the intercession of the Mother of God in times of fear and difficulty. The rosary was an external physical manifestation of religious spirituality and is embodied in the symbols and imagery of Mother Ireland of the period.

On the Thursday of Easter week, the group in the GPO sent Leslie Price to St Mary's pro-cathedral in Marlborough Street to get a priest for a dying Volunteer. She met with Fr John Flanagan and he agreed to come with her. When he arrived, he was nominated chaplain to the Volunteers and gave a general absolution to the whole garrison. Gertie Colley Murphy, a member of Cumann na mBan, recalled that the general absolution took place in the canteen where the catering corps had organised a dining-room. On that particular day, the men and women were told to assemble in the dining-room:

> The priest said he had the power to give general absolution in danger of death and considered everyone in this building was in danger of death so he told us to kneel down and say an Act of Contrition while he gave absolution. This was a most impressive scene, men of all walks in life, most of them unshaven, unwashed, and yet all so serious. I had a tray load of mugs, which I had to balance on the corner of a table. Here I might mention we girls had our rosary beads hanging around our necks all the time.[37]

Similar scenes took place in the College of Surgeons. William Partridge led the rosary every evening and de Markievicz wrote a verse called 'The Rosary College of Surgeons'. For these men and women the spiritual aspect of their daily lives became an integral aspect of their particular nationalism. From 1916, Irish nationalism took on a distinct turn towards an exclusive Catholicism. Those women like Sarah Purser and Beatrice Elvery and their Protestant friends, who had been at the cutting edge of the evolving neo-Celtic imagery during the late nineteenth century, became marginalised and the significance of their contribution was almost lost.

When the bombardment of Sackville Street and in particular the GPO became fierce and the building began to burn, the decision was made to evacuate the women from the GPO. This evacuation became essential because there was a large quantity of ammunition and home-made bombs in the building and there was danger of an explosion. Patrick Pearse called together the women who were still in the GPO, thanked them and praised them for their work and their help. Elizabeth O'Farrell, Julia Grennan and Winifred Carney remained and the other women left in two separate groups.

Gertie Colley Murphy led the first group of women and she explained that Desmond Fitzgerald called her aside and Pearse gave her a large Red Cross flag attached to a flagpole. He ordered her and Bridie Connolly to lead the other women up Henry Street to Jervis Street Hospital and seek admission. Colley Murphy recalled:

> As the door of the GPO was just about to be opened, Pearse called out, 'girl with the flag march at the centre of the street'. It was only a matter of seconds before the others joined me, but my legs felt like jelly. We turned into Henry Street to be confronted with our first barricade. I scrambled up and held the flag on the top while the others got through at the sides or ends. Amy Wisely held the flag while I got around. We had I think three such barricades before reaching the turn into Jervis Street.[38]

They were refused admission to Jervis Street Hospital. They retraced their steps and then moved through several army checkpoints, clambering over many barricades before they were placed under a military escort and marched to the Broadstone railway station.

Here they were given tea and biscuits before they were interviewed one at a time by a colonel and other officers about the events inside the GPO. The colonel then gave each one a signed pass and allowed them to go home. This trek was almost two miles and they were not fired upon due to the protection afforded them by the Red Cross flag.

Louise Gavan Duffy was with the second group to leave the GPO and it was also led by 'someone carrying a Red Cross flag'.[39] This group comprised seven or eight women, some rebels who were wounded (one was being carried in a sheet) and a few who were unscathed. They were accompanied by Fr Flanagan. This group was also ordered to go to Jervis Street Hospital. The able-bodied rebels burrowed through several buildings and the entire group emerged at about 7 p.m. in a laneway which gave them access to Middle Abbey Street away from the firing line and close to the hospital. Some of the men were wearing the Red Cross insignia. Halfway down the laneway they were stopped by a detachment of British soldiers and an officer. 'Father Flanagan pointed out the Red Cross flag and the wounded men' and told the soldiers they were taking them to Jervis Street Hospital.[40] The soldiers then escorted the group to the hospital. According to Molly Reynolds, it was at this point that the British soldiers 'arrested the Red Cross men and men with minor wounds'.[41] The British officer organised for the women to spend the night in the dispensary waiting-room. The following morning, after a breakfast of tea and bread, they were told to go home. The surrender had not taken place yet and they did not all go home. Leslie Price recalled that as they left the hospital, she decided to go to the garrison at Jacob's Factory 'to see what they were going to do there'.[42]

During this time the main group of the rebels and the leaders had retreated to Moore Street. They left the GPO by crossing to Henry Place and entered buildings wherever they could. In the ensuing mayhem, several civilians were killed. According to

Volunteer Joe Good, the group of rebels retreating from the GPO had suffered several casualties and they began to break into houses around Moore Street. In Henry Place, Good recalled he 'heard one of them shout "Stand Clear" and then burst the lock of one door with a shot or shots. Unfortunately, a girl and her father were trying to open the door. Both were hit, she fatally.'[43] This was the home of the McKane family and the girl, Bridget McKane, was fifteen years old. She received a fatal gunshot wound to her head. Good recalled seeing a piece of her skull on the ground and he said that it was, 'about the size of an orange; it was clean and white as I imagined a baby's would be'. For some reason Good 'slipped it into my mac pocket so that no one would discover it'.[44] The most poignant part of this story was that Bridget's mother, Margaret McKane, continued cooking, trying to improvise some sort of breakfast for everyone and cooking 'a very large quantity of potatoes, which was all the food she had'.[45]

Good said there was a 'Red Cross Man' with him when he entered the building. This was Seamus Donegan, who was a member of the Kimmage garrison. Good said that it was while he was in the McKane's home that 'he put on a Red Cross armlet because there was some thought that it might be efficacious, certainly it gave me more liberty of movement'.[46]

When the rebels finally left the GPO, Winifred Carney, Julia Grennan and Elizabeth O'Farrell left with them. When the decision was taken by the leaders to capitulate, O'Farrell was chosen to carry the message of surrender to the British army post at the top of Moore Street. Before she left the building, Seán McDermott ordered her to procure a white flag, which he then hung out of a window to ensure that the British soldiers would not fire on her. O'Farrell left the building at about 12.45 p.m. carrying the flag and wearing her nurse's uniform with the Red Cross insignia on her front and on her arm. She walked along Moore Street towards the army post and, on reaching it, informed the officer that she 'brought a verbal message from Pearse to the Commander of the British Forces to the effect that he [Pearse] would like to treat with him'.[47] That officer then turned to another and ordered him to remove the Red Cross insignia from her clothes and to search her in case she was a spy. The Red Cross insignia was cut from her armband and her apron. The search yielded two pairs of scissors, some sweets, some bread and cake. At this point she was deemed a prisoner and held for about an hour until Brigadier General William Lowe arrived.

O'Farrell repeated the message of surrender to Lowe and he responded by ordering her to return to Pearse and inform him that Brigadier General Lowe would not 'treat with him until he made an unconditional surrender', adding that 'if she did not return within the half-hour hostilities must continue'.[48] A written note to this effect was given to her to pass on to Pearse. The note read:

To Patrick Pearse; 29 April 1916, 4.40 p.m.
A woman has come in and tells me you wish to negotiate with me. I am prepared to receive you in Britain Street at the north end, provided that you surrender unconditionally. You will proceed up Moore Street accompanied by the woman who brings you this note, under a white flag.[49]

The leaders of the rebel army discussed the situation and sent O'Farrell back up Moore Street with their reply. Apparently Brigadier General Lowe was angry with her when she returned because she was half a minute late. O'Farrell did not know what was in the note. Brigadier General Lowe read it and again sent her back to Pearse with the verbal message, that if she did not return accompanied by Pearse with Connolly on a stretcher, he would resume hostilities. After receiving this message at about 3.30 p.m., Pearse, accompanied by O'Farrell, walked up the street and surrendered to Brigadier General Lowe.

For the fourth time that day, O'Farrell walked down Moore Street to the GPO garrison, carrying written instructions on how to surrender. Julia Grennan, in her account of the time just before the surrender at Moore Street, recalled that:

> A number of the men gathered in the back drawing-room and knelt to say the rosary. This picture will never fade from my memory. They knelt holding the rifles they so soon were to surrender in their left hands, the beads in the other. We then marched out ... The GPO was still burning fiercely.[50]

After the surrender of the GPO garrison, Brigadier General Lowe decided to use O'Farrell to deliver the surrender to the other garrisons. She was told to take the order of surrender to the Four Courts garrison. She walked from Moore Street through Parnell Street and Capel Street. She was challenged several times by British soldiers and every time she had to explain herself. She had to turn back at Little Mary Street and retrace her steps to the site of the surrender at the top of Moore Lane, where was she given a military escort to the Four Courts. From this point, she continued alone until she reached a barricade at Chancery Street, where she met Fr Columbus of the friary on Church Street. Here Captain de Courcy Wheeler was detailed to accompany her to the Four Courts, where Commandant Daly accepted the order to surrender. O'Farrell then returned by the same route to Sackville Street; it was now 7.15 p.m. At this point, O'Farrell was taken by Captain de Courcy Wheeler to a building on the corner of Sackville Street and Parnell Street that belonged to the National Bank, to stay overnight. From her window she could see the 300 to 400 Volunteers who had surrendered that day in the grounds of the Rotunda Hospital. Julia Grennan and Winifred Carney were with this group. The following day O'Farrell's solitary journey began again.

At 8 a.m. on Saturday morning, Captain de Courcy Wheeler produced typewritten copies of the surrender and brought Elizabeth O'Farrell to the centre of Grafton Street, from where she walked to the College of Surgeons, carrying a white flag. She was told that Mallin was sleeping and that de Markievicz was next in command. De Markievicz was surprised at the order and refused to allow O'Farrell to meet Mallin. O'Farrell passed the order of surrender to de Markievicz to give to Mallin, who accepted it as leader of the garrison.

Following this surrender, O'Farrell was taken by Captain de Courcy Wheeler to Butt Bridge to begin the journey to the Boland's Mills garrison. De Courcy Wheeler refused to accompany her past Butt Bridge because there were too many railway lines where he would be exposed to enemy fire and they did not know exactly where the Volunteers were. He left her at the bridge and she started the journey by approaching the military barricade of British soldiers who were lined across the top of Westland Row. They 'began screaming at her to go back', but she said that she kept going and 'kept on waving my white flag and the paper'.[51] When she reached the top of the street an officer sent a soldier with her to enable her to pass through the military lines at Holles Street and Merrion Square. She enquired from the soldier as to where the Volunteers were firing from and he told her the gasometer at Macken Street. She then walked down Holles Street, around Wentworth Place and into Harmony Row and continued to walk down under the railway bridge in South Brunswick Street and over the gas works. She tried to enter these works but failed, so she then went along Barrow Street towards the railway bridge, where she encountered some Volunteers she knew. Enquiring from them as to de Valera's whereabouts they told her he was 'at the Grand Canal Dispensary'.[52]

When O'Farrell finally located the dispensary building on Barrow Street, it was so heavily barricaded that she had to be lifted inside by some of the Volunteers. Eamon de Valera was shaving when she was brought in and he came out to talk to her with the towel still around his neck. O'Farrell recalled that when 'de Valera came to me, at first I think he thought the thing was a hoax, but by the time some of my Volunteer friends came in he realised I was to be trusted'.[53] However, he refused to accept the order to surrender because he would only take orders from Commandant Thomas MacDonagh, his immediate superior officer, leaving O'Farrell to muse that 'after all my trouble in finding him I had to go off again'.[54] O'Farrell returned towards the city to report to Captain de Courcy Wheeler who escorted her to the garrison at Jacob's Factory, which was under the command of Thomas MacDonagh. De Courcy Wheeler left O'Farrell at Bride Street and she walked alone through the firing line to Jacob's Factory at Peter Street. When she eventually gained entry, she was blindfolded for about five minutes before she was allowed to talk to MacDonagh. He told her he would not take orders from a prisoner. Apparently he refused to obey because the order contained the signature of James Connolly. He refused to recognise Connolly's position as a leader of the revolution. The same issue arose at Church Street, which was part of the Four Courts garrison.

According to Fr Augustine and Fr Aloysius, two Franciscan friars who described themselves as chaplains to the rebel army and who were in dialogue with the rebels inside the garrisons, there was a clear distinction made by Connolly about the original surrender document. Fr Augustine said that on 30 April 1916 at 7 p.m. he 'went with Aloysius to Dublin Castle to seek a permit from Brigadier General Lowe to enable them to visit Patrick Pearse who was being held at Arbour Hill Military prison'. Lowe received them very courteously and promptly granted them the permit. He also suggested to them that they should see James Connolly, who was being held in the Castle in the Red Cross hospital. Both men agreed. Augustine said of the meeting in Connolly's room that:

Approaching his bedside, I asked him if the surrender document said to have been signed by Pearse was genuine and he assured me in the affirmative. 'Did you also sign it, I then asked?' He said 'Yes.' Then as I turned to leave him, he said, 'But only for the men under my command.' These words are indelibly imprinted on my memory … The General was a gentleman: he recognised the delicacy of the situation.[55]

Aloysius concurred with this story to a large degree and added his perception of Connolly's words:

In our presence (General Lowe), asked Connolly if his signature to the letter advising surrender was genuine. Connolly's reply was 'yes, to prevent needless slaughter'… He added that he spoke only for his own men.[56]

Both friars were then taken to Arbour Hill to meet with Pearse, who told them he had already signed a surrender document for another friar who he named as Fr Columbus. However, he wrote another one for the garrison at Jacob's Factory. Meanwhile, de Valera had marched his men to Sir Patrick Dun's Hospital where he surrendered himself and his men. By 6 p.m. on Saturday 29 April 1916, the surrender was complete. Elizabeth O'Farrell had finished her final task and was taken to Ship Street Barracks at Dublin Castle.

In the immediate aftermath of the rebellion, the rebels expressed shock at the negative reaction they received from the citizens of Dublin. This reaction was ascribed to one group of people, namely those women of the poorer class whose husbands were in the British army and who were known as 'separation women', so-called because they were receiving separation allowances from the British government. In the wake of the rebellion they were subjected to venomous insults and the term became one of significant derision.

Following the rebellion, the term 'separation women' came to apply in particular to the poor women of Dublin city slums. The impression created by subsequent histories is that because of these women Dublin was somehow an aberration in terms of the rest of the country, where pro-English sentiments were concerned. However, as there were about 200,000 Irishmen in the British army, the payment of the separation allowance was not confined to the Dublin region. Subsequently, after 1916 and the emerging propaganda that criticised these women and their families, there was a loss of interest by nationalist women in the issue of poverty and their philanthropic flirtation with the poor ended.

While those women on separation allowances were more than likely very angry, they were not the only angry citizens in Dublin. Many people severely affected by the fighting of Easter week had reason to feel aggrieved. In Dublin an estimated '259 civilians were killed and 1,728 were wounded'.[57]

TABLE 5: FIGURES FOR ALL THOSE REPORTED KILLED AND WOUNDED DURING THE REBELLION

Category	Killed	Wounded
British military officers	17	46
British military other ranks	99	322
Civilians & rebels	318 (59 rebels, 259 civilians)	2217
DMP	3	7
RIC officers	2	0
RIC other ranks	11	22
Total	450	2614

Source: Colonial Office files, CO 903/19, Part 2, p. 39.

There were twenty-eight children under the age of fifteen killed by gunfire.

TABLE 6: THE TWENTY-EIGHT CHILDREN WHO DIED DURING THE REBELLION

First Name	Surname	Address	Age
Christina	Caffrey	27b Corporation Street	2
John Francis	Foster	18 Manor Place	2
William	Mullen	5 Moore Place	9
Walter	Scott	Irvine Tce, Church Road	9
Christopher	Cathcart	28 Charlemont Street	10
Bridget	Stewart	36 Pembroke Place	11
Phillip	Walsh	10 Hackett's Court	11
M.	Doyle	7 Whitefriar Street	12
Patrick	Featherstone	1 Long Lane	12
George Percy	Sainsbury	54 Haroldville Tce	12
John Henry	McNamara	York Street	12
Mary	Kelly	128 Townsend Street	13
n/s	Kavanagh	4 North King Street	13
J.	Andrews	8 Stephens Place	14
J.	Healy	188 Phibsborough Road	14
Eleanor	Warbrook	7 Fumbally Lane	14
J.	Creevan	St Aloysius Road	14
Mary A.	Brunswick	57 Lr Wellington Street	15
J.	Dunphy	Adelaide Hospital	15
Bridget	McKane	10 Henry Place	15
Mary	Raymond	8 St Mary's Abbey	15
C.	Whelan	30 Nth Great Georges Street	15
Bridget	Allen	27 Arran Quay	16

C.	Corrigan	Nth Fredrick Street	16
Christopher	Hickey	168 North King Street	16
Joseph	Jessop	3 Upr Gloucester Street	16
P.	Ryan	2 Sitric Place	16
Margaret M.	Veale	103 Haddington Road	16

Source: The Irish Times *and General Register Office (GRO) Dublin.*

On the first day, three children were killed. The youngest was John Francis Foster, who was two years old. He died when a bullet entered his head 'at level of his ears'; he had been shot on Church Street and died there without receiving medical assistance. Christopher Cathcart, who was ten years old and lived in Charlemont Street, died at Portobello Barracks due to a haemorrhage caused by a 'gunshot wound'. The third child to die that day was Patrick Featherstone, who was twelve years old. He was hit by a bullet in his thigh and he died at Jervis Street Hospital from 'shock and haemorrhage'.

On 28 April, as rebels were evacuated from the GPO through Moore Place, nine-year-old William Mullen who lived there was shot in the thorax and died in his home. In Corporation Street, Christina Caffrey, who was two years old, died in her home after she was hit by a bullet which first struck her mother Sarah in the hand and then hit the infant.

Elsewhere, citizens suffered trauma as fighting broke out around their homes and workplaces. Twenty-five men under Seán Heuston took over the Mendicity Institute, which was a charity on Usher's Quay, and used it as an outpost. This charity fed the poor and destitute of the city. The rebels arrived at dinnertime and put the diners out of the building. The occupants, the staff and the superintendent's family were put out at the point of a bayonet. The 3rd Battalion Irish Volunteers, under the leadership of Éamonn Ceannt invaded the South Dublin Union (SDU), which housed over 5,000 paupers. The SDU complex became a veritable battlefield. On this occasion there was no time to move any of the residents, so everyone simply tried to stay out of the way of bullets. Nurse Margaret Kehoe died after she received four bullet wounds while attempting to protect her patients. She was forty-eight years old and had worked in the SDU for many years. She was a native of Carlow and was not a member of Cumann na mBan. It was obvious that there was a plan to occupy the SDU for strategic reasons. About a week before the rebellion, 'Ceannt visited a Miss White who worked and lived in the SDU to collect a toy gramophone for his son'.[58] White reported to the matron Annie Mannion after the rebellion that:

> During his visit, he asked for a tour of the grounds, and Mr Dooley, a ward master took him though the garden infirmary. Ceannt simply walked around and examined the views that could be obtained from the windows.[59]

The fact that there were so many people within the complex was clearly not a concern. Ceannt, who lived in Dolphin's Terrace at Dolphin's Barn, 'within firing range of the SDU', was fully aware of the danger to civilians.[60] He had taken the precaution of moving his wife, child and mother-in-law away from home to stay with Kathleen Brugha. Áine had time to pack for her son and mother and had 'forwarded all their clothes and food to Brugha's house some days before the rebellion'.[61] It appears that the poor of Dublin were not given these same considerations.

Some business in the heart of the city used a system of live-in caretakers to ensure security. These caretakers were allowed accommodation above the business premises and many families lost jobs, homes and possessions in the ensuing fires. In the immediate area of the city centre, several families had small businesses over which they lived and they too lost everything. These people had every reason to feel angry.

However, in the wake of the execution of the leaders and the subsequent propaganda, their dissension was silenced. The executions began on 3 May and ended on 12 May. Those executed were Patrick Pearse, James Connolly, Thomas Clarke, Thomas MacDonagh, Joseph Plunkett, Éamonn Ceannt, Seán McDermott, Micheál O'Hanrahan, Seán Heuston, Ned Daly, William Pearse, Con Colbert, Major John MacBride and Michael Mallin; Thomas Kent was executed in Cork. As the courts martial took place, the almost daily announcement of executions had the effect of engendering an emotional response within the population, which manifested as anger. This quickly displaced the existing anger away from the rebels and onto the British government.

A total of 3,430 men and 79 women were arrested by the British military. There were 171 rebels tried by courts martial, of which 90 took place between 2–9 May 1916.

TABLE 7: A BREAKDOWN OF THE NUMBERS OF MEN AND
WOMEN WHO WERE ARRESTED IN 1916

Description	Number
Men released	1,424
Women released	73
Tried by courts martial (men)	170
Tried by courts martial (women)	1
Men interned	1,836
Women interned/deported	5
Total	3,509

Source: The Irish Times 1916 rebellion handbook, *The Home Office report (PRO, HO-144-1453-311980) and the card catalogue of the prisoners of the rebellion 1916 (NAI).*

Joe McGallogly recalled of his court martial that he was court-martialled with Seán McGarry, J.J. Walsh and Willie Pearse, with the latter wearing uniform. McGallogly recalled that Lieutenant King, whom he had taken prisoner during the rebellion at Princes Street, gave evidence against him and said that 'he had also seen the other three in the GPO'.[62] J.J. Walsh told the court he had no official position in the Volunteers and William Pearse explained he was merely a personal attaché of his brother. Seán McGarry and McGallogly remained silent. Immediately after the court martial the men were moved, with eighteen other men, to Kilmainham Gaol while the courts decided their fate. McGallogly recalled that during the early hours of the following morning, an officer of the British army came to his cell to inform him of the sentence. He recorded the exchange:

> You have been tried, found guilty and sentenced to death. Do you understand? I said yes. He paused a second or two and then continued, out of consideration of mercy the sentence has been commuted to penal servitude for ten years. Do you understand? Again, I said yes. He told the others to shake me and I was duly shaken.[63]

The officer asked McGallogly if he wanted anything to eat and they gave him three army ration biscuits. Joe McGallogly fell asleep and did not hear the executions a few hours later.

De Markievicz was tried by court martial on 4 May 1916. There were two witnesses for the prosecution: Walter McHugh, a seventeen-year-old pageboy who worked in the University Club on St Stephen's Green, and Captain de Courcy Wheeler who took the surrender of the garrison. McHugh in his evidence said that at around 12.45 p.m. on Easter Monday, he saw de Markievicz drive into the Green and stop opposite the club:

She leaned out of the car and gave orders to one of the rebels who was at the gate of St Stephen's Green. The accused then went away in the motor. I saw the accused a little time afterwards. When I saw her, she was standing behind the monument in St Stephen's Green. She had an automatic pistol in her hands. I saw her fire the pistol at Dr Daly who was looking out of the window ... Dr Daly was in uniform. The accused at the time was dressed in a man's uniform as she is now.[64]

De Markievicz availed of her right to question the witness:

Q: Where were you standing when you saw me fire this shot?
A: On the steps of the club.
Q: How could you see what I was firing at?
A: I could see that the gun in your hands was pointing upwards towards the club.
Q: Did you see Captain Daly looking out of the window at the time when the shot was fired?
A: No – but I had seen him looking out about 10 minutes before. The gun when fired by the accused was pointed in the direction of Captain Daly's window.[65]

Captain de Courcy Wheeler in his evidence stated that on being informed that the rebels at the College of Surgeons were ready to surrender, he went to the college accompanied by an NCO under a white flag. Michael Mallin accompanied by de Markievicz came out to meet him. Captain de Courcy Wheeler had ordered the rebels to disarm inside the college but de Markievicz ignored the order and according to the captain came out of the College of Surgeons armed with a Mauser pistol and ammunition, which she gave to him. De Courcy Wheeler inspected the assembled rebels and then, turning to de Markievicz, asked her 'if she wished to be driven away in a motor, but she refused and said she preferred to remain with her men, as she was second in command'.[66] De

Markievicz declined to question de Courcy Wheeler. She made a statement instead, saying, 'I have no witness to call at my trial, what I did was for the freedom of Ireland in believing there was a fighting chance'.[67] She was sentenced to death, then reprieved because of British reluctance to execute a woman and her sentence was commuted to penal servitude.

William Wylie, who was a member of the prosecution for a number of the courts martial, made an interesting observation about de Markievicz at her court martial. Wylie was born in Dublin in 1881 and his family moved to Coleraine when he was an infant. He studied law in Dublin as a young man and was called to the bar in 1905.[68] By 1915, he was an officer in the Trinity Officer Training Corps (OTC). He was in Kerry when the rebellion began and returned to Dublin. When the courts martial were being set up, he was appointed a member of the prosecution. He said of de Markievicz:

> We quite expected she would make a scene and throw things at the court. In fact, I saw the General getting out his revolver and putting it on the table beside him. He need not have troubled. She curled up completely. 'I am only a woman, you cannot shoot a woman, and you must not shoot a woman.' She never stopped moaning the whole time she was in the courtroom ... I think we all felt slightly disgusted. She had been preaching ... death and glory die for your country etc., and yet she was literally crawling. I will not say any more it revolts me still.[69]

After her trial, Countess de Markievicz was removed from Richmond Barracks to Kilmainham Gaol, still wearing her uniform. When she saw the other women prisoners at a distance, Brigid Foley said that Countess de Markievicz shouted across to them 'penal servitude for me' and described her as appearing 'to be delighted with herself'.[70]

Meanwhile Joseph Plunkett had been tried on 2 May and executed the following morning at dawn. Before he was shot he was allowed to marry Grace Gifford in the chapel at Kilmainham Gaol. According to Grace Gifford Plunkett, she became engaged on 2 December 1915 and she claimed they 'had no immediate plans to marry'.[71] She was not involved in the nationalist movement, though her sister Nellie was involved with the ICA. Another sister, Sydney, was a journalist who worked under the pseudonym John Brennan. She had joined INE in its early years and contributed articles to the organisation's paper, *Bean na hÉireann*. A third sister, Muriel, was married to Thomas MacDonagh. MacDonagh was one of the men executed after the rebellion and he and Muriel had two small children. Gifford said Joseph Plunkett was keen to be married and wanted them to marry during Lent. However, she was 'on the point of becoming a Catholic' (she converted to Catholicism in April 1916) and thought this would be 'a fearful thing to do', so she suggested they get married at Easter, but he responded 'we may be running a revolution then'.[72] During Easter week, Joseph Plunkett managed to send her two notes, which explained his sudden keenness to marry. Because she had been 'thrown out of her home', he believed they should marry so that she would be taken care of if anything happened to him, but in another part of her recollection she said that 'Joe wanted them to marry so they could go into the Rising together'.[73]

On 3 May, Gifford went to Kilmainham Gaol with a wedding ring and was taken to the Catholic chapel. Joseph Plunkett was brought in and his handcuffs removed. Fr McCarthy, the prison chaplain and a friar at the Priory of St James, married the couple and Plunkett's handcuffs were put back on him. The couple were not allowed any time alone together 'so did not have any private conversation' and Grace said, 'I just came away'.[74] That evening she returned to the prison, where, in the company of a guard, they spent ten minutes together. This was the last time they met.

After her marriage, Grace was living at Larkfield House in Kimmage. Geraldine Plunkett Dillon said that one day when she visited Grace at Larkfield she went into her bedroom and saw 'a large white chamber pot full of blood and a foetus'.[75] At a time, especially within middle-class society, when an unwed mother was a social pariah and Grace was facing a fate almost worse than death, the hasty marriage in Kilmainham Gaol makes sense. Although this is a plausible reason for the timing of the marriage, we cannot be sure it was the actual motive.

On 8 May the trials of Eamon de Valera, James Connolly and Seán McDermott were due to be held. De Valera's trial went ahead on 8 May and he was sentenced to death, but this was reduced to servitude for life 'for reasons that remain unclear'.[76] The trial of Connolly and McDermott was postponed to the following day. They were both sentenced to death and General Maxwell assented to this decision. These two men were the last to be executed, their sentences carried out on 12 May.

TABLE 8: THE SENTENCES METED OUT BY THE DUBLIN COURTS MARTIAL AND THOSE REPRIEVED BY GENERAL MAXWELL

Sentence by Court Martial	Number of rebels
Death	15
Death reduced to penal servitude for life	10
Death reduced to various lengths of imprisonment from 6 months to 20 years	156
Total	181

Source: The card catalogue of the rebellion of 1916 held in the National Archive Dublin and Home Office papers PRO London.

There were seventy-seven women arrested. A number of these women were members of the INE branch of Cumann na mBan from the Marrowbone Lane garrison, which had been under the command of Éamonn Ceannt. They were the only group of women to insist on surrendering with the men. As the garrison prepared to surrender, Captain Ó Murcada told the women they could go home. Rose McNamara and Marcella Cosgrove, the leaders of the women, refused, insisting, 'we came with you, we will surrender with you'. The women then marched out behind the men.[77] When Lily O'Brennan heard the order to the men to empty their pockets, she quietly tore up the diary she had been keeping. As the column of rebels marched towards St Patrick's Park, a cordon of British soldiers began to close in. O'Brennan recorded that Rose McNamara's voice rang out that they were surrendering with the men. Immediately the cordon opened and the women passed into St Patrick's Park. When they were halted there was total silence and to their left they saw Commandant Ceannt and the 4th Battalion. After the surrender was formalised, the women were lined up between the 3rd and 4th Battalions of the Irish Volunteers and made to march to Richmond Barracks. As the rebels marched along British soldiers surrounded them and O'Brennan recorded that there was a soldier to guard each rebel. She said:

> As we looked ahead at our disarmed Volunteers enclosed in a British arsenal, our hearts beat in defiance. With one accord, the women raised their voices and Ireland's great ballad, 'God Save Ireland', burst from their lips.[78]

As they marched, the women kept singing and went through a repertoire of songs, which led O'Brennan to comment, 'yes the Inghinidhe had a wonderful store'. As they walked O'Brennan dropped the pieces of her torn up diary.[79] When the women reached Richmond Barracks they were placed in the married quarters for two days and then moved to Kilmainham Gaol.

After the garrison at City Hall surrendered, the women there were marched through the Castle Yard to Ship Street Barracks and put into cells in the basement area. Kathleen Lynn recorded that they received quite a good dinner on the first day. Over the following days the quality of the food deteriorated. Dublin Castle was a Red Cross hospital for recovering British soldiers and the influx of so many prisoners at Ship Street Barracks, located within the Dublin Castle complex, meant food shortages became a serious problem. The rebellion had made it difficult for the British army to source food and consequently, the prisoners received army ration biscuits, but the soldiers shared their food with the women:

> When the military were able … some of them broke into one of the houses nearby; and the sergeant came in one evening with his pockets full of oranges, which he gave us. We thought we had never tasted anything so delicious as these oranges.[80]

According to Molony, the soldiers guarding them 'were decent enough and often brought them a dish of fried bacon and bread'.[81] One experience the women found difficult was coping with vermin. Kathleen Lynn said that within twenty-four hours they were covered in fleas. She never slept during her time in Ship Street because of the fleas:

> The scratching was not so bad in the day-time but at night-time it was perfectly awful. I always was very sensitive to that sort of thing. I used to marvel how the other girls seemed to sleep. They did not seem to mind, I was the only one, and even Miss Molony could.[82]

Lynn decided to instigate a daily de-lousing regime. The women were held at Ship Street Barracks for three days and then moved to Richmond Barracks. After a few days, they were transferred with de Markievicz to Kilmainham Gaol. At Kilmainham, Lynn shared a cell with Madeleine Ffrench Mullen and Helena Molony. Kilmainham was apparently somewhat more comfortable than Ship Street. By degrees, Lynn was able to get rid of her fleas. 'I must have been able to undress because I remember picking my undergarments. So, by degrees I got rid of the vermin'.[83]

Even in prison, social protocol was followed. At Kilmainham Gaol, each cell received one basin of water for its inhabitants and Lynn recorded that, 'I being the doctor used it first, Miss Ffrench Mullen second, and Miss Molony was last. We all had some sort of a wash, so that was something'.[84] Some of the women heard the shots at dawn when the executions took place, while others slept through them. One week later the authorities released sixty-nine women and kept eight women in custody. De Markievicz was unhappy with this and told her sister Eva Gore Booth that she believed 'the released girls must have played a very deep game, for all those who mattered were released a day or two after they were arrested'.[85]

After a few weeks, the eight women were transferred to Mountjoy Jail. Here they were each allocated a single cell and were allowed visitors and parcels. They were 'inundated with all sorts of presents and luxuries', but Lynn complained that 'the only thing we longed for was clean bread and butter. We had all sorts of cakes but we wanted something plain.'[86] After a short time they were allowed to have free association and were able to mix in the exercise yard. On 26 June 1916, Winifred Carney, Helena Molony, Maria Perolz, Brigid Foley and Ellen O'Ryan, were moved to Lewes Prison in England:

An order was made by the Secretary of State under regulation 14b of the Defence of the Realm Act [DORA] directing that she shall be interned in Lewes prison, the order is made on the ground that she is of hostile association and is reasonably suspected of having favoured, promoted or assisted an armed insurrection against his majesty.[87]

Countess Plunkett and Kathleen Lynn were deported to England under section 14e of DORA. Countess Plunkett and her husband were deported to Oxford and Kathleen Lynn was deported to Bath. The deportation order required that they should live at a specific address in England agreed by the authorities and report regularly to the local police. Refusing to comply with the deportation would have led to internment.

Meanwhile, the British authorities set up an advisory committee to investigate the cases of some of the prisoners. In the House of Commons on 12 July 1916, Home Secretary Herbert Samuel announced that the committee had decided that a large number of men who took part in the rebellion 'were kept in ignorance by their leaders and thought they were being called up for a route march on Easter Monday'.[88] Following this announcement, 860 men and two women were released. The two women were Maria Perolz and Brigid Foley. Perolz later said that they had been treated well in Lewes Prison, but that Helena Molony had instructed them 'not to say we were well treated'.[89] Helena Molony, Winifred Carney and Ellen O'Ryan were then transferred from Lewes to Aylesbury Prison. At this point, Countess de Markievicz was still being held in Mountjoy Jail and was not transferred to Aylesbury Prison until 7 August.[90]

Within weeks of her deportation, Kathleen Lynn heard that her sister was ill with typhoid fever. She received permission from the Home Secretary to return to Ireland to nurse her. When her sister began to recover Lynn returned to England. Meanwhile, General Maxwell recommended that Lynn should be released and allowed to return to Ireland because he 'believed she was no doubt under the influence of others'.[91] By the end of August, Lynn was allowed to return to Ireland.

At this time Carney, Molony, O'Ryan and de Markievicz were the only women still in prison. In August 1916, Carney requested permission to return home because her family had written to inform her that her mother was ill. This request was refused. Later in November, she was informed she would be released if she signed an undertaking of good behaviour, but she refused to sign the form and returned it to the authorities.[92] Ellen O'Ryan was released on 17 October 1916 and Carney and Molony were released in the general release of female interned prisoners on 23 December 1916. De Markievicz remained in Aylesbury Prison because she had been sentenced to penal servitude.

In late 1916, Cumann na mBan held a convention at Sinn Féin headquarters, which was presided over by Louise Gavan Duffy. According to Nancy Wyse Power, the attendance was 'between fifteen and twenty women who were mostly from Dublin'.[93] She said that de Markievicz was elected president (despite the fact that she was not a member) and that Philomena Plunkett and Min Ryan were elected secretaries. However, according to Nancy's mother, Jennie Wyse Power, the secretaries 'were Ellen O'Ryan and Philomena Plunkett, with Mrs O'Rahilly elected vice-president'.[94]

Kathleen Clarke and Sorcha McMahon called a general meeting of the Central branch. Clarke, in her autobiography *Revolutionary Woman,* said the meeting was stormy and a heated discussion took place between those members who were involved in the rebellion and those who were not. The questions being bandied about by the women were, 'Where were you? Were you out? If not, why not?'[95] A motion was then proposed that those who did not take part in the rebellion should be expelled. Clarke says that some members showed intense bitterness towards members who had not taken part in the rebellion. A row was averted when Clarke simply ignored the motion and told the members that they should, 'close ranks, forget our failures and get to work'.[96] They heeded her and went on to work together. However, this undercurrent of one-upmanship continued to exist within the organisation.

Cumann na mBan began a campaign to try to keep the issue of the executions and internments in the public consciousness. They organised protests each Sunday outside the church of St Mary of the Angels at Church Street and repeated this every Sunday for some weeks. The women also turned their attention to trying to help the widows and children of the executed men. They had been deeply affected by the execution of the leaders of the rebellion and it fuelled a determination in them to carry on the fight for freedom. In this effort, they were superb. In their determination to help the widows by initiating a dependants' fund, they were in fact following in the footsteps of the Fenian women of the previous century.

6

KEEPING THE FLAME ALIVE: THE IRISH NATIONAL AID ASSOCIATION AND VOLUNTEER DEPENDENTS' FUND

In the wake of the rebellion in 1916, many of the families of the men who were executed and imprisoned experienced severe economic hardship. As relatives of the rebels, they were excluded from the initiatives set up by the British government to help civilians.

In *Revolutionary Woman*, Kathleen Clarke said that before the rebellion her husband Tom gave her £3,000 in case it was needed by relatives of the men. In the aftermath of the rebellion, with the executions and imprisonment of so many men, this amount was insufficient. Within weeks, Clarke launched the Irish Volunteer Dependants' Fund (IVDF), took the position of president and appointed Sorcha McMahon as secretary and Eilís McRaghniall as treasurer. She appointed an executive committee comprising women who had been bereaved by the executions. They were Áine Ceannt, Margaret Pearse, Muriel MacDonagh, Eileen O'Hanrahan, Madge Daly and Lil Colbert. Clarke said she deliberately chose female relatives of the executed men because John Redmond of the Irish

Parliamentary Party would not object to them. This opinion appears to be based on the premise that with these particular women on the committee he would not be so crass as to criticise the IVDF. The committee began its work by distributing the £3,000 to some of the widows and families of the executed men and then began a fundraising campaign.

At the same time a second aid committee, the Irish National Aid Association (INAA), was formed in May 1916, 'to provide for those in Dublin and certain other parts of Ireland, who have suffered as the result of the recent Insurrection'.[1] This fund was more democratic than the IVDF because the executive committee was elected and a constitution was also drawn up. It proposed to support the dependants of the men who were executed, the men killed in action and the men who were imprisoned and interned. The INAA believed that the last group would not be released for a long time and, consequently, that an all-encompassing fund for all the families was necessary. Kathleen Clarke was hostile to the INAA because she believed it was controlled by the Irish Parliamentary Party. The INAA held their first meeting on 28 May and an executive committee was elected comprising Louise Gavan Duffy, Fred J. Allan, Michael Davitt and Thomas J. Cullen. The constitution was drawn up and, in a manner similar to the earlier traditional Irish associations, a ladies' sub-committee was set up to draw women into the organisation, which was copper-fastened by rule four of the constitution, which stated:

> A ladies' sub-committee shall be appointed to inquire into and report on claims and to distribute grants. Reports on claims to be submitted to the Executive Committee, who shall decide on the grants to be made; but an emergency grant shall be advanced each week to the ladies' sub-committee to enable special cases to be immediately dealt with.[2]

The INAA planned to support the families indefinitely. On this basis, they calculated they would need more than £40,000 during the first year and another £30,000 would be needed for families who required long-term help.

The IVDF and the INAA administered aid within a common sphere and as a result were duplicating each other's work. Both committees also had a fundraising campaign in operation in various parts of the country. On 6 July 1916, the INAA wrote to the IVDF inviting it to send three or four of its members to a meeting to discuss their work and compare their respective registers of needy families, 'to prevent overlapping, and still more particularly to prevent anyone being neglected'.[3] Apart from the problem of overlapping, the INAA found some families who were neglected, 'owing no doubt to the fact that our committee believed that the other was dealing with the case'.[4] In their letter to the IVDF, the INAA expressed the hope that they would be equally anxious to solve this problem.

The impetus for this appeal to the IVDF came about because the INAA had approached a meeting of the bishops at Maynooth and requested them to authorise a parish church collection throughout Ireland. The request was rejected by one vote because both committees were running a public appeal and the bishops believed they 'could not side with either'.[5] The INAA believed that co-operation by both committees would be mutually advantageous and of more benefit to the families they were trying to help. The INAA also reassured the women of the IVDF that 'the distribution of the (INAA) funds' would be as 'strictly guarded as their fund' and furthermore, clause four of the INAA constitution would ensure that the distribution of aid would be 'left in the hands of the ladies' sub-committee'.[6] Louise Gavan Duffy, Fred J. Allan, Michael Davitt and Thomas J. Cullen signed the letter. At this point, the IVDF and the INAA had raised £13,415 and £14,459 respectively.

Pragmatism won out and, on 11 August 1916, the representatives of both the IVDF and the INAA met in the Gresham Hotel in Dublin to discuss amalgamation. This conference brought together the IVDF, the INAA and the Irish Relief Committee of America (IRCA). The IRCA was represented at the meeting by John Archdeacon Murphy of Buffalo, New York, who was a representative of the IRB, and a Mr Gill. The two men brought a large sum of money from America. Murphy and Gill presided at the meeting. The representatives of the IVDF were Daniel O'Hegarty, John MacDonagh, John Murphy, Dr Groran, Sorcha McMahon, Eileen O'Hanrahan, Kitty O'Doherty, Madge Daly, Patrick P.T. Keohane, Patrick Belton and J.J. O'Kelly. The INAA was represented by Fr Richard Bowden, administrator of the pro-cathedral, Dublin, Louise Gavan Duffy, Patrick Corrigan, Matt Russell, Michael Davitt, Louis Ely O'Carroll, George Nesbitt and F.J. Allan. On a motion proposed by Madge Daly of the IVDF and seconded by Louise Gavan Duffy of the INAA, both associations were amalgamated. The Bishop of Dublin, Rev. Dr Walsh, was invited to become honorary president.

The new executive committee was elected with Fr Richard Bowden and Patrick Keohane appointed president and vice-president. There were four members appointed to the executive committee: Bowden, Corrigan, McMahon and O'Kelly. After some discussion, it was agreed to have seven honorary secretaries: Michael Davitt, Fred Allan, T.J. Cullen, Patrick Belton, Jennie Wyse Power, Kitty O'Doherty and Louise Gavan Duffy. A specific sub-committee was formed to distribute the money brought from America and it later became known as the Permanent Grants Committee. The first full meeting of the new executive committee took place three days later, where three representatives of the Dublin Trades Council were added to the executive: Thomas Farren, Thomas MacPartlin and Thomas Lawlor. In this manner the members of the Irish Citizen Army were drawn into the aid programme. It was at this meeting that the organisation was named officially as the Irish National Aid Association and Volunteer Dependents' Fund (INAAVDF). The draft constitution was discussed and amended.[7]

The female members of the executive committee were authorised to bring together a new ladies sub-committee and to draw its membership from the now defunct IVDF and INAA. The ladies sub-committee was renamed the Ladies Distribution Committee (LDC) and it was allocated a representation of one on the executive committee of the INAAVDF. Thomas Farren and Daniel O'Hegarty were then appointed to work with the LDC in a consultative capacity to prevent the possibility of duplication.[8] The LDC became the major conduit through which money was channelled to families in need. Grants were made for rent, clothes, boots, milk, insurance policies, railway fares, a surgical boot, an artificial eye and the admission of a child to a convalescent home. Money was also granted to families to enable them to redeem any possessions they pawned in times of dire financial distress. By early September 1916 the LDC had dealt with about 750 cases in Dublin alone. By the end of 1916, the women were paying out each week an average of £800, of which £600 was distributed in Dublin and £200 outside the city. This money came from fundraising outside Ireland and within the country itself. Throughout the country they organised committees at parish level and created branches of the INAAVDF. A national organiser, Liam Clarke, was appointed for this work. The first parish collection, which took place on 19 August 1916, yielded £968.[9]

In September 1916 the executive of the INAAVDF recorded that subscriptions were just below £1,000 a week; by the end of the year it was £2,000 each week; by January 1917 it was £5,000 a week; and in the first week in July 1917, they received over £10,000.

The INAAVDF planned to send women to the USA to raise funds, but this plan ran into difficulties because martial law was still in operation and anyone planning to leave the country had to apply for permission through the military authorities. General Maxwell was generally not inclined towards allowing women connected in any way with the rebellion to travel to the USA.

In June 1916, Lillie Connolly had applied in Belfast for a passport to travel with some of her children to the USA. Robert Dunlop of the Belfast RIC objected strenuously, because he believed:

> Her family have always taken an active part in the extreme movement, such as attending meetings of Cumann na mBan, Gaelic League, Irish Volunteers, etc., her house had been the meeting place of leading Sinn Féiners and such persons as the Countess Markievicz, O'Rahilly, Seán McDermott and Denis McCullough.[10]

The RIC also claimed that when explosives were stolen in Motherwell in Scotland, they were brought into Ireland through Belfast to Dublin and that the person carrying the material stayed in the Connolly household. Lillie and one of her daughters were also observed buying supplies of lint and bandages, which they sent to Dublin before the rebellion. Dunlop concluded that 'from their actions and associates, they clearly hold the same views as the late James Connolly, and there cannot be any doubt that once in America, they will lend their aid to anything that goes to injure Great Britain'. Yet he clearly felt some doubt over the correct course of action as he ends his report by saying: 'Then on the other hand, perhaps they could do less harm in the USA than if they were left in Ireland.'[11]

Sir Horace Plunkett had taken an interest in the Connolly family and promised General Maxwell that he would introduce Lillie to people in the USA who would enable her to find a way of earning her living. Maxwell recommended that Lillie be allowed to travel to the USA, saying 'I have seen her and she appears to be a decent and humble woman who would be incapable of platform oratory in America'.[12] However, the RIC won this battle and Lillie Connolly was refused a passport.

In early August 1916, Nora Connolly and Margaret Skinnider left Liverpool for the USA. Both women were born in Scotland and had been able to get a passport in Edinburgh. The police believed Connolly was carrying documentation:

> ... regarding the rebellion and the subsequent events, as well as papers in cipher, giving the existing conditions of the IRB organisation and its plans. It is expected she will return to Dublin in the course of three or four months.[13]

On 20 September 1916, General Maxwell made an order prohibiting Connolly from returning to Ireland. When Connolly and Skinnider arrived in the USA, they began a series of fundraising lecture tours on behalf of the INAAVDF.

Grace Plunkett sought permission to travel to the USA to work, but the authorities refused to grant her a permit. She was living at this time at Larkfield House in Kimmage. She wrote a letter of complaint about the refusal to the authorities, claiming, 'I had no connection before, during, or since the rebellion, to any political organisation. I have never written in any journals connected with same or made speeches in their interest.' She concluded that if her marriage was 'the reason for this refusal and if this act branded me as a suspect why was I not cautioned before doing so that this would be the result?'[14]

Plunkett also explained that she had been contemplating travelling to the USA for some time before the rebellion. She insisted that this application for a passport to travel and work in the USA was *bona fide*. She promised that if given a passport she would sign an undertaking not to make public speeches in the USA. At this point Plunkett describes the refusal as an 'unjust victimisation'. Having made a convincing case, she spoiled it all by asking for a photograph of the entry in the Kilmainham register recording her marriage and showing both signatures, which made it look like she was actually planning to lecture in the USA. She was informed that she 'could have a marriage certificate by applying to the General Registrar Office for a mere two shillings and seven pence'.[15]

Plunkett kept up a correspondence on the issue and by December the military declared they had no problem allowing her to have a passport, but decided against asking her to sign an undertaking not to participate in anti-British activities while in the USA. The police believed that if she was asked to sign the undertaking, it might make her appear important 'in the eyes of the Irish Americans and enable her to make capital out of the undertaking'.[16] If she was allowed to 'go freely the fact would more or less detract from any perceived importance she might have if she did engage in any propaganda work'.[17] The final point that weighed in her favour was that she had not participated actively in nationalist politics at any point before or in the immediate aftermath of the rebellion. In January 1917, she was granted permission to travel, but after all the effort she did not go to the USA.

Hanna Sheehy Skeffington was also unable to get a passport, so she forged her identity and managed to get a passport for herself and her son in the names of 'Mrs Gribben and Eugene Gribben'.[18] The INAAVDF funded the trip. They travelled on the ship *Cameronia* from Glasgow, arriving in New York on 18 December 1916 and they went to stay with Margaret Skinnider, who at this time had an address in Brooklyn.

The death of Sheehy Skeffington's husband was one of the many tragedies of the rebellion. Francis Sheehy Skeffington had been arrested while trying to prevent looting. While being held in custody at Portobello Barracks, he was shot dead by Captain J. Bowen Colthurst. At a subsequent court martial, Bowen Colthurst was found guilty of murder, but found to be insane. This event catapulted Hanna into nationalist republican politics. Up to this time she was always adamant she was non-political, her sole purpose being to get the vote for women. From her involvement in fundraising for the INAAVDF, she became immersed in nationalist republican politics. Sheehy Skeffington spoke at over 250 meetings across the USA 'to civic groups, university students, peace groups, socialists, suffragists and Irish-American organisations'.[19] John J. Splain, the national vice-president of the Friends of Irish Freedom, described her mode of operation:

> Mrs Skeffington in particular found sympathetic ears; she toured the country drawing large audiences who paid to hear the story of her husband's brutal killing, told with a simple pathos that gave it force ... Oswald Garrison Villard, editor of the influential *New York Evening Post* was so stirred by her recital that he opened his columns to her and found outlets for her pen.[20]

Sheehy Skeffington's ability to raise money is described in a letter from the USA, written by a woman called Flora. She said, 'Mrs Skeffington is doing fine, lecturing round the country, even in Chicago. She makes the Americans cry, some feel in their hearts, some in their pockets.'[21] Copies of the *Irish Volunteer* ballad, the 'Soldiers Song', which had been the written by Peadar Kearney, were 'sold at these meetings for 50 cents each'.[22]

Nora Connolly, Margaret Skinnider and Hanna Sheehy Skeffington were paid their living and travel expenses by the INAAVDF. The women travelled extensively and raised large sums of money. Funds also came from Australia and the Archbishop of Melbourne, Rev. Dr Mannix, sent £1,500 to the fund. In New York, an organisation called Cumann na mBan Inc. was launched, the sole purpose being to raise money to be sent to Ireland. While in America, both Nora Connolly and Margaret Skinnider produced books on Ireland. In New York in 1917, Skinnider published *Doing My Bit For Ireland* and in 1918 Connolly published *The Unbroken Tradition*.

In early September 1916, the vice-chairman of the INAAVDF suggested that permanent provision should be made for the dependants of the men who were executed. The committee decided to put aside £20,000 for this purpose and invested the money in Dublin Corporation stock. In 1917, when the money began to arrive in large amounts, they allocated to each widow the sum of £1,500, which she could accept as one lump, or have invested on her behalf. In order to create an equitable system of payment for each family, the INAAVDF drew together the information from the IVDF and the INAA to ascertain how much money the families had already received.

The INAAVDF recorded the circumstances of every family and the amount of money they had been granted by the fund. Tom Clarke left a widow, Kathleen, and three sons aged between twelve and six. She received £250 from the USA and decided to take the £1,500 in one grant.[23] James Connolly left a widow, Lillie, and five children. The eldest child, Nora, was in her early twenties and the youngest child was fifteen. They also had a daughter who was described as 'too delicate to work' and she remained at home with Lillie.[24] Before the rebellion, the Connolly family had a total income of £5 8s a week. This was made up from James' pay, which was £2, and the wages of his two daughters Nora and Ina, who worked in a mill in Belfast. Lillie Connolly told the LDC that £2 a week would be sufficient to keep herself and her children. She received £50 from the IVDF and £250 from the American Fund. Archdeacon Murphy also gave her a private donation of £25. She chose to have the £1,500 invested.

Éamonn Ceannt left a wife, Áine, and a ten-year-old son named David. Before the rebellion Éamon had worked as a clerk with the Dublin Corporation treasurer's department. His salary was £220 a year. Áine told the committee that she would like to work at intensive gardening or market gardening. She received £50 from IVDF, £250 from the American Fund and she chose to have the £1,500 invested.

Michael Mallin left a wife, Una, and five children: three sons and two daughters aged between twelve years and two months. His wife was given a weekly grant of £1 7s, but after an interview with Thomas Farren, this was raised to £2 10s. She received £100 from the American Fund and she decided to have the £1,500 invested on her behalf. Mrs Mallin, however, was very concerned about her children's education and Thomas Farren thought that the fund should accept responsibility for them and defray the cost of their education from the interest on her £1,500.

Thomas MacDonagh left a widow, Muriel, and two children: a son aged four and a daughter age two. Muriel told the LDC 'she required £4 a week for herself her children and a maid' and she 'received £50 from the American Fund'.[25] The INAAVDF accounts show that the committee rented a house in Skerries in the summer of 1917, so that the women and children could have a holiday. While swimming in the sea Muriel drowned. There is no record to show if the fund put aside any money for the children.

Michael O'Rahilly, known as The O'Rahilly, was fatally wounded when he led a charge up Moore Street towards a British army barricade. His widow wrote to the INAAVDF and informed them that her income remained unchanged and so she did not need any help.

Grace Gifford Plunkett received £100 from the American Fund, which was paid to her quarterly. This was reviewed again in August 1917, when she 'was given another £100, which was paid to her in monthly instalments of £5 until 1 March 1919'.[26] The increase in income might be the reason why she decided not to go to America.

The INAAVDF also became involved in providing for the education of children affected by the death of their fathers. An education sub-committee was set up, to make 'provision for the education for the children of the men executed, killed in action, or sentenced to penal servitude'.[27] This sub-committee comprised Fr Aloysius, OSFC, Fr Eugene Nevin and Fr John Flanagan, CC, based in the Dublin diocese and Fr Patrick Browne, based in St Patrick's College, Maynooth. The other members of the committee were Mrs O'Doherty, Mrs Bradley, Louise Gavan Duffy, Nancy Wyse Power, Miss Neary, Miss Corrigan, Thomas Farren, P.T. Keohane, John MacDonagh and Louis E. O'Carroll. The education sub-committee calculated that there were sixty-seven children (thirty-nine boys and twenty-eight girls), ranging in age from eighteen months to fifteen years, whose fathers had been executed or killed. Altogether, seventy-five rebels died and ten were sentenced to penal servitude for life. The executive committee believed the children had a permanent claim on the fund. Most of the boys were sent to St Enda's and the fund paid the fees. The girls were sent to a wide range of boarding schools. Lillie Connolly refused to allow her son Roddy to be sent to St Enda's and arranged an alternative education for him.

Apart from taking financial responsibility for the families of the married men, the committee considered the families of the single men who were executed. It was common during this period that sons were often the sole financial support for the family, particularly where the father was deceased. Sometimes this support extended to sisters as well as mothers. During this period of social transition, some families, particularly at the lower middle-class level, believed respectability meant keeping daughters at home until marriage. Consequently, the men of these families were the main family support. With their sisters still at home and not engaging in paid employment, it often precluded the son from marrying until his sisters married, as he carried the financial responsibility for his sisters.

The INAAVDF system of aid extended to include these families. Patrick and Willie Pearse had supported their mother and sister, both named Margaret. The fund gave them a total of £1,750 between October 1917 and March 1918. Both women kept St Enda's school open and the fund sent many children to the school.

Seán Heuston had also supported his mother and sister. His sister, who worked in a shop, was described as very delicate because 'she suffered from rheumatism'.[28] Both women received a total of £800 from the fund.

Micheál O'Hanrahan, who was executed, worked in the *Irish Volunteer* office as a clerk. His older brother Henry was an insurance agent and both men had supported their mother and three sisters. Henry had been sentenced to penal servitude for life. Their mother received £300 and the three sisters received £300 to help them run a shop. They were also granted £6 a week.

Con Colbert worked as a clerk in Kennedy's Bakery and supported his sister, who was described as very delicate. She received '£150 from the American Fund'. Seán McDermott and Thomas Kent were 'deemed to have no dependants'.[29]

Three men who do not fit into any of the above categories were Major John MacBride, William Partridge and Roger Casement. The entry for MacBride states that he had one son, but written in brackets are the words 'reserve case' and there was no payment recorded. William Partridge died after he was released from prison and his family was granted £1 a week and was included in the investment scheme. Two sisters known as the Misses Bannister, and who were described as Roger Casement's nieces, received a grant of £100 each.

The INAAVDF then turned its attention to the men left without employment due to their imprisonment. Several hundred men found themselves in this position. Some of these men were released from prison in the summer of 1916. The INAAVDF began to keep a register and by 26 August 1916, discovered that 250 men were making claims for aid. Some of the men had been employed by the

Guinness Brewery and the committee decided to try to have them reinstated. They took up each case on an individual basis and within three weeks were successful in having 150 men re-employed.

In November 1916, the executive examined the problem facing civil servants, who 'lost lucrative appointments because of their participation in the Rising' and decided they should receive help.[30] Twenty-six civil servants had contacted the committee. Of this number, seven were married and nineteen unmarried. Their salaries varied from £60 to £200 a year and two of the men are recorded as each having an income over £300. At a meeting on 20 November 1916, it was recorded that six of these men had obtained employment. A total of £4,475 was then disbursed to the other twenty men and their families. Men who lost pensionable posts in places like the Great Southern and Western Railway, the Guinness Brewery and those who had lost permanent appointments in large drapery stores and firms were treated on the same basis as the civil servants.

The Irish Relief Committee had been set up in London and Manchester by Art O'Brien, George Gavan Duffy and Fintan Murphy to organise aid for the men still in prisons in England. They were in constant communication with the INAAVDF committee in Dublin. At the end of November, O'Brien reported that the Manchester Committee was preparing to spend £100 at Christmas time on the deportees. The Liverpool and Manchester committees were also working to raise money to augment the available funds. The INAAVDF committee set aside £250 for special expenditure through the London committee and arrangements were made to dispense grants through the Dublin committee to prisoners on parole.

Just before Christmas 1916, approximately 600 male internees were released unexpectedly from Frongoch internment camp and Reading Jail. The LDC supplied money to help the men take care of various needs like clothes, boots, railway fares, country rest, hospital treatment, medicine, dentists' fees, opticians' bills, rent, tools and insurance premiums. In addition, the fund paid for some of the men who had tuberculosis to be treated at the Peamount Sanatorium, which was founded by Lady Aberdeen and the WNHA in 1906. Good medical care obviously enabled them to ignore their former objections to this association. By the end of 1916, the fund gave grants to some men who could not reclaim their jobs, enabling them to set up businesses. These businesses covered a wide spectrum from wheel and wagon works to a timber-cutting business, a furniture factory and shops dealing in tobacco, vegetables, fruit, fish and poultry. More than one grant was made for fancy goods stores and insurance books. Money was also granted for a shirt factory, a tailoring workroom, a boot making and boot repair business and hairdressing. Applications for fares to America were turned down.[31]

In late 1916, Liam Clarke resigned as national organiser of the INAAVDF and was replaced by Michael Staines. Patrick McGrath, who was general office manager at committee headquarters, resigned and was replaced by Michael Collins, who at this time was the IRB centre (leader) for the Dublin area. Both these posts were paid positions. This job gave Michael Collins access to the people who were central within the complex network of parish committees throughout the country and he ensured that the work of the fund was meticulously recorded. Collins also had access to information and, as information represented power, he was now at the centre of intelligence regarding the fast changing political arena in Ireland.

When the INAAVDF held its first annual convention in April 1917, there were thirty-four delegates representing various parish committees. Of this number, eight were women: Kathleen Treacy, Margaret M. O'Toole, Kathleen Browne, Agnes Buckley, Kit Ryan, Eilís Mallon, Min Mulcahy and Ellen O'Ryan.

Three months later, on 17 June, the British government released the last prisoners. This unexpected release meant that the INAAVDF was no longer necessary and on 23 July 1917, the executive decided to close the fund and a decision was taken to notify everyone in receipt of a grant that the payment would cease within the month. By the end of July, all activity on the prisoner sub-committee had ceased. When Thomas Ashe and Thomas Hunter sought help for some of the men released from Lewes Jail, the LDC undertook this work. The final closing date of the INAAVDF was set for 1 November 1917 and the executive made efforts to expedite all the money collected on their behalf. They decided to make one last appeal for more money before finally closing the fund and on 1 August 1917 they circulated an appeal, which read:

> The Executive ... undertake that all monies subscribed between this and 1 November 1917, shall be devoted in their entirety to augmenting the Fund specially intended to make provision for the future of the Mothers, Widows, Dependants, and Orphans of the men who made the Supreme Sacrifice for Ireland in 1916, and offered their lives to awaken the dormant spirit of their countrymen ... That sacrifice has not been in vain.[32]

All new funds would then be circulated before the closing date in November. The fund had helped to develop and encourage a growing spirit within the general population as to the importance of looking after its patriots and their families. Another section of the appeal explained that:

> Already a new spirit is abroad in the Land ... Ireland stands erect once more, claiming her Freedom as a God-given right, and we may well hope that the conception of our Independence can never again be misunderstood by the Countries of the World ... The debt which Ireland owes her latest Martyrs can never be repaid: the care of their Mothers, Wives, and Children, and of

their seriously wounded Comrades is a Sacred Trust in which the Irish People will not fail.[33]

By March 1918, the fund was closed entirely and its documents and ledgers were prepared for transfer to the auditors. To avoid further expense, the salaried staff members were dismissed. Their employment was terminated in May 1918, with Michael Collins' employment terminating in July 1918. The fund had raised a total of £134,520.

The INAAVDF operated as an all-encompassing support for nationalists affected by the rebellion. Its major significance was that by providing financial support for the prisoners and their families it began a process of cohesiveness within the nationalist movement on which Sinn Féin was enabled to grow. Aside from its financial role, the significance of the INAAVDF was that its parish-based fundraising activities gave a new impetus to the growing separatist movement and the 1916 rebellion was central to its propaganda.

7

STAKING A CLAIM IN
REPUBLICAN POLITICS 1917

The British government began to release some of the political prisoners held in England in December 1916. A month later, on 15 January 1917, the Home Office in London added Count and Countess Plunkett to this general release.[1] A police report recorded that when Countess Plunkett arrived at Westland Row railway station on 10 February 1917, she was met 'by about fifty ladies who wore Sinn Féin badges and rosettes and they gave her three cheers, as she drove away in a cab towards her residence'.[2]

Count Plunkett immediately put himself forward in a by-election in North Roscommon. Technically an independent, Plunkett received support from Sinn Féin and other republicans and nationalists. He won the election 3,022 votes to 1,708, but he refused to take his seat in the parliament at Westminster. Instead, he organised a conference of republican and nationalist organisations at the Mansion House in Dublin on 19 April 1917, which was billed as 'a meeting of the Irish assembly'.[3]

According to F.S.L. Lyons in his work *Ireland Since the Famine*, Plunkett's intention was 'to bring the various republican organisations together, to frame a national policy within the umbrella of the old Sinn Féin'.[4] Arthur Griffith had also resumed publication of the paper *Nationality* with £200 he received from James O'Meara of Kilkenny.

Pádraig O'Keeffe in his witness statement to the Bureau of Military History said that in January and February 1917 he was part of a group of men who met on a casual basis at the Sinn Féin party headquarters and they decided to reorganise the party. They formed a new committee and appointed Seán Campbell and Seán Fitzgibbon honorary secretaries. Seán Milroy was appointed director of organisation and Dan McCarthy was appointed director of elections. Pádraig O'Keeffe was appointed as the office manager. The men managed to raise about £500 and this money was used to pay the wages of the committee. Each man was paid £1 a week and Milroy was paid his expenses. The Sinn Féin party had taken on a strong semblance of organisation.

996

IRISH ASSEMBLY

MANSION HOUSE, DUBLIN

APRIL THE NINETEENTH, 1917, AT 11.30 a.m.

ADMIT

Delegate _____

Council _____

ᵹ0 SAORAIÞ ᴅIA éIRE.

Mrs J. McGuinness, invitation card to the meeting of the 'Irish assembly'.
Source: Bureau of Military History, Military Archive.

By the time Count Plunkett held his meeting at the Mansion House it was known officially as the 'Irish Assembly', but the meeting was not a harmonious event. Count Plunkett presided at the assembly, but instead of negotiating with the growing Sinn Féin organisation, he launched a new organisation naming it the Liberty League. After a very heated debate and, according to Michael Laffan in his work *The Resurrection of Ireland*, an imminent 'split in the classic Irish tradition', the assembly came to an agreement and formed a nine member composite committee, which represented all the groups at the meeting.[5] This composite committee became known as 'the council of nine'. Those elected to 'the council of nine' were Count and Countess Plunkett of the Liberty League; Fr Michael O'Flanagan, Cathal Brugha, Thomas Dillon and William O'Brien of the United Irish League (UIL); and Thomas Kelly, Arthur Griffith and Séan Milroy representing Sinn Féin. They published an eight-point declaration of their aspirations in the national newspapers:

That we proclaim Ireland to be a separate nation.

That we assert Ireland's right to freedom from all foreign control, denying the authority of any foreign parliament to make laws for Ireland.

That we reaffirm the right of the Irish people to declare their will as law and enforce their decisions in their own land without let or hindrance from any country.

That maintaining the status of Ireland as a distinct nation, we demand representation at the Peace Conference.

That it is the duty of the nations taking part in the Peace Conference to guarantee the liberty of the nations calling for their intervention, releasing the small nations from the control of the greater powers.

That our claim to complete independence is founded on human rights and the law of nations.

That we declare that Ireland has never yielded, but has ever fought against foreign rule.

That we hereby bind ourselves to use every means in our power to attain complete liberty for our country.[6]

The 'council of nine' discussed holding a national plebiscite, to enable them to make a claim to a right to representation as an independent nation at the peace conference that would take place at the end of the war in Europe. Dr Thomas Dillon, the son-in-law of the Plunketts, was appointed director of the plebiscite.

The fact that there was just one woman on 'the council of nine' angered the active political women and they set about organising themselves to stake their claim to representation on the committee. They called an impromptu meeting to discuss this and then set a date for a more formal meeting at the home of Countess Plunkett on 12 May 1917. Áine Ceannt chaired the meeting and Madeleine Ffrench Mullen acted as secretary. Cumann na mBan was represented by some members of its executive and three representatives from its Dublin-based branches: the Central branch, the INE branch and the Fairview branch. Helena Molony and Maria Perolz were present as representatives of the IWWU. From this, a lobby group was formed who called themselves 'a conference of Women Delegates to the all Ireland Conference of 19 April 1917 (WDIC)'.

In her address to the group, Countess Plunkett explained how the national plebiscite was going to be conducted:

> Five representatives were to be chosen from each parish or half parish and these representatives would collect signatures, and when 5,000 have been collected, a meeting would be called to elect the district representative. The district representative would in turn elect members for a council of 2,000, who would choose the representatives for the Peace conference.[7]

The signatures for the plebiscite were to be 'collected house-by-house by men and women on equal terms'.[8] Madeleine Ffrench Mullen was directed to write to Dr Dillon and tell him that women were equally eligible with men for appointment to parish committees. Countess Plunkett was concerned about 'the vagueness of the young men in Ireland, who did not know how to claim their right to vote' and she suggested that:

> The group should set up a programme of instruction to teach these young men how to register for the franchise so aiding in the election of republican candidates, and to enable them to prepare themselves for the exercise of the privilege later.[9]

This led to a discussion on suffrage. Some of the women believed it was too soon to discuss the issue of the franchise, while others expressed the hope that the group 'would not imitate suffragist methods'.[10] One woman pointed out that Count Plunkett had based his policies on the republican proclamation of 1916, which 'had granted rights to all citizens regardless of sex, so there would be no talk of struggling for the vote after English or other methods, because the vote had already been granted to Irishmen and Irishwomen'.[11] The meeting ended with an agreement by the women to meet occasionally to discuss any subjects of importance that might arise that would affect women. The WDIC was not a formal association, it was lobby group for active political women and while some of them were members of Cumann na mBan, they retained a separation between the political and the military.

On 17 June 1917, the British government released the remaining republican prisoners who returned home to a tumultuous welcome. Áine Ceannt recalled that when word came that the prisoners were being released, people began to drift towards the North Wall. She said that they roused the female students of Scoil Bhríde which was located close St Enda's in Rathfarnham. Then the group called at the home of Phyllis Ryan with the news and from there they went to the to the North Wall where they spent the night singing. At about 6 a.m., they received news that the men were going to arrive at Westland Row railway station and a general stampede ensued 'to Westland Row, from where the men had a triumphal procession to O'Mahony's Hotel in Gardiner's Row'.[12]

A recurring issue in the primary source material from this time is the conviction of most of the women that Eoin MacNeill was responsible for the military failure of the rebellion. Consequently, they found it difficult to forgive him. While waiting at Westland Row, Áine Ceannt saw Fr Joe Breen from Kerry, who was walking with a tall, clean-shaven man with tight-cropped hair. She approached the men under the impression that the ex-prisoner was Austin Stack, but then realised it was in fact Eoin MacNeill. Ceannt was shocked, because she remembered him as 'a patriarchal-looking man with a long beard' and she exclaimed 'God bless us' and turned away, but on instant reflection she decided 'this was a very unchristian thing to do' and turning back she said, 'Fáilte romhat', to which he replied in Irish and she then walked away from him.[13]

Countess de Markievicz was released on 18 June and returned to Dublin three days later, where she received a welcome bordering on adulation. She was collected at Westland Row by Kathleen Lynn and stayed at Lynn's home for a short time because she was homeless. After the rebellion, the agent dealing with the tenancy of her house in Rathmines had written to her regarding giving up the tenancy.[14]

Within two days of their return to Dublin, a large number of the ex-prisoners received a grant of £20 each from the INAAVDF to enable them to have a holiday. Eamon de Valera and Desmond Fitzgerald were each given £40. Some days later, other lump sums were distributed, ranging from £250 to £500. Eamon de Valera, Countess de Markievicz and William T. Cosgrave each received £500. Seán McEntee and Austin Stack each received £400 and Desmond Fitzgerald received £250. The INAAVDF also provided a public reception for the ex-prisoners. John MacDonagh, secretary of the reception sub-committee, sent an invitation to all the ex-prisoners. To augment the 'welcome home fund' John MacDonagh invited a select number of people to attend the reception at five shillings each.[15] The reception was held at the Mansion House on 14 July 1917 and was deemed to have been a great success.

Between April and early June 1918, 'the council of nine' met about five times. At some point in this period, Sinn Féin and the Liberty League amalgamated and a new executive of twelve members was formed, comprising six members from each organisation. They adopted the name Sinn Féin and agreed that Griffith should retain the presidency. They kept the existing Sinn Féin constitution until they organised a convention. Countess Plunkett retained her place on this new executive. Cumann na mBan had sought representation, but this was refused on the basis that only 'societies standing for Sinn Féin, and those alone, could be represented'.[16] During the first two weeks of July, the executive was expanded when six ex-prisoners were co-opted, so the council membership was expanded to eighteen. Countess de Markievicz was one of the ex-prisoners and she was co-opted to the executive, which brought female representation on the council to two.

During this period, republican propaganda focused on Countess de Markievicz and Eamon de Valera, implying that they were the only people who were sentenced to death and reprieved. In fact, ten people who had been tried by the general courts martial and sentenced to death were reprieved by General Maxwell and instead received penal servitude for life.

By mid-1917, de Markievicz and de Valera had become the centre of a developing and palpable sense of spiritual triumphalism. Late in 1916, portrait photographs of the executed men and some of those who were reprieved were reproduced as postcards and sold to the public. A postcard photograph was reproduced of Countess de Markievicz that had been taken around 1903 when she first settled with her husband in Dublin. The photograph helped to enhance the burgeoning fable of the Anglo-Irish lady who abandoned her class to champion the plight of the masses and so an icon was born.

In June 1917, de Valera put himself forward as the republican candidate for a by-election in East Clare. Aware of the divisions within the republican movement since the rebellion, de Valera invited Eoin MacNeill to accompany him on his election campaign. He also conducted an intense personal campaign, which operated with 'military precision and as a military campaign'.[17] He addressed the crowds, which contained a significant number of Irish Volunteers, and the meetings ended with the singing of 'The Soldier's Song'. With the political support of Sinn Féin, de Valera won the by-election on 17 July 1917.

The growing republican movement at this point did not have a readily identifiable public face because the executions had decapitated the separatist leadership. Arthur Griffith, though president of the Sinn Féin party, was not suitable because he had not participated in the rebellion. The movement needed a figure that could encompass the post 1916 situation and the aspiration to a new Ireland. Somewhere in the machinations of the movement, a decision was made that de Valera suited this purpose. According to Pádraig O'Keeffe, the honorary secretary of Sinn Féin, on 26 July 1917 he was instructed to invite Eamon de Valera to the weekly meeting of the party's standing committee. De Valera accepted the invitation and attended, and O'Keeffe said that as far as he was aware, 'this was the first contact de Valera had with the Sinn Féin organisation'.[18] When O'Keeffe made this statement to the Bureau of Military History, he wrote to Joe McGrath and Eamon de Valera and asked them to corroborate the story. McGrath said he could not remember this incident mainly because of the time lag. Eamon de Valera simply returned the letter through his aide-de-camp Lieutenant Colonel Seán Brennan, who informed O'Keeffe that 'Mr de Valera had no comment to make on its contents'.[19]

The following month a by-election was held in Kilkenny and the republicans considered this an opportunity to consolidate the victory of Roscommon and East Clare. William T. Cosgrave was the chosen candidate. In the aftermath of the rebellion Cosgrave, like de Valera, had been sentenced to death and reprieved with a sentence of penal servitude for life. Two members of the Kilkenny branch of Cumann na mBan were selected to act on the election committee. In a style similar to the operation in East Clare, Eamon de Valera and William Cosgrave addressed the major public meetings, with the Irish Volunteers and Cumann na mBan parading.

By this time the public perception of de Valera as figurehead of the republican movement was copper-fastened, with de Markievicz holding a parallel role with regard to the women. De Markievicz had moved away from any association with Jim Larkin and James Connolly and attached herself to de Valera. Their deification was growing as the propaganda created a sense of mystery around them. In particular, de Valera's reprieve from execution became a spiritual issue and was perceived almost as some kind of miracle. By the time the last of the ex-prisoners arrived back in Ireland, they found the work of drawing together the various shades of republican politics had been completed in their absence and a new unified Sinn Féin party was now in existence with de Valera as the figurehead of the movement.

Meanwhile, Countess de Markievicz was making a countrywide tour. All her public speeches centred on her participation in the rebellion in 1916. This enhanced the growing body of mythology that was forming around her. At Ballaghadreen, County Roscommon, she told her audience:

Easter week was the proudest moment of my life. We went out on Easter week because we leaders were well posted and we knew we would be arrested on Tuesday. We knew, too, that a Bill to conscript Ireland was already printed. We stopped all that by going out.

Where would you boys be if conscription had passed? You would
be manuring the soil in Flanders, Gallipoli and elsewhere.[20]

During her speech at Newcastle West, she said:

The only evidence against her was that of a little boy brought up
in an Industrial school who could not tell the truth. On being put
a few questions by her, he commenced to cry and would tell no
more.[21]

There is no evidence that the young man cried. There was also a
second witness at her trial, Captain de Courcy Wheeler, on whose
evidence she was found guilty. In her public speeches, she never
mentioned him, but often referred to the young boy in a denigrating
manner. The burgeoning iconography surrounding Countess de
Markievicz had by this time eclipsed Maud Gonne MacBride.

On 30 September 1917, de Markievicz attended the funeral
of Thomas Ashe. Ashe had been part of a protest against the
authorities' ban on the holding of public meetings, the wearing
of military uniforms and the carrying of weapons. A number of
republicans were arrested for breaching the law and imprisoned,
and they demanded to be treated as political prisoners. When
this was refused, they went on a hunger strike. Force-feeding was
introduced and Ashe was moved from Mountjoy Jail to the Mater
Hospital, where an attempt to force-feed him failed.

His funeral was organised by the Wolfe Tone Memorial Committee. With a crowd estimated at 30,000, it became a significant
public demonstration for Sinn Féin, the Irish Volunteers and
Cumann na mBan. Michael Collins attended and wore the uniform of the Irish Volunteers. The *Daily Mail* newspaper reported
that Countess de Markievicz arrived dressed in 'the uniform of
the Irish Volunteers with her officer rank advertised by the Sam
Browne belt she wore'.[22] An accompanying photograph shows her

wearing a long skirt with a military jacket. It appears on first sight to be a Cumann na mBan uniform, however, the collar badge is that of the Irish Citizen Army. She appeared to believe she could straddle all the existing political organisations.

In the meantime, Countess Plunkett had failed to keep the WDIC up to date on the newly reformed Sinn Féin party. They learned about it almost by accident and at a meeting on 23 July, the women expressed their anger with her. It is amazing that women like Jennie Wyse Power, Kathleen Lynn and Helena Molony did not know what was happening in the wider political arena. Countess de Markievicz was staying at Kathleen Lynn's house, yet Lynn remained ignorant of these events. It was becoming apparent that de Markievicz was not particularly interested in a collective women's political campaign. The WDIC decided to demand an allocation of six places on the Sinn Féin executive on the same basis as the ex-prisoners group. The demand was sent in the form of a resolution which read, 'taking into consideration the numbers of members of your executive, we, representing the various interests of the great bulk of the women of Ireland, propose a representation of six to be chosen by our body'.[23] The Sinn Féin executive refused to discuss the issue. During this time, Countess Plunkett became ill and was unable to attend the meetings of the Sinn Féin executive and the WDIC proposed that Lynn should replace Plunkett as a proxy. After a full discussion, the group appointed Lynn, subject to the approval of Countess Plunkett, who assented. Kathleen Lynn took every opportunity to fight for women's right to have an equal place in republican politics.

At the WDIC meeting on 23 July, Madeleine Ffrench Mullen suggested it might be a good idea to encourage all existing women's organisations in Ireland to affiliate with them and thereby create an umbrella organisation. After some discussion it was decided that Cumann na mBan, with so many 'branches countrywide, were in a better position to do this work'.[24] While the WDIC was adamant that they were a political group distinct from Cumann na mBan, they were not willing to spearhead or form a national political forum for Irishwomen.

At this time, Sinn Féin was experiencing phenomenal growth throughout the country. Men and women with no previous involvement with nationalism or republicanism joined the party. By September 1917, Kathleen Lynn was regularly attending the Sinn Féin executive meetings in lieu of Countess Plunkett. Having failed to engage successfully with Sinn Féin in July 1917 on the issue of co-opting at least six women onto the party's executive, the WDIC renewed their demand in late September.[25] On this occasion the executive of Sinn Féin agreed to co-opt four ladies, with two conditions attached, which were that the women selected should not represent any other organisation and that they should join a Sinn Féin club. At a meeting of the WDIC, a discussion ensued on the desirability or otherwise of all members of the WDIC joining their local Sinn Féin club. After a lengthy debate they decided it would be a good idea to join a club. However, Countess Plunkett, a member of the Liberty League, dissented from this decision. The secretary, Madeleine Ffrench Mullen, received instructions to write to the Sinn Féin executive and inform them that the four new delegates, Áine Ceannt, Jennie Wyse Power, Countess Plunkett and Helena Molony, would attend the next meeting. At the following meeting of the WDIC, Lynn complained 'that just two of the women had attended the Sinn Féin executive meeting'.[26] The absent women claimed that pressure of work prevented them attending and Lynn urged them to make a greater effort to attend future meetings.

Meanwhile at the meeting of the WDIC on 25 September, Madeleine Ffrench Mullen 'informed the meeting that she, with Dr Lynn, had written a small article urging the women to assert their political rights, which had been given to them by the republican proclamation in 1916. They had sent the article to

Nationality but it was not published'.[27] The women decided to have the article printed as a handbill or pamphlet and have it distributed throughout the country. They printed 25,000 copies and in order to defray the cost of printing they decided to raise money by holding a raffle for a republican flag.

On 16 October 1917, nine days before the Sinn Féin convention was to meet, the WDIC realised that without a formal structured organisation they would find it difficult to approach female delegates at the convention to canvass for their support. They convened a meeting and agreed to create an agenda that would explain their aspirations. They named the agenda 'Political Organisation of Women' and it contained 'a copy of a hastily drafted constitution, a report of the first meeting of the WDIC and an explanation of their fundraising activities'.[28] Having ascertained there were twelve female delegates due to attend the Sinn Féin convention, they organised a reception for them at Countess Plunkett's home, where each delegate would be presented with a copy of the agenda.

By this time, Countess Plunkett's health had improved. She resumed her position on the Sinn Féin executive and Lynn had to step down. The WDIC believed that because Lynn was responsible for having a resolution placed on their behalf on the agenda, she should attend the convention. Áine Ceannt withdrew from the delegation to allow Lynn to attend. Subsequently, Jennie Wyse Power, Kathleen Lynn, Countess Plunkett and Helena Molony represented the WDIC at the Sinn Féin convention.

On 24 October 1917, the weekend of the Sinn Féin convention, Cumann na mBan held their fourth annual convention. From this year forward, the organisation always held their annual convention on the same weekend as Sinn Féin and the Irish Volunteers. The membership of Cumann na mBan was growing and they claimed to have 100 branches, which was more than a two-fold increase from the eve of the rebellion. The Cumann na mBan convention elected Countess de Markievicz as president and Nancy O'Rahilly as vice-president. The new elected executive committee were Kathleen Clarke, Áine Ceannt, Elizabeth Bloxham, Louise Gavan Duffy, Mabel Fitzgerald, Jennie Wyse Power, Mrs D. McCullough, Mary MacSwiney and Miss M.T. Walsh, with Niamh Plunkett and Máire Ní Riain elected the joint secretaries.[29]

At the opening of the Sinn Féin convention on 25 October 1917, Thomas Dillon, addressed the convention and said that:

> The Roscommon election was the first opportunity that occurred to test the feeling of the country and the co-operation of Sinn Féin with the Irish Volunteers and the Labour Party, assisted by local people, succeeded in bringing about the return of the first representative pledged to Irish Independence and abstention from the British Parliament ... The tremendous victories of East Clare and Kilkenny city were the first fruits of the amalgamation of all the national and political organisations into one.[30]

Dillon also told the delegates that the party had 1,200 affiliated Sinn Féin clubs, which represented a membership of over 250,000. There were 1,700 delegates at the convention representing 1,009 clubs.

Arthur Griffith, in his presidential address, spoke of the peace conference expected to take place when the war in Europe ended. He explained to the delegates that he believed Ireland should have a place at the conference in its own right. However, as it stood, Ireland was precluded from attending the conference because it did not have a constituent assembly in its own right. He went on to explain that a general election would be necessary to attain this position, but he doubted the British government was going to give them that opportunity for some time. Consequently, he said that Sinn Féin would:

> ... constitute themselves a constituent assembly of Ireland, backed up by the moral strength and material power of the Irish people,

to act for Ireland and speak in Ireland's name at the future peace conference.[31]

Based on the success of the by-elections and the fervour engendered by their campaign, and with a membership estimated at 250,000, this new Sinn Féin believed they had the remit of the population to create a constituent assembly and speak and act on behalf of a new Irish nation. Article four of the proposed new constitution made this intention clear, where it stated that:

> No law made without the authority and consent of the Irish people is or ever can be binding on their conscience. Therefore, in accordance with the Resolution of Sinn Féin adopted in Convention in 1905, a Constituent Assembly shall be convoked comprising persons chosen by the Irish Constituencies as the supreme National authority to speak and act in the name of the Irish people and to devise and formulate measures for the welfare of the whole people of Ireland.[32]

The plan was to constitute a new assembly after Sinn Féin and its supporters conducted a new nationwide plebiscite. The plebiscite was modelled to some degree on the one instigated at the Mansion House conference in early 1917. The plan was that every local constituency throughout the country would elect a delegate and these delegates would then meet and set up a new independent Irish national assembly. He went on to explain to the delegates that they were:

> Remaking this organisation of Sinn Féin for the real purpose and object … of the setting up of that assembly, once we have it we will have a centre round which the people can rally and a centre which the world will listen to.[33]

The next item on the agenda was the ratification of the new

constitution. Cathal Brugha explained that the executive had 'spent three nights arguing and deciding on the wording and although we may have our differences we are all united on this point that we stand henceforth for an Irish Republic. We believe this can be achieved by the weapon we have wielded in this suggested constitution.'[34] Here he was referring to the meeting held at his home in early October 1917, after the weekly meeting of the Sinn Féin Standing Committee, when, after a brief conversation with Joe McGrath and O'Mahony, Cathal Brugha left the building accompanied by Eamon de Valera, Arthur Griffith, Joe McGrath and John O'Mahony. Patrick O'Keeffe said he discovered later that they had gone to Cathal Brugha's house in Rathmines and that:

> The following morning (Friday) at about 11 a.m. Mr Griffith handed me a slip of paper, on which was written a working agreement signed by Messers Brugha, de Valera and Griffith, with a request from Mr Griffith that I bring it before the next meeting of the standing committee. This I did, and it was passed without amendment by the standing committee. When the meeting was over, I got Mr Brugha and Mr de Valera and Mr Griffith to initial the agreement. The organisation worked smoothly until the Ard Fheis of 25th and 26th of October 1917.[35]

At the second Sinn Féin Ard Fheis an interesting debate took place before the vote was taken on the ratification of the new constitution. Seán O'Twomey from Cork proposed that the convention should insist 'on the right of Irishmen to drill and arm to defend the rights of Ireland and that men of military age be educated in the use of arms'.[36] Tadhg Barry from Cork seconded this, adding that 'all members of Sinn Féin should be able to use arms'.[37] Griffith expressed his belief that this amendment would run contrary to the constitution, which caused an unnamed delegate to say:

Many young men joined Sinn Féin because they regarded it as a purely political organisation. I know several of these young men have no idea of training themselves in the use of arms. They are simply going on the spirit abroad and I do not see any good can come of this resolution.[38]

De Markievicz contributed to the debate saying:

I, as a member of a military organisation, would very much dislike to have a lot of young men hunted into my organisation who are not prepared to fight. Any man, boy or girl who wants to fight can get into a military organisation, but I say there is work for them in a political one. I oppose this amendment for the simple reason when you get into a scrap the men who want it will be there, but the men who don't want to fight who happened to be there, will be under the bed.[39]

Fr O'Flanagan contributed to the debate by saying he believed 'that the amendment was the equivalent of suggesting conscription and he opposed it'.[40] Griffith came up with a solution to the dilemma: 'O'Twomey's proposal should be viewed as a simple expression of opinion and not an effort to change the constitution'.[41] Seán O'Twomey agreed with this interpretation. Consequently, the Sinn Féin party remained a political entity separate from the militant section of republican nationalism.

Fr Gaynor from Ennis, County Clare, who represented the United Irish League (UIL), believed the convention 'should form a provisional government in opposition to Dublin Castle and the British government and call themselves the Irish Parliament, not Sinn Féin'.[42] In reply, Griffith pointed out that Gaynor's proposition was in direct opposition to the section of the proposed new constitution which stated 'that a constituent assembly shall be convoked after the election by the constituencies'.[43] De

Valera argued that the 'organisation was a national organisation in the broadest sense of the term, but could not be regarded as a constituent assembly'.[44] Griffith intervened to say that when the convention was finished they could 'choose representatives and convoke the assembly as soon as possible'.[45]

Rosamund Jacob, a delegate from Waterford, asked how the franchise would work, because women and clergymen were excluded. Griffith replied that 'he was of the opinion that clergymen and women must be equally available as voters and representatives'.[46] Gaynor then agreed to withdraw his motion 'providing immediate steps were taken to convene the constituent assembly'.[47] This was agreed.

Kathleen Lynn put forward the resolution on behalf of the WDIC, 'that in the Sinn Féin organisation men is understood to mean men and women and that in all speeches and leaflets, men and women should be mentioned'.[48] She went on to explain:

> I think that this resolution is very important in a gathering of this kind. Up to this, women have been debarred from taking any active part in the government of the country, and I do not think that the result has been very flattering to men. The government would not be what it is today if women had been given their proper share in it.[49]

Jennie Wyse Power seconded Lynn's motion. Griffith supported it and expressed the hope that the convention would support it. It was passed unanimously. While women had access to membership of Sinn Féin from its foundation in 1905, it was implicit rather than written. After 1917, the issue of political equality was an accepted part of Sinn Féin policy. Ambiguity about the theoretical position of women within the political sphere of the republican movement was over. The constitution was then passed unanimously by the convention.

Before the end of the first day's session, two proposed schemes of organisation were put forward, one by Eamon de Valera and the other by Cathal Brugha. After a brief discussion, the scheme put forward by de Valera was passed unanimously. Within this scheme of organisation, qualification for membership was open to 'all adults of Irish birth or parentage irrespective of sex, class or creed, who accepted the constitution of Sinn Féin'.[50] Those excluded from membership were members of the British armed forces, people with British government pensions and any other person who took an oath of allegiance to the British government. The new party was organised in layers of interdependent sections, whereby no one man or women could take control. In addition, for the first time, the Irish language was used in a Sinn Féin constitution. The Ard Fheis was the major decision-making body of the party. It elected the officer board, which was made up of a president, four vice-presidents, two secretaries and two treasurers. The Ard Fheis also elected the executive board of twenty-four members. The local Comhairle Ceanntair (district council) was made up of members who were elected by their respective cumainn.

The constitution stated 'that when the Ard Fheis was not in session the supreme direction and government of the party resided in the Ard Chomhairle, which was convened within five to seven weeks after the Ard Fheis'.[51] The Ard Chomhairle was made up of members of the officer board, the executive board and one member from each Comhairle Ceanntair. In certain circumstances, the scheme also allowed for the co-option of up to twenty members. This aspect of the party's constitution became vital to the survival of the party and it was vital for the women because it was a means by which they could gain a place on the Ard Chomhairle without having to be elected by the membership.

Before the election for the officer board began, a major row erupted when de Markievicz protested against Eoin MacNeill's name being on the nomination list. Her objection was based on her belief that he was responsible for the failure of the rebellion in 1916. She began by saying:

> I regret I have a disagreeable duty to perform. I wish to protest against one name that has been put forward on the executive, namely that of John [Eoin] MacNeill. I consider it my duty not only to the memory of the dead, but to the men and women who remain behind to work under the leadership.[52]

Seán McEntee tried to interrupt her on a point of order, but Griffith stopped him saying de Markievicz was entitled to speak. She insisted she was not going to make an attack on MacNeill. McEntee interrupted again to point out that if the convention allowed this to happen, then they would have to discuss all nominations. Griffith reiterated that delegates were entitled to discuss any nomination, but he regretted that the matter had been introduced. He gave de Markievicz the floor and she then set about castigating MacNeill for putting the notice in the newspaper cancelling the rebellion. Invoking James Connolly, she said that she was 'told by Connolly that MacNeill cut the ground from under our feet when we were going out to fight for Ireland in Easter week'.[53] At this point, the shout of 'chair, chair' came from the delegates. Ignoring them, de Markievicz continued her vitriolic attack.

Griffith expressed regret that she believed it was her duty to raise this issue. He explained to the convention that she had informed him before the meeting that she was going to make the protest and he had asked her not to do it. He said:

> I myself believe that John [Eoin] MacNeill, in the position he was in, with the great responsibility on his shoulders, did duty to Ireland as it came to him without fear ... none of you know the history of it ... when the onus was put upon him, and he was faced with the responsibility, as it seemed to him, of offering up

the young men of Ireland as a holocaust, he did his best to save the young men of Ireland. (Cheers). The men who went out in Easter week were brave and noble men who risked and gave their lives for Ireland, but Eoin MacNeill risked the misunderstanding and obloquy of his own people in intervening as he did.[54]

Arthur Griffith expressed the opinion that MacNeill could not have acted otherwise and reiterated, 'I will not stand by and see one man whom I know, sentenced and put out of Irish public life'.[55] Eamon de Valera's input to the row was to say that 'he understood MacNeill's reasons for his actions were honest and that he had done his duty for Ireland as he conceived it'. He continued:

> I believe I am the only living man who knows what happened ... there is no tribunal that would do otherwise than acquit John [Eoin] MacNeill of anything like cowardice or dishonour ... I am perfectly convinced that John MacNeill did not act otherwise than as a good Irishman. Had I the slightest doubt in my mind of that I certainly would not have had him on my platform in Ennis.[56]

Helena Molony spoke next and said she believed 'that de Markievicz's only desire was to save Ireland from any mistake in the future. There are people present who quite agree with her but have not the same courage as Madame de Markievicz.'[57] This brought a response from James Lennon who interrupted to enquire if the discussion about 'saving the country from the same mistake meant that Sinn Féin was contemplating another rebellion'.[58] There is no record that this received a response.

Kathleen Clarke also spoke in support of de Markievicz. Before the convention, de Markievicz approached Clarke seeking her support, but she refused. As the discussion became more heated, Clarke changed her mind. She explained her reasons for the change of heart in *Revolutionary Woman*. She perceived that the discussion was becoming hostile to de Markievicz and observed, 'if there had been rotten eggs or anything else handy they would have been flung at her' and 'the thing was hard to understand, and under the circumstances I felt bound to stand by her'.[59] At this time, de Markievicz was publicly admired and possibly overestimated her political influence within Sinn Féin, but she succeeded in her ploy. Eoin MacNeill withdrew his name from the list of candidates for the officer board.

The election of the officer board then proceeded. Eamon de Valera and Arthur Griffith were proposed as president, but Griffith withdrew allowing de Valera to be elected unopposed. Áine Ceannt who was at the convention said that:

> Arthur Griffith who had been the guiding brain in establishing Sinn Féin, and who had been its president, voluntarily retired from that office in favour of de Valera. It was a gracious act.[60]

Griffith consented to act as vice-president. The other officers elected were Fr Michael O'Flanagan, Count Plunkett, Austin Stack, Darrell Figgis, William T. Cosgrave and Laurence Ginnell MP (treasurer). MacNeill's name remained on the list of candidates for election to the party executive committee and he topped the poll, 200 votes ahead of his nearest rival, Cathal Brugha. Four women were successful: Countess de Markievicz, Kathleen Lynn, Kathleen Clarke and Countess Plunkett.

The source of funding for the new party was to come from membership fees. This was set 'at one shilling per year with one-third (four pence) to be channelled to each local Comhairle Ceanntair, and the remaining three-fourths (nine pence) channelled to the Ard Chomhairle'.[61] This would pay for the administrative functions of the party and the salaries of senior party officials. Each cumann also had to send an annual affiliation fee of £2 to headquarters and had the power to raise extra funds for its own needs.

This issue of fundraising generated another heated exchange. One delegate expressed the opinion that the 'small farmers would not pay [a] one-shilling membership fee and some of the Sinn Féin clubs would become bankrupt'.[62] A second delegate responded with 'we are up against a big proposition and we cannot work without money. If our small farmers are not willing to give one shilling a year for general expenses then I say this is all a waste of time.'[63] A third contributor to the debate said that they had 'a lot to contend with in going amongst the small farmers in the west, where one man pays a shilling and a rich neighbour pays nothing. It is not a pleasant thing going around to collect even a penny a week.'[64] A fourth contributor intervened, saying 'as a small farmer I thoroughly disagree with the speaker'. He complained that the remark cast a bad reflection on the farmers of the south and west because it suggested that they were too miserly to pay the annual subscription of one shilling. He went on to call the delegate a liar and at this point Eamon de Valera intervened, saying 'nobody at this convention is going to say that any delegate is a liar, you must withdraw'.[65] The delegate withdrew his comment and de Valera continued, saying that 'as long as the Ard Chomhairle gets nine pence we are satisfied'.[66] The funding proposals were passed and the collection of the membership fees subsequently acquired the name Sinn Féin Shilling Fund.

It is important to point out that if men had difficulty with this financial commitment then women had even more difficulty paying because they were always paid less than men. Women who worked on the family farms and in the family business were also affected because in most cases they did not receive wages. The same applied to all those young men, and some not so young men, who described themselves as 'farmer's sons' and were completely dependent on their parents for money.

On the weekend of the Sinn Féin convention, the Irish Volunteers held a separate, secret convention and redrew their constitution.[67]

Eamon de Valera was elected president and Cathal Brugha became chief of staff. Within a few short months, Eamon de Valera had become the leader and figurehead of the civil and military arms of the Irish republican movement.

Within days of the Sinn Féin convention, the WDIC held a general conference and finally adopted a constitution, according to which they were to be known as Coiste na dTeachtaire.[68] Those elected to its standing committee were Kathleen Clarke, Áine Ceannt, Jennie Wyse Power, Kathleen Lynn, Madeleine Ffrench Mullen, Helena Molony, Maria Perolz, Mabel Fitzgerald, Miss Davis and Mrs Kennedy. Mrs Ginnell was elected secretary and Countess Plunkett was elected treasurer. Sometime between late October and 13 November they, 'consulted an Irish scholar about the name of the organisation and changed its name it to Cumann na dTeachtaire'.[69] There were twelve members of the standing committee, which included a treasurer and secretary, but all members of the organisation were entitled to attend standing committee meetings. Within a group everyone is deemed equal but the downside of this is that factions can develop, which enable the dominant personality rather than a leader to emerge. Within a structured organisation with a constitution and rules, a more democratic atmosphere prevails and it is easier for an individual with leadership skills to emerge. Allowing every member of Cumann na dTeachtaire to attend the standing committee meetings had the effect of negating the new hierarchical structure. Having gone to the trouble of drawing up a constitution, they effectively remained a group.

Cumann na dTeachtaire discussed the possibility of launching 'a women's paper as a part of a publicity campaign to draw more attention to women's position in the new government'.[70] However, they decided against this because the work involved would be time-consuming and they decided instead to produce occasional leaflets and short articles and have them published in local newspapers.

Again, they discussed the possibility of linking up with other women's societies, but did not pursue the issue. A discussion on various methods of fundraising took place and eventually it was decided to take a country produce stall at the Aonach (the annual sale of work held under the auspices of Sinn Féin) on 11 December. The raffle for the republican flag was still ongoing and they hoped to chose the winner of the raffle at the Aonach.

The Sinn Féin Ard Chomhairle was due to convene on 19 December 1917 to elect the party standing committee and, in late November, the women of Cumann na dTeachtaire decided to pursue their claim for representation on the committee. Kathleen Lynn suggested that each member should consider which activities would be most suited to women, so they could make a case for representation and she instructed the women to produce a list of suitable women. The list produced read:

Organisation: Maud Gonne MacBride, Mrs Wilson, Miss Helena Molony, Mrs R. Ely O'Carroll, Miss Lily O'Brennan.

Agriculture: Miss Barton, Miss Williams, Miss Ellen Ryan and Mrs K. Brown.

Education: Louise Gavan Duffy, Miss E. Eden, Miss L. King, Miss Pearse and Miss Ffrench Mullen.

Health: Dr K. Lynn, Miss Adrian, Dr K. Dillon, Dr M. McKenna, Dr Alice Barry and Miss Cunningham.

Poor Law: Mrs Wyse Power, C. Plunkett, Miss Mulhall, Miss Maria Perolz, Miss Shanahan, Mrs Humphreys and Miss O'Rahilly.

Publicity: Miss Cavanagh, Miss Eilís Somers, Miss McKenna, Miss Chrissie Doyle, Madame de Markievicz, Mrs Ginnell and Mrs D. Fitzgerald.[71]

On 11 December 1917, the last day for nominations for the Ard Chomhairle, the women still had not discussed or selected suitable names from the list. At the Aonach, they hastily convened a meeting in the bathroom of the Mansion House to discuss the situation and decided to send the complete list to the Ard Chomhairle in the form of a resolution. The resolution was sent in the names of Kathleen Lynn and Countess de Markievicz. Sinn Féin's new constitution did not allow groups to operate within the party, so a resolution in the name of Cumann na dTeachtaire would not have been accepted. The women also 'sent out a special whip to all women delegates who were attending the Ard Chomhairle, instructing them to support their nominations'.[72]

The Ard Chomhairle convened on 19 December 1917 and elected a standing committee. Each member of the standing committee was appointed director with a specific area of responsibility.

TABLE 9: FIRST STANDING COMMITTEE OF THE 2ND SINN FÉIN PARTY ELECTED 19 DECEMBER 1917

Name	Directorships
Frank Lawless	Agriculture
Eoin MacNeill	Education
Diarmuid Lynch	Food
Eamon de Valera	Foreign Affairs & peace conference
S.M. O'Meara (co-opted)	Industries
Madame de Markievicz & Cathal O'Shannon (co-opted)	Labour
T. Kelly & Jennie Wyse Power (both co-opted)	Local Government
J. McDonagh	National Finance
Thomas Dillon	Director Plebiscite
Dr Hayes & Dr Lynn	Public Health
Michael O'Callaghan	Trade and Commerce

Source: Preamble to the Sinn Féin convention report 1918 in the Colonial Office, PRO, London.

Ernie O'Malley said 'these directors were appointed to organise what would later become departments of government'.[73] Áine Ceannt believed 'that from this period the Sinn Féin Standing Committee was to all intents and purposes the government of Ireland'.[74] Cumann na dTeachtaire expressed contentment with the fact that three women were now members of the standing committee. Although Countess de Markievicz was not a member of Cumann na dTeachtaire, this did not prevent them from congratulating themselves and declaring that 'the women were appointed to different departments as a result of our representation'.[75]

Thomas Dillon began to set in motion the mechanism for conducting the national plebiscite. Since the formation of the INAAVDF parish committees in late 1916, the rank and file had become adept at using the parish unit to good effect. Dillon had specific voting forms printed for the work, and the men and women set to work canvassing and collecting support from each household. Áine Ceannt described the printed forms 'as a document left at all the houses asking the people if they wished Ireland to be an Irish Republic'.[76]

On 1 February 1918, Cumann na dTeachtaire finally held the raffle for the republican flag. It is not recorded how much money was raised, but on 26 March, Ffrench Mullen reported that the flag had not been claimed. She was instructed to put an advertisement in *Nationality* to the effect that if the flag remained unclaimed by 7 April they would dispose of it.

The women of Cumann na dTeachtaire continued to work as individuals within Sinn Féin and Cumann na mBan. By 1918, they were united in their vision of a new Irish nation and operated on two separate levels of engagement, the military and the political. It appears that the new politics of the embryonic Irish nation were truly national and apparently inclusive, and these women were determined to be part of it. The leading women within republican politics were now on the cusp of a great adventure as their involvement in the new body politic became normalised. Within a year, they would perceive themselves as an integral constituent of the developing ideology of a new Irish nation.

8

ATTAINING THEIR
ASPIRATION

In February 1918, Kathleen Lynn and Thomas Hayes, Sinn Féin's co-directors of health, produced their first health circular, which was addressed to 'all the Sanitary Authorities of the nation, to national organisations and to our fellow countrymen'. It dealt solely with the issue of the venereal disease in Ireland. The circular opened with an apology, which stated that:

> While recognising the possible indelicacy of discussing publicly this unpleasant subject, we think that such a consideration should not deter us from warning our people of the imminence and gravity of this great black plague.[1]

Venereal disease was a problem worldwide and particularly in Europe, where the rise in the number of people diagnosed with the disease was associated with the war. Lynn and Hayes warned that when the war in Europe ended an estimated 100,000 Irishmen would be returning to Ireland and that at least 15,000 of them would be carrying the disease. Both doctors went on to state that it was 'a great social evil which threatens us individually and racially'.[2] The circular also claimed that venereal disease, 'was unknown in Ireland outside the British military centres. Among a people like the Irish, whose blood has no immunity, contagion could not be avoided and tens of thousands of unborn Irish children will come into the world stamped with the stigma of this foulest and most shameful of diseases.'[3] This circular is emphatic that this was a threat more serious than tuberculosis and it described in detail the ravages of syphilis on women and children. It also made the claim that syphilis could be caught by sharing 'cups, glasses, tobacco pipes, baths, razors, hair brushes, combs etc. that have been used by a diseased person'.[4]

The purpose of the leaflet was to insist that all the 'soldier's returning to Ireland should be tested, and those found to be infected detained in institutions, until they were pronounced free from the contagion'.[5] While they acknowledged that this could be construed as an infringement on the rights of the individual, they believed the greater good to be more important. There is also an implicit tone in the circular that only British soldiers carried venereal disease and the insinuation that the Irish nation was a place of moral and physical rectitude and was in need of protection. It does not elucidate exactly who comprised this Irish nation, but it did state that:

> Irish people themselves must see to it that their Small Nationality will not have her living children and her yet unborn children, stricken with a blighting curse. We must realise our responsibility on this vital matter. We owe it to the next generation, we owe it to the race that we will not be guilty of a hideous national sin.[6]

The circular was distributed to all municipal and county councils, doctors, politicians and clergymen of all denominations throughout the country.

Despite their efforts there was, nonetheless, a serious problem with venereal disease. During 1917 and early 1918, efforts were made to deal with the problem, when the Local Government

Board (LGB) put into force section 148 of the Public Health (Ireland) Act, 1878. This enabled 'each local authority to instigate a programme to deal with the problem'.[7] The Irish LGB was set up in 1872 and brought together into one department the Poor Law Commissioners and other functions of the Public Health Act of 1866. The LGB comprised the chief secretary for Ireland (president), the under-secretary, a vice-president (permanent head of the department) and two commissioners. Within its remit, the LGB had responsibility for the supervision and the operation of the Poor Law Act in Ireland. It also supervised and audited the accounts of local authorities. 'Under the terms of the Public Health Act, 1874, towns with a population of over 6,000 were created urban sanitary districts, while Boards of Guardians became the rural sanitary authorities'.[8] The LGB channelled funds to the urban sanitary districts and the Boards of Guardians for public health.

In 1918, Dublin Corporation instructed its medical officers, Dr Charles Cameron and Dr M.J. Russell, to prepare and devise a strategy 'for a scheme for the treatment of venereal disease in Dublin'.[9] Both doctors suggested 'that one fully equipped institution should be set up to give patients continuous and systematic treatment, and prevent the possibility of patients conveying infection to others'.[10] The governors of Dr Stevens' Hospital agreed to have this facility based in their hospital. The Lock Hospital was excluded from the scheme. According to Cameron, this hospital had a capacity of 100 beds, but only thirty-two beds were in use. He concluded that 'this institution dealt principally with the prostitute class, and provides the necessary treatment so this class of patient is amply provided for, and need not be considered in this scheme'.[11]

At a meeting of Cumann na dTeachtaire on 26 February 1918, a discussion on the issue of venereal disease arose, but Countess Plunkett was more concerned with the inadequate provision of public lavatories for women in the city. There was apparently a major problem associated with public lavatories because women of ill repute frequented them, creating a problem for the general 'respectable' female population. The women instructed Kathleen Lynn in her capacity as co-director of health for Sinn Féin to bring the matter before the relevant Dublin Corporation authority. The group then moved on to discuss the problem of venereal disease, which was prompted by a discussion in the newspapers about the 'impact of the disease on the lives of Frenchwomen'.[12] The women of Cumann na dTeachtaire believed that venereal disease was a menace in Dublin and the time had come to do something about the problem. They organised a 'conference of Irishwomen's societies of every shade and political opinion' to discuss 'what measure they could adopt to combat this problem'.[13]

The Irish Women's Suffrage and Local Government Association (IWSLGA) was convening a conference on 18 March 1918 at the Mansion House and Cumann na dTeachtaire asked Mrs Stephenson of the IWSLGA if her organisation would co-operate in enabling the two conferences to be held on consecutive days. On 19 March 1918, under the auspices of Cumann na dTeachtaire, a conference of women's societies met at the Mansion House to discuss a programme for combating the spread of venereal disease in Ireland. The women at the meeting represented several organisations: Mrs Stephenson of the IWSLGA, Miss Griffin of the Irish Women's Reform League (IWRL), Mrs Riordan, Lil Ní Griffith and Maud Townsend of the Génna Fiodoyne (Wild Geese), Mrs Cuff of the Infant Aid Society, Dr Alice Barry from the WNHA and Meg Connory and Mrs D. Cogley of the IWFL.[14] Cumann na mBan was represented by Mabel Fitzgerald, Máire Ní Riain and Kathleen Clarke. Madeleine Ffrench Mullen represented Cumann na dTeachtaire and Kathleen Lynn represented Sinn Féin. Mrs Stephenson chaired the meeting. The Irish Women's Suffrage Federation and the United Irishwomen sent letters regretting their inability to take part in the conference but wishing them every success.'Dr Mary Strangeman, from Waterford, Catherine Quinlin from Tralee, Dr K. Dillon from Mullingar and Dr E. Fleury from Dublin sent regrets'.[15]

Dr Lynn read a paper to the conference about the dangers of venereal disease and in the discussion that followed made a few suggestions about educating the public about it. The women instigated the founding of the Irish Society for the Combating of the Spread of Venereal Disease (ISCVD), an ad hoc committee, the initial remit of which was to educate the populace about the dangers of venereal disease. Dr Alice Barry proposed a resolution, which was passed unanimously, 'that this conference of Irishwomen note with appreciation, that the corporation of Dublin and Belfast have taken up the question of venereal disease, and urge those bodies to see that every soldier who lands at Irish ports be guaranteed free from disease'.[16]

Dr Alice Barry is an interesting woman because she managed to straddle the line between working for the WNHA, while simultaneously being an active member of the ISCVD committee. Barry was the WNHA 'Medical Superintendent of work for woman and children' and her office was located at the WNHA headquarters at 9 Ely Place in Dublin.[17] She was also a member of its Invalid Children's Aid Committee, which 'organised care for invalid children living in their own homes'.[18]

The ISCVD met formally for the first time at 12 p.m. on 9 April at the office of the Génna Fiodoyne, which was located at 23 Kildare Street in Dublin.[19] The women 'insisted they were not antagonistic towards the existing English society, but believed that the matter in Ireland was urgent and that an Irish society could deal with the problem more efficiently.'

Cumann na dTeachtaire, meanwhile, received a report from Lynn on the issue of women and public lavatories. She had met with the corporation authorities to discuss the problem and reported that a scheme had been agreed, whereby newsagents 'at suitable points throughout the city could be registered and empowered to keep a public lavatory for women, and to paste up a notice to that effect'.[20] The corporation agreed to appoint a female inspector and, subject to inspection, make a grant to each shopkeeper to cover the cost of installing or altering their premises. The women approved this plan and they appointed two members of the committee to make a list of shops at suitable points in the city. However, this plan never came to fruition, mainly because Cumann na dTeachtaire held only one more meeting that year. Dublin Corporation simply reopened the public lavatories and asked the DMP to put on extra patrols.

On 2 April 1918, Cumann na dTeachtaire held its second annual general meeting and finally adopted a formal constitution. Kathleen Lynn read a report to the meeting about the events that took place at the founding of the ISCVD in March 1918 and addressed a few words to them on the subject of venereal disease. She urged the group, particularly the members from the country districts, to take all the necessary precautionary measures and 'do all in their power to educate those around them to the dangers of venereal disease and try to influence their local LGB to take all necessary action regarding the issue'.[21]

The initial aim of the ISCVD was to devise a scheme of education to teach the population how to combat the spread of venereal disease. One member of the committee suggested that they should affiliate to the Dublin Watch Committee (DWC), founded in January 1916 after a conference was held to discuss immorality and drunkenness in Dublin. The conference was held by an umbrella organisation made up of six separate committees, 'concerned with the issues of housing, drunkenness, immorality, money-lending, gambling and acts against children'.[22] Its remit was to work towards combating the loose morals of a section of the populace and it was equally concerned with the issue of venereal disease. In January 1917, under the auspices of the DWC, a series of lectures were organised and delivered by Maude Royden from London 'on moral education and the social prevention of venereal disease'.[23] The DWC also organised lectures on the subject in working-class areas of the city. At the annual convention of the DWC in 1918, Mrs Kingsly Tarpy spoke on behalf of the ISCVD about the 'evils of venereal disease and urged Irish people to return to their old high standard of morality'.[24]

The ISCVD approached Dublin Corporation and the LGB for a grant to help them devise a scheme of education. One of the committee members suggested that they should seek a grant, which was available from the British government, to enable them to cover at least 75 per cent of their expenses. The majority were not in favour of this suggestion on the basis that 'accepting money from the British government would tie the hands of the committee'.[25]

At a subsequent meeting of the ISCVD Maud Gonne MacBride presented the contents of a letter she received, pertaining to the village of Artane in County Dublin, which said that the village was 'crowded with war babies and some of them were suffering from syphilis'.[26] MacBride did not give the identity of the writer of this letter. A discussion ensued about the problem of 'syphilitic infants' and the callousness of various societies who 'board these infected infants on families ignorant of this danger'.[27] Miss O'Brien brought forward a resolution, which was seconded by Lynn:

> In view of the great dangers to the community of the boarding out of syphilitic infants by philanthropic and other institutions, we would recommend local authorities under the Children's Act, 1908 to require societies and others responsible, to have such infants immediately removed for treatment to hospitals, on diagnosis of the disease by the medical officer of the district.[28]

Mrs Ginnell in her capacity as secretary of the ISCVD was instructed to send this missive to the various hospital boards around the country and ask them what provision they had made 'for the treatment of syphilitic infants in their hospitals'.[29] Miss Griffin told the committee that the Lock Hospital was the only hospital that admitted infants, but their admission policy was that an infant had to be accompanied by its mother. The women became very concerned with motherless infants in various workhouses and those boarded in the community with families. These infants became the central core of the activities of the ISCVD in their campaign to combat venereal disease in Ireland. Effectively they labelled all children born outside of marriage with the disease, as well as those infants boarded out from the workhouses and those resident in workhouses and orphanages. By intimating that these infants were the progeny of diseased, unmarried women, the ISCVD campaign placed unmarried mothers and their children beyond the margins of social respectability in the new Irish nation.

At this time the ISCVD was still an ad hoc committee and in May 1918 they decided to form an organised committee under the title Sláinte na nGael. The new committee's mission statement was that they had 'come together, to combat the spread of venereal disease in Ireland, so likely to come from the presence of troops coming back from the front'.[30] They also hoped to attract doctors, nurses and others interested in the health of Ireland onto the committee. A new executive committee was elected: Miss Griffin, Maud Gonne MacBride, Mrs Reddin, Mrs Ginnell, Mrs O'Moore, Miss G. Griffin, Alice Barry and Madeleine Ffrench Mullen. A discussion ensued on the plight of motherless infants with symptoms of congenital syphilis and a decision was taken to approach Dublin Corporation again to insist that they 'take a house and put a qualified nurse in charge, so that there may be some treatment for syphilitic infants'.[31]

At the following meeting, the group decided against calling

the organisation Sláinte na nGael. Some weeks later, they formally renamed the group the Committee for the Protection of Ireland from Venereal Disease (CPIVD). They had the name translated into Irish, calling it 'Coiste Cosanta na hÉireann Ó aicíd na h-ainmhéine', which was printed on their official notepaper.[32]

coisce cosanca na héireann ó aicío na hainnhéine
[Committee for Protection of Ireland from Venereal Disease.]

sráid cilleдara a' 23aó
(Kildare Street, No. 23.)

27th August 1918.

Sir,

In view of the great want which exists at present and which as time goes on will become more and more urgent it is proposed to open a small hospital for the treatment of infants suffering from syphilis.

We all realise that the number of such infants is alarmingly on the increase, especially in the case of boarded out war babies.

Such infants are a terrible danger to the families who receive them, and there is at present no institution at which they can be effectively treated. The above Committee hope to secure the premises formerly occupied by the Domestic Training Institute in Charlemont St, which are admirably suited for the purpose; having an annex which could be used as a Nurses' home and a laundry as well as a large airy house.

If possible, the Committee wish to buy out the house, about £500 would be required for this purpose. It would be an immense saving for future years, and would well repay the initial outlay.

The Committee, would require about £1000 for fitting, furnishing and rent, herewith make an urgent appeal for generous subscriptions for this most humane object and one on which the future welfare of the race so largely depends. The Public may rest assured that every penny of the money will be used directly for this most worthy object, all the organization being carried on by voluntary assistants.

M. ffrench Mullen
Hon. Sec,

Fundraising letter (CPIVD). Source: Hannah Sheehy Skeffington papers (NLI, MS 22 682).

Meanwhile, Lynn had met with Dr Russell, the deputy medical officer with Dublin Corporation, and reported that he was very supportive of their proposals and if the women 'submitted their literature to the corporation he would give every help towards having it printed'.[33] However, without explanation, the women changed their plan. They decided instead to acquire a building in the neighbourhood of Dr Stevens' Hospital for use as a temporary house of treatment, before approaching Dublin Corporation for financial support. This new plan received impetus from a case that was brought to their attention of an infant suffering from congenital venereal disease who had been sent to London for treatment at a 'cost of two pounds two shillings irrespective of other expenses'.[34] The CPIVD believed that money would be saved if a facility for such children existed in Ireland.

While the women were concentrating their efforts on the issue of children and venereal disease, the war in Europe was dragging on. On 10 April 1918, Prime Minster Lloyd George introduced the Military Service Bill in the House of Commons. This bill did not impose conscription directly on Ireland, but it gave the British government the power to apply it by Order of Council whenever they believed it was necessary. The threat of conscription served as a potent unifying force for diverse sections in Irish society. On 18 April 1918, a conference was called which encompassed a wide spectrum of organisations and as a result of this a unanimous declaration against conscription in Ireland was made. It said in part that:

The passing of the Conscription Bill by the British House of Commons must be regarded as a declaration of war on the Irish nation … the attempt to enforce it will be an unwarrantable aggression, which we call upon all Irishmen to resist, by the most effective means at their disposal.[35]

The almost total opposition to conscription gave Sinn Féin an additional platform on which to build support. However, on 17 May 1918, the authorities arrested the leaders of Sinn Féin. The pretext of these arrests was 'that Sinn Féin was conspiring with the

Germans against Britain' and this subsequently became known as the German Plot.[36] There is no evidence that there was a German Plot. F.S.L. Lyons described the episode 'as a colourful excuse for shutting up the principle opponents of the conscription'.[37] From early April 1918, the Ard Chomhairle had been aware that arrests were a strong possibility. At a meeting of the Ard Chomhairle on 4 April 1918, Darrell Figgis proposed a resolution, which was carried unanimously, that the emergency committees of Comhairlí Ceanntair should be authorised to co-opt a replacement for any member of the Ard Chomhairle who might be arrested. This was the first time the co-option clause from the party's constitution was used. Under this clause, each member of the Ard Chomhairle and its standing committee was allowed to nominate a replacement in the event of their prolonged absence. For example, Countess de Markievicz nominated Nancy Wyse Power as her deputy. This allowed Sinn Féin to keep replacing party officers who were arrested, enabling the party to continue functioning. Without the co-option clause, Sinn Féin would certainly have been decapitated. The warning of impending arrests gave the standing committee time to co-opt a new leadership and this made the transition in the party leadership appear seamless. That so many of the main players in Sinn Féin did not go into hiding when they became aware of the impending arrests, indicates that either they did not believe the story, or that it suited the party to have its leaders arrested. The ensuing propaganda gave Sinn Féin more support because it appeared the British government was trying to break the party.

There was one other possible reason for these arrests: the progress of the national plebiscite. Thomas Dillon, director of the plebiscite, had the work at an advanced stage when he was arrested. The government could not ignore the possibility that Sinn Féin might convoke a republican constituent assembly. On Dillon's arrest, the responsibility for the plebiscite was taken over by Seán T. O'Kelly. That the plebiscite was the possible reason for the arrests becomes clear when the list of those arrested is examined. Sixty-eight of those arrested were the principal officers of the party at national and local level.

TABLE 10: THE BREAKDOWN BY COUNTY OF THE ARRESTS OF LEADING MEMBERS OF SINN FÉIN

County	Numbers arrested
Dublin	24
Cork	8
Galway	8
Cavan	4
Louth	3
Belfast	3
Kerry	3
Wexford	2
Tipperary	2
Sligo	2
Roscommon	2
Mayo	2
Kilkenny	1
Tyrone	1
Monaghan	1
Westmeath	1
Offaly	1
Clare	1
Total arrested	**69**

Source: Minutes of the Sinn Féin SC, 20 May 1918.

Three women were arrested: Kathleen Clarke, Countess de Markievicz and Maud Gonne MacBride. The latter was not a member of Sinn Féin, but in early 1918, MacBride decided to settle permanently in Ireland and had been observed by police surveillance visiting the Sinn Féin headquarters.

Kathleen Lynn only evaded capture because 'Joe Clarke helped her to slip out the back of Sinn Féin headquarters'.[38] The authorities issued an order for her arrest under 14b of DORA, which accused her of being a 'person suspected of acting, having acted, and being about to act in a manner prejudicial to the public safety and the Defence of the Realm'.[39] The order also stated that when arrested she should be interned in Frongoch. Lynn went on the run, but managed to continue attending executive meetings of the CPIVD and the Sinn Féin Standing Committee.

Within two days of the arrests, the new officer board of Sinn Féin met, with Seán T. O'Kelly in the chair. Jennie Wyse Power and George Nesbitt were appointed joint treasurers. Others co-opted were Louise Gavan Duffy, Miss Eilís Somers, Miss Kearney, Nancy Wyse Power and Áine Ceannt.[40] On 4 June, the new Ard Chomhairle decided to reduce the workload of the standing committee by creating four new departments. They appointed new directors: Director of Organisation and the Plebiscite, Seán T. O'Kelly; Director of Elections, Robert Brennan; Director of Propaganda, Rev. Michael O'Flanagan; and Director of Food, Phil McMahon.

The arrests did not affect the anti-conscription campaign, which continued apace. In fact, the arrests actually appear to have added extra impetus to the campaign. Cumann na mBan organised several anti-conscription meetings, distributed leaflets, painted slogans on walls and collected signatures of sympathisers. They also made a specific pledge that stated:

> Because the enforcement of conscription of any people without their consent is tyranny, we are resolved to resist the conscription of Irishmen. We will not fill the places of men deprived of their

work through refusing enforced military service. We will do all in our power to help the families of the men who suffer through refusing enforced military service.[41]

Cumann na mBan began to view themselves as the main women's organisation in Ireland and developed a strong sense of ownership about some aspects of the anti-conscription campaign.

The historian Alice Stopford Green, along with Helen Curran and Agnes O'Farrelly, formed a committee to plan a campaign which would enable Irish women to express their opposition to conscription. Stopford Green sought and received permission from Dublin Corporation to have City Hall 'placed at the disposal of women desiring to sign the pledge against conscription'.[42] The date for this event was set for 9 June and it was named 'Women's Day'.[43] The Women's Day committee then invited other women's organisations to a meeting to plan a united campaign. Nancy Wyse Power, secretary of Cumann na mBan, described the Women's Day committee as 'a committee of odds and ends, which led the executive of Cumann na mBan to believe that the demonstration might prove inadequate'.[44] A representation from Cumann na mBan attended the meeting and Wyse Power explained to Stopford Green 'that Cumann na mBan proposed to take over the project and run it themselves'.[45] Wyse Power recalled that 'Mrs Green was in the chair, and the original organisers must have felt some irritation at seeing their idea snatched from them, but they made little opposition, as I pointed out that with our widespread organisation we were in a position to arrange a nationwide demonstration'.[46] Cumann na mBan hijacked the Women's Day committee and the campaign and renamed it 'Lá na mBan' (Day of Women).

The event took the form of 'a procession of various women's organisations walking to City Hall, where they signed a protest against conscription'.[47] The members of Cumann na mBan 'took part in the procession as a distinct group and marched in uniform carrying haversacks and water bottles'.[48] The Protestant Women's Anti-Conscription Society handed in a list of about 75 signatures. The largest contingent of women came from the IWWU, who handed in 'a list of 2,400 signatures'.[49] This event was replicated all over the country. In Midleton, County Cork, 1,000 women marched and in Killarney, 2,000 women and girls held a procession. At the end of the meetings they recited the rosary in Irish. In Limerick, the Dominican fathers loaned the women a statute of the Virgin and Child to erect a temporary shrine. 'Father Connolly, the administrator of St Johns, and Father Hayes CC, led the crowd in a recital of the rosary, while the women sang hymns'.[50] Meanwhile, Sinn Féin cumainn began 'setting up parish defence committees to collect funds for the anti-conscription campaign'.[51] Cumann na mBan also held a flag day to raise funds for the campaign, using the slogan 'Women Won't Blackleg' (become scab labour by taking on the men's jobs).[52]

The CPIVD, meanwhile, was still pursuing its plan to treat motherless infants diagnosed with congenital syphilis. The two women delegated to find a suitable building for use as a house of treatment, reported that they had found a building at 37 Charlemont Street, which was formerly a Church of Ireland school of Domestic Economy. Mrs Butterly, Mrs O'Moore and Madeleine Ffrench Mullen were delegated to inspect it. The building was considered suitable 'because it had an annex, which could be used as a nurse's home and a laundry. The committee needed £500 to buy the house and £1,000 for fittings and furnishings.'[53]

The building had an annual ground rent of £22 7s 6d. In addition, a building contractor estimated that it would cost between £300 and £400 to render it suitable for use. Mrs O'Moore made an offer of £350 for the premises, but the leaseholder asked for £600. Mrs Reddin then informed the committee that the North Dublin Union (NDU) workhouse was in the process of being taken over by the British military authorities for use as a barracks and the union would be disposing of its furniture and fittings. Mrs Butterly, who was a guardian of the NDU and a member of its Children's Admissions Board, was delegated to examine the 'place with a view to making an offer for cots, beds, bedding and anything else she thought likely to be of use'.[54] She reported that the beds and bedding from the NDU could be had at reasonable terms and that the master of the union was supportive. However, the LGB refused to allow the NDU to dispose of any of the material in this manner and insisted that everything was to be auctioned off by a reputable auctioneer.

In August, the CPIVD launched a fundraising campaign to raise money for the purchase of 37 Charlemont Street. In a letter to Hanna Sheehy Skeffington, Madeleine Ffrench Mullen made it clear that the committee was planning to use the building as 'a small hospital for the treatment of infants suffering from syphilis'.[55] The letter stated:

> We all realise that the number of such babies is alarmingly on the increase, especially in the case of boarded out babies. Such infants are a terrible danger to the families who receive them, and there is at present no institution at which they can be effectively treated.[56]

In September, the committee learned 'that a lady who wished to remain anonymous, had purchased 37 Charlemont Street', but that this lady was willing to rent the building to them 'at a sum that would cover the ground rent and a reasonable percentage of the purchase price until the committee were in a position to buy the house out'.[57] This was a straightforward business arrangement, not an act of charity. The Irish Land registry shows that the new owner of the building was Ethel Rhodes. Rhodes, who was born in Tipperary, was a member of the Society of Friends and lived with her mother in Rathgar. She was a friend of Kathleen Lynn, who was still on the run.

Another health issue had also become a major problem by late 1918. An epidemic of Spanish flu had broken out in Ireland and reached its peak in October of that year. At this point, Rathmines Town Council, Dublin, called a special meeting to discuss the situation. A resolution was proposed 'that in the interests of suffering humanity we demand the release of Dr Kathleen Lynn, Dr Hayes, Dr Cusack and Dr McNab'.[58] Because Lynn had literally dropped out of sight, the councillors were apparently under the impression that she had been interned. The councillors wrote a letter to the Chief Secretary for Ireland, Edward Shortt, and within days of the letter being sent, Lynn returned to her home and was immediately arrested and taken to Arbour Hill Prison. Charles Cameron, on behalf of the hospitals committee of Dublin Corporation, wrote to the under-secretary and asked him to release Lynn, and he suggested that she should 'be asked to sign an undertaking to confine herself to medical work'.[59] This request was passed on to Chief Secretary Shortt and on 31 October he ordered that Lynn should be released on the condition that she signed the undertaking. She agreed to sign it and was subsequently released. The wording of the undertaking stated: 'I Kathleen Lynn undertake on my honour if released from custody to take no part in politics, and not to leave the area of the Dublin Metropolitan Police'.[60]

One of her first actions on her release was to attend the Sinn Féin Ard Fheis and in her capacity as director of health she addressed the convention. In reference to the Sinn Féin health leaflet she said:

> I wish to point out that the evil we prophesied has already fallen upon us. All over the country, syphilis is showing itself, introduced by soldiers on leave and the huge British Garrison quartered on our poor land.[61]

This is more or less the same kind of propaganda that had been around since Maud Gonne MacBride introduced it with her anti-British propaganda in 1899–1900. However, Lynn introduced a new aspect to the issue:

> Another source of infection is the increasing number of war babies sent over here from England to be boarded out. These babies have been known to infect whole households with syphilis. I can only warn the public of the danger and point out the way to escape contagion, and this I shall continue to so do at every point.[62]

The CPIVD was experiencing great difficulty in collecting money and gaining support from the public, and they were legally tied to the agreement with Ethel Rhodes, which appears to have been an early version of public-private partnership. After some discussion, the committee changed their plan of opening a house of treatment and decided instead to open 'a general hospital for all infants, with a portion of the building to be set aside for the syphilitic infants'.[63] This suggestion met with the approval of Alice Barry, who believed a general hospital for infants would meet with wider support. On 17 October 1918, Miss Griffin, Alice Barry and Ethel Rhodes were appointed trustees, to take responsibility for the building at 37 Charlemont Street. Rhodes retained her anonymity as the owner of the building.

In October 1918, during the influenza epidemic, the CPIVD opened the building as an emergency nursing home. Lynn recalled that the top floor dormitories 'were full of pigeons and were filthy, but the women of the Irish Citizen Army of one accord, on a Sunday, came to that derelict house and cleaned it up'.[64] An appeal for lint, beds and bedding was made, and on receiving a good response to the appeal, the women 'began to admit adults suffering from flu'.[65] Lynn recorded that none of her patients died and stated:

> We had some patients that were very bad, among them Mrs

Cathal Brugha who at that time was pregnant. We had Michael Staines there. His friends in the Irish Volunteers were constantly trying to visit him, but I refused permission.[66]

This last comment indicates that some of the patients in Charlemont Street were perhaps republicans on the run.

When the CPIVD committee met on the 7 November 1918, there were five patients still in the building. The committee believed that because they opened the building to flu patients during the epidemic, they 'had lost nothing and there had been some gain to the proposed Infant Hospital'.[67] They decided not to take any new adult patients and returned to their plans for opening a hospital for infants.

At this time Kathleen Clarke, Countess de Markievicz and Maud Gonne MacBride were still incarcerated in Holloway Prison in London. While in Holloway, the three women did not develop any sense of camaraderie. Kathleen Clarke, in *Revolutionary Woman*, described her encounter with some aspects of upper-class social distinctions:

> When we were out for exercise, Madame de Markievicz and Madame MacBride walked up and down ... discussing their mutual friends and acquaintances and disputing as to which of them was of higher social status. Madame de Markievicz claimed that she was far above Madame MacBride: she belonged to the inner circle of the Vice Regal Lodge set, while Madame MacBride was only on the fringe of it.[68]

From the first day, Clarke found de Markievicz irritating. She sensed a certain tone of patronage in de Markievicz's attitude towards her, with the latter persistently asking Clarke, 'why on earth did they arrest such a quiet, insignificant person as yourself?' Clarke said she responded that 'when people important like her [de Markievicz] were in prison somebody had to carry on' and furthermore, she was 'not in prison as a result of going on platforms and making speeches asking for arrest'.[69] Clarke had a point. After her release from prison in June 1917, de Markievicz had immediately embarked on a country-wide speaking tour.

TABLE 11: COUNTESS DE MARKIEVICZ'S TOUR OF IRELAND

Date	Town	County
24 July 1917	Ballaghadereen	Roscommon
12 August 1917	Clonakilty	Cork
9 September 1917	Trim	Meath
10 September 1917	Trim	Meath
15 September 1917	Newcastle West	Limerick
16 September 1917	Newcastle West	Limerick
16 September 1917	Bruree	Limerick
17 September 1917	Ennis	Clare
23 September 1917	Rathfarnham	Dublin
7 October 1917	Castlewellan	Down
14 October 1917	Bantry	Cork
20 October 1917	Listowel	Kerry
19 October 1917	Tralee	Kerry
21 October 1917	Athea	Limerick
1 November 1917	Clonmel	Tipperary
2 November 1917	Waterford	Waterford
4 November 1917	Carrick-on-Suir	Tipperary

Source: RIC reports (PRO, CO/904–23), pp. 68-111.

Clarke's charge, that de Markievicz courted imprisonment, is borne out by the general contents of these speeches. For example, at Trim she said:

Maud Gonne with some of the members of Inghinidhe na hÉireann *c.*1905.
Source: Kilmainham Gaol Museum.

Left: Elizabeth Maguire, a member of Drumcondra Cumann na mBan 1918–
1921.
Right: Elizabeth's Active Service certificate. *Photo Courtesy Richard O'Driscoll.*

Dr Kathleen Lynn, founder member of the Women Delegates to the All Ireland Conference and the Committee for the Protection of Ireland from Venereal Disease. She was elected Sinn Féin co-director of health in 1918 and was one of the four vice-presidents of the party in 1921.

Mrs Jennie Wyse Power, a founder member of Inghinidhe na hÉireann in 1901, executive member of the Sinn Féin league in 1908 and a founder of Cumann na mBan in 1914. She was co-treasurer of the Sinn Féin party 1920–22 and founded Cumann na Saoirse in 1922.

Left: Marcella Cosgrove, a member of the INE branch of Cumann na mBan. *Source: Kilmainham Gaol Museum.*

Below left: Emily Elliot wearing her Cumann na mBan uniform with the official brooch and first aid armlet. She was a member of the GPO garrison during the 1916 Rising. *Source: Kilmainham Gaol Museum.*

Below right: Eilís Ní Riain wearing the Cumann na mBan uniform with the official brooch. She was a member of the Colmcille Branch. *Source: Bureau of Military History 1913–1921 (CD/202/1) Military Archives.*

Hannah Sheehy Skeffington, suffragist and founder of the Irish Women's Franchise League in 1908. In 1921 she was elected one of the four vice-presidents of Sinn Féin and appointed the party's national organiser.

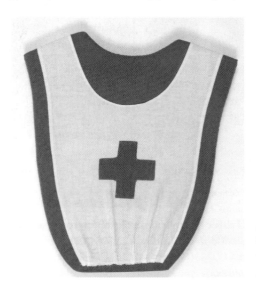

A Cumann na mBan Red Cross apron front belonging to Eva Burke. *Source: National Museum.*

Countess de Markievicz making one of her public appearances.

Pro-Treaty Cumann na mBan in Cork. *Source: Conlon Collection, Cork Public Museum.*

The women of the Irish Citizen Army, Cumann na mBan and the Clan na Gael girls in late 1916 at Ely House.

1st row from left: Madeleine Ffrench Mullen, Miss Foley, Dr Kathleen Lynn.

2nd row from left: Rose McNamara, Kathleen Kenny, M.J. Walsh, (unknown), Mrs Lawless, Jenny Milner, Eileen Walsh, Louie Kennedy, May Byrne, Annie Cooney.

3rd row from left: M. Moore, K. Lane, Sarah Kealy, Gertie Colley Murphy, Mary O'Hanrahan, A. Wisely, B. Murtagh, Cilla Quigley, Julia Grennan, Stasia Twomey, B. Walsh.

4th row from left: Nora Thornton, Rose Mullally, Sheila O'Hanlon, Moira Quigley, Margaret O'Flaherty, Josie McGowan, Eileen Cooney, Josie O'Keeffe.

5th row from left: Lucy Smyth, Nora Foley, P. Morkan, D. Sullivan, M. Elliot, Mary O'Sullivan, Tilly Simpson, Mrs Cathleen Treston.

6th (back) row from left: May Kelly, Brigid Brady, Jennie Shanahan, Kathleen Barrett, Rosie Hackett, Margaret Ryan, Brigid Davis, C. Caffery, Patricia Hoey.

Left side of the group: Madge Fagan or A. Tobin, Aoife Taafe, Marcella Cosgrove, (unknown), Miss Foley.

Right side of the group: May Kelly, Máire Ní Shiublaigh, Lily O'Brennan, Elizabeth O'Farrell, Nora O'Daly, Mary Murray.

Source: Nancy Wyse Power, Bureau of Military History papers, Military Archives, Dublin.

Fellow rebels, when coming from Dublin today, one thing I noticed was the Republican colours everywhere I looked. I saw the yellow cornfields, green fields and the white cloud: yellow green and white, the Sinn Féin colours ... I made a vow when leaving prison that I would never go on a platform without talking sedition, and then if they want me they can have me, jail is not such a bad place ... Of course all this is sedition, and I may be back again in prison any day, but I am prepared.[70]

Kathleen Clarke was upset at being separated from her children. She refused to eat the prison food and consequently became ill. The matron of Holloway Prison enquired of her if she wished to have her meals brought in from outside the prison, as de Markievicz had been doing. Clarke refused because she believed 'that those who sent me here are responsible for my well being and everything I need to keep me in good health'.[71] Clarke asked de Markievicz about what the matron had said regarding the food. De Markievicz replied 'that she had been recovering from measles when she was arrested and was afraid that the prison diet would hinder her recovery'.[72] When Clarke's weight plummeted, the prison doctor put her on a prison hospital diet, which she found easier to digest.

In July 1918, the prison authorities moved the three women to a more modern part of the prison where they were each allocated a cell and allowed to associate. They also had access to a garden for exercise. The prison governor commented, 'with these amenities it is hoped that there will be no further complaints'.[73]

In August, de Markievicz received a visit from her sister Eva. The visit was supervised by the governor of Holloway, Mr Waller, and he recounted that de Markievicz told her sister of 'being brought to England by military escort with fixed bayonets and loaded re-volvers and the order to shoot if she attempted to escape'.[74] Eva was instructed to 'badger the censor and enquire why her letters were held up, and why male internees were allowed much larger sheets of writing paper than the female prisoners'.[75]

In September, Clarke and de Markievicz informed the governor of the prison that they would 'decline to receive visits from their friends and relatives, if their visitors had to sign the usual undertaking' not to discuss any political issues or pass on information that might be construed as political.[76] However, this did not prevent them receiving three letters and one parcel each week. By this time de Markievicz was becoming bored and she asked Eva to send her 'watercolours and etching materials'.[77] She also asked for some picture postcards because they did not 'count as letters and also some books of pictures to help me get ideas for my painting'.[78] Later in the winter, Eva sent her a fur coat. During her time in Holloway de Markievicz was still president of Cumann na mBan but she signed her letters with 'Countess de Markievicz IRA'.[79]

MacBride took a different attitude to her imprisonment. She did not have a problem with friends and relatives signing the undertaking. In a letter to the authorities in early July 1918, she complained that she had 'been kidnapped in the streets of Dublin by five suspicious ruffians, who had no warrant for my arrest' and she demanded a solicitor.[80] She gave the authorities the address of her daughter Iseult who she described as her adopted daughter. At this time Iseult was living in London. Gonne MacBride never acknowledged in public that Iseult was her biological daughter. Iseult began to write a steady stream of letters to the prison authorities concerning her mother. Gonne also complained about feeling unwell. The prison medical officer Francis E. Forward examined Gonne MacBride and made his report on 8 July:

Apart from her rheumatism, which she has been subjected to for the last few months or so, and for which she received medical treatment when necessary, her general health was very fair, and as far as one can judge there is no deterioration in rheumatism since her reception here.[81]

MacBride continued to eat little, but she did not go on hunger strike. On 28 August, the report of the prison deputy medical officer, F.J. Wilfred Sass, indicated that she had lost twelve pounds in weight since her initial incarceration. This was a loss of about one pound each week, indicating she was on a low calorie diet. MacBride was fifty-two at this time. She was then put on the prison hospital diet. Around 6 September, MacBride was examined by Symes Thompson, physician to the Great Northern Central Hospital, who reported that 'she was suffering from a generalised urticarial rash which covered her limbs and trunk, and her left lung was cause for concern, but there was no sign of active disease'.[82] This report was sent to the prison medical officer Francis Forward who, in his report to the Home Office, stated that:

> MacBride's convalescence was retarded by her not taking sufficient nourishment. At one time she expressed her intention of going on hunger strike, and for several days she took very little food, but during the last 48 hours she has taken quite a fair quantity, and I think now she has given up the idea.[83]

On 14 September, she was examined again by the deputy medical officer Dr Sass, who reported that MacBride told him she had experienced night sweats on two occasions, but he believed this was due to the fact that she had taken 'hot milk and brandy before retiring'.[84] The prison hospital diet included a daily measure of brandy. He also indicated that the rash she had been suffering from was fading, that her general condition was fair and there was no sign of lung disease. Her mental condition was deemed normal 'although she was worrying a good deal about her children'.[85] Her son Seán MacBride was fourteen at this time and her daughter

Iseult was twenty-four. The doctor also recorded that MacBride had lost more weight and was now sixteen pounds lighter than at her initial incarceration in May. He attributed the loss of weight to a fever and the fact 'that she was eating less than usual'.[86]

Ten days later, MacBride was allowed to have a consultation with her solicitor. The governor, in his report of this meeting, said that she informed the solicitor that when she was examined by the prison medical officer he told her 'she had a few spots, which were drug spots'. This was apparently an allergy to a drug she was taking which manifests as a series of tiny red spots or hives all over the body, known as urticaria. It can also be a symptom of the menopause. This made her very indignant and she proceeded to tell the solicitor 'that the prison was a dumping ground for all kinds of cases of syphilis', at which point the prison governor, R.N. Paton, who was monitoring the interview, 'cautioned her that the visit would be stopped unless that subject was dropped'.[87]

Meanwhile Seán MacBride and Iseult Gonne kept up a series of letters demanding her release. Within a few weeks, after several more medical reports which indicated that her health was becoming a cause for concern, she was examined by Mr F.W. Thunnicliffe, MD, a physician from Kings College Hospital, in London. He concluded 'that she needed active medical care and open air treatment in a suitable climate'.[88]

Two days later, F.J. Stevenson of the prison service wrote to the British Home Office and informed them that he believed MacBride 'should be released because remaining in Holloway could be fatal'.[89] He also pointed out 'that her long absence abroad had already detracted from her political influence in Ireland and her release would not be dangerous, whereas if she died in prison an impetus would be given to Sinn Féin'.[90] On 29 October, MacBride was sent to a nursing home in London. After six days she became concerned about the cost of the nursing home because she could not afford the fees and asked permission 'to move to the home of W.B. Yeats in London'; this was refused.[91] She left the nursing home without permission and went to Yeats' home, from where she wrote letters to the newspapers 'complaining about her treatment in Holloway'.[92]

The prison authorities contacted a sanatorium in Ipswich and asked them to accept MacBride as a patient. They were willing to accept her at the usual rate of forty-five shillings a week. The sanatorium had a vacant bed and could admit her immediately, but they qualified this with the proviso that she be 'given to understand that this sanatorium was primarily for the working classes, and that she would be treated in every way the same as the other patients and could not be guaranteed a separate ward'.[93] On 28 November 1918, an order was made under 14b of DORA 'that she forthwith proceed to the County Borough of Ipswich, in the county of Suffolk, and do remain and reside in the said County Borough of Suffolk or within a radius of five miles of the sanatorium'.[94] Within weeks she managed to slip out of Suffolk and arrived back in Dublin.

When in late 1917 the INAAVDF decided to cease collecting, Hanna Sheehy Skeffington, Nora Connolly and Margaret Skinnider sought permission to return to Ireland from the USA. Permission was in the process of being granted, when the commander in chief of the British forces in Ireland objected most strenuously on the basis that if 'these three ladies [are allowed] to enter Ireland they will undoubtedly at once become, if not active agitators, figureheads for the encouragement of disloyal propaganda'.[95] After substantial correspondence between Sir C. Spring Rice, the British envoy in Washington, and the British under-secretary's office in Dublin, the women were allowed to travel to Liverpool but were refused permission to enter Ireland.

In early July 1918, Nora Connolly, Margaret Skinnider and Hanna Sheehy Skeffington with her son Owen, 'left New York on the ship SS *Matagama*'.[96] The ship docked at Liverpool on 10

July 1918 and they were brought before a military tribunal for questioning, where 'Sheehy Skeffington and Connolly refused to give an address of residence in Britain'.[97] Skinnider indicated she was returning home to Glasgow. The women's bags were searched but nothing incriminating was found. They were each served with a notice that prohibited them from travelling to Ireland. Connolly decided to travel to Glasgow with Skinnider and stay at her home. Sheehy Skeffington travelled to London. By August, Sheehy Skeffington decided to ignore the order prohibiting her from entering Ireland and travelled to Dublin. She was arrested under regulation 14b of DORA and taken to Holloway Prison, where she immediately began a hunger strike. Within days the order was revoked and she was released. She travelled back to Ireland on 17 August 1918.

Nora Connolly, who was still in Glasgow, wrote an angry letter to the authorities asking them to revoke the order prohibiting her from returning to Ireland as they had done for Sheehy Skeffington. This was rejected. Connolly wrote a second time and demanded an explanation:

When I was given my passport from America, I was told that I would be allowed home subject to the same restrictions as Mrs Sheehy Skeffington, but she is at home and I am still detained here. How can that be justified? Is it because she is a greater menace to the peace of the government than I, or is it because she has a greater following and more influence than I can lay claims to have? Or am I kept here simply because I am the eldest daughter of a man the English government executed? Having allowed Mrs Skeffington home, what sane or justifiable reason can you possible have for keeping me here?[98]

Connolly had a point: the case of Sheehy Skeffington did receive a lot of attention from the press, but Connolly and Skinnider were not mentioned. The office of the lord lieutenant informed her that they were unable to comply with her request. Connolly was forced to remain in Scotland and only returned to Ireland sometime in 1919. It was implied in press reports that Sheehy Skeffington travelled back to Ireland with her son Owen at that time – there was no mention of Skinnider or Connolly.

On 28/29 September 1918, Cumann na mBan held its fourth annual convention. There were 150 delegates present. Áine Ceannt took the chair because de Markievicz was still in prison. Niamh Plunkett, who was secretary of the organisation, reported that the organisation had over 600 branches. Within a year, the number of branches had risen from a very modest 100. Plunkett claimed this was because the organisation had appointed Alice Cashel as national organiser. However, Nancy Wyse Power ascribed the growth to the anti-conscription campaign. She believed 'the threat of conscription in the spring and summer of 1918 caused a sudden and unmanageable increase in the number of branches'.[99] The increase was probably due to a combination of both. Cumann na mBan's anti-conscription campaign was very emotive and it gave the organisation a wider public profile than ever before. It appears that many young women responded on an emotional level and they joined the organisation as a result.

TABLE 12: THE CUMANN NA MBAN ORGANISERS APPOINTED BETWEEN NOVEMBER 1917 AND NOVEMBER 1918 AND THE COUNTIES WHERE THEY FORMED NEW BRANCHES

Name	Areas of responsibility
Áine Ceannt	Tralee, Kerry
Alice Cashel	Donegal-Tyrone-Cavan-Monaghan-Galway-Mayo-Roscommon
Ellen O'Ryan	Waterford & South Wexford

Jennie Wyse Power	Kells, Meath
Leslie Price	West Cork
Lily O'Brennan	Longford and West Wicklow
Louise Gavan Duffy	South Armagh
Niamh Plunkett	County Cork

Source: Cumann na mBan 1918 convention report and the statement of Alice Cashel to the Bureau of Military History.

As well as the national organisers, several branch secretaries also became involved in starting new branches. They were Miss O'Riordan, Cahirsiveen, Co. Kerry; Miss Hurley, Tralee, Co. Kerry; Miss Brigid O'Mullane, Sligo; Miss Mullen, Monaghan; Miss Power, Tipperary; Miss O'Brien and Miss O'Leary, Cork.[100]

It was at this convention that a decision was taken to bring the organisation within the directive of the Irish Volunteers. In February 1918, the executive of Cumann na mBan had expressed their concern that their local branches were being perceived as women's Sinn Féin Clubs because of their public profile in the by-election campaigns of 1917. Concerned that its membership might be 'in danger of losing sight of the reason for which they had been founded', the executive decided to redress the situation.[101] The women drew up a directive called 'Military Activities' and issued it to all its branches. It dictated that:

Captains of branches should put themselves under the orders of the local Irish Volunteer officer and convey these orders to the members of the branch and see that they are carried out ... the captains of the branches comprising a district council, should form a military committee in touch with the Battalion Council in the event of military operations being necessary.[102]

The district council was essentially a form of military committee, which would operate as an attachment to their relevant battalion council for the purposes of planning military operations.

However, over the period of February to October 1918, just one district council was organised. This was in Dublin and comprised 'seven officers, namely captains and adjutants of the seven branches in the city'.[103] These were the Central branch, the INE branch, the Colmcille branch, Fairview (renamed the Four Martyrs branch), the James Street branch, Ranelagh (renamed the Éamonn Ceannt branch) and a branch named University College Dublin.

Having tried and failed to impose the 'Military Activities' directive on the membership, the executive sought to have it inserted into the constitution. The executive proposed a resolution that 'for the purpose of military organisation and operations, captains of branches shall take orders from the local Volunteer Commander'.[104] The plan was to bring the Irish Volunteers and Cumann na mBan closer by implementing the concept of the district council. This council would operate within each battalion company and would comprise a captain and secretary from each branch of Cumann na mBan and men of the corresponding ranks of the Irish Volunteers. Alice Cashel, who represented Galway, objected to the plan and enquired if it meant 'that a captain from the Irish Volunteers would have an input into the election of a captain in Cumann na mBan'.[105] Miss Matthews from the Dundalk branch also objected and complained that a row had erupted in a branch in County Louth, when a member of the Irish Volunteers interfered in the appointment of its officers. After some discussion it was clarified that 'the election of the officers in Cumann na mBan, was a matter in which outsiders could have no say'.[106] Three members of the executive, Máire Ní Riain, Leslie Price and Niamh Bean Uí Laoghaire, defended the resolution. They explained 'that the military activities of Cumann na mBan were meaningless without the Irish Volunteers and it was essential that they organise

Cumann na mBan to fit in with the men's activities'.[107] The executive's resolution was passed unanimously. The work of the organisation was now effectively being subsumed into the activities of the Irish Volunteers.

In August 1918, Lloyd George announced a general election for December. At this time, Seán T. O'Kelly, the director of the national plebiscite, presented a report on its progress:

> So far as I have been able to discover, the Plebiscite has been already completed by a great number of cumainn. Cumainn that have not already done so, are directed to notify me no later than the 15 September, as to the

Books of the National Plebiscite 1917–1918. Source: Robert Barton papers, MA BMH, CD 264.5.3-3.1.

> result of their efforts. [Each] Comhairle Ceanntair is directed to have tabulated and sent on to the Director of the Plebiscite a full statement of the results of the Plebiscite in their respective areas. The Plebiscite books are to be carefully stored in safe custody until further orders. As the information here asked for may be required in connection with the forthcoming general election, it is particularly requested, that this matter be attended to without further delay.[108]

The work of organising of the plebiscite had enabled Sinn Féin to reach into to every village, hamlet, town and city in the country. It is possible to speculate that by 1918 the collection of the signatures for the plebiscite had politicised a significant section of the population and subsequently gave Sinn Féin an enhanced position with regard to the election campaign.

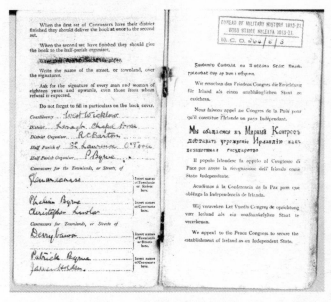

Books of the National Plebiscite 1917–1918. Source: Robert Barton papers, MA BMH, CD 264.5.3-3.1.

An intriguing aspect of the plebiscite has surfaced in the papers of Robert Barton. He organised the collection of the plebiscite in west Wicklow and the men who collected the signatures kept a 'Black Book' recording those individuals who refused to sign the document.[109]

The collection of signatures nationwide facilitated politicisation at all levels of Irish society. The passing of the Representation of the People Act (1918), granted the franchise to all males over twenty-one and females over thirty years. This increased the Irish electorate from just over 700,000 to over 2 million people and made a democratic revolution possible.

The 'Black Book' used to record those in west Wicklow who refused to sign the National Plebiscite. Source: Robert Barton papers, BMH, Military Archive, CD 264 53.

Sinn Féin began the selection process of nominating candidates for the election. Each candidate was nominated and ratified by their Comhairle Ceanntair *in absentia*. Three women were nominated: Countess de Markievicz was nominated and ratified by St Patrick's Comhairle Ceanntair in Dublin, Winifred Carney was nominated and ratified by the Belfast Comhairle Ceanntair, and the Harbour Division Comhairle Ceanntair nominated Hanna Sheehy Skeffington as a candidate, but she 'declined to go forward'.[110]

Cumann na mBan supported the election campaign whole-heartedly. Throughout the country, members of the organisation accepted responsibility for printing and distributing election leaflets. They pasted up posters and canvassed each household in their own specific areas of operation. Individual branches of Cumann na mBan also took on the work of arranging representatives to address public election meetings for Sinn Féin. On polling day in several rural areas the members helped their local Irish Volunteer companies to provide transport and refreshments for old people, and they worked at polling booths throughout the country, also providing meals for the election workers. Cumann na mBan was the main female support organisation working for the success of Sinn Féin in the election. This view is supported by Jennie Wyse Power, who observed that most of the 'women workers at the election were drawn from the ranks of Cumann na mBan'.[111] Sinn Féin won 73 out of 135 seats, 46 of these held by men still in prison. The women within the republican movement now faced into the future in a triumphant and optimistic mood because they believed they would have a well-deserved and equitable role in the creation of a new Irish Republic.

9

WAR 1919–1921

The success of the Sinn Féin party in the general election of December 1918 meant that they could now set about fulfilling their plan to convoke a constituent assembly. On 21 January 1919, twenty-seven members of Sinn Féin, who had won seats in the general election, met at the Mansion House and convoked the parliament of the Irish Republic (Dáil Éireann). The proceedings, which were held in the Irish language and lasted about two hours, were described as momentous by F.S.L. Lyons in *Ireland Since the Famine*.[1] The Declaration of Independence and the message to the free nations of the world 'were presented in the Irish and English languages'.[2] This document reiterated the claim by Sinn Féin that the Irish Republic should have a place at the pending peace talks in Versailles. However, Dáil Éireann was an illegal assembly, so gaining international recognition was going to be exceptionally difficult. The Democratic Programme of the Irish government was presented in English and Irish; a constitution was produced 'in Irish only and was adopted'.[3] At this time, the Irish population was predominantly English speaking and producing the constitution exclusively in the Irish language indicates the disregard in which these politicians held the general population.

The assembly met again the following day in private session and, in a show of hypocrisy, they held this meeting entirely in the

English language, presumably because some of them could not speak or write in the Irish language. Cathal Brugha was elected president *pro tem*. The appointment of Eoin MacNeill as Minister for Finance was approved, with only Piaras Béaslaí dissenting. Others appointed to ministries were Michael Collins to Home Affairs, Count Plunkett to Foreign Affairs and Richard Mulcahy to National Defence. Seán T. O'Kelly was appointed speaker of the assembly. The members of the Dáil were to be known as Teactaí Dála (TDs). Countess de Markievicz was the sole female representative and the women of Cumann na dTeachtaire were unhappy that the assembly had just one female representative. However, Cumann na dTeachtaire had not played any role in the general election campaign and consequently had not developed a public profile. So while they were unhappy that they did not have a significant presence in the assembly, it was due to their own inaction. Nine days after the Dáil convened, the women met to discuss the situation and decided that they should work towards redressing the situation at local level. They drew up a list of women that they deemed suitable and sent it to all local Comhairlí Ceanntair of Sinn Féin, 'to ensure that before the selection of candidates at local elections commenced, the women of Ireland would have more equitable representation than in Dáil Éireann'.[4] This list comprised Kathleen Lynn, Hanna Sheehy Skeffington, Kathleen Clarke, Áine Ceannt and Countess Plunkett, all based in Dublin; Madge Daly in Limerick; Winifred Carney in Belfast; Rosamund Jacob in Waterford; and Alice Cashel in Galway. The list was circulated to the relevant Comhairlí Ceanntair with the demand that they consider these women as candidates.

The group also discussed sending a circular to each Sinn Féin club, urging them to ensure that female candidates were selected for the local elections. Another issue that concerned them was the lack of competent female public speakers in Ireland. They had often discussed this issue, but it had never moved beyond discussion. They decided to ask Hanna Sheehy Skeffington to undertake the task of teaching public speaking and they set up classes at a cost of two shillings and sixpence for a course. Their other concern at this meeting was their failure to make plans to celebrate the feast day of St Brigid on 1 February. They believed St Brigid 'was a good suffragist' and expressed regret at their lapse, but they decided to make plans for a high mass in her honour the following year. Meanwhile, they decided that all the members of Cumann na dTeachtaire should attend a special service that had been organised by a 'Protestant suffrage society'.[5] St Brigid did not get her high mass because Cumann na dTeachtaire never met again. Without explanation, the organisation simply ceased to exist. A possible reason for the disappearance of Cumann na dTeachtaire is that Sinn Féin did not allow distinct groups to operate within the party.

The issue of women operating in republican politics, as a group, was not addressed again. Cumann na mBan was the only female republican organisation in existence, but their insistence that they were part of the republican army, left them on the margins of political activity. The CPIVD, which had been spawned by Cumann na dTeachtaire, met for the last time on 13 February 1919. On the following day it was reformed as the hospital board of St Ultan's Infant Hospital. This board comprised some of the members of the CPIVD, including Madeleine Ffrench Mullen and Kathleen Lynn, who were secretary and chairperson respectively, of the committee.

In February 1919, Eamon de Valera was helped to escape from Lewes Jail by Michael Collins and Harry Boland. He returned to Dublin and went into hiding. In March many of the prisoners held in jails in England were released. The Dáil reassembled on 1 April 1919, with fifty-two members present, including Eamon de Valera and Countess de Markievicz. The morning session was held in private and was taken up with discussions about the prisoners still being held in England and ministerial reports on the payment of the TDs' daily expenses. Seán McEntee moved an amendment, which was seconded by de Markievicz, that TDs should be 'allowed the price of a third-class return rail ticket, and 15/- per day when attending the Dáil'.[6] The publication of an official government *Gazette* was entrusted to Laurence Ginnell. With the basic issues of housekeeping sorted out, the session adjourned until the afternoon.

The afternoon session was a public one. This was mostly taken up with amendments, one of which came from de Valera and it was seconded by de Markievicz, 'that no deputy shall make a personal charge against another, nor use offensive remarks about another'.[7] This was carried. At the end of this session, Cathal Brugha resigned his position as president *pro tem* of Dáil Éireann and Eamon de Valera was unanimously elected in his stead. The following day the government ministers were nominated and elected: Secretary for Home Affairs, Arthur Griffith; Secretary of Defence, Cathal Brugha; Foreign Affairs, Count Plunkett; Labour, Countess de Markievicz; Industries, Eoin MacNeill; Finance, Michael Collins; and Local Government, Liam Cosgrave.[8] Countess de Markievicz remained the sole female member of the cabinet.

In the early months of the Dáil, de Markievicz's input was small and did not follow any distinct pattern. The only specific mention of women and their lives was on 10 April 1919, when Eoin MacNeill in his capacity as Minister for Industries addressed the assembly. He stated, 'no woman should retain any occupation which is harmful to her health or morals, but if employed they should receive the same pay as men for equal work'.[9] This was said in the context of the issue of the workers' right to a decent living wage.

On 1 June 1919, the Dáil initiated a National Loan. Five days later de Valera left for the USA accompanied by Harry Boland to initiate a campaign towards gaining support for the National Loan and to gain recognition for the Irish Republic. Seán T. O'Kelly and

George Gavan Duffy were nominated to travel to Paris to put the case of the Irish Republic before the peace conference at Versailles. In de Valera's absence, Arthur Griffith was elected deputy president of the Dáil. During the following eighteen months, while de Valera was absent, Griffith was effectively the *de facto* president of Dáil Éireann.

On 19 June 1919, Dáil Éireann launched the National Loan prospectus, which it was hoped would raise £250,000. This money would enable the Dáil to function. The bonds were to be issued in denominations of £1, £5, £10, £20, £50 and £100, and the general population were invited to subscribe. The purpose of this range of certificates was to enable individuals on small incomes to subscribe. Each certificate would qualify for a 5 per cent rate of interest paid half-yearly. The National Loan was marketed as the means by which the general population could contribute to and have control of the future of Ireland. The appeal for subscriptions was published 'in national newspapers'.[10] Apart from seeking funds for the administration of the Dáil, the appeal also declared that subscribing to the fund would:

> Recover Ireland for the Irish ... re-people the land ... abolish the slums ... send Ireland's ships to every port and put her flag on every sea ... garner the harvest of the seas ... set the hammer ringing on the anvil ... set the looms spinning ... plant the hillsides and the wastes ... drain the bogs ... save every girl and boy for Ireland.[11]

The rank and file of Cumann na mBan became involved in the drive to sell the bonds certificates. They undertook to sell them in a house-to-house canvass. Because so many people could not afford to purchase them outright, the members of Cumann na mBan devised a method of sale by instalment. This involved collecting subscriptions on a weekly basis until the full amount of the bond was paid. This system appears unusual now, but the women believed this was necessary because of 'the scarcity of money among the very people who were most inclined to invest in the Dáil'.[12]

When de Valera arrived in the USA, 'his first public address was made under the auspices of the Friends of Irish Freedom (FOIF)'.[13] The FOIF emerged from the First Irish Race Convention summoned by Judge Cohalan and John Devoy in New York, in March 1916. Its remit was 'to educate Americans on the issue of the Irish question and try to influence world opinion at the end of the war'.[14] In June 1916, the Pádraig H. Pearse branch of the FOIF was founded in Washington. When America entered the war in Europe in 1917, the organisation ceased its activities and resumed them at the end of the war in 1918. Harry Boland presented the prospectus for the Irish National Loan to the FOIF and they informed him that it conflicted with American law. They advised de Valera to consider changing it to a National Certificate campaign. De Valera was unhappy with this advice and refused to make the change, which led to some argument between him and the FOIF.

De Valera then travelled to San Francisco, where he received the same advice. The relationship between Cohalan, Devoy and de Valera was never harmonious and soon led to a split. At Boland's request the FOIF set up a fundraising sub-committee to help him with the National Loan campaign. The FOIF put their national headquarters at Boland's disposal. This office became the base from which de Valera's lecture tours were arranged. After some months, de Valera conceded that the bond campaign should be changed to a certificate campaign and he began planning the new campaign.

The FOIF was led to believe that de Valera's new campaign would be operational by September 1919, so they closed down their fundraising sub-committee. However, de Valera's campaign did not get off the ground until January 1920, so between September 1919 and January 1920 the FOIF was financially supporting de Valera and his entourage, as well as Seán T. O'Kelly and George Gavan

Duffy, the two envoys in Paris. The FOIF also sent money directly to Ireland. In total during this period they sent:

	Dols
Cash sent to Ireland direct	$115,000
Cash to Irish envoys in Paris (O'Kelly and Duffy)	$21,500
Cash to President de Valera for expenses in America	$26,748
Advance to President de Valera for Irish Bond Certificates campaign	$100,000
TOTAL	$263,248 [15]

In November 1920, de Valera initiated the American Association for the Recognition of the Irish Republic (AARIR). Twelve days later, 'the Pádraig Pearse branch of the FOIF became part of the AARIR'.[16]

Meanwhile, back in Ireland, the population was experiencing a gradual slide into war. At Soloheadbeg on 21 January 1919, the first shots were fired in what became known as the Anglo-Irish War or War of Independence. The Irish Volunteers needed arms and ammunition and they decided to source them from the RIC. This led to attacks on police barracks and anti-police propaganda, a campaign given further impetus by de Valera, who, before he had left Ireland in early 1919, said at a public session of Dáil Éireann:

> Members of the police forces acting in this country, as part of the British occupation, and as agents of the British government, be ostracised socially by the people of Ireland ... They are spies in our midst. Their history is a continuity of brutal treason against their own people.[17]

In August 1919, the Minister for Defence, Cathal Brugha, moved a motion in the Dáil, 'that all the deputies of the Dáil, the Irish

Volunteers and the officers and clerks of the Dáil should take an oath of allegiance to Dáil Éireann'. He did not specify Cumann na mBan, but the organisation came under the description of 'any other body or individual who in the opinion of the Dáil should take the same Oath'.[18] The wording of the oath was:

> I ... do solemnly swear (or affirm) that I do not and shall not yield a voluntary support to any pretended Government, authority or power within Ireland hostile and inimical thereto, and I do further swear (or affirm) that to the best of my knowledge and ability, I will support and defend the Irish Republic and the government of the Irish Republic, which is Dáil Éireann, against all enemies, foreign and domestic, and I will bear true faith and allegiance to the same, and that I take this obligation freely without any mental reservation or purpose of evasion, so help me, God.[19]

Brugha explained that 'the object aimed at was to unify the whole body in this country'.[20] However, the Irish Volunteers' constitution prevented them from being subject to any other body but their own executive. Brugha, who was chief of staff of the Irish Volunteers, told the Dáil that at their next convention that 'it would be proposed that they ask them as the standing army to swear allegiance to the Dáil'.[21] The motion was carried by thirty votes to five. From about this time the Irish Volunteers became known as the Irish Republican Army (IRA). Within weeks, the British government denounced the Dáil, Sinn Féin, Cumann na mBan and the Irish Volunteers. The Volunteers did not hold a convention following this, so by default the IRA remained outside the control of the Dáil.

At this time, Countess de Markievicz was in Cork Jail. She had been arrested on 13 June 1919 and was charged three days later with addressing a proscribed meeting at Newmarket in Cork. She received a sentence of four months in prison, which she served in

Cork Jail. While she was incarcerated, the members of the local branches of Cumann na mBan prepared, cooked and delivered a meal to her every day. In expressing her appreciation to her sister Eva, de Markievicz said:

> This is the most comfortable jail I have been in yet. There is a nice garden … I have heaps of friends here, who send me in lots of very good food – in fact – all my meals. Our people are such darlings. In Dublin [Mountjoy Jail] my meals were sent in and at Mallow, a girl gave me a teapot of lovely tea and some cakes to keep me going.[22]

In July she received a visit from the visiting committee of the General Prison Board for Ireland. They came to ascertain if she had any complaints about her position; she told them 'that she had not'.[23] In their report the committee observed that de Markievicz 'was in good health and content in her circumstances with her present lot'.[24] During her time in this jail, she signed her letters 'Countess de Markievicz, Irish Citizen Army'.[25]

In July 1919, the Lord Lieutenant, Lord French proscribed Sinn Féin, the IRA, Cumann na mBan and the Gaelic League. In October, Cumann na mBan decided to challenge the ban and hold their annual convention at the Mansion House in Dublin. To prevent the convention from being held, the police placed a cordon around the Mansion House. Inspector Barrett of the DMP was in charge, with a sergeant and twenty policemen under his command. As some of women arrived at Dawson Street, they lingered a few moments and went away again. Maud Gonne MacBride was observed arriving and leaving again, and Countess Plunkett arrived on a tricycle. Countess de Markievicz, who had been released from jail two days earlier, 'arrived by tram accompanied by a low-sized, dark-sallow-complexioned lady wearing glasses'.[26] As de Markievicz walked towards the Mansion House, she was stopped by Inspector Barrett and informed that she could not enter the building. She responded to him with the words, 'I am a member of the Irish Government elected by the Irish people, I want to see the lord mayor'.[27] She also informed him that she was Minister for Labour. Barrett enquired from her a second time if she was connected with the proposed meeting and received the response:

> What an impertinent question ... do you represent the hirelings of the British government? What Irishmen. I got four months in Cork for telling the people about you, and I'm glad I did so. You won't let me in, then, very well, I have been here to test it, and I hope you won't be badly punished.[28]

In his report on the incident, Barrett expressed the opinion that this 'veiled threat showed her consciousness of the assassin gangs of the Irish Volunteers, in whom she is in all probability more interested, as her career of crime would indicate, than with labour'.[29]

Some women lingered in the vicinity and walked up and down the street until about 3 p.m., before dispersing. Cumann na mBan had their headquarters in Dawson Street at this time, but the police were unaware of this. The women who were observed lingering around the Mansion House were passing the information to their fellow members that the convention was now going 'to take place at the premises of the Gaelic League in 25 Parnell Square'.[30] The convention went on for two days. On the day the convention ended, Constable Downing of the DMP, who was based at Chancery Lane police barracks, was shot and fatally wounded while on patrol in High Street. Inspector Barrett wrote in his report that 'he believed her [de Markievicz] veiled threat was responsible for this death'.[31] He went on to say that 'the release of this pestilential harridan was appropriately celebrated by the brutal murder of Constable Downing'.[32] Barrett believed de Markievicz was 'of the extreme section and a grave danger as long as she is at large'.[33]

The IRA were by this time waging a continuous campaign against the RIC. The police force was decimated by the constant attacks and this led to a decision by Lloyd George in March 1920 to supplement the declining membership of the RIC and the DMP. Members of a new force were recruited in England, from the ranks of demobilised British soldiers. Due to a shortage of uniforms, they were issued with a uniform 'which was a mix of the green khaki military trousers and the dark green tunics of the RIC'.[34] They became known as the Black and Tans, and they were detailed to operate in areas of intense republican activity in Clare, Cork, Dublin, Galway, Kerry, Kilkenny, Limerick, Mayo, Meath and Tipperary. Some months later, auxiliaries were recruited from among the demobilised officer rank of the British army. This force operated as the officer corps and numbered 1,500 cadets, who were divided into fifteen companies of 100 men and were in effect replacements for the officer corps of the RIC. J.J. Lee stated that while this number was not numerous enough 'to impose a real reign of terror' they did commit numerous atrocities.[35] However, the arrival of these men intensified the warfare considerably and forced the IRA volunteers to go on the run. Joost Augusteijn says the IRA men began to group together almost spontaneously for security. In June 1920, at an IRA GHQ meeting, the idea of forming Active Service Units (ASU) was discussed by Michael Collins and Richard Mulcahy. 'An ASU was a small squad of men formed within each battalion area' to plan and carry out attacks on the British military.[36] By October, the units were given greater scope when GHQ ordered all brigade areas to set up flying columns. These columns operated in wider geographical areas than the ASUs. The members of Cumann na mBan continued to use the expression ASU when referring to both groups of men.

From late 1919, the members of Cumann na mBan accepted responsibility for conveying food supplies to ASU bases and IRA training camps. In Dublin, Eilís Ní Riain, a member of the Central branch Cumann na mBan recalled that they 'collected comforts for men on the run, organised safe houses and first aid stations'.[37] In Carlow town, Annie Murphy acquired food and carried it by bicycle to the IRA training camp at Duckett's Grove, some miles from the town.[38] The women also brought food to prisoners and smuggled letters in and out of prisons. This was not easy work. In many cases they were subjected to 'foul language and sometimes personal violence'.[39] The women were trained in the care, maintenance and use of guns. This aspect of their work had been inserted into the constitution of Cumann na mBan at the convention in 1918. By a resolution from the Ranelagh branch, it was passed unanimously 'that rifle practice with the cleaning of, and unloading of rifles, be included among the military activities of the organisation', with the addendum 'where practicable'.[40]

The members of Cumann na mBan also became responsible for creating and protecting the IRA arms dumps. Planning ambushes involved the co-operation of Cumann na mBan because in many instances the women carried the guns and ammunition to and from the site of ambushes. Sighle Hartnett, who lived in Kenmare, recalled that she carried 'dispatches, and arms to the Volunteers, and made black powder at the back of a chemists shop'.[41] Annie Murphy in Carlow, 'stored rifles, revolvers and ammunition' in her house for the local Volunteer company and 'assisted the company captain in securing a box of bombs'.[42] Her house was also used as a safe house for men on the run. In Wexford, Charlotte Heney was involved in keeping arms dumps in a stable on her family's farm. She was responsible for 'collecting arms, keeping them clean and ready for use; this particular arms dump was in constant use until 1922'.[43]

In the area of the 1st Western Division IRA, the work of the women was a significant factor in enabling the ASUs to operate. Apart from carrying dispatches, they worked as scouts and gathered intelligence, which was 'highly dangerous and they did far more than the soldiers'.[44] The men in the ASUs came to depend on the women for basic care. The officer commanding the 1st Western Division said of this work:

> Where they got enough money to do all this is a mystery to me, but they did it. When almost everybody deserted us during the Christmas panic, these girls stood by us and at the height of the terror we found that the more dangerous the work the more willing they were to do it. Without their assistance … life would have been more unpleasant than it already was.[45]

One aspect of the work of Cumann na mBan was to relieve British soldiers of their arms and ammunition. Margaret Brodrick Nicholson from Galway city was involved in this activity, which involved enticing 'British soldiers down to the docks, to enable the Volunteers to relieve them of their arms'.[46] She said she hated doing this work and found it embarrassing 'because one of the Volunteers was her brother'.[47] Nicholson also recounted an episode when her hair was cut off by a Black and Tan patrol. The patrol came to her home and asked for her specifically by name. She recalled:

> I was upstairs and called down from the top of the stairs and said, 'Surely I am allowed to dress myself?' They replied, 'No come down as you are' … [I] went down and snatched a coat from the hall stand. My mother shouted after me, 'Be brave Peg' … I thought they were going to shoot me, but they took me outside and closed the door, then grabbed my hair saying what wonderful curls you have, and then proceeded to cut off my hair to the scalp, with a very blunt scissors. I might say they did not handle me too roughly, which is strange to say, there was no further comment until they were finished, when they pushed me towards the door and said good night.[48]

On the following day, Nicholson went to a barber to have her head shaved so that her hair would grow back properly. According to Nicholson, there was a public house in Eyre Square, which was frequented by Black and Tans and the girls who mixed with them 'were warned by the local Volunteers about publicly associating themselves with the RIC and the Tans'. However, she added, 'nothing was done to molest these girls, but their whole families cleared out around the period of the Truce and were never heard of again'.[49]

The social organisation of the sexes at this time made it easier for women to buy food and cook in their homes without attracting attention. Several friendships and many romances developed. Joost Augusteijn, while writing his book, interviewed individuals (who remain anonymous) who told him that the usual rituals of courting were transcended and 'that there were some unconfirmed reports of illegitimate children being born'.[50] John Healy recounted how his uncle had made two young women pregnant while he was with an ASU unit.[51]

An unmarried woman or girl in a small rural area would not openly have a full sexual relationship. Pregnancy would have meant a social death, so it would have to remain secret. To be unmarried and pregnant meant social ostracism, and if an unmarried member of Cumann na mBan became pregnant, she would have been drummed out of the organisation. If the putative father refused to marry her, she had only two options: she could give birth in the local workhouse; or, if she could raise the money, move away and give birth in secret.

An interesting case surfaced in Westmeath where a young woman brought a case before a republican court against a member of the IRA named as Flanagan, who she claimed seduced her and she subsequently gave birth. Flanagan was ordered by the court to pay the young woman '£200 and failing this, a grant of 30/– per week was to be paid for the maintenance of the child'.[52] Every young female understood the consequence of sex before marriage and there was little sympathy for the unmarried mother, regardless of the fact that she was fighting for her country. There were also many hasty marriages. As Countess de Markievicz told her sister in a letter, 'people got married on the run and many babies were born, whose fathers were on the run'.[53] Finding substantial primary sources about this issue is very difficult because of the necessary secrecy on the part of the female.

Women outside the Cumann na mBan organisation also became immersed in this war. An example of this is the story of Siobhán Lankford. She became involved in an intelligence network, which was largely created by Michael Collins. It is not possible to estimate how many people were involved in the network, but its members came from various backgrounds and occupations: railway workers, hotel porters, typists, civil servants, nurses and doctors. While working for the Mallow post office Lankford had been involved in setting up a Gaelic League club as a cover for IRA activity and she became an integral part of the intelligence network for the Cork no. 2 Brigade, IRA. When each telegram reached a post office, it was always written out in duplicate, one for the customer and a copy for filing in the post office. Lankford would slip a third piece of paper underneath the two sheets of paper and then slip it into her pocket and pass it on to her IRA contact.

While the military campaign was progressing, in the political arena the former members of Cumann na dTeachtaire were anxious to be nominated as candidates for Sinn Féin for the forthcoming local elections, which were to be held in January 1920. At the outset of the election campaign, in November 1919, Sinn Féin drew up an oath, which it was obligatory to swear before the party would ratify any potential candidate. This read: 'I ... recognise the Republic established by the will and vote of the Irish people, as the legitimate government of Ireland.'[54] Any potential candidate who refused to take this oath would not receive any support from the party. In addition, election expenses were channelled to Sinn Féin from Dáil Éireann; so signing the oath was a way of obtaining campaign funding.

In 1919 the republican government had appointed William Thomas Cosgrave as the Minister for Local Government, with Kevin O'Higgins as his assistant. Both men built up close contacts with local councils and officials all over the country and consequently, when the local elections took place in January and June 1920, 'Sinn Féin won a sweeping victory'.[55] Some of the former members of Cumann na dTeachtaire were successful in gaining a place on Dublin Corporation, including Jennie Wyse Power and Kathleen Clarke. In the township of Rathmines/Rathgar, Kathleen Lynn, Madeleine Ffrench Mullen, Áine Ceannt and Min Mulcahy were successful. Alice Cashel was successful in Galway and succeeded in being appointed vice-chairperson of the council. As Cumann na dTeachtaire no longer existed, it can be assumed that each woman fought individually for a nomination from the relevant Comhairle Ceanntair of Sinn Féin and signed the oath. Hanna Sheehy Skeffington was also successful in gaining a place on Dublin Corporation.

There were 127 corporations and councils in the country. By June 1920, 'Sinn Féin controlled seventy-two councils and shared their authority in a further twenty-six. They dominated 28 out of 32 county councils, 182 out of 206 rural district councils, and all but 16 of the 154 Poor Law Boards'.[56] Flushed with success, several councils withdrew from the LGB, in order to become part of the Republican government's planned new system of local government. The LGB retaliated by withdrawing funds. This had a catastrophic effect on the country.

A brief examination of the situation in Dublin, gives an inkling of how the situation developed across the country and its effect on people's lives, particularly those at the lower end of the social stratum. On 4 September 1920, the president of the LGB wrote to Dublin Corporation and informed them that it was going to withdraw its financial support. This money was supplementary to the local rates tax. Without this support, 'Dublin Corporation was facing a shortfall of £200,000' and cutbacks became inevitable.[57] Dublin Corporation immediately discontinued the funding of school meals, closed three of its treatment centres for tuberculosis and withheld payment of supplementary grants to the Richmond Asylum and the Dublin Union. The Dublin Union was the official name given to the amalgamated SDU and NDU in 1918. 'From 1 October 1920, the corporation was forced to suspend the wages and salaries of its employees'.[58]

Across the country (except in the northern counties) each county, in both rural and urban areas, was affected. In Dáil Éireann, the members of the government were content in their method of pursuing the freedom of the country, but outside the Dáil the country was falling apart. By late 1920, the withdrawal of the support of the LGB, along with the general misery created by the ongoing violence and mayhem, made the lives of the civilian population unbearable. The personal lives of families within all sections of society were disintegrating. As the warfare between the IRA and the Black and Tans intensified, many businesses, farms and family homes were burned down, and innumerable people lost paid employment. The withdrawal of the local councils from the LGB and the subsequent loss of income, meant the various Poor Law Unions were short of funds, so they could not give aid to the people who were affected. The economy had almost ground to a halt and citizens without work had no money to pay bills or buy food. In several areas of the country the now endemic poverty led to cases of typhus. An article in the *Irish Exile* on 8 July 1921, based on a report by Margaret Connory said, 'Typhus is a dirt disease. You cannot expect people to pay for soap and cleaning material who have not the wherewithal to put bread in their mouths.'

By December 1920, it was becoming clear that the population was in dire need of economic aid. John J. Splain, who was the national vice-president of the FOIF, said that 'de Valera had in his personal control millions of dollars raised by the Bond Certificate Campaign in America. When asked to donate $20,000 to relieve distress or help restore devastated Irish towns, he refused'.[59]

The American Committee for Relief in Ireland (ACRI) was founded in December 1920 to raise money and provide relief to the civilian population in Ireland. This committee was formed by William J. Moloney with several supporters, one of whom was L. Hollingsworth Wood, a member of the Religious Society of Friends in America, and they began a systematic fundraising campaign.[60] Meanwhile, Eamon de Valera, who was back in Ireland by late December 1920, was trying to involve himself in these developments. On 1 January 1921, he wrote to Harry Boland and told him he was going to create a new organisation and name it the 'Irish White Cross':

> Arrived safe after a little excitement … am settling to work to establish Irish White Cross: this name will avoid international complications … and we can look later to have it recognised by Geneva, as a Red Cross … I will try and get prominent women such as Lord Midleton's sister [Albina Broderick], Mrs Desparde, Miss Spring Rice as well as prominent people in the Society of Friends involved as well etc., so as to tone down the strong political colour that our own will give.[61]

Almost two weeks later, on 13 January 1921, Boland reported to de Valera that he had attended a meeting of the ACRI: 'I have not officially announced that I am here as your representative, and I think it advisable not to do so.'[62]

Some time in January 1921, Hollingsworth Wood, on behalf of the ACRI, contacted James Douglas, a member of the Society of Friends in Dublin, and informed him that he was 'sending him $25,000' that was to be used to help people who were suffering due to the war. Douglas was also informed 'that he had been chosen as the recipient of the money because the ACRI was anxious that the fund should be kept free from politics'.[63] Hollingsworth Wood also contacted the Lord Mayor of Dublin, Laurence O'Neill, to discuss the fund and O'Neill in turn contacted de Valera to discuss the situation. On 1 February 1921, the IWC was formed as a non-political and non-sectarian organisation. Laurence O'Neill was elected chairman, James Douglas was made treasurer, James McNeill secretary and Lionel Smith-Gordon was made chairman of the Standing Committee. The president of the IWC was His Eminence Michael, Cardinal Logue. It was through the IWC that the ACRI distributed money in Ireland.

The IWC and ACRI made a joint appeal for money and emphasised the multi-dimensional political and religious ethos of the organisation. Within a few months, the fund had raised approximately $5,000,000. In her work, *United States Foreign Policy and Ireland*, Bernadette Whelan states that 'in total $4,907,102.70 was sent to the Irish White Cross Society between 7 January 1921 and 28 June 1922, in fifty-two instalments'.[64]

The IWC had a complex system of committees and sub-committees, which enabled it to draw its representatives from 'practically every section of the political and religious beliefs of the Irish community'.[65] The fund had nine trustees. James Douglas recalled in his memoir that to make it clear that the IWC had the support of republicans, 'it should include some prominent leaders from Sinn Féin on its executive council'.[66] Michael Collins, Arthur Griffith and William T. Cosgrave were appointed as trustees. The other six appointed were the Archbishop of Dublin, Dr William Walsh, Thomas Johnson, James G. Douglas, George Russell, Mrs Mary Alden Childers and Joseph T. Wigham, MD.

The IWC also had an executive committee with a membership

of twenty-five, of which eight were women. The decision to create a fund that was representative of the wider population and not confined solely to republicans is highlighted by the choice of women on the executive committee. Three of these women were not republican: Miss E.M. Cunningham, MA, Mrs T.M. Kettle and Miss J. Wigham. The republican female members were Kathleen Clarke, Maud Gonne MacBride, Madame O'Rahilly, Jennie Wyse Power and Áine Ceannt. Apart from MacBride, the women brought with them their experience gained in working for the Ladies Distribution Committee of the INAAVDF. The IWC appointed a general council, which comprised ninety-six nominees from organisations with an interest in the fund. To add to its all-embracing ethos, Henry Kennedy, DSO, was appointed a director of the IWC. Kennedy held the Distinguished Service Order for his service in the British army. In addition, 'Captain David Robinson, DSO, was appointed to the post of whole time secretary'.[67] Robinson was a former British officer who had joined the Irish Volunteers in 1918. He was now a practising solicitor.

While the various IWC sub-committees worked together successfully in bringing relief to many people, the IWC report published in 1924 indicates that they did not develop a meeting of minds in the political sense:

> As private citizens they differed fundamentally … in their corporate capacity their sole function was to work for the relief of their suffering fellow countrymen. That they succeeded in their task is proved by the fact that widely as they differed among themselves on public matters, not one of them resigned from the society.[68]

Twelve days after the IWC was set up, a delegation of seven men arrived in Ireland under the auspices of the ACRI 'to ascertain the nature and extent of the need for relief'.[69] The delegation comprised the chairman and secretary of the ACRI, C.J. France, a lawyer from Seattle, Washington, and Samuel McCoy from Connecticut. There were also five men from the Society of Friends in America. The delegation remained in Ireland until 31 March. During 'these forty nine days, the delegation conducted an investigation into the economic distress' of the civilian population.[70] They then presented an extensive report, which indicated that there were three fundamental causes of distress: the burning of homes, the destruction of industries, and the 'subsequent loss of employment and great distress for many families'.[71] The burning of creameries led to very severe economic hardship for farmers and their employees. It was estimated that approximately 15,000 farming families were affected by the destruction of fifty-five co-operative creameries.

Harry Boland in the meantime, kept de Valera appraised of almost every move made by the ACRI. On 25 February, the day before the IWC was to be officially launched at the Mansion House in Dublin, Boland informed de Valera 'that the ACRI was prepared to co-operate with the IWC'.[72] On 26 February 1921, at the Mansion House, the IWC and the ACRI published a joint appeal to the Irish population and enumerated why the aid was needed. They estimated that over 7,000 men were in prison and that endemic violence had reduced 100,000 people to destitution with 'no alternative left to them but the support of charity, or escape from their miseries by death from want and hunger'.[73] The IWC made it clear in its public appeal that the organisation aimed to help everyone, regardless of political or religious affiliation: 'the appeal which we make today is made not in the name of any section of a people, but in the name of humanity, no political distinctions exist in suffering and none must exist in its relief'.[74] The areas in which aid was to be distributed were defined:

The relief of distress and hardship in the case of individual or groups of persons deprived of the means of livelihood.
The restoration or repair of buildings and the replacement or

repair of furniture, fittings, machinery, implements, or personal attacks.

The purchase or provision of stock-in-trade or raw materials to replace stocks or materials removed or destroyed.

The provision of employment by the organisation of works or otherwise.[75]

Initially, many republicans assumed the IWC were another republican organisation similar to the INAAVDF, but there was a fundamental difference between the two. The IWC and the ACRI were adamant that neither active members of the IRA nor men on the run would receive money from the fund. These men remained the responsibility of Dáil Éireann, which channelled money to them through a Republican government sub-committee officially called the 'prisoner's committee' and this comprised members of Sinn Féin, the IRA and Cumann na mBan.

The distribution of funds from the IWC to individual families was made at parish level. The parish unit, which was so successful in building the republican movement at grass roots level, was now brought into use by the IWC. This was a recognition of the fact that the parish was the centre of most local activity and the best source for knowledge of local conditions throughout the country. The parish priest in each committee acted as chairman. This was a practical decision because all members of the parish committee worked in a voluntary capacity.

The determination by de Valera to hold onto the funds generated by the AARIR for the administration of the republican government and to supply the needs of the IRA, meant that the IWC became the main support of the civilian population and this included the dependent families of the men of the IRA. The IWC was humanitarian and obviously decided that these families should receive help. The aid was channelled to them through the Irish Republican Prisoners' Dependents' Fund committee (IRPDF), which comprised members of Sinn Féin, the IRA and Cumann na mBan.[76]

In 1920 Cumann na mBan held its annual convention in secret. The 'Carmelite Fathers at Whitefriar Street, allowed them to use a large room attached to their church', where, according to Eilís Ní Riain, 'Cumann na mBan assembled as a women's sodality'.[77] The convention lasted for two days. Countess de Markievicz, who was at this point incarcerated in Mountjoy Jail, was elected president. The four vice-presidents were widows and mothers of men who died in 1916: Madame O'Rahilly, Mrs Kathleen Clarke, Mrs Margaret Pearse and Mrs Áine Ceannt.[78] Sorcha McMahon and Nancy Wyse Power were elected joint secretaries. The rest of the executive were Eileen McGrane, Jennie Wyse Power, Lou Kennedy, Min Ryan, Eilís Ní Riain and Lily O'Brennan from Dublin; Mollie O'Reilly from County Dublin; Leslie Price from Cork; and Phyllis Ryan from Wexford. The executive met weekly at a different venue each time.

When the Dáil was set up in 1919, most of its female secretarial staff came from the ranks of Cumann na mBan. In late 1920, Lily O'Brennan and Nancy Wyse Power, who both worked for Dáil Éireann, resigned from the executive of Cumann na mBan because the work of the Dáil was taking up too much of their time. Lily O'Brennan was also involved in finding hiding places for wounded men. When they both resigned, Florence O'Sullivan and Miss McGavock were co-opted to fill the vacancies.

During the Anglo-Irish War, the number of women arrested and imprisoned was small. Nancy Wyse Power believed this was because 'the authorities were not disposed to paying any attention to women, unless they were caught red-handed in the commission of some offence'.[79] By 1921, the number of republican women arrested was just forty-six. Sentences meted out ranged from fines to ten years with hard labour. When the activities they were involved in are taken into consideration, this was a small number.

**TABLE 13: THE SEVENTEEN WOMEN WHO WERE TRIED
AND SENTENCED BY COURT MARTIAL BETWEEN LATE 1920
AND EARLY 1921**

Name	Sentence	Location detained
Eithne Coyle	1 year hard labour	Mountjoy Jail
Lillian Hawes	1 year	Mountjoy Jail
Jean Quinn	1 year	Scotland
Linda Kearns	10 years hard labour	Mountjoy Jail
Mdm de Markievicz	2 years hard labour	Mountjoy Jail
Eileen Keogh	2 years hard labour	Wexford
Kathleen Hicks	3 months	Mountjoy Jail
A. McMahon	6 months	Mountjoy Jail
Ada English	9 months with hard labour	Galway
Sighle Rigney	9 months	Mountjoy Jail
Mary Bowles	Detained in reformatory	Cork
Miss O'Leary	Fine £1	
Miss Moloney	Fine £2	
Madge Daly	Fine £20	Limerick
Una Daly	Fine £40	
Mrs Ryan	Fine £50/3 months	Mountjoy Jail
Alice Cashel	6 months with hard labour	Galway

Source: Lil Conlon, Cumann na mBan and the Women of Ireland.

The most severe sentence passed was on Linda Kearns, who received ten years. She was arrested when she was caught driving a car carrying three men, ten rifles with loaded magazines, a Webley gun, two police belts, a police pouch, a haversack, a Maxim gun belt, 328 rounds of ammunition and some automatic pistol ammunition. Three of the rifles, the automatic pistol and a portion of the police equipment were identified as belonging to a police patrol that had been ambushed at Moneygold. An RIC sergeant and two constables had been killed outright in the attack, and one policeman was mortally injured.[80]

The shortest sentence, three months, was imposed on Kathleen Hicks, a shop assistant from Dublin, who was charged with having seditious literature at her workplace.

In Cork, Mary Bowles from Clogheen 'was charged with trying to hide a Lewis gun in a field, while a military raid was in progress'.[81] On being searched, Mary 'was found to be wearing steel body armour strapped to her shoulders, which was fastened at the sides. She was also in possession of a service revolver and an automatic pistol; both were loaded in every chamber'.[82] Because she was under-age, she was sentenced 'to be detained in a Roman Catholic Reformatory, until she attained the age of nineteen'.[83]

Other women received fines for less serious offences. Una Daly in Limerick was fined £40 because she removed a British military proclamation posted on her bakery premises. Madge Daly 'was fined £20 for not having a list of the occupants of her house pinned on the back of her front door'.[84]

A total of twenty-eight women were held on remand (they were released without trial following the Truce). In Cork, Kate, Madge and Lily Cotter, along with Kate Crowley from Carrigtwohill, County Cork, who were all aged between seventeen and twenty years, were accused of 'intent to murder some military on 23 June 1921, near Glanmire'.[85]

An insight into the experiences of the women who were imprisoned can be gleaned from Sighle Rigney's account of her time in Mountjoy Jail. Her description of life in prison with de Markievicz and other women is an indication of how they coped with their imprisonment. Rigney became a member of Sinn Féin in 1919. She worked as a courier delivering notices of the sittings of Sinn Féin courts. She distributed leaflets during election campaigns, 'wrote up election lists, and checked up the electoral register'.[86] In November 1920 she was sent by Sinn Féin to work at 6 Mespil Road as a cook/housekeeper for Michael Collins. Rigney remained there until late December 1920. This house was the home of Patricia Hoey, a former civil servant who had been sacked for her involvement with republican activities. At this time, she was employed as an assistant by the joint propaganda department of Dáil Éireann and Sinn Féin.

On 31 January 1921, Rigney was arrested after a group of auxiliaries and Black and Tans searched her home in Clontarf in Dublin and found two guns and ammunition. She was removed to Mountjoy Jail, where she was placed on remand in B Wing with Eithne Coyle and Ellen McGrane. Within a month Rigney was taken to the North Dublin Union Barracks where she was tried with 'having two revolvers and twenty-three rounds of ammunition. The revolvers were well oiled and in good condition.'[87] She was sentenced to two years imprisonment with hard labour, which was commuted to nine months. She was then moved to the C Wing section of Mountjoy Jail, where de Markievicz was the sole prisoner at this point. De Markievicz had been tried in December 1920, after the British authorities had captured documents belonging to Na Fianna which bore her signature. She was arrested and charged that:

> Together with E. Martin and others unknown, she had organised, promoted assisted and encouraged, a certain organisation known as Fianna Éireann in the committing of crimes and murders of members of His Majesty's Forces, and unlawful drilling of men, and carrying and using firearms.[88]

She was sentenced to two years hard labour, which involved working a garden plot within the women's prison. This plot was a square, enclosed on one side by barbed wire and prison buildings on the other three sides. According to Rigney, de Markievicz gave her advice on how to manage the guards. In sharp contrast to her self-portrayed public image of constant challenge to authority, her mode of operation was actually one of acquiescence. Rigney said that:

> Countess de Markievicz gave me a few hints/tips on how to manage the guards … and we got use of the whole C Wing library. This provided a welcome change, we were allowed one book per week, but the wardress in charge of it used to smuggle us more than our allowance from time to time, and we hid them under our mattresses.[89]

After a few weeks they were joined by Eithne Coyle and Eileen Keogh, who had been sentenced to one and two years respectively with hard labour. Under the tutelage of Coyle, an Irish speaker from Falcarragh in Donegal, they began Irish lessons.

After the summer months of 1921, the women acquired two extra guards. This came about because an attempt had been made to rescue Seán MacEoin, who was in the male section of the prison and under sentence of death. The guards were redoubled everywhere and two members of the Black and Tans patrolled the area where the women had their daily exercise. Rigney described the two new guards as 'ill-looking specimens, and … always known to us as the Poisoned Pup, Sambo/Satan, they always came around with revolvers'.[90] These two guards were not allowed inside the garden plot, and the women were constantly trying to find ways to taunt them. One day Eileen Keogh decided that the women should have a flag flying on their garden plot and Rigney said that:

> She pulled up one of the flower stakes, and a large green cabbage leaf from a bed (this was the garden Madame I worked in when

we were in first). Then she spied an old piece of newspaper outside on the path … She decided to get a bunch of dandelions, so before our warders was [*sic*] aware of the fact, Miss Keogh had dashed through the gate into the field, pulled the dandelions, picked up the paper and was back again, before we realised she was out.[91]

Keogh tied the paper, the dandelion and the cabbage leaf onto a garden stake and hoisted it to the 'post on one side of our gate, and a cheer was given by the other female prisoners in the exercise yard, and we settled down to our usual way'.[92] This action was successful in taunting the two guards, who tried to have it removed, but according to Rigney, the prison wardress did not have any problem with the flag and 'she allowed us to keep it'.[93] As the prisoners began to return to their cells, 'Keogh took the flag down and marched back inside, leading the group. Inside her cell, she pushed it through the window'.[94] The following morning, the women again marched out with Keogh in front carrying the flag. She hoisted it into a large stone flower urn in the centre of the garden plot and the women sat around it:

> Meanwhile the army continued to stare, eventually, as they were not getting anywhere they moved off at 4 p.m., the governor again did his rounds as he passed us each evening he just touched his glove to his hat. On this particular evening, he did the same, and there was a loud cheer from our gang, as they cried, 'he saluted the flag'.[95]

The women did not achieve anything concrete with this form of protest, but evidently they felt secure enough in their situation to taunt the two Black and Tans. Their counterparts within the civilian population did not experience such freedom. The women within the elite of the republican movement were fast losing touch with the reality of the daily lives of women all over the country.

10

THE WAR ON WOMEN

One aspect of the war missing from the historiography of the War of Independence is the issue of 'the war on women' (by both sides) in the form of physical and sexual abuse. This has not been adequately addressed and has never been discussed in a historical context, perhaps because public discussion of sexual assault and rape in war is a modern phenomenon. While being careful not to place the context of the modern world onto this period, it is necessary to record that women and their families suffered a terror that was not confined to armed conflict. Caught between the violence of the reprisals perpetuated by the IRA and the Black and Tans, the lives of women within the population descended into a living nightmare.

The period of the reign of terror by the Black and Tans in Ireland is well recorded. J.J. Lee, in *Ireland 1912–1985*, stated that 'the new recruits were too few to impose a real reign of terror but numerous enough to commit sufficient atrocities to provoke nationalist opinion in Ireland and America, and to outrage British liberal opinion'.[1] The historiography for this period maintains that the Black and Tans did not assault women physically or sexually. This appears to have had its origins in a statement made by Sir Hamar Greenwood, Chief Secretary for Ireland, in the House of Commons in February 1921. In response to a letter from Eamon de

Valera that accused the British military and the police of outrages against women, Sir Hamar Greenwood said:

> [It was the] most serious charge that can be laid at the door of any white man. We have over 60,000 armed men in Ireland, and there has never been one bit of evidence produced to show that there has been any outrage of this kind. The House will understand that if there could be a case got up against the soldiers or policemen it would be gladly produced with all its loathsome details to harm this Government and besmirch the name of these gallant men who are the representatives of this House in trying to put down the greatest conspiracy this country has been faced with for many years.[2]

When the report of the American Commission on Conditions in Ireland was published in 1921, it appeared to take its lead on the subject from Sir Hamar Greenwood. The commission said that while they had received evidence about women and girls being searched, their bedrooms entered by force in the middle of the night and accounts of them having their hair cut off, they did not receive any statement or charge of rape against the imperial troops. It continued:

> The fact that for four and a half years an army of at least 78,000 British was occupying Ireland without provoking charges of major sensual [i.e. sexual] offences against Irish women is remarkable. It would appear to be the more remarkable when that army is proved to contain drunkards, highway robbers, gunmen and petty thieves. It would seem to the commission that the credit for the sparing of Irish womanhood must be attributed at least in part to the officers commanding the Imperial British Forces in Ireland.[3]

The American Commission on Conditions in Ireland sat in

New York to collect evidence from witnesses about conditions in Ireland. However, it was perceived as a biased and pro-Republican commission and was subsequently boycotted by a significant section of the population who were outside republican politics; it thus presented a one-sided view.

There was another commission simultaneously examining conditions in Ireland, which actually travelled to Ireland. This was the British Labour Party Commission to Ireland (BLPCI) and it addressed all aspects of terror and violence in Ireland and, in particular, the war on women by both sides, in the form of physical and sexual abuse. Because the BLPCI explored the violence from all sections of the conflict, especially with regard to violence towards women, it is an excellent primary source on this subject.

Sometime between late 1920 and early 1921, a pamphlet was published under the name of Hanna Sheehy Skeffington by the office of the Irish diplomatic mission in Washington. This pamphlet was titled: 'Statements of Atrocities against Women in Ireland made and signed by Mrs Hanna Sheehy Skeffington'.[4] The sources for this pamphlet were taken from various newspapers like the *Daily News*, the *Manchester Guardian* and the *Herald*. Sheehy Skeffington also used material gathered by the members of Irish Women's Franchise League and from her own personal experiences or observations.[5]

Margaret Connory, who was a member of the IWFL, also conducted an investigation into this issue in the south and west of Ireland in June 1921 on behalf of the IWC. The resulting material was published in the English-based newspaper *Irish Exile* in April and July 1921 under the title 'Outrages on Irish women'.[6] Connory spent twenty-nine days conducting oral interviews in Cork city and the outlying districts of Macroom, Mallow and Bantry; she also visited Dungarvan in Waterford, Tralee, Ballymacelligott in Kerry, Ennis in Clare and Limerick city. She wrote of many cases of women and small children being put out of their homes, generally in the middle of the night, clad only in their nightclothes. More serious, is her description of the experiences of women who were raped and sexually assaulted. Most raids by the Black and Tans took place after the official curfew and she recorded that within the general population:

> Women and children were in a constant state of depression and nervous breakdown, and in the case of expectant mothers, it produces very grave results for the mothers and children ... Women know that it is during curfew hours attempts of a sexual character have been made, it is difficult to appreciate the effects which this continued strain is producing upon the health of women.[7]

Margaret Connory believed that this problem was not confined to a small number of areas, but was an issue throughout the country. However, most of the women she talked to about their experiences shrank from allowing their stories to be told publicly.

The British Labour Party set up their commission in November 1920, in the wake of the party's failure to make the British government accept responsibility for the continuing war in Ireland. When the party instigated the commission it had a double remit, which was to condemn British government policy in Ireland and to examine the use of violence ('reprisals') directed towards the civilian population by the British forces in Ireland.[8] In their report, the commission used the word 'reprisal' when referring to all acts of violence against the civilian population. This report was published as the *Report of the Labour Commission to Ireland*.

The BLPCI delegation said that they believed that the terror being experienced by the population of Ireland would have 'far-reaching effects on the health of the population' because a significant proportion of the population was 'all nerves'.[9] They also recorded their repulsion at the discovery of the level of violence perpetuated by the crown forces and said that:

The atmosphere of terrorism which has been created and the provocative behaviour of armed servants of the Crown, quite apart from the specific 'reprisals', are sufficient in themselves to arouse in our hearts feelings of the deepest horror and shame.[10]

The specific issue of violence against women was examined by the BLPCI and it found that, in general, getting information was problematic because women were reluctant to report it. They said:

The rough and brutal treatment of women is by no means the worst that is to be said against the men in the service of the British Crown. It is however extremely difficult to obtain direct evidence of incidents affecting females, for the women of Ireland are reticent on such subjects.[11]

Lady Augusta Gregory echoed this in her diaries, where she recorded that within the general population and in particular in rural areas, women had ceased walking on the roads 'because the Black and Tans were out for drink and women'.[12] In isolated parts of the country, young girls and women had no protection whatsoever.

The BLPCI was given permission to read RIC reports and statements from women who found the courage to report the violence perpetuated against them by both sides in the conflict. Interestingly, this specific information is copied in the papers of Oscar Traynor, Richard Willis, John Bolster and Fintan Murphy, all of whom were involved as combatants in the War of Independence. They gave the material to the Bureau of Military History. It is probable that these four men, in keeping this information and passing it on to the bureau, were anxious that this aspect of the war should be recorded.

The BLPCI delegation said that assaults on women were common and reported one incident to highlight the casual manner in which the Black and Tans inflicted terror. A group of Black and

Tans were raiding a house, when they entered the bedroom of a young girl and made her get out of bed. In the ensuing struggle her nightdress was ripped open from top to bottom. The report went on to say that:

> The cases of physical violence and brutal treatment, which we have cited, are, like the examples of other crimes, which we have given, but examples. We could refer to more cases, but we believe that the reader of this report will agree with us that they suffice to show the infamous deeds which have been done in the name of law and order.[13]

The same incident is recorded in more detail by Hanna Sheehy Skeffington. She stated that the young woman was obliged to dress (under protest) while the men invaded her room and was 'then taken in a lorry with drunken police and kept all night'. She went on the say, 'she is young and pretty but was a complete nervous wreck for weeks after this experience'.[14] Sheehy Skeffington also reported acts of terror inflicted on the wives, widows and sisters of men on the run saying:

> I mention the frequent raids upon Mrs Maurice Collins, Parnell Street, Dublin (see Erskine Childers' pamphlet Military rule in Ireland), Mrs Kent widow of Eamonn Kent shot in 1916, Mrs Pearse (house at St Enda's destroyed as 'reprisal'), Mrs Cathal Brugha, wife of speaker of Dáil Éireann (to her house bloodhounds were brought), Mrs Wyse Power, members of the Sinn Féin executive.[15]

The BLPCI recorded several accounts of terror inflicted on families of lesser-known men. One of the stories is that of Mary Kelly from Enniscorthy in Wexford. She reported that her brother 'was on the run' and there was a raid on her home by the military. She warned her brother, who escaped through a window at the back of the house. He was fired on by the military but kept running and about twelve of the military followed him. They returned two hours later without him and Mary said that a member of the party who seemed to be in command, shouted to her:

'I want you'. I didn't reply and he repeated the words, with the order to some of the others 'bring her here'. Two of the party dragged me over to him when he caught me by the arms and dragged me out into the field away from the others. Here he placed me standing against the door of the outhouse (all the time name-calling and swearing). He produced a revolver, told me to look at it, asked me where and when I saw it last, telling me it belonged to my brother whom he had shot and left lying in a bog.[16]

Then she said he caught her roughly by the hair and told her to name the man who had escaped through the window and when she refused, he struck her 'a heavy blow across the face', but when she remained silent 'he caught her by the hair, forced her down on her knees and told her to prepare to die'. She refused to give him information and he then placed the revolver to her breast and struck her another blow on the face, which sent her to the ground stunned. When she recovered a little she went into the yard where the men were ill-treating her father and were in the process of taking him out into a field. She said:

Fearing he would shoot my father I insisted on going with him, but several of the party held me back, twisting my arms and using me very roughly. On hearing a shot being fired in the place where my father was I fainted … I next remember the house being searched, my mother and myself being ordered out and a bomb being placed on the kitchen floor … After about ten minutes delay the man in charge told us we could go inside now as the house was safe and that we would find my brother's dead body in a bog two miles away. After which they left. PS I made no mention of insults curses and threats all this time.[17]

In another case, the commission investigated the burning of a farm. They visited the farmstead and found the farmhouse and outhouses (except for a small fowl-house) in ruins. The tenant farmer was a seventy-two-year-old woman whose son was on the run. She lived at the farm with two daughters and an eight-year-old boy. The members of the commission discovered the latter living in the fowl-house. The two daughters told the commission that two police officers and a number of men in plain clothes had come to the farm and enquired as to the whereabouts of their brother. He was not there and the women and child were ordered to clear out. The sisters and the old lady left the house partially dressed and without boots, as the 'men poured petrol on the furniture, the outhouses, pigsty and on the pigs and poultry'.[18] The buildings were burned to the ground and about forty of the fowl were burned to death, but the women managed to save the pigs. The family spent the night in a field. Subsequently, they were reduced to living in the fowl-house and the old lady was sent to the workhouse.[19]

Hanna Sheehy Skeffington also tackled the everyday assaults inflicted on women by the military. Apart from the case of the young woman whose nightdress was ripped open, she cited a case in Tipperary which was reported by a sister of the Ursuline Convent in Thurles, who said that a girl who 'refused to walk with soldiers was taken forcibly and kept for three days in barracks'.[20] She also mentioned that there were several cases of attempted rape and in one incident a young girl was raped in the presence of her father. Lady Gregory related that her doctor, Dr Foley, told her that across Clare and Galway young girls were violated by Black and Tans but, afraid of publicity, the families kept quiet to protect their wives and daughters.

Throughout the country the warfare had descended into tit-for-tat reprisals, which left the population helpless, and as the terror ground on, women and children were sucked into the mayhem and reduced to abject terror. The most common form of assault on women and girls was the shaving or cutting of their hair, and this usually was carried out using some form of physical violence. Both sides indulged in this practice for the pettiest of reasons and it grew more common as reprisal became the form of warfare used most often against the civilian population.

On the opposite side, the republican war on the RIC extended to their families as well. The BLPCI did emphasise, however, 'that in the overall terrorisation of the population this was not carried out on a scale comparable with the terrorisation of the mass of the Irish people' and continued that 'the policy of this particular victimisation was regrettable because it tended to embitter the relations between the constabulary and the Irish people'.[21] This was no comfort to the wives, children and girlfriends of the RIC. Domestic servants employed in RIC barracks also bore the brunt of the violence. As the RIC barracks were attacked and burned out, the families of RIC sergeants were in many cases made homeless and citizens were afraid to help the women and their children because they feared being burned out themselves. This fear was realistic. A policeman's widow who was planning to take a sergeant's wife into her home as a lodger, was warned by an anonymous letter not to take 'this woman into her house' and that if she ignored the warning her house would be burned and she would be shot.[22] The commission told the story of a police sergeant's wife who was reduced to living in a wooden outhouse after her home had been destroyed. The report said:

> Thirty masked men came to the evacuated huts and burned them. The sergeant's wife and her sister resided in one section of the hut. The raiders gave them five minutes to clear out, and they were not allowed to take anything away ... The neighbours refused them

admittance, thus compelling them to remain in the little wash-house all night and until 11 a.m. the following day, where they were found by the District Inspector and party who investigated the outrage.[23]

A vacated barracks that another RIC sergeant was living in, was invaded by fourteen men who marched him out of the building and forced him to face a wall while they removed his four children to a neighbouring house. He protested that his daughter had influenza, but the raiders told him that she 'must be removed as these were times when many were suffering'.[24] The barracks was then set alight.

One constable's wife was visited by fifty men with blackened faces who were carrying rifles and shotguns, and they ordered her and her six children out of their house. The woman and her children were marched to a nearby house and this householder was ordered to keep her for the night. The men went back to the constable's house and set it alight, destroying everything. The wife of another constable reported that about twenty armed men entered her home and seized her and her four children who were under six years of age, and put them out on the road. Their furniture was then put outside. It was raining heavily and the mother sought refuge at the local post office, but the raiders told her that she would not be allowed to remain in the parish another night, so she 'cycled in the rain in a deplorable condition, to where her husband was stationed'.[25]

The girlfriends and acquaintances of RIC and DMP men were also targeted. In Dublin, a Miss Price received two threatening letters telling her that if she continued to keep company with an RIC constable she would be punished. Another young woman reported that about twenty men forced their way into her home, grabbed her, knocked her down and cut off her hair with tailor's scissors. The raiders then proceeded to another house nearby where another young woman had her hair cut off and was warned 'not to have anything any more to do with the police'.[26] On another occasion, two sisters were visited by a group of armed men at night-time and they were taken outside in their night attire and marched some distance away where they were court-martialled for 'walking with the Peelers'.[27] They were found guilty and sentenced 'to be shot, but this was mitigated and their hair cut off instead'. The reason given for this outrage was that 'these girls were friendly towards the police'.[28]

Barrack servants had a particularly hard time. In July 1921, a woman who had already been injured in the conflict, received an anonymous letter warning her that if she continued working for the police, the IRA would take steps to have her removed from the locality. In another instance, seven or eight masked men invaded the home of a barrack servant, dragged her outside and cut her hair off. They did this because she ignored a warning she had been given to leave police employment. Another servant was removed from her lodgings by armed and masked men, who gagged her and then took her to a field where they cut off her hair, while simultaneously kicking her all over her body. Her crime was that she had taken the job when another woman had left due to the boycott of the police. On 7 August 1920, four men entered the home of another woman and seized her by the hands and feet, while another put his hands over her mouth. They then put 'three pig rings into her buttocks with pincers'.[29] Her crime was that she supplied goods to the police.

The IRA also committed crimes against women within the general civilian population. On 20 September 1921, two men held up a woman at Mountain View Road in Ranelagh, accused her of 'having expressed anti-Sinn Féin sentiments' and then 'cut off her hair'.[30]

It was not just republican men who were involved. There is one particular report where a raiding party included women. On

2 October 1920, two women and three men entered the home of a couple named Bowes at Cadogan Road in Dublin and while one of the men held a revolver on the husband, one of the women cut off Mrs Bowes' hair. There was no reason given for this particular act of violence.

In Kenmare on April 1921, a young woman was dragged from her aunt's house by a large group and marched through the streets in a torchlight procession before having her hair cut off. Shots were fired in her direction but she was not hit. She was discovered by the police in a dazed condition and required medical treatment. Her crime was that on the preceding night there was a party of police on duty in the village and she was apparently observed exchanging 'a few words with the constables'.[31]

Women suspected of being spies were also dealt with in the various IRA brigade areas. Some of the brigade areas made their own rules and consequently treatment of women varied across the country. In Cork, on 9 November 1920, the adjutant general of the Cork No 2 Brigade issued a directive on the subject of 'women spies':[32]

Where there is evidence that a woman is a spy or is doing petty spy work, the brigade commander whose area is involved will set up a Court of Inquiry to examine the evidence against her. If the court finds her guilty of the charge, she shall then be advised accordingly, and except in the case of an Irishwoman, be ordered to leave the country within 7 days. It shall be intimated to her that only consideration of her sex prevents the infliction of the statuary punishment of death.

Following this, a formal public statement was made in the form of a poster or leaflet warning women that if they were caught spying 'they would be neutralised'.[33]

In July 1921, the *Irish Exile* published an article on the abuse of women in Ireland. The report said that in Cork the home of a married couple had been invaded by two men in uniform and wearing masks. The husband, in his statement to the police, said the men had English accents, were wearing police uniforms and had white linen cloth masks across their faces. His wife was in an advanced state of pregnancy and one of the men ordered her out of her bedroom, and she pleaded with him 'not to do anything to me as I was near my confinement. He said, "Never mind", he caught hold of me, pushed me into the back kitchen, and closed the door.'[34] The husband was being held prisoner in the bedroom by the second man who was wielding a gun. In the kitchen the woman tore the mask off her assailant's face 'and cracking a match put it to his face to have a look at him. He ordered me to put the match out saying "you are courageous".' Despite her 'every resistance he then succeeded in criminally assaulting and raping me'.[35] She said that he ordered her to go back to her room, where she went very quickly and informed her husband of everything that had occurred. The couple reported the incident to the police at Shandon.[36]

In another report in the same paper there is a story of a young woman who was assaulted by a member of Black and Tans while they were searching her home. She stated that one of the men:

> … kept running his hands all over my body … but I kept moving away from him until finally he raised my nightgown above my waist and kept it in that position for several minutes. All the time he was going through the actions of searching me, putting his hand in under my blouse and all around my body and he kept repeating that I was not to be alarmed and that he would do me no harm because he was a married man with five children. Finally he dropped the gown and resumed his search …

She then went to her parent's room for safety, but he followed and assaulted her a second time.

Margaret Connory recorded the emotional trauma experienced by some women at the constant personal searches by the Black and Tans, whereby anyone could be stopped on the street and searched. Connory explained that these searches were:

> ... carried on very extensively in different places and were regarded with the utmost horror and repugnance. In poor districts, those affected are subjected to a close and sometimes very offensive and suggestive form of search. These searches take place in private houses, in trains, in barracks, at courts ... and sometimes on the streets, or some section of a town is isolated for this purpose ... Even very old women and invalids are not excepted, thus in some cases procuring great mental and physical distress.[37]

When the Black and Tans began to use female searchers, Connory observed that the whole issue was greatly aggravated by the widely held belief within the population that the women who engaged 'in this unpleasant work are not such as one would choose to come into close personal contact with'.[38] These women searchers were recruited in England, though it is not clear when this practice started. However, by 1921 the use of female searchers was accepted practice.

Margaret Connory was critical of the IWC parish committees because of their general lack of female membership. She believed the assaults on women remained unrecorded because 'men with the best will in the world, were not competent to deal with cases of sexual assaults'.[39] She also suggested that the IWC should try to avail of the services of the district nurses to deal with this issue. However, a point missed by Connory, was that the meetings and the work of the parish committees was voluntary and had to be done in the evenings. Many women were reluctant to leave the relative safety of their homes because it could be misconstrued and was consequently too dangerous, which is one very cogent explanation for the lack of women on these committees. The unspoken but palpable terror within the female population had the effect of spreading a profound feeling of dread amongst large numbers of women in the districts where rape and sexual assaults occurred.

There is no evidence that Margaret Connory and the elite republican women from Dublin, interviewed any women who were attacked by the republican side.

Hanna Sheehy Skeffington, in her pamphlet, had some very interesting observations to make about prostitutes. She said that the only women who had freedom of movement after curfew were prostitutes 'who are presumably seen as a military necessity'.[40] She said that in Dublin the women were:

> ... taken about by military police in lorries and often kept in barracks for days (this happened recently in Portobello Barracks) and at Rathmines police station to my own knowledge ... The officers take the better class of 'joy ride' at curfew ... Many of these women are paid to act as spies and recently one testified in a murder case against an Irish Volunteer. She was supposed to be a servant in an officer's house, but was a prostitute in [the] Secret Service Army.[41]

She ended the pamphlet by saying that English societies were taking action on this matter in the interests of public health and safety. However, Sheehy Skeffington did not explain how she knew the difference between innocent women, like the girl attacked by the Black and Tans, and the women she claimed were prostitutes who were also being taken away in the middle of the night in military lorries.

In early 1921, Hanna Sheehy Skeffington organised a deputation from the Irish section of the Women's International League for Peace and Freedom, to travel to the Imperial Conference due to be held in London in May and 'present a pamphlet [on the abuse] by distributing it to the individual premiers of the British Empire at the conference'.[42] The Women's International League for Peace and Freedom (WILPF) was an international women's organisation, which had its headquarters in Geneva. The WILPF was:

> An organisation which is active in twenty different countries in Europe, America and Australia and is made up of people who believe that we are not obliged to choose between violence on the one hand and passive acceptance on the other; who, on the contrary believe that courage, determination, moral power, generous indignation and active goodwill can achieve their ends without violence.[43]

Mrs Dix and Rosamund Jacob were the secretaries of its Irish section and the deputation was made up of five members of the Irish section. Sheehy Skeffington approached Michael Collins and asked him for £100 to enable the delegation to travel to London to present a pamphlet to the leaders of the Commonwealth countries who were meeting in London. While Collins and de Valera did not believe this would be effective propaganda, they were none-theless willing to give them the money. Collins in a report to de Valera said:

> If I had the time to send you a note about this thing, I would not have favoured this expenditure, although I think we shall take every opportunity of striking at the Premiers from the English colonies, I am not sure however that we shall get value in this particular instance, nor indeed that the case will be presented effectively.[44]

De Valera concurred with this opinion but decided that as the 'deputation is composed of the ladies I heard were going, the protest they make will be in every way worthy. If proper publicity is given to their protest, it will have an influence on the women in other countries'.[45] Yet in another memo to Art O'Brien in London, de Valera expressed the belief that this protest could only be a publicity stunt. He told O'Brien that if he should see Mrs Sheehy Skeffington, to 'impress on her the line that she should indicate to the premiers of the various commonwealth countries, that they must share the responsibility for the acts of the British government'.[46]

Soon, national amnesia in republicans, both male and female, reduced the experiences of many Irishwomen to mere speculation. They were then conveniently forgotten. Meanwhile, the elite women, now triumphant at their rise within republican politics, remained unaware of the 'war on women' and the horror to which these women's lives had descended.

11

From Triumph to Fury

In late December 1920, Eamon de Valera returned to Ireland amidst speculation that feelers for peace were being discussed in his absence. On the day de Valera reached Ireland, 23 December 1920, the Government of Ireland Act 1920, received royal assent, having passed through both houses of parliament in London. Under the provisions of the Act, two parliaments were to be created in Ireland, one in Belfast to govern the north-eastern counties and one in Dublin to govern the remaining twenty-six counties. Both parliaments would take an oath of allegiance to the king. The Act also provided for a Council of Ireland to be set up as a forum for discussion on matters of common interest to north and south. It was due to come into force in May 1921, after a general election was held in both areas of the country.

While de Valera was on his journey back to Ireland, Mary MacSwiney and Donal O'Callaghan were simultaneously travelling in the opposite direction as stowaways on the SS *Coppage*. MacSwiney came to national prominence due to the death of her brother Terence, who died on 25 October 1920. He had endured a seventy-four day hunger strike while being held in jail in London. MacSwiney arrived in Washington on 7 December. According to Rossa F. Downing, who was the local organiser for the AARIR in Washington DC, she was 'welcomed by an enthusiastic crowd, which he estimated at 15,000'.[1] Not everyone in the USA was happy to see MacSwiney; Harry Boland, in a letter to de Valera, expressed his unhappiness with the development and he told him that 'the arrival of O'Callaghan and MacSwiney as stowaways has caused us very serious embarrassment'.[2] MacSwiney remained in the USA and became involved in republican propaganda. The death of her brother Terence had enabled her to gain a foothold in national politics, whereas before this she was only a local political activist.

According to Rossa F. Downing, 'MacSwiney gave a speech in Washington, in the wake of the burning of Cork by the Black and Tans', which was billed as the 'Relief of Mallow Fund' and was initiated into the exhilaration of speech-making in the USA.[3] Carried away by her success in raising emotions and funds from her American audiences, she wrote to the Dáil and demanded money to help her to continue working in the USA. She also demanded that the Dáil send more women to join her and she enclosed a list of the names of women that she deemed would be suitable. She nominated Kathleen O'Callaghan, Nancy Wyse Power, Alice Cashel and Anna Walsh. She did not want Hanna Sheehy Skeffington 'because she got herself mixed up in American domestic politics, Nora Connolly has the same drawback and would tie us up with labour'.[4] MacSwiney donned the mantle of the Irish republican martyr in the name of her brother and in this guise she became one of the most vitriolic of female republicans.

In May 1921, under the terms of the Government of Ireland Act 1920, two general elections took place in Ireland. In the twenty-six counties the election took place on 19 May and in Northern Ireland the election took place on 24 May. In the twenty-six counties, just four seats from 128 constituencies were contested, for the constituency of Dublin University, and these were won by southern Unionists. The remaining 124 uncontested seats went to the Sinn Féin candidates. In Northern Ireland the total number of seats available was fifty-two; unionist candidates gained forty seats and the remaining twelve were divided between Sinn Féin candidates and other nationalists.

Meanwhile, Sinn Féin refused to convene a Home Rule parliament under the terms of the Government of Ireland Act and instead convened the second Dáil Éireann. This assembly had five women members: Countess de Markievicz, Margaret Pearse for Dublin, Kathleen O'Callaghan for Limerick city, Mary MacSwiney for Cork city and Ada English for Galway.

King George officially opened the parliament of Northern Ireland on 22 June 1920. In Dublin that same day, the British military made a raid on a house called Glenavy in Mount Merrion and seized hundreds of documents pertaining to the work of the Dáil. De Valera used Glenavy as an office, where he worked with Seán Harling and his secretary Kathleen O'Connell. Batt O'Connor, who was a senior officer with the IRA, 'had constructed a secret dump in a rockery in the garden',[5] but on the day the building was raided, Harling, de Valera and O'Connell were working on Dáil business and had the box of papers inside the house. When the raid began they did not have the time to hide the box. Harling, who escaped capture, recalled that he was in the study with de Valera when he saw:

> A detachment of soldiers extended across the meadow advancing in the direction of the house. I told the president we had not the time to dump the Deed box, which was always on the study floor. The president instructed me to get away. So I crossed the back meadow to the grounds of Professor MacNeill's house and onto Nutley Avenue.[6]

Eamon de Valera and Kathleen O'Connell were arrested. The documents in the box were removed and the British now had 'a significant amount of information about all aspects of the working of the Dáil and the IRA'.[7] Harling reported the arrests to Michael

Collins, who informed him that de Valera had been taken to Dublin Castle before being moved to Portobello Barracks in Rathmines. Harling was instructed by Collins to go into hiding 'in a house in Rathmines and stay there'.[8] Harling recalled that while he was at the house, a worker from Portobello Barracks came to the house and 'informed him that the long fellow [de Valera] was having a posh time in the officer's quarters'.[9] De Valera was released within twenty-four hours of his arrest.

Within two days of his release from custody, de Valera received a letter from the British Prime Minister, Lloyd George. Harling delivered the letter to de Valera and he recalls 'that on reading it' de Valera told him, 'it looks Seán, as if we would be in the Vice Regal very shortly'. According to Harling, the letter was addressed to, 'Eamon de Valera representative of the Irish People, Mansion House, Ireland'.[10] It was an invitation to a meeting in London and an invitation was sent simultaneously to Sir James Craig, who was the premier of Northern Ireland. A cabinet meeting was called and a decision was taken to publish the contents of the letter in the Sunday newspapers.

Instead of replying immediately to Lloyd George, de Valera wrote on 28 June to James Craig, Sir Robert Woods, Sir Maurice E. Dockrell and Mr Andrew Jameson and invited them to meet with him as the representatives of the unionist community in Ireland. He did this, he said, because any response he made to Lloyd George would 'affect the lives and fortunes of the political minority in this island, no less than those of the majority'.[11] James Craig declined the invitation because he had already accepted Lloyd George's invitation to London, but the other men met with de Valera. After the conference, an official report was issued on 8 July, which said in part that 'it would be impossible to conduct negotiations with any hope of achieving satisfactory results unless there was a cessation of bloodshed in Ireland … A letter … from Mr Lloyd George was read, concurring in this view and indicating the willingness of the

British government to assent to a suspension of active operations on both sides … It is expected that an announcement of a truce to take effect from Monday next, will be made early tomorrow.'[12]

The Truce began at noon on 11 July 1921 and three days later de Valera travelled to London. He had several meetings with Lloyd George in this time and later, during August and September, a series of letters passed between both sides. During the Truce, many republican prisoners were released from jails. The IWC gave the sum of £10,000 to the Republican Prisoners Dependants' Fund to 'enable it to meet the very pressing needs of hundreds of released men'. Áine Ceannt who worked for the IWC recalled that:

> When the prison doors opened they were, themselves, free men. Many of them were unable to travel to their homes for want of money to pay their fares. In many cases men had to be provided with clothing, not merely for the sake of comfort, but often for the sake of decency.[13]

The need for care did not end at the prison gates. Many of the men needed extra support. There were two main reasons for this. According to Ceannt:

> Some of the men were unable to get work, while others could not work, because their health was broken due to their confinement in frequently insanitary prisons and internment camps. Some of the bad health was caused by the results of beatings or bullet wounds. Others needed surgery to have bullets removed. Several had broken teeth or broken noses, and others had to be fitted with artificial limbs.[14]

Around this time, the women on the IWC executive committee were becoming concerned that some people within the republican movement considered their work mundane and unimportant. At a

meeting between the Northern Irish Republican Prisoners' Fund
(IRP) and the IWC, two members of the NIRP delegation asked
Jennie Wyse Power and Nancy O'Rahilly 'to help them to seek out
families in need, by undertaking a tour of the country, at the expense of the IRP'.[15] Jennie Wyse Power, in a letter to her daughter
Nancy, exclaimed 'I had never met them before; they added insult
to injury by asking us to tour the country, at their expense, to find
cases of neglect. Nancy O'Rahilly asked them was it messengers
they wanted.'[16]

After the initial contact between Lloyd George and de Valera
in July, exploratory meetings were held in London. Michael
Laffan, in his work *The Resurrection of Ireland*, examined in detail
all the correspondence between de Valera and Lloyd George. He
said that 'when de Valera entered these discussions he described
himself not as president, but as spokesman for the Irish nation',
since Lloyd George would not have met him if he had used the
title president.[17] A reading of the *Official Correspondence Relating
to the Peace Negotiations June–September 1921*, makes it clear that
Lloyd George was offering dominion status for the twenty-
six counties and nothing else. Laffan says 'that de Valera never
rejected the prime ministers insistence that there could be no
settlement except on the basis of southern Ireland becoming a
dominion'.[18] He also says that de Valera was committed to an
imaginative and far-sighted scheme of his own creation, that
of an external association between Ireland and Britain, but that
'he failed to communicate to his colleagues the strength of his
feelings on this subject'.[19] What is not in doubt is that de Valera
knew before the delegation left Ireland that the offer of an Irish
Republic was not on the table for discussion.

By October 1921, after protracted discussions, five plenipotentiaries were appointed to act on behalf of Dáil Éireann and
they travelled to London to discuss a peace settlement. Those
appointed were Arthur Griffith, Michael Collins, Robert Barton,

Eamon Duggan and George Gavan Duffy. Lily O'Brennan of Cumann na mBan was one of the secretaries accompanying the delegation. A significant entourage accompanied them, which prompted Jennie Wyse Power to comment in a letter to her daughter, 'the delegation including cooks, typists, porters, and messengers, etc. have gone'.[20] Jennie Wyse Power wrote several letters to her daughter Nancy from the period August 1921 to July 1922 as Nancy was in Germany working with John Chartres, the Sinn Féin foreign office representative in Berlin.

The relatively peaceful lull of the Truce afforded Cumann na mBan, the IRA and Sinn Féin some breathing space to reassess their organisations. In July, Cumann na mBan recorded that there were 839 branches. This was the largest number of branches since organisation was founded in 1914.

TABLE 14: THE DEVELOPMENT OF CUMANN NA MBAN 1914–1921

Year	Branches
1914	16
1915	21
1916	40
1917	100
1918	650
1919	No figure available
1920	300
1921	839

Source: Cumann na mBan convention documents 1914–1921 and captured documents from St Monica's Mother and Baby Club in Dublin on 7 February 1923, Irish Volunteer 1914–1916.

Cumann na mBan held its annual convention on 22–23 October 1921 and the secretary reported that the convention in 1920 'had only 120 delegates, while, today we have nearly 400' and 'last year our affiliated branches numbered nearly 300 and today, we have nearly 800'.[21] The convention in 1921 recorded that there were 353 delegates present representing the organisation by county and province.

TABLE 15: NUMBER OF DELEGATES AT THE 1921 CUMANN NA mBAN CONVENTION

Province	Number of delegates recorded as in attendance
Leinster	123
Ulster	46
Munster	158
Connacht	20
Scotland	2
England	4
Total	353

Source: Cumann na mBan convention document, 1921.

However, just 208 branches had paid affiliation fees, which would indicate that since the beginning of the Truce in July the organisation was already in serious decline. Under the Cumann na mBan constitution, no branch was entitled to representation at the convention unless its affiliation fees were paid at least one month prior to the date of the convention. Consequently, only those branches that had paid the affiliation fees could participate in making policy decisions. It has to be assumed that this convention represented at most only 208 branches of the organisation.

Countess de Markievicz, who was released from prison at the beginning of the Truce, addressed the convention. She told the delegates:

I say to you, each one, how proud and glad I am to be among you
again, and how pleased I was when I came out of prison of the
great work done while I was in Mountjoy doing nothing at all. I
want to tell you how proud I am of the girls who stood in the gap
of danger during the time of distress and war last winter.[22]

She continued:

There was a generous chorus of praise from all parts of Ireland
for the girls of Cumann na mBan on the way they had worked
through the winter … When the history of Ireland is to be written,
the name of Cumann na mBan will be a name that will go down
to your children and your children's children, and the organisation
will stand as a memorial to the Irish People as a great organisation
of the past. That is what I have been told about you, and that is
what I want to tell you today.[23]

The convention had a palpable sense of triumphalism despite the
declining membership of Cumann na mBan.

During the period of the Truce, the IRA and Cumann na mBan
took the opportunity to restructure their respective organisations
and improve their working relationship. In October 1921, Cumann
na mBan organised a series of classes for delegates, over a five-day
period, at the end of the annual convention. The classes took place
at the Technical School and at the Gaelic League rooms, both in
Parnell Square, where the women were taught a range of subjects
from first aid to cooking and the care of guns and ammunition.
The organisation also began to implement and develop the concept
of the district council, to enable them to work more closely with
the IRA. At this time, the IRA put into operation the plan it had
devised in April 1921, which was to create separate divisions and
streamline the organisation. By December 1921, fifteen divisions
were operating in Ireland and there were some brigades operating

in Scotland and England. The Cumann na mBan district councils
were organised to work within each IRA battalion.

The Sinn Féin Ard Fheis was held in late October 1921 and
a new Árd Chomhairle standing committee was elected. There
were six women elected: Kathleen Lynn, Áine Ceannt, Countess
Markievicz, Jennie Wyse Power and Hanna Sheehy Skeffington.
Lynn was elected as one of the four vice-presidents of the
party. Hanna Sheehy Skeffington was appointed as the party's
national organiser and Áine Ceannt was appointed director of
communications.[24] When Sheehy Skeffington tendered her
resignation because she could not attend meetings every Thursday
at 8 p.m., the committee changed their meeting time to 4 p.m. to
accommodate her. One of the most striking things about the Ard
Fheis is the decline in support for Countess de Markievicz. She
was not elected to any office within the party, whereas Kathleen
Lynn's work was gaining her admiration and respect within Sinn
Féin and she was elected a vice-president of the party.

At the local level, women were joining Sinn Féin cumainn,
which were also known as 'Sinn Féin Clubs'.[25] A police report
estimated 'that by 31 October 1921, there were 1,457 Sinn Féin
Clubs with an estimated membership of 129,152, of which
120,994 were men and 8,158 were women'.[26]

During the period between October and the signing of the
Treaty in London on 6 December, to some degree life continued
as normal, with scores being settled and speculation and gossip
about what was going on in London enlivening many people's
daily conversations. On 7 December, one day after the Treaty was
signed in London, Wyse Power wrote to her daughter:

> So, it is all over or perhaps only beginning … A rift is anticipated
> … Collins would go to the country on it if there were any divisions
> … The oath of allegiance is what sticks.

Women particularly seem strong, you remember Maggie

Synott, and she is out for Blood. I hear poor Miss Annie is in tears! Oh, there will be talk and if it ends with talk all right.[27]

Jennie Wyse Power also told Nancy that for the first time in her life she hesitated in taking sides, 'until I know all, I cannot make my mind easy on the subject'.[28]

The executive of Cumann na mBan met to discuss the issue and amid an intense argument, Jennie Wyse Power proposed a motion 'that the discussion should be postponed until after the Dáil met'.[29] This was passed by nine votes to eight. The nine who supported Wyse Power's motion were Min and Phyllis Ryan, Nancy and Annie O'Rahilly, Eileen Aughney, Mairéen Deigan, Jo Aherne and Leslie Price. The eight who opposed the resolution were de Markievicz, Margaret Skinnider, Sighle Humphreys, Una Gordon, Bridie Connolly and three other women who are not named. After the vote was taken, de Markievicz proposed an amendment, which was 'that the discussion should be postponed until after the Dáil met and they should declare confidence in de Valera'. Wyse Power withdrew her original motion on the condition that de Markievicz's 'amendment be given into de Valera's hands, and not published'.[30] This was agreed by the meeting.

During this time Jennie Wyse Power had a conversation about de Valera and the Treaty with Seán T. O'Kelly, who expressed the opinion that:

> The plenipotentiaries had done their best and could not get more … he sees the formation of a Republican Party, and says he will form it. I pointed out to him that this would be useless unless it was inside the parliament, and that I could not see how they could enter it because of the oath; he seemed to think that too could be got over.[31]

The annual Sinn Féin Aonach, which was held on 6 December,

became the centre of gossip. Jennie Wyse Power wrote to Nancy saying, 'The talk would drive you mad, and I feel I could not face it again'. She went on to say that the female members of the Dáil 'were all on de Valera's side and were very free in their criticism with anyone who disagreed with them', but despite this, 'it was generally presumed the Dáil would carry the Treaty … but what then?'[32]

The debate in the Dáil on the ratification of the Treaty began on 14 December 1921. At the first meeting, de Valera set the tone of the debate by explaining his perspective on the plenipotentiaries. From this first meeting, it quickly became clear that the already obvious divisions were beginning to grow like a canker. The debate descended into a morass of meaningless words, with members of the Dáil – with few exceptions – constantly referring to the 'people of Ireland' or 'the plain people of Ireland', as though the whole population was an abstract concept.

On 20 December 1920, Kathleen O'Callaghan was the first woman to speak. She was the widow of Michael O'Callaghan, the former mayor of Limerick. Her husband was killed in March 1921, when a Black and Tan search party entered their home. She asserted her right to speak because of his death. She castigated Fionán Lynch, TD for Kerry and West Limerick, who had spoken just before her. In his speech, Lynch alluded to the emotional ambience in the Dáil chamber saying, 'we have had a great deal of emotion here and a great deal of emotional speeches about the dead. I say for myself, that the bones of the dead have been rattled indecently in the face of this assembly.'[33] O'Callaghan took him to task saying:

The last Deputy talked about indecent rattling of the bones of the dead in this assembly. Since I came up to Dublin for this session I have been told, with a view to changing my vote I suppose, that my husband was never a republican. I challenge any Deputy in this

Dáil to deny my husband's devotion to the Republic, a devotion he sealed with his blood.[34]

In defence of her own republican credentials, she told the assembly that for her the issue was one 'of principle, a matter of conscience, and a matter of right and wrong'. O'Callaghan admitted that the delegates who went to London had full powers to negotiate and conclude a Treaty, but was still critical of the actions they took. At this point her language took on a tone of self-deprecation, as she told the assembly, 'I am only a plain person, a person of plain intelligence, and I understood they were to submit the final draft to the cabinet and the president before signing'. She went on say that her mind was now 'sharpened by sorrow, I came here for the last five days, and I listened to arguments which left my attitude unchanged'. Coming back to the issue of the oath of allegiance, she reiterated:

> When I asked the question as to the nature of the oath, every legal man in this assembly, and many who were not legal or logical, tried to explain it. I still fail to see how in swearing an oath of allegiance to the Free State, I can avoid King George.[35]

O'Callaghan gave a second reason why she was voting against the Treaty, which was that 'the people of Limerick who elected me to the second Dáil, two months after my husband's murder, know that I will stand by my convictions and by my oath to the Irish people during the general election in May 1921'. It is interesting that she believed the people of Limerick had a choice in an uncontested election.

Confident of the support of the other female deputies, she explained that none of the women were open to canvass on the issue and were totally united in their opposition to the Treaty. In defending the stance of the women in the Dáil, she initially said that they were not voting against the Treaty because they were 'warped by a deep personal loss'. Then in an immediate contradiction, enumerating their collective losses, she said:

> It was the mother of the Pearses who made them what they were. The sister of Terence MacSwiney influenced her brother, and is now carrying on his life's work. Deputy Mrs Clarke, the widow of Tom Clarke, was bred in the Fenian household of her uncle, John Daly of Limerick. The women of An Dáil are women of character, and they will vote for principle, not for expediency.[36]

O'Callaghan continued by saying 'those who know me and my sorrow' know 'what little bitterness I feel against the actual murderers of my husband', which appears to indicate forgiveness towards the men who killed him. She elaborated, telling the assembly that her husband's killers remained free because she had not sought to have him avenged by Irish Republican Army bullets. She went on to explain that she felt bitter because 'the thing [Republic] he and I cared about and worked for, the thing I lost my happiness for, should be voted away by young men, the young soldiers in whom we had such hope'. She went on to say that the republican plot in which her husband was buried was republican ground. In summary, she told the Dáil that they were making history and their decision would have a far-reaching effect on the country. She appealed to them for 'God's sake to think well, and stand for principle and against the Treaty'.[37]

On the following day, Mary MacSwiney rose to make her contribution. Her opening words were:

> It has been said by many Deputies when they rose to speak, that they would try to keep the House as short a time as possible. I, too, shall do that, but I am sorry that I cannot promise that it will be very short, for I rise to speak with the deepest and fullest sense of my responsibility.[38]

MacSwiney then proceeded to speak for two hours and forty minutes. Her speech became a diatribe of republican rhetoric, laced by a hectoring and insulting tone of condescension towards all who were in favour of the Treaty within the general population as well as in the Dáil. Her first salvo was a personal promise, that if the Free State came into existence she would be its first rebel. She made a promise 'that they will have the pleasure or the pain, as it pleases them, of imprisoning me as one of their first and most deliberate and irreconcilable rebels'.[39] She promised she would never teach in a school under their control. Expanding further, she said 'she would only teach a child in her control the republican doctrine and keep their souls clean'.[40]

At one point, she moved to protect de Valera and Document 2 from criticism. De Valera had presented this document at a private meeting of the Dáil on 15 December, as an alternative to the Treaty. The document became central to many arguments and distorted the actual debate. Apparently, some observers believed he was 'trying to draw a red herring across the track of the discussion'.[41] The basic difference between the Treaty and Document 2 was that the former placed Ireland within the empire with dominion status and the latter sought to amend the Treaty by proposing external association with the empire. It also sought the omission of both the oath of allegiance and the post of governor general. The issue of Document 2 has been discussed and dissected by several historians over the decades. However, for the general population, which was kept in ignorance of its contents, the discussion was completely meaningless. F.S.L. Lyons explored the issue of Document 2 in detail:

> De Valera, who led the attack on the Treaty, could not achieve verbal clarity on the issue. This was partly due to his obsessive preoccupation with the meaning of words which led him into intricacies of speech where deputies found it hard to follow

him, but still more because he laboured under the disadvantage of having to attack the Treaty without having yet convincingly demonstrated that what he put forward in its place was sufficiently different to justify throwing overboard the London agreement.[42]

J.J. Lee in *Ireland 1912–1985* held a more benign view of de Valera and Document 2. He said that it 'contained the best terms de Valera dared to contemplate'.[43] In discussing the difference between the Treaty and external association put forward in Document 2, Lee said, 'the shading here proved far too subtle for either doctrinaire Irish republicans or doctrinaire Irish British royalists'.[44]

When the pro-Treaty side insisted that the document should be made public, de Valera withdrew it. MacSwiney lauded de Valera for this action, saying, 'he took what, to my mind, was the only straight and honourable course'.[45] By his withdrawal of Document 2, MacSwiney believed de Valera brought the discussion back to the real issue, which was acceptance or non-acceptance of the Treaty. (MacSwiney was conveniently ignoring the fact that the issue of Document 2 had been introduced by de Valera.) Continuing her tirade, she declared 'there was only one oath and this was the one to the Republic, anything else was a betrayal'.[46] Document 2 remained secret until Griffith eventually released its contents to the newspapers on 4 January 1922. By this time it had become meaningless.

MacSwiney's other main concern was the post of the governor general. She explained in minute detail her concern that the wives, sisters, daughters, and in some cases, mothers of the deputies, would receive invitations to drawing-room levees at the governor general's residence. She was concerned that he would use these social functions as a bait to draw the 'women of Ireland in and enable them to socialise for the first time by consent of the Irish people, at functions representing the British King'. She continued, 'I love my people, every single one of them; I love the country, and I have faith in the people, but I am under no delusions about any of us. We are not a race of archangels'.[47] Her opinion of Irish women was not high and she appeared to believe Irish women, like children, had to be protected from themselves. In her summary, she said:

> I know the women of Ireland, I know what they will say to the men that want to surrender, and therefore I beg of you to take the decision to throw out that Treaty. Register your votes against it, and do not commit the one unforgivable crime that has ever been committed by the representatives of the people of Ireland.[48]

When she finally sat down, de Valera announced that they would have to sit the following day and night, to try and finish the debate before Christmas. This brought a suggestion from Michael Colivet, that the whips on both sides should collect the names of people wishing to speak and arrange a time schedule; otherwise, the debate would drag on for another two weeks. Alluding to MacSwiney, he said he believed not everyone would speak for three hours, adding, 'any member of the assembly could express themselves if they wished in ten or fifteen minutes'.[49]

Jennie Wyse Power, who had been at the debate, was beginning to wilt. She wrote to Nancy on the following day that 'last evening at the Dáil was so terrible that I had not courage to go today. I now feel everything is hopeless and that the country or its interests are entirely forgotten. The idea of trying to amend the Treaty to prove that your position was a correct one is childish' and she added, 'the sorrow in the Dáil chamber was so intense that all hope of uniting the country had dissipated'.[50]

The day after MacSwiney's speech, a meeting of some members of the executive of Cumann na mBan took place at her flat in Dublin. The pretext of the meeting was to discuss the new paper produced by the organisation, which was called *Cumann na mBan*. MacSwiney wanted the paper distributed immediately. Some of the women objected on the basis that distribution of the paper would force some of them into the position of having to take sides on the issue of the Treaty. After a vote was taken, it was decided by seven votes to five to distribute the paper.

Mairéen Deigan immediately tendered her resignation. She was against the Treaty, but in an effort to maintain unity in the organisation, she was reluctant to take sides publicly. In an effort to prevent Deigan's resignation, Mrs Nagg (this name is a pseudonym – her real identity is not clear) rescinded the vote. However, Jennie Wyse Power pointed out to Nagg that the vote could not be rescinded without a notice of motion. Nagg ignored Wyse Power and rescinded the vote, whereupon Leslie Price intervened and told the meeting that if they did not stop the discussion 'the organisation was gone'.[51] Cumann na mBan was falling victim to the fast developing factionalism within the republican movement. Wyse Power told Nancy 'that none of the big people were present, or the two Ryans' and she concluded her letter saying 'that the organisation was on the brink of disruption'.[52] The two Ryans were Min, who was married to Richard Mulcahy, and her sister Phyllis, who was married to Seán T. O'Kelly. Both sisters found themselves on opposite sides of the Treaty debate.

On 22 December, Kathleen Clarke rose to speak. She began by saying, 'I rise to support the motion of the president to reject this Treaty' and continued:

> [I have] listened very carefully from the first meeting to the discussion and could not see how the Treaty brought peace with England, and freedom to Ireland … if this Treaty was ratified, it would divide people and the same old division will go on, those who will enter the British Empire and those who will not, and so England's old game of divide and conquer goes on.[53]

In a manner similar to O'Callaghan, she used self-deprecation to make her point, telling the assembly that there was not 'power enough to force me, nor eloquence enough to influence me in the whole British Empire into taking that Oath, though I am only a frail scrap of humanity. I took an Oath to the Irish Republic, solemnly, reverently, meaning every word. I shall never go back from that'.[54] She then gave an account of her last moments with her husband Tom Clarke. Kathleen was temporarily imprisoned in Kilmainham Gaol in the immediate aftermath of the 1916 rebellion. She was initially held in Dublin Castle, but said that she was:

> Roused from my rest on the floor, and taken under armed escort to Kilmainham Gaol to see my husband for the last time … He informed me he was to be shot at dawn. Was he in despair like the man who spoke of him on Tuesday? Not he. His head was up; his eyes flashing; his years seemed to have slipped from him; victory was in every line of him. Tell the Irish people, he said, that my comrades and I believe we have saved the soul of Ireland.[55]

Clarke went on to tell the assembly that although she had been in great emotional trauma at his imminent death, she 'gloried in him' and she 'gloried in the men who have carried on the fight since, every one of them'. It was on this basis that she believed 'a vote in favour of the Treaty was wrong'.

Rumour and gossip were rife about all aspects of the Treaty and rumour of a personal nature was circulated about Michael Collins. Kathleen Clarke informed Jennie Wyse Power that an anonymous letter was in circulation in Dublin to the effect that 'there was another Kitty O'Shea in the Gresham' (referring to Charles Stewart Parnell's notorious affair which destroyed his political career) and 'said lady it stated was sapping the manhood of Collins'.[56] The woman was Moya Llewelyn Davis, who had booked into the Gresham Hotel where Collins was based. Wyse Power told Collins about the letter and he spoke to Davis, who moved away immediately. Collins then refused to entertain any correspondence from her, except though his friend and colleague Batt O'Connor. According to Wyse Power, Llewelyn Davis was subsequently shunned by Collins' friends and colleagues.

The debate resumed after the Christmas break, on the 3 January 1922. The anti-Treaty group upped the stakes on this day by publishing the first edition of the anti-Treaty paper, *The Republic of Ireland*, subtitled *Poblacht na hÉireann*. Later that day Countess de Markievicz rose to make her speech. She told the assembly: 'I rise today to oppose with all the force of my will, with all the force of my whole existence, this so-called Treaty, this Home Rule Bill covered over with the sugar of a Treaty.'[57] She went on to tell the assembly that the main reasons for her opposition were her principles as a republican, which she had pledged 'to the teeth for freedom for Ireland'. The proposed constitution for the Free State government had a provision for a second chamber and de Markievicz objected to this aspect of the Treaty because she believed it was a sop to southern unionists. Here her speech took off on a tangent, becoming a monologue of abuse against all landowners and the Anglo-Irish ascendancy. She claimed they were more or less all southern unionists, stating that:

> They are the people who have combined together against the workers of Ireland, who have used the English soldiers, the English police, and every institution in the country to ruin the farmer, and more especially the small farmer, and to send the people of Ireland to drift in the emigrant ships and to die of horrible disease or to sink to the bottom of the Atlantic.[58]

The self-appointed defender of the working class took her tirade into a confused invocation of James Connolly, when she claimed that she believed in the ideal of a workers' republic:

I say that that is one of the things that England wishes to prevent. She would sooner give us Home Rule than a democratic Republic. It is the capitalists' interests in England and Ireland that are pushing this Treaty to block the march of the working people in England and Ireland. Now, we were offered a Treaty in the first place because England was in a tight place.[59]

She spoke in this vein for some time, before finally coming to her position on the oath of allegiance, which was essentially that, as a republican, she objected to the king. She said:

… the King really stands in politics for his Prime Minister, the court of which he also is the head and centre, the pivot around which he turns – well it is not one of the things that tends to elevate and improve the country. It tends to develop all sorts of corruption, all sorts of luxury and all sorts of immorality.[60]

She told the assembly that she should have been included in the negotiation team that went to London, on the basis that:

You all know me, you know that my people came over here in Henry VIII's time, and by that bad black drop of English blood in me, I know the English that is the truth. I say it is because of that black drop in me that I know the English personally better perhaps than the people who went over on the delegation.[61]

De Markievicz then descended to insults when she broached the subject of the marriage of Princess Mary. She suggested that the pending wedding of the Princess Mary 'was going to be called off because she was to marry Michael Collins, who will be appointed first governor of our Saorstát na hÉireann'. With regard to the criticism that they were rattling the bones of the dead, she protested, asking, 'where would Ireland stand without the noble dead?' She then returned to one of her favourite themes, the cancellation of the rebellion by Eoin MacNeill. She told the assembly that when it was cancelled James Connolly had told her, 'there is only one sort of responsibility I am afraid of and that is preventing the men and women of Ireland fighting and dying for Ireland if they are so minded'. Claiming that these were Connolly's last words to her, she continued:

> I have always thought of that since, and I have always felt that that was a message which I had to deliver to the people of Ireland. We hear a great deal of the renewal of warfare. I am of quite a pacific mind. I don't like to kill. I don't like death, but I am not afraid to die and, not being afraid to die myself … I fear dishonour; I don't fear death, and I feel at all events that death is preferable to dishonour … and sooner than see the people of Ireland take that oath meaning to build up your Republic on a lie, I would sooner say to the people of Ireland: Stand by me and fight to the death … I have seen the stars, and I am not going to follow a flickering will-o'-the-wisp.[62]

Claiming to know intimately the bravery of the soldiers of Ireland, she declared herself willing to 'stand humbly behind them, these men who have given themselves for Ireland'. Her willingness to take a position in the rearguard indicates, perhaps, that her aspiration to become Ireland's Joan of Arc had taken a battering by this time. Summing up, she told the assembly that she believed that the freedom of Ireland was 'worth blood, and worth my blood, and I will willingly give it for it, and I appeal to the men of the Dáil to stand true, stand true to Ireland, stand true to your oath, and put a little trust in God'.[63] Michael Collins' response to the remark about the Princess Mary was that he would 'not allow without challenge, any Deputy in the assembly of my nation to insult any lady either of this nation, or of any other nation'.[64] Countess de Markievicz did not respond.

Margaret Pearse spoke the day after de Markievicz. Her speech was short and to the point. She told Dáil Éireann:

I rise to support the motion of our President for the rejection of this Treaty. My reasons for doing so are various, but my first reason for doing so I would like to explain here today is on my son's account. It has been said here on several occasions that Pádraig Pearse would have accepted this Treaty. I deny it.[65]

She also believed that her younger son Willie would not have accepted the Treaty either. She explained to the assembly that since 1916 (except for the Black and Tan period) she had 'comfortable, nice, happy nights and happy days because I knew my boys had done right and I knew I had done right in giving them freely for their country'. On a personal level, she could not renege on her oath because her catechism, 'taught to her in childhood that it was perjury to break an oath' and she believed she 'would be perjuring herself if she broke her oath to Dáil Éireann'.[66] Believing she knew what was in the hearts of Irishwomen, she explained that she had travelled through Ireland in recent years and knew:

The sorrows of the wives of Ireland. I have studied them, no one studied them more, and let no one here say that these women from their hearts could say they accept that Treaty. They say it through fear; they say it through fear of the aeroplanes and all that has been said to them.[67]

The reference to aeroplanes is interesting because since the end of the war in Europe, planes were coming into use as weapons of war. The British military was now using planes in Ireland as part of its weaponry. Rumour of the abilities of these machines, fuelled by fear of the relatively new and unknown, would have been frightening to many civilians throughout the country. In her summary, Pearse, like the other women, tackled the issue of rattling the bones of the dead and told the assembly:

Remember, the day will come soon, I hope, Free State or otherwise when those bones shall be lifted as if they were the bones of saints. We won't let them rattle. No! But we will hold what they upheld, and no matter what anyone says I feel that I and others here have a right to speak in the name of their dead.[68]

This ended the input of the women in the Treaty debates. Their speeches were a combination of emotional entreaty on behalf of dead men and hectoring on behalf of the same dead men. Their speeches at times also included a significant amount of tortuous verbiage.

The vote on the Treaty took place on the 7 January 1922. It was carried by sixty-four votes in favour of the Treaty to fifty-seven against. Before the debate ended, Cathal Brugha spoke against the Treaty. His speech was a tirade similar to that of MacSwiney and de Markievicz, though his language was more explicit and insulting. Wyse Power said:

It was the most dreadful public utterance I ever listened to, apparently made to prejudice Collins, even Brugha's followers interposed to ask him to restrain himself. Some of them say the speech gained some waverers for the Treaty. It was vicious and malignant and his face reminded me of a hound striking his fangs in an inferior animal and then licking its lips to satisfy itself that it had drawn blood ... Oh the sorrow of it all ... de Valera broke down, and there was dead silence in the chamber.[69]

Jennie Wyse Power's letters contain a strong sense of the wide chasm that now opened in Irish politics. The fury unleashed by the debates in the Dáil left a rumbling that was to culminate in a civil war. With or without acceptance of the Treaty, the population was to be subjected to warfare and bloodletting, created by these men and women who had lost all direction. This chasm began to permeate all aspects of life in Ireland.

Within republican politics, the fury of both sides was to culminate in a split that reached out across every aspect of life in Ireland. One of the saddest observations by Jennie Wyse Power was that many of de Valera's supporters really did believe that he had an alternative plan. She told her daughter Nancy that 'the extraordinary thing is that many intelligent people believe that de Valera is playing an arranged game to get more from England'.[70] However, by this time, the slide into civil war was completely beyond his control as he was now a puppet of other people's machinations. The general population, lauded in 1920–21, who supported by a majority the Anglo-Irish Treaty, would now be vilified as the row intensified and war once more resumed.

12

FEBRUARY 1922: STRIDING TOWARDS A POLITICAL ABYSS

On 3 January 1922, four days before the vote was taken in Dáil Éireann to decide the fate of the Anglo-Irish Treaty, the anti-Treaty group began a programme of propaganda, with the launch of *The Republic of Ireland* (*Poblacht na hÉireann*) newspaper. The editorial staff were Liam Mellows, editor, Frank Gallagher, assistant editor, and Joseph McDonagh, manager. The committee of directors comprised Cathal Brugha, Austin Stack, Liam Mellows, J.J. O'Kelly (Sceilg), Constance de Markievicz, Mary MacSwiney, Seán Etchingham, Seán T. O'Kelly, Mrs O'Callaghan, Robert Brennan and Erskine Childers.[1] Apart from its mission to disseminate anti-Treaty propaganda, the paper also made an appeal for funds. They set up a fund called the 'Uphold the Republic Fund', to enable those members of the public who were anti-Treaty to subscribe 'on behalf of Dáil Éireann and to refuse the surrender of Ireland's declared independence'.[2]

Seven days after the vote on the Treaty, the sixty-four members of the second Dáil who supported the Anglo-Irish Treaty assembled at the Mansion House. They formed the Provisional Government of the Irish Free State and elected an executive council. Those elected to the council were Michael Collins, William T. Cosgrave, Eamon Duggan, Kevin O'Higgins, Seamus Hogan, Patrick McGrath,

Eoin MacNeill and Fionán Lynch. Michael Collins was elected chairman of the council.

On 17 January 1922, the Ard Chomhairle of Sinn Féin was convened to elect a new standing committee to act on its behalf. This was the first meeting of the Ard Chomhairle since it was elected the previous October at the Sinn Féin Ard Fheis. The Ard Chomhairle had a membership of nearly seventy, which was drawn from the party's officer board, its executive and the representatives of all Comhairlí Ceanntair. The election yielded a predominantly pro-Treaty standing committee, which indicates that at senior level the party was positive towards the Treaty. Peter Pyne, who closely studied the minutes of the Sinn Féin Standing Committee for the years 1919–26, said that 'by late January 1922, the party was overwhelmingly pro-Treaty'.[3] The Ard Chomhairle also decided to call an extraordinary Ard Fheis for 7 February, to enable the party membership to:

> … authoritatively and decisively interpret the Constitution of the Organisation with special reference to the situation created by the articles of Agreement for a Treaty between Great Britain and Ireland, signed in London on the 6 December 1921, and its approval by Dáil Éireann by sixty-four votes to fifty-seven, so as to decide the policy of the organisation in view of possible forthcoming elections.[4]

A general election was pending on 16 June, which would enable the official setting up of the Irish Free State parliament. This election was also the first opportunity the population had to make its opinion known.

At a meeting of the Sinn Féin Standing Committee on 31 January, Michael Collins put forward a motion, which was seconded by Seán McCaoilth, 'that any member of Sinn Féin who had not enrolled before 31 December 1921, could not vote for the selection of delegates to the Ard Fheis'.[5] This was later amended, 'to allow internees or prisoners not released before 31 December 1921, to have a right to vote'. Collins also proposed that the standing committee should 'recommend to the Ard Fheis, that the vote on acceptance or non-acceptance of the Treaty should be by ballot'.[6] Kevin O'Sheil seconded this. Austin Stack proposed an amendment to the resolution, that the voting should be open, and Áine Ceannt seconded it. This amendment also received the support of Kathleen Lynn and Hanna Sheehy Skeffington. However, when the voting took place they were in a minority and Collins' motion was passed.

While in public apparent efforts were being made to preserve some kind of unity within the party, the anti-Treaty faction continued its campaign through *Poblacht na hÉireann*. Seán T. O'Kelly was the main mover in this and he circulated a document to all branches of Sinn Féin, which stated:

> I know you are doing your best to ensure that meetings of Sinn Féin Cumainn in your Comhairle Ceanntair area, for the selection of delegates to the forthcoming Ard Fheis, are properly convened and efforts should also be made to uphold the Republic delegates elected.[7]

Four days before this, Jennie Wyse Power said she heard on the grapevine 'that little Seán T. O'Kelly is now feeling very badly' because 'things are not as smooth as he anticipated when he told me the republican party would go into the parliament and take an oath under protest'.[8]

In a second letter to the members of Sinn Féin, O'Kelly instructed:

> Where the republicans form a majority in Cumainn and Comhairlí Ceanntair, they should elect delegates to the Ard Fheis who can be relied upon to support the existing Republic. If the majority ...

should prove to be on the side which seeks to subvert the Republic the names of the republican members of those bodies should be noted and meetings held and the name of some members to be forwarded at once to Messers Seán T. O'Kelly and Harry Boland.[9]

On 3 February, the Sinn Féin Standing Committee postponed the Ard Fheis until 22 February because of an ongoing rail strike and this allowed some breathing space.

Sometime between 3 February and the Ard Fheis meeting of 22 February, the anti-Treaty side met and formed an organisation called Cumann na Poblachta. The group elected three trustees: J.J. O'Kelly (Sceilg), Cathal Brugha and Austin Stack. Cumann na Poblachta affirmed its allegiance to the proclamation of 1916 and to the Declaration of Independence of 21 January 1919. Their remit was published in *Poblacht na hÉireann* and stated:

> Convinced that the union of national forces necessary for national success can be secured only on the basis of the existing Republic, for which so many young lives have been offered, so many sacrifices made, and as much suffering endured, and determined that the Republic shall not die, the republican members of Dáil Éireann have decided to found and accordingly launch Cumann na Poblachta.[10]

F.S.L. Lyons incorrectly dates the formation of Cumann na Poblachta as 15 March 1922.[11] Jennie Wyse Power, in a letter to her daughter Nancy, dates its formation sometime in the middle of February. In a letter dated 24 February 1922, she discussed the new headquarter offices of Cumann na Poblachta in Suffolk Street in Dublin. Observing the amount of money the new group was spending, she said that it was able to rent offices in Suffolk Street for use as headquarters at £550 a year, buy new furniture and employ six typists. She ended with the comment, 'the republican party are in a most expensive mood'.[12] While de Valera and his followers described Cumann na Poblachta as an organisation and were careful not to use the words 'political party', it was perceived as the political party of the anti-Treaty side.

The three trustees of Cumann na Poblachta went to the USA on a fundraising campaign, accompanied by Countess de Markievicz and Kathleen Barry. Countess de Markievicz was living on a meagre income and had apparently a style of dress that reflected her state of relative penury. For her journey to the USA she had a new range of Irish-style clothes made specially, which led Jennie Wyse Power to comment, 'I am glad to say she is getting a decent outfit for the journey' and also to remark rather nastily that de Markievicz, who had bad teeth, was getting 'her teeth settled'.[13] The Cumann na Poblachta delegation arrived in New York on St Patrick's Day 1922. J.J. O'Kelly, recounting in 1948 why de Valera had sent the delegation to the USA, said that:

> He felt that we could not use any of the Sinn Féin funds … I remember definitely that he left on my mind the impression that we could not have access to the to the Sinn Féin funds … We went to the United States, and issued an appeal for funds over the names of Austin Stack and myself, under the auspices of Cumann na Poblachta, which appeared on the heading of our stationery for the years I spent in the United States.[14]

The delegation operated under the auspices of the AARIR, which was launched by de Valera and Harry Boland in 1920. J.J. O'Kelly said 'that with the support of Clan na Gael, they raised a substantial amount of money'.[15]

The Dáil was not the only organisation split by the issue of the Treaty. In February 1922, Cumann na mBan experienced the second split in its history. During the Treaty debates, the press reported extensively on the four women in the Dáil. They subsequently came to represent the public face of the dissenting female voice. These women, and in particular Countess de Markievicz and Mary MacSwiney, came to be associated solely with Cumann na mBan. On 11 January 1922, twenty-six members of the Cumann na mBan executive met to discuss the Treaty and they voted twenty-four to two against acceptance. The two women who supported it were Jennie Wyse Power and a Miss Mullan from Monaghan.[16] Wyse Power resigned from the executive. 'Mary MacSwiney, Madge Daly and Madame de Markievicz asked her not to resign', but she simply 'asked them to get on with business and leave her alone'.[17] The executive believed a special convention 'was rendered necessary because of paragraph five of the organisation's constitution', which stated that 'the role of Cumann na mBan was to organise the women of Ireland, to carry out the orders of Dáil Éireann'. Therefore, the organisation 'could not pledge loyalty to the Free State government, without first holding a national convention'.[18] The convention was called for 29 January 1922, pending the availability of de Markievicz.

Unlike Sinn Féin, the Cumann na mBan executive did not allow discussion. Mary MacSwiney and Countess de Markievicz were determined that the organisation would be the first republican organisation to vote against the Treaty and thereby lead the vanguard for the anti-Treaty side. A week before the convention was held it was discovered 'that de Markievicz was not going to be in Dublin that day' and it was postponed until 5 February.[19] Meanwhile, Mary MacSwiney wrote to the branches in Cork and instructed them to:

> … call a special meeting of their branches to discuss the executive resolution. Because the majority of the Deputies of Dáil Éireann have declared for the Free State and this may lead to decrees subversive of the constitution of Cumann na mBan.[20]

She also told them that 'in view of the grave importance of the decisions involved, the executive earnestly hope that each branch will make a special effort to send a delegate'.[21]

At rank and file level, Cumann na mBan was riven by the arguments about the Treaty. The implosion, which took place within the organisation in Cork city, is an example of how the organisation was affected throughout the country. A week before the special convention, the Cumann na mBan Cork district council held a meeting to discuss their differences. The meeting was attended by twenty-three delegates, representing branches from Bishopstown, Blackpool, Blackrock, Clogheen, Dublin Pike, Cork city (Poblacht na hÉireann branch), Pouladuff, Shandon, St Finbarr's, St Patrick's and Cork University. A motion was put forward by the Poblacht na hÉireann branch that:

> The Cork district council reaffirms its allegiance to the Irish Republic and condemns without qualification the betrayal of the Republic by the signing of the Treaty in London on December 6 1922 ... furthermore it repudiates the action of the sixty-four men who were elected to represent the Republic of Ireland and have foresworn their allegiance to the Republic in voting for this settlement.[22]

This report was sent by Nora Ní Brianin to the *Cork Examiner* and it also stated that a poll was taken on the motion that was defeated by sixteen to seven votes.[23] Three days later, on 2 February, a complaint from May Conlon (who signed her name as Bealtine Ní Coindealbain) of the Blarney district council was published to the effect that Ní Brianin was incorrect and that the motion was in fact 'defeated by ten to seven'.[24] Two days later Ní Brianin reported that on investigation 'five of the branches concurred with May Conlon'.[25] Ní Brianin decided that due to this disagreement she would call a special meeting to enquire into the matter. The following day a letter from Cait Ní Mhurcadha, representing the Brothers Delaney branch, Dublin Pike, was published. This letter reiterated that there had not been a 'withdrawal of allegiance to the Republic on their part, but as in the past, they would adhere to the one principle'.[26] Regardless of the confusion, it is clear that the majority of the Cork district council was pro-Treaty.

The most successful and enduring propaganda of this period comes from the vote of the Cumann na mBan special convention, which was held on 5 February 1922. *The Irish Times* and the *Irish Independent* published detailed reports of the convention, with the latter paper reporting that:

> At the special convention of Cumann na mBan in Dublin yesterday, a resolution of adherence to the republican policy was carried by 419 to 63 for an amendment advocating working for the republic through the Free State.[27]

Based on the publication of the above figures, Florence O'Donoghue in his book *No Other Law,* interpreted this as Cumann na mBan 'registering a practically unanimous vote against the Treaty at their convention'.[28] This perspective has endured to the present.

These figures, accepted without question or careful scrutiny, have subsequently become the accepted story of the voting pattern at the convention. This has remained unchanged since 1922. F.S.L. Lyons in *Ireland Since the Famine* said:

> Mention should also be made at this point of the revitalised women's organisation, the Cumann na mBan, with Countess Markievicz at its head. It was fiercely, even virulently, republican and followed closely the line taken during the Treaty debates by such speakers as Kathleen Clarke, Mary MacSwiney and Erskine Childers.[29]

Ireland Since the Famine is a very important work for any study of this period of Irish history because F.S.L. Lyons' forensic approach to sources is also supported by a balanced discussion. That a historian of his calibre did not discover this was republican propaganda shows how successful the dissemination of this particular piece of misinformation was.

A more careful reading of the newspaper reports in *The Irish Times* and *Irish Independent* elicits the fact that these figures actually refer to an amendment made by Jennie Wyse Power and that the vote against the Treaty was made by a show of hands.

The special convention of Cumann na mBan was preceded by a social evening for the delegates on 4 February 1922, in Dublin. This was organised by the executive of Cumann na mBan who apparently took care to exclude members 'whom they knew to be pro-Treaty'.[30] Jennie Wyse Power attended the event, refusing to be bullied into staying away, and described it as a warm-up for the convention. She said de Markievicz had 'addressed the delegates, telling them out plain to lead for the Republic'.[31] The following day the delegates gathered and a significant number of them were wearing the uniform of Cumann na mBan. According to *The Irish Times* and *Irish Independent*, there were 600 delegates present, with 200 missing because of a rail strike affecting the Cork and Kerry area. Countess de Markievicz opened the convention saying 'that as president she could not make a political speech' and that 'all that she could say was that they were being asked to reaffirm their allegiance to the Irish Republic and that the question before them was whether they would remain republican or accept Dominion Status'.[32]

Mary MacSwiney then proposed that 'Cumann na mBan reaffirms its allegiance to the Republic of Ireland, and therefore cannot support the Articles of Agreement signed in London, 6 December 1921'.[33] The motion was seconded by Miss Breen and several other delegates spoke in favour of it. Wyse Power then proposed her amendment:

> We reaffirm our allegiance to the republic, but realising that the Treaty signed in London will, if accepted by the Irish people, be a big step along the road, to that end, we declare we will not work obstructively to those who support the Treaty, (1) either in their putting the Treaty before the people, or (2) in their subsequent working of it, should the majority of the people accept the Treaty at a general election. And we also declare that in such an election this organisation shall not take a party side as between men who have worked so nobly and given proof of their loyalty to the Republic.[34]

She also told the convention that 'the decision they were being asked to make was unfair and premature' and said the organisation was being premature and as they were in fact an auxiliary 'to the IRA they should wait until the men decided what they were going to do'.[35] She continued amidst interruptions of women shouting 'Yes' and 'No' and asked the women were they going to support only republican candidates and openly oppose Irishmen who had fought and nobly worked for the Irish Republic? De Markievicz called for order and Wyse Power continued, saying that she had 'nothing to put before them in the way of a heroic record, except that her life had been spent in drudgery for the service of Ireland'. This was a sideswipe at de Markievicz, whom Wyse Power said, 'had during many of the public debates about the Treaty, ranted about her deeds'.[36] Wyse Power concluded her speech and told the meeting that they should wait and follow the example of the IRA who were remaining neutral and had yet to make a decision. The IRA and Sinn Féin had postponed their convention because of the rail strike, but a secondary reason was to allow those who had not paid their affiliation to do so. In her summary, Wyse Power appealed to the convention to declare that Cumann na mBan would not take sides in any future election. Wyse Power's amendment was seconded by Min Mulcahy, and in her speech she appealed to the women not to take sides in the election so as to avoid creating bitterness. She also said:

> There was a good deal of unworthy talk, and she was sorry that it came mostly from women about men's motives. People had even been called traitors (cries of no). Men who had been their heroes were now charged with all vices with which men could be afflicted.[37]

Mulcahy, in a final appeal to the convention, told the delegates that the Irish Republic could be gained by the Free State. A few more women spoke in favour of Wyse Power's amendment, which was then put to a vote, but it was defeated by 419 to 63, with some abstentions. With a calculated 600 delegates present at the convention, it appears that 118 delegates abstained from voting on this motion. Following this, the vote on MacSwiney's original motion took place, but not before she wound up the debate. In her speech, she paid tribute to 'Wyse Power's work in the cause of Irish freedom', but expressed surprise to hear her advocate that 'they should wait for the men's decision'. She said:

> Of all the people in Ireland, Wyse Power was the last person who should take such a stand because she was fighting for the right of women to take their places in the councils of the nation, when many of the delegates were in their cradles ... this right had now been granted, and women were entitled to voice their opinion whether the men do so or not, and if the IRA became a Free State army were they going to work for them (cries of NO), therefore why wait for the men? Rather let it be their place to give them a lead if they needed it.[38]

A question was posed from the floor about Cumann na mBan remaining neutral, and de Valera's Document 2, to which MacSwiney replied 'that asking Cumann na mBan to remain neutral was akin to asking her to stand neutral while a murderer stabbed her mother to death'. Making reference to de Valera's Document 2, she continued, 'there is no Document 2, it is as dead as the Treaty'. MacSwiney's motion that 'Cumann na mBan reaffirm its allegiance to the Republic of Ireland, and therefore cannot support the Articles of Agreement signed in London, 6 December 1921' was then 'put forward as a substantive motion and was carried by a show of hands'.[39] This was the actual vote that determined the organisation's position on the Republic versus the Treaty and the actual numbers have never been divulged.

The convention moved to the next item on the agenda, which was an amendment of the organisation's constitution. Mrs Margaret Pearse, one of the four vice-presidents of the organisation, then moved a motion to amend paragraph five of the constitution of Cumann na mBan, to read:

> Cumann na mBan was to organise the women of Ireland to support at the forthcoming elections, only those candidates who stand true to the Republic proclaimed in 1916, and established as a functioning government in 1919, and that no branch of Cumann na mBan can give any help to a candidate standing for the Free State.[40]

She continued 'that if she had made any other resolution she would be ashamed of herself, considering that she had given her all for the Republic'. She assured the convention that she did not have anything against those men who agreed with the Treaty and that:

> She firmly believed that they had done their best, but they had erred as bold children do, they did not do what they were told. Had they done what they were told, they would be the happy nation she had always been looking forward to.[41]

In the final speech of the convention, de Markievicz told the women they 'should pledge themselves never to allow the flag of the Republic to be used by any party that stood for anything less than complete independence'.[42] In reply to a question from a delegate, she said she also believed that those who refused to conform to the constitution of Cumann na mBan could not remain in the organisation.

Cumann na mBan did not allow any reporters into their convention. They sent a report on the outcome to the newspapers for publication and it was published among others in *The Irish Times*, the *Irish Independent* and *An Poblacht*. The newspapers all reported that 'were 600 delegates present with 200 missing because of a rail strike affecting the Cork and Kerry area'. The report also said that the convention voted 'to reject the Treaty by 413 to 63 votes', which is a total of 476 delegates. There is no mention of the remaining 124 delegates who attended.

However, the special convention of Cumann na mBan produced documents that tell a very different story, and these were sent by Sighle Humphreys and Eileen Aughney to the editor of *An Poblacht*. These documents show that 312 and not 413 delegates supported MacSwiney's substantive motion against the Treaty.[43] In addition, the documentation indicates that the number of members prevented from travelling because of the rail strike was not 200, but a mere 33 women.[44]

Another important aspect of this convention is that it broke one of the rules of the constitution of Cumann na mBan which made the meeting and the vote invalid. This issue hinges on the non-payment of affiliation fees by the majority of the branches represented at the convention. The constitution of Cumann na mBan of 1921 states 'that no branch shall be entitled to representation at the convention unless it has been affiliated at least one month prior to the date of the convention'. Each year after the annual convention, the branches renewed their affiliation by paying an affiliation fee. If this was not paid, their membership was invalid. For example, at the convention in October 1921, the organisation claimed to have 839 branches, but just 208 had paid the fee, so according to the constitution it actually had just 208 branches. Although affiliation fees were usually paid after each annual convention, there was a flexible time scale for payment, but in January 1921, in their rush to be the first organisation to vote against the Treaty, the leadership did not allow sufficient time for branches to pay their fees.

By February 1922, just seventeen branches had paid their affiliation fees and of this group, just six sent delegates. Therefore, according to the rules of Cumann na mBan's constitution, just six branches at the special convention had voting rights. Consequently, the documents produced by Humphreys and Aughney show that the special convention on 5 February 1922 was constitutionally invalid. Subsequent propaganda has obscured this fact and also the reality that the organisation had been in serious decline since late 1921. At this point Cumann na mBan cannot with any accuracy be described as an anti-Treaty organisation.

This did not worry the executive, nor were de Markievicz and MacSwiney deterred from claiming an overall victory for the anti-Treaty section of the organisation. The documents produced by Humphreys and Aughney only recorded one vote against the Treaty. There is no documentation showing how many were actually in favour. In addition, it is essential to record that 312 branches were represented, which left 528 unaccounted for. Consequently, the vote at the convention cannot be considered a democratic representation of the organisation. According to Jennie Wyse Power, those members who voted in favour of the Treaty were taunted with 'shouts of traitor' as they left the convention.[45] Jennie Wyse Power, Elizabeth Bloxham and Louise Gavan Duffy, who were three of the founder members of Cumann na mBan, left at this time. Wyse Power believed the convention 'had the further effect of limiting Cumann na mBan to purely military work'.[46] This was the second split within the organisation since it was formed in 1914 and led Wyse Power to comment, 'I feel I have seen Cumann na mBan from its cradle almost to its grave'.[47]

In the following week, the Cork district council held a meeting to discuss the future of the organisation in the city. Mary MacSwiney informed them that she was coming to address them, but the women refused her admission. They also expressed their feelings on her long speech at the Treaty debates, saying 'they were not willing to allow themselves to be subjected to a two and a half hour harangue of invective, similar to that delivered to the Dáil'.[48] The rank and file members now simply walked away from the organisation and from the executive, which had become elitist. The executive, based in Dublin, had lost touch with the work and experiences of these women during the Anglo-Irish War. Because the executive was predominantly anti-Treaty, they were in a position to hold onto the name Cumann na mBan. However, it was a hollow victory because from this time forward the organisation was a rump. After the split, the pro-Treaty members of the organisation had a dilemma: they no longer had a forum from which they could express their point of view.

In early March 1922, a small group of women came together at 70 St Stephen's Green in Dublin and formed an alternative organisation. Later, at a public meeting at the Mansion House on 13 March 1922, Jennie Wyse Power said:

> That it was right and proper that Irish women should publicly declare their allegiance to the Free State because an idea had gone abroad that all women were against the Treaty ... the women of Ireland, not a noisy faction of them, stood where they always stood, on the bedrock of Irish nationality.[49]

Cumann na Saoirse emerged from this meeting. Jennie Wyse Power and Louise Gavan Duffy were the main movers behind this idea. Cumann na Saoirse gave a platform to women who wanted to support the Treaty. It did not attract big numbers, but it did work during the Civil War in aid of the Irish Free State. In its early stages, the Irish Free State Criminal Investigation Department did not quite trust this organisation and kept a file on it. One notebook belonging to a member of the CID contained 'the names and address of fifty-seven members in the Dublin area'.[50] By 20 July 1922 the organisation was obviously accepted by the Free State authorities, because at a meeting of the executive council a report was read which stated 'that schemes for the assistance of and provision of comforts for wounded soldiers were being organised by Cumann na Saoirse'.[51] The executive council subsequently gave Cumann na Saoirse a grant of £100 for the provision of comforts for wounded soldiers.

In Cork, a row erupted over the use of the name Cumann na mBan. The pro-Treaty members in Cork refused to use the name Cumann na Saoirse and insisted they were entitled to keep the original name. The Cork district council, which was predominantly pro-Treaty, refused to change their name and retained the name Cumann na mBan. On 6 March 1922, May Conlon placed a notice in the *Cork Examiner* to publicise a meeting for women who were pro-Treaty, which read:

> Secretaries of branches of Cumann na mBan in the city and county in favour of the Treaty or perhaps desirous of forming branches in districts at present unrepresented are invited to communicate with the secretary at 75 Grand Parade Cork.[52]

This brought a swift response from headquarters in Dublin. On the following day, a letter was published from Sighle Humphreys at Dublin headquarters, notifying the branch secretaries that: 'May Conlon was no longer a member of Cumann na mBan and that any meeting summoned by her purporting to be a meeting of

the organisation was illegal' and that a new secretary of the Cork
district council had been appointed. The new secretary was Máire
Ní Achaoirinn and the members of Cumann na mBan in Cork
were ordered to address all communication to her. This notice
was placed at the behest of Mary MacSwiney, who had asked the
executive to place it in their name. She was reluctant 'to use her own
name because it would be interpreted as a personal quarrel within
the Cork membership'.[53] She wrote two more letters. The first was
a demand sent to the executive that they contact May Conlon, the
leader of the pro-Treaty section, because:

> Miss Conlon has already begun writing to country branches
> – probably with view to lining them up for the Free State and
> creating the idea that there is no split in Cumann na mBan,
> except personal rivalry with branches is being carefully spread …
> the abysmal ignorance in some of the country districts about the
> Treaty is appalling.[54]

Her second letter was addressed directly to May Conlon, but she
sent it via the executive in Dublin and insisted that they transcribe
it before sending it to Conlon so it would appear as though it came
from them. They complied with this demand. This letter said in
part:

> I am desired by the executive of Cumann na mBan to inform
> you that they have learned that you have issued a summons for a
> meeting of the Cork District Cumann na mBan, that such action
> is illegal on your part, and that any further attempt to use the
> name of this organisation will be dealt with by the courts of the
> Republic. You are requested to hand over, without delay, all books
> and correspondence in your possession dealing with Cumann na
> mBan to Máire Corcoran.[55]

Conlon simply ignored the letters. MacSwiney then resorted to writing to the editor of the *Cork Examiner*:

> As the overwhelming majority at the All-Ireland Convention of Cumann na mBan in February 1922, declared its allegiance to the Republic ... those persons who were formerly members of Cumann na mBan, but who now support the Treaty, have long ceased to be members of our organisation ... I therefore inform you that no mention of Cumann na mBan is to be made in your paper as taking part in any proceedings in favour of the Free State ... you have my authority, as a member of the executive, for refusing to print the name of our organisation in connection with such proceedings, and my warning that proceedings will be taken if it is so used.[56]

The editor complied with her order. MacSwiney then informed the executive that:

> The editor of the *Cork Examiner* has eventually taken my letter of Sunday to heart ... I think it would be well if you wrote to him also, from Dublin, warning him not to publish any reference to Cumann na mBan in connection with the names of Miss Conlon and Miss Duggan.[57]

The row remained bitter, but the pro-Treaty members of Cumann na mBan in Cork were determined they were not going to be bullied by MacSwiney.

Meanwhile, the Sinn Féin Ard Fheis convened on 22 February 1922, when the delegates devised a written agreement to enable the party to adjourn for three months. The purpose of the agreement was to try and avoid a division within the party, and also 'avert the danger to the country of an immediate election and give an opportunity to the signatories of the London Agreement to draft a Constitution'.[58] It was also decided that the party's officer board would act as the Ard Comhairle standing committee from this time. In an emotional letter to her daughter Nancy, Jennie Wyse Power described the ambience of the meeting saying:

> Well the Treaty now is in such a position, that perhaps the game is up, and only for the country I would like to see the instrument laid at rest, and let the fighting men and women take up the running.[59]

She also told Nancy that before de Valera signed the agreement he had 'sent for Mary MacSwiney to see if she would she be satisfied, of course everyone says that she is the virtual leader and he is completely in her hands', which 'is a tribute to her strength'.[60] De Valera, Michael Collins, Arthur Griffith and Austin Stack finally signed the agreement. Describing the end of the meeting, Wyse Power said:

> The country people went home delighted, little knowing that there is no peace agreement. Before the Ard Fheis separated, Seán T. O'Kelly used the platform to call his party together. I wanted Griffith to do the same but he refrained. The de Valera followers were supplied with the Tipperary IRA manifesto in pamphlet form to bring home with them. This is an outrage and of course, it is an incitement to smash the army.[61]

While Sinn Féin was still intact as a political party, unity was very tenuous. Nevertheless, unlike Cumann na mBan, Sinn Féin tried to hold the organisation together by not having a vote on the issue of the Treaty.

The IRA convention, which was to take place on 26 March 1922, was prohibited by the Free State government because they believed this convention had been:

... proposed to endeavour to remove the Army from under control of the government elected by the people, which is Dáil Éireann. Such a proposal is illegal and you are hereby instructed that the holding of the Convention is forbidden.[62]

The anti-Treaty members of the IRA went ahead and held the convention. On 9 April they assembled at the Mansion House, adopted a new constitution and elected a new executive. Neither de Valera nor Cathal Brugha was elected. According to Florence O'Donoghue, the new IRA executive comprised Liam Lynch, Liam Mellows, Rory O'Connor, Joe McKelvey, Florence O'Donoghue, Seán Moylan, Seán Hegerty, Liam Deasy, Seamus Robinson, Ernie O'Malley, Peadar O'Donnell, Joe O'Connor, Frank Barrett, Tom Maguire, P.J. Ruttledge and Tom Hales.[63] At the conclusion of the convention, the executive met and appointed Liam Lynch chief of staff. An army council of seven was also appointed but O'Donoghue could only name some. They were Liam Lynch, Rory O'Connor, Liam Mellows and Joe McKelvey; he speculated that the other three were Ernie O'Malley, Seamus Robinson and Peadar O'Donnell.[64] The new IRA claimed their legitimacy emanated from the proclamation of 1916, the declaration of the Irish Republic in 1919 and the second Dáil Éireann created in 1921. By the end of March 1922, the IRA and Cumann na mBan had both fragmented.

TABLE 16: THE REPRESENTATIVES AT THE CONVENTION OF CUMANN NA MBAN ON THE 6 FEBRUARY 1922 AND THE IRA CONVENTION HELD ON 28 MARCH 1922

IRA divisions	IRA delegate numbers	Cumann na mBan delegate numbers
First Southern	54	44
Second Southern	28	50

Third Southern	10	31
First Western	13	11
Second Western	18	18
Third Western	18	
Fourth Western	20	4
First Northern	5	
Second Northern	2	8
Third Northern	3	19
Fourth Northern	2	4
Fifth Northern Division	0	19
First Midland	2	17
First Eastern	1	19
Dublin Brigade/ Dublin South Brigade & Carlow	16	29
Third Eastern /Northern & Southern Wexford Brigade	9	22
English Brigades	6	4
Scottish Brigade	2	4
Unidentified	2	9
Total	**211**	**312**

Source: Florence O'Donoghue, No Other Law *and the documents captured at St Monica's Mother and Baby club in Wereburgh Street in April 1923, held at the BMH Military Archive, Dublin.*

This table shows that membership within Cumann na mBan's First Northern Brigade had almost collapsed; while the IRA Fifth Northern Division was defunct, but its counterpart in Cumann na mBan still recorded nineteen branches. The only consistency in the voting pattern of both conventions was in the First and Second Southern and First and Second Western Divisions. Nevertheless, a study of the attendance of their respective conventions indicates that only a slight pattern of agreement existed between both organisations, geographically speaking.

Within seven months of its convention of October 1921, when
they claimed to have over 800 branches, Cumann na mBan now had
133.[65] Of this number, forty-three were new branches that had been
formed since the special convention in February 1922. This indicates
that Cumann na mBan had lost 749, or 89 per cent, of its branches.
This does not mean that the 89 per cent were pro-Treaty. There is
a strong possibility that the rank and file were simply war weary or
perhaps preferred to remain neutral.

Within months, Cumann na mBan and the political women of
the anti-Treaty side found themselves part of a Republican Triad,
which came together to fight the Irish Free State. In this division
lay the seeds to the demise of women in republican politics in
Ireland.

APPENDIX 1

The members of the citizens committee who organised the children's party for Queen Victoria on 7 April 1900.

Title	Name	Title	Name
Mrs	Alston	Mrs	Jones
Miss	Alston	Miss	Jones
Mrs	Arnold	Miss	Jones (no. 2)
Lady	Arnott	Mrs	Kenny
Mrs Graham	Bailey	Lady Annette	La Touche
Miss	Barry	Lady	Martin
Mrs	Browne	Mrs	McAuley Fitzgibbon
Mrs	Bulger	Miss	Montgomery
The Misses	Calderwood	Miss	Montgomery (no. 2)
Miss	Carson Rea	Mrs	Mooney
Miss	Church	Mrs	Newcomen
Mrs	Conolly Norman	Miss	O'Farrell
Mrs	Cooke	Miss	O'Farrell (no. 2)
Mrs	Crossley	Miss	O'Farrell (no. 3)
Mrs	Dallas Pratt	Lady Mayoress	Pile
Mrs	Dockrell	Miss	Plews
Mrs	Dwyer	Mrs	Plews
Mrs	Egan	Miss	Rathbourne
Countess Elizabeth	Fingall	Mrs	Richard
Mrs Henry	Fitzgibbon	Mrs	Rowe
Mrs	Fitzpatrick	Miss	Royce
Mrs S.O.A.	Fitzpatrick	Miss Isabel	Sexton
Hon Mrs	Foljambe	Miss	Seymour

Mrs	French		Mrs	Tolerton
Miss	French		Miss	Towers
Mrs W.J.	Goulding		Miss	Young
Miss	Smith			

Source: M.J.F. McCarthy, Five years in Ireland.

APPENDIX 2

The members of the committee for the Patriotic Children's Treat on 1 July 1900. The names in bold are those who participated in founding INE.

Title	Name
Mrs	Boylan
Miss	Brady
Miss	Browne
Mrs	Byrne
Miss Harriet Rose	**Byrne**
Miss	Clarke
Miss	Clegg
Miss	Conneiff
Miss	Connelly
Miss	Cosgrove
Miss	Cross
Miss	Dempsey
Miss	**Devlin**
Mrs Henry	Dixon
Miss	Donnolly
Mrs	Echlin
Mrs J.F.	Egan
Miss	Fanning
Miss	Fitzgerald
Miss	Gibb
Miss Maud	**Gonne**
Miss	Griffith
Miss	Haberlin
Miss	Hanratty
Miss	Higgins
Miss	Hyland

Title	Name
Mrs	Tier
Miss Alice	Furlong
Miss	O'Farrelly
Miss	**O'Kennedy**
Mrs	**O'Leary Curtis**
Misses	Pearse (2)
Miss Maria	**Perolz**
Miss Delia	Perolz
Miss Anna	Perolz
Miss	Potter (no. 1)
Miss	Potter (no. 2)
Miss	Power
Miss	Purtell
Miss	Quaid
Mrs M.J.	**Quinn**
Miss	**Quinn (no. 2)**
Miss	Rice
Miss	Robinson
Miss	Ronan
Miss	Rooney
Miss	Ross
Miss	Rothwell
Mrs	Ryan
Miss L.	Ryan
Miss Nora	Ryan
Misses	Ryder (2)

Miss	Kilmartin		Miss	Sheehan
Miss	Larkin		Miss	Sheils
Miss	Manning		Miss	Sheridan
Madame Brigid	Marie		Miss Annie	Smyth
Miss	McGlade		Miss Margaret	Smyth
Miss	McGuinness		Mrs	Sullivan
Miss	McNamara		Miss	Sullivan
Miss	**Meagher**		Miss May	Tierney
Miss	**Morgan (no. 2)**		Miss E.	Tierney
Miss	**Morgan (no. 1)**		Miss	Wheatley
Miss	Mulvey		Miss	Whelan
Miss	Murphy		Miss	White
Mrs	**O'Beirne**		Miss Nancy	Wyse Power
Miss	O'Brien		**Mrs Jennie**	**Wyse Power**

Source: United Irishman, *March 1900 to November 1900.*

Appendix 3

The constitution of the Irish Citizen Army and the army council.

That the first and last principle of the Irish Citizen Army is the avowal that the ownership of Ireland, moral and material, is vested of right in the people of Ireland.

That the Irish Citizen Army shall stand for the absolute unity of Irish nationhood, and shall support the rights and liberties of the democracies of all nations.

That one of its objects shall be to sink all difference of birth, property, and creed under the common name of the Irish people.

That the Irish Citizen Army shall be open to all who accept the principle of equal rights and opportunities for the Ireland people [*sic*].

A further clause was added, on the motion of the Countess de Markievicz and Thomas Healy, which read:

Before being enrolled, every applicant must, if eligible, be a member of his trade union, such union to be recognised by the Irish Trade Union Congress.

Army Council:
Chairman: Captain Jack White.
Vice-Chairmen: Jim Larkin, P.T. Daly, Councillor W. Partridge, Thomas Foran, Francis Sheehy Skeffington.
Hon. Secretary: Seán O'Casey.
Hon. Treasurers: Countess Markievicz and Richard Brannigan.

Committee: T. Healy, M. Mullin J. Bohan, T.C.P. Morgan, T. Burke, T. Blair, J. Poole, J. McGowan, T. Kennedy, P. O'Brien, P.J. Fox, John Shelly, P. Coady, T. Fogarty.

Source: Seán O'Casey, The Story of the Irish Citizen Army, *p. 14.*

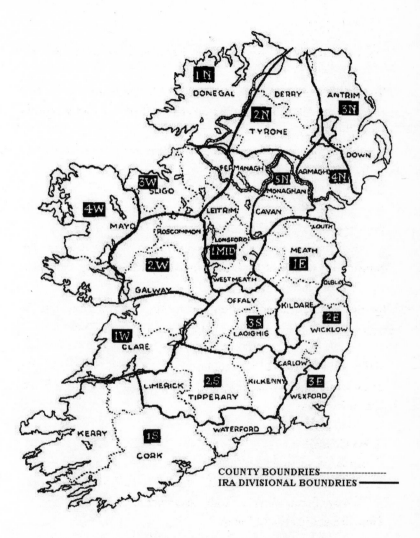

Map of IRA Divisions 1921.

(Florence O'Donoghue, No Other Law, *p. 198)*

APPENDIX 4

The names of the women who were involved in action during Easter week. The table has 140 names, some with their organisation and branch affiliation. It was not possible to ascertain what garrison all of these women were working in.

Title	First Name	Surname	Organisation	Garrisons 1916
Miss	Nano	Aiken		
Miss	Eilís/Eileen	Aughney		
Miss	Kathleen	Barrett		
Mrs	Kitty	Barrett		
Miss	Eibhlin D.C.	Barry		
Miss	Brigid	Brady	ICA	City Hall
Miss	Martha	Brown		
Miss	Kitty	Brown		
Miss	Eileen	Byrne		
Miss	Katie	Byrne	INE Branch	Distillery Marrowbone Lane
Miss	Winnie	Byrne	INE Branch	Distillery Marrowbone Lane
Miss	May	Byrne	INE Branch	Distillery Marrowbone Lane
Miss	Chris	Caffery	ICA	St Stephen's Green/Surgeons
Miss	Winifred	Carney	ICA	GPO
Miss	May	Carron		
Miss	Brigid	Carron	Central Branch	GPO/Four Courts
Miss	Gertie	Colley	Fairview Branch	
Mrs		Conlon	Central Branch	Four Courts Church St
Mrs		Connolly	ICA	City Hall

Miss	May	Cooney		
Miss	Lily	Cooney		
Miss	Annie	Cooney	INE Branch	Distillery Marrowbone Lane
Miss	Eileen	Cooney	INE Branch	Distillery Marrowbone Lane
Miss	Lily	Cooney	INE Branch	Distillery Marrowbone Lane
Miss	Marcella	Cosgrove	INE Branch	Distillery Marrowbone Lane
Miss	Peg	Cuddidhy	INE Branch	Courier
Miss	Brigid	Davis	ICA	City Hall
Countess	Constance	de Markievicz	ICA	St Stephen's Green/Surgeons
Miss	May	Derham		
Miss	Mary	Devereux	ICA	St Stephen's Green/Surgeons
Miss	Emily	Elliot		
Miss	M.	Elliot		
Miss	Ellen	Ennis		
Miss	Nellie	Ennis	Central Branch	GPO/Four Courts
Miss	M.	Fagan		
Mrs	Anna	Fahy	Central Branch	Four Courts Church St
Miss	Madeleine	Ffrench Mullen	ICA	St Stephen's Green/Surgeons
Miss	Kathleen	Fleming		
Miss	Nora	Foley		
Miss	Katie	Foley		
Miss	Brigid	Foley		
Miss	May	Gahan		
Miss	Nora	Gavan	Central Branch	GPO/Four Courts
Miss	Nellie	Gifford	ICA	St Stephen's Green/Surgeons

Miss	Brigid	Gough	ICA	St Stephen's Green/Surgeons
Miss	Julia/Sheila	Grennan	INE Branch	GPO/Four Courts
Miss	Rosanna/ Rosie	Hackett	ICA	St Stephen's Green/Surgeons
Mrs		Hayes	Central Branch	Four Courts Church St
Miss	Brigid	Hegerty	INE Branch	Distillery Marrowbone Lane
Miss	Patricia	Hoey		
Miss	Mary/Molly	Hyland	ICA	St Stephen's Green/Surgeons
Mrs	Maggie	Joyce	ICA	St Stephen's Green/Surgeons
Miss	Sarah	Kealy		
Misses	May & Martha	Kelly		
Mrs	Annie	Kelly	ICA	St Stephen's Green/Surgeons
Miss	Katie	Kelly	INE Branch	Distillery Marrowbone Lane
Miss	Josephine	Kelly	INE Branch	Distillery Marrowbone Lane
Miss	Lily	Kempson	ICA	St Stephen's Green/Surgeons
Miss	Margaret L.	Kennedy	INE Branch	Distillery Marrowbone Lane
Miss	Kathleen	Kenny	Central Branch	Four Courts Church St
Miss	Bridie	Kenny	INE Branch	Distillery Marrowbone Lane
Miss	K.	Lane		
Mrs		Lawless		
Miss	Catherine	Liston		
Miss	Mary	Liston		

Miss	Bessie	Lynch	ICA	City Hall
Dr	Kathleen	Lynn	ICA	City Hall
Miss	Bridget	Lyons		
Miss	Kathleen	Maher		
Miss	Brigid	Martin	Central Branch	Four Courts Church St
Miss	Kathleen	Martin	ICA	Four Courts Church St
Miss	B.	Masterson	INE Branch	Distillery Marrowbone Lane
Miss	Josie	McGowan	INE Branch	Distillery Marrowbone Lane
Miss	Rose	McGuinness	Central Branch	Four Courts
Mrs	Joe	McGuinness	Central Branch	GPO/Four Courts
Miss	May/Mary	McLoughlin	Clan na Gael	GPO/St Stephens Green
Miss	Sorcha	McMahon	Central Branch	GPO/Four Courts
Miss	Rose	McNamara	INE Branch	Distillery Marrowbone Lane
Miss	Agnes	McNamee	INE Branch	Distillery Marrowbone Lane
Miss	Flossie/Florence	Meade	Central Branch	GPO/Four Courts
Miss	G.	Milner		
Miss	Jenny	Milner		
Miss	Carrie	Mitchell	Central Branch	GPO/Four Courts
Miss	Helena	Molony	ICA	City Hall
Miss	Mary	Moore		
Miss	Phyllis	Morkan		Four Courts Church St
Mrs	Pauline	Morkan	Central Branch	GPO/Four Courts

Miss	Rose	Mullally	INE Branch	Distillery Marrowbone Lane
Miss	Lily	Murnane	Central Branch	Four Courts Church St
Mrs		Murphy	INE Branch	Four Courts Church St
Miss	May (Mary)	Murray		
Miss	Brigid	Murtagh		
Miss	Máire	Ní Shiublaigh		
Miss	Emily	Norgrove	ICA	City Hall
Mrs	Annie	Norgrove	ICA	City Hall
Miss	Lily	O'Brennan	Central Branch	
Miss	Nora	O'Daly		
Miss	Elizabeth	O'Farrell	INE Branch	GPO
Miss	Margaret	O'Flaherty	INE Branch	Distillery Marrowbone Lane
Miss	Sheila	O'Hanlon	INE Branch	Distillery Marrowbone Lane
Miss	Molly	O'Hanlon	INE Branch	Distillery Marrowbone Lane
Miss	Eily	O'Hanrahan		
Miss	Emily	O'Keeffe	INE Branch	Distillery Marrowbone Lane
Miss	Josie	O'Keeffe	INE Branch	Distillery Marrowbone Lane
Miss	Mollie	O'Reilly	ICA	City Hall
Miss	Lousia	O'Sullivan		
Miss	Mollie	O'Sullivan	Central Branch	GPO/Four Courts
Miss	Dolly	O'Sullivan	Central Branch	GPO/Four Courts
Mrs		Parker	Central Branch	Four Courts Church St

Miss	Maria	Perolz		Courier
Miss	Leslie	Price		
Miss	Josephine	Purfield		Boland's
Miss	Priscilla	Quigley	INE Branch	Distillery Marrowbone Lane
Miss	Moira	Quigley	INE Branch	Distillery Marrowbone Lane
Miss	Josephine	Quigley	INE Branch	Distillery Marrowbone Lane
Miss	Áine	Ryan		GPO/Four Courts
Miss	Min	Ryan	Central Branch	GPO/Four Courts
Miss	Margaret	Ryan	ICA	St Stephen's Green/Surgeons
Miss	Phyllis	Ryan	ICA	GPO/Four Courts
Miss	Eilís	Ryan (Ní Riain)	Colmcille Branch	GPO
Miss	Kathleen	Seery	ICA	St Stephen's Green/Surgeons
Miss	Jennie	Shanahan	ICA	City Hall
Mrs	Hanna	Sheehy Skeffington	GPO/St Stephen's Green	
Miss	Matilda	Simpson		
Miss	Margaret	Skinnider	ICA	St Stephen's Green/Surgeons
Miss	Lucy	Smyth		
Mrs	Josephine	Spicer	INE Branch	
Miss	D.	Sullivan		
Miss	Mary	Sullivan	INE Branch	
Miss	Aoife	Taaffe		
Miss	Nora	Thornton		
Miss	Catherine (Cathleen)	Treston		
Miss	Stasia	Twomey		

Miss	B.	Walsh		Four Courts Church St
Miss	Martha	Walsh	ICA	GPO
Miss	Kate/ Kathleen	Walsh	ICA	GPO
Mrs	Joe	Walsh	INE Branch	GPO/Four Courts
Miss	Eileen	Walsh	INE Branch	Four Courts Church St
Miss	Nancy	Wyse Power		

Source: This table was constructed from several sources. These were Military Bureau Papers, which are held in the National Archive and Military Archive; some of these papers are also held at the Allen Library and Kilmainham Gaol because individuals donated their personal copies to these repositories. Other sources used were the papers of Sighle Humphreys, Eithne Coyle and Mary MacSwiney, held in UCDAD, and the memoir of Gertie Colley Murphy held at Kilmainham Gaol.

APPENDIX 5

Regulation 14e of the Defence of the Realm Act, 31 August 1916.

DEFENCE OF THE REALM REGULATION 14e
Your attention is drawn to the following regulation:

A Secretary of State or the Admiralty or the Army Council may Prohibit from going to Ireland any person who is not a British subject or who being a British subject has since the last day of March, 1916 come or may hereafter come to the United Kingdom from parts beyond the seas and if any person so Prohibited embarks at any port in Great Britain for the purpose of going to Ireland or is subsequently found in Ireland he shall be guilty of a summary offence against these regulations and where an Aliens Officer has reason to suspect that any person is attempting to embark on any ship in contravention of this regulation he may prevent the embarkation of that person.

1.   When a British subject has been served with a notice prohibiting him from going to Ireland, you will be informed, either by a telegram from the Aliens Officer at the port at which he has arrived in the United Kingdom, or by a notice from me. You should thereupon take steps to prevent him from embarking at your port for Ireland.

2.   When a British subject is to be prohibited from going to Ireland, but has not been served with a notice, you will be informed by a notice from me. If he presents himself at your port for embarkation to Ireland he should be refused leave to embark, and if he states that no notice of prohibition has been served on him, you should serve one upon him and if he has a passport you

should endorse it "Prohibited from going to Ireland". A book of prohibition forms will be sent to you. A carbon copy of every form served should be sent to me.

W. HALDANE PORTER.
HM Inspector under the Aliens Act.

Source: Defence of the Realm Act 14e. 16 August 1916.

APPENDIX 6

Constitution of the Irish National Aid Association Volunteer and Dependents' Fund (INAAVDF).

1. The objects of the Association are to make adequate provision for the families and dependants of the men who were executed, of those who fell in action, of those who were sentenced to penal servitude, in connection with the Insurrection of Easter, 1916; and, in addition, to provide for the necessities of those others who suffered by reason of participation, or suspicion of participation, in the Insurrection.

2. The Executive shall consist of the twenty-four members elected by the two Associations now amalgamated, together with five representatives to be elected by the Dublin Trades Council, and two representatives from each province to be elected by the branches of the Association and co-opted by the Executive.

3. Weekly meetings shall be held on Tuesdays at 8 p.m. Seven members shall form a quorum.

4. Any member who fails to attend at least six ordinary meetings of the Executive, in each half-year, without adequate reason, automatically ceases to be a member.

5. The Executive shall have power to appoint sub-committees to deal with the departmental work of the Association, all such sub-committees to report to the Executive at each meeting.

6. The Executive shall have power to deal with vacancies, or other necessary changes, in its membership, by a majority vote of not less than two-thirds of those present at a meeting of which five clear days notice in writing of the special purpose of the meeting, shall have been given to each member.

7. The Executive shall issue a Half-Yearly Report with a duly audited Statement of Accounts.

8. The Executive shall summon a Conference, for advisory purposes, of representatives of the local Aid associations at such times as may be deemed necessary.

Source: Financial report INAAVDF (Catholic Bulletin, vol. ix, no. 8, August 1919).

Appendix 7

Cumann na dTeachtaire Constitution, 2 April 1918.

Objects
1. To safeguard the political rights of Irishwomen.
2. To ensure adequate representation for them in the Republican Government.
3. To urge and facilitate the appointment of women to Public Boards throughout the country.
4. To educate Irishwomen in the rights of duties and citizenship.

Rules
1. General meeting to be held annually on the desire of three-quarters of the members.
2. A standing committee to be elected to carry on the whole of the association meeting once a month or oftener if necessary.
3. Any member of the association to be entitled to attend meetings to lay suggestions before the committee.
4. The standing committee has the power to adopt any representative women not happening to be a delegate.
5. All republican women elected to public boards through the country to be offered the option of being co-opted as a member.
6. The women delegates should be prepared to confer with other Irishwomen's societies whenever it can be accomplished without sacrifice of principle because they are convinced that the bringing together of all Irishwomen to discuss matters of common interest on a neutral platform could not be but beneficial to all parties.

Source: Minute Book of the Conference of women delegates at the Mansion House, 17 April 1917 (WDIC), 2 April 1918 (NLI MS 21/194/47).

Appendix 8

Concept of District Council of Cumann na mBan 1918.

1. The District Council to correspond to the IRA Battalion Company and consist of a Captain and Secretary from each branch of Cumann na mBan within each battalion area.
2. The District Council would be called into existence by local branches of the organisation or by the executive. It would elect a Chairman, Secretary and Treasurer, would meet once a month and be subject to the executive of Cumann na mBan.
3. The Secretary of each District Council accepted responsibility for the all branches within her specific battalion area. The purpose of this arrangement was that the District Council would co-ordinate the work of local branches and thereby prevent overlapping, to extend the organisation by appointing local organisers and to arrange for instructors and lecturers to visit the branches.
4. Every branch of the organisation through its secretaries shall submit a written monthly report to her local District Council. In turn, the secretary of the District Council would report to GHQ monthly the conditions of branches in the battalion area.
5. Each month the secretary of the District Council and one other member of the District Council would inspect each branch in battalion.
6. All orders given by the District Council would be binding on the branches within its remit.
7. Each District Council should arrange a first aid for branches included in its district and one doctor who should examine all the branches. After the examination, a special course shall be held for those who pass, to provide lecturers for branches unable to get a doctor.

Source: Cumann na mBan convention report, 28 September 1918 (UDCAD, Humphreys papers, p106/1128).

Appendix 9

Attendance at the meetings of the WDIC and Cumann na dTeachtaire from 1917–1919.

The group met on eleven occasions.

Name	Attendance
Bloxham, Miss	11
Ffrench Mullen, Miss	11
Ginnell, Mrs	9
Kennedy, Miss	9
Lynn, Dr K.	9
Clarke, Mrs Kathleen	6
Fitzgerald, Mrs	6
Ceannt, Mrs	5
Davies, Mrs	3
Plunkett, Miss	3
Plunkett, Miss (2)	3
Shanaghan, Mrs	3
Davis, Miss	2
Duggan, Mrs	2
Kennedy, Mrs	2
Molony, Miss	2
O'Brennan, Miss	2
Perolz, Miss	2
Wyse Power, Mrs	2
Barton, Miss	1
De Markievicz, Countess	1

Doherty, Mrs	1
Gavan Duffy, Miss	1
MacSwiney, Mary	1
O'Grady, Mrs	1
O'Riordan, Mrs	1

Source: Minute Book of the WDIC and Cumann na dTeachtaire, 23 July 1917 to 30 April 1919 (NLI MS 21/194/47).

APPENDIX 10

Constitution of the Irish section of the Women's International League for Peace and Freedom

The league has national sections in twenty different countries in Europe, America and Australia, is made up of people who believe that we are not obliged to choose between violence on the one hand and passive acceptance on the other; who, on the contrary believe that courage, determination, moral power, generous indignation and active goodwill can achieve their ends without violence.

We believe that experience condemns force as a self-defeating weapon and that new methods free from violence must be worked out, to end abuses and to undo wrongs as well as achieve positive ends.

The nations are beset by fear of future wars, but the choice as to whether these things shall occur lies in the wills of men and women. Those who serve peace must serve it as ardently as those who make war, serve war.

Secretaries of the Irish section: Mrs Dix, 36 Highfield Rd and Miss Jacob, 122a St Stephen's Green

International HQ 6 Rue du Vieux College, Geneva

Subscriptions 2/- per year

Source: Women's International League for Peace and Freedom, Irish section (NLI WDIC minute book, MS 21/194/47)

APPENDIX 11

Cumann na mBan branches by county, July–November 1921

Area	No. of Branches
Cork County	99
Kerry	97
Wexford	42
Kilkenny	39
Leitrim	36
Roscommon	32
Laois	27
Limerick	27
Clare	26
Offaly	23
Carlow	22
Waterford	22
Louth	21
Longford	20
Westmeath	20
Cavan	19
Wicklow	19
Meath	18
Mayo	17
Galway	14
Kildare	14
Tipperary	14
Glasgow	13
Sligo	13
Dublin	11
Cork city	8
Fingal, Dublin	8
Dublin South County	8
Scotland	8

Antrim	7
Down	7
Armagh	6
Manchester, England	6
Donegal	5
Tyrone	5
London	4
England	3
Derry	2
Liverpool, England	2

Source: Documents captured during the Civil War at the WHNA St Monica's Mother and Baby Club in Werebergh Street, Dublin. These papers are part of the Captured Documents collection held in the Military Archive in Dublin.

ENDNOTES

INTRODUCTION

1 Constance de Markievicz is usually described in the literature as Markievicz. But I have discovered that she always signed herself de Markievicz. See discussion in Ann Matthews, 'Vanguard of the Revolution' in Ruan O'Donnell (ed.), *The impact of the 1916 Rising: Among the nations*, p. 25.

CHAPTER 1

1 Sylke Lehne, 'Fenianism – A Male Business: a case study of Mary Jane O'Donovan Rossa 1845–1916' (henceforth Sylke Lehne, 'Fenianism – a male business'), p. 25.

2 *Ibid.*

3 *Ibid.*, p. 113.

4 *Ibid.*

5 Katharine Tynan, *Twenty-Five Years: Reminiscences*, p. 76.

6 Jenny Wyse Power in Nancy Wyse Power, witness statement (Military Archive, Bureau Military History (henceforth MA BMH), WS 541, Appendix.

7 *Ibid.*

8 Brigid Martin, witness statement (MA BMH, WS 398), p. 2.

9 Áine Ceannt witness statement (MA BMH, WS 264), p. 1.

10 *Ibid.*

11 John Merriman, *A History of Modern Europe* Vol. II, p. 871.

12 *Ibid.*

13 Senia Pašeta, *Before the Revolution*, p. 28.

14 Siobhán Lankford, *The Hope and the Sadness*, p. 69.

15   *Ibid.,* p. 70.

16   John Coolahan, *Irish Education: history and structure*, p. 103.

17   Mary Colum, *Life and the Dream*, p. 61.

18   Mona Hearn, *Below Stairs*, p. 31.

19   Census of population household returns 1911, www.nationalarchives.ie.

20   *Ibid.*

21   Joost Augusteijn, *From Public Defiance to Guerrilla Warfare*, p. 357.

22   Ann Matthews, Clonbern Parish database, Census of population household returns 1911 (Clonbern Parish Project, 1997).

23   *Ibid.*

24   Michael Taaffe, *Those days are gone away*, p. 149.

25   John O'Grady, *The Life and Work of Sarah Purser*, p. 29.

26   *Ibid.,* p. 103. Irish Ireland is a generic term for the forms of cultural nationalism that took shape during the 1890s and in the first decade of the twentieth-century. See UCC web page, www.multitext.ucc. ie – Multitext project in Irish history: Movements of political and social reform 1870–1914.

27   Nora Robertson, *Crowned Harp*, p. 73. The Kildare Street Club was an exclusive gentleman's club.

28   *Ibid.*

29   Beatrice, Lady Glenavy, *Today We Will Only Gossip*, p. 13.

30   *Ibid.*

31   Mary Colum, *Life and the Dream*, pp. 94–5.

32   *Ibid.*

33   Sheila Turner Johnson, *Alice*, p. 87.

34   *Evening Telegraph*, 28 March 1900.

35   South Dublin Union, Board of Guardians minute book, 24 March 1900 (NAI, A/G/79).

36   *Ibid.* It is unclear why they refused the jam, but the pleasure of poor workhouse children was irrelevant to the political point being made.

37   Royal Irish Constabulary (RIC), police report, 15 April 1900 Public Record Office London (PRO) Colonial Office papers (henceforth cited CO), 904/202.

38 *United Irishman*, 16 June 1900.

39 *Ibid.*

40 *Ibid.*, 7 July 1900.

41 *Ibid.*, 3 Oct. 1900.

42 *Ibid.*, 12 May 1900.

43 Maud Gonne MacBride, *Servant of the Queen*, p. 278.

44 Kathleen Behan, *Mother of all the Behans*, p. 48.

CHAPTER 2

1 Conrad A. Balliett, 'The Lives – and Lies – of Maud Gonne', p. 17

2 Edith Frith Gonne, Last Will and Testament, General Register Office (hereafter GRO), London.

3 *The Irish Times*, 2 April 1868, p. 3.

4 Edith Frith Gonne, death certificate, GRO, London.

5 *The Irish Times*, 1 February 1871.

6 Maud Gonne MacBride, *Servant of the Queen*, pp. 9–10.

7 *The Irish Times*, 13 May 1871.

8 Maud Gonne MacBride, *Servant of the Queen*, pp. 11–12 .

9 *Ibid.*

10 Thomas Gonne, British Army service papers (PRO, WO 76/12) p. 152.

11 *The Irish Times*, 24 Feb. 1879; J.W. Fortescue, *History of the 17th Lancers*, p. 174.

12 Conrad A. Balliett, 'The Lives – and Lies – of Maud Gonne', p. 21.

13 *Regulations of the King's Army* (London, 1925), p. 49.

14 *Ibid.*

15 *Thom's Directory* 1885, p. 133.

16 *Ibid.*, 1886, p. 797; Conrad A. Balliett, The Lives – and Lies – of Maud Gonne', p. 21.

17 Maud Gonne MacBride, *Servant of the Queen*, p. 26.

18 *The Irish Times*, 27 January 1886.

19 *Ibid.*, 6 March 1886.

20 *Ibid.*, 18 March 1886.

21 Maud Gonne MacBride, *Servant of the Queen*, p. 31.

22 *Ibid.*

23 Susan Griffin, *The Book of Courtesans*, pp. 1–17 & pp. 251–7.

24 Maud Gonne MacBride, *Servant of the Queen*, pp. 32–3.

25 *Ibid.*

26 Nora Robertson, *The Crowned Harp*, p. 37.

27 Thomas Gonne, death certificate, GRO Dublin.

28 Nora Robertson, *The Crowned Harp*, p. 37.

29 Maud Gonne MacBride, *Servant of the Queen*, p. 56.

30 Judith Thurman, *A Life of Colette*, p. 163.

31 Maud Gonne MacBride, *Servant of the Queen*, p. 57.

32 *Ibid,* p. 60.

33 Bertrand Joly, 'The Jeunesse Antisémite et Nationaliste 1894–1904' in Robert Tombs (ed.), *Nationhood and Nationalism in France*, pp. 147–8.

34 Maud Gonne MacBride, *Servant of the Queen,* pp. 61–2.

35 *Ibid.*, p. 72.

36 Margaret Ward, *Maud Gonne: A Life*, pp. 17–18.

37 *The Irish Times,* 27 Oct. 1888.

38 *Ibid.*, 12 Nov. 1888.

39 *Ibid.*, 6 Dec. 1888.

40 Conrad A. Balliett, The Lives – and Lies – of Maud Gonne', p. 27.

41 Maud Gonne MacBride, *Servant of the Queen*, p. 55. The word ukase means that she was effectively disowned by her family.

42 Gerd Krumeich, 'Joan of Arc between right and left' in Robert Tombs (ed.), *Nationhood and Nationalism in France*, p. 66.

43 W.B. Yeats, *Autobiographies*, pp. 123–4.

44 *United Irishman*, 14 October 1899.

45 *Ibid.*

46 *Ibid.*, 23 Sept. 1899.

47 Bertrand Joly, 'The Jeunesse Antisémite et Nationaliste 1894–1904' in Robert Tombs (ed.), *Nationhood and Nationalism in France*, pp. 147–8.

48 *Ibid.*

49 *United Irishman,* 21 October 1899.

50 *Ibid.,* 27 Oct. 1900.

51 *Ibid.*

52 RIC police report, 23 Oct. 1900 (PRO, CO 904/202).

53 *United Irishman,* 13 Oct. 1900.

54 Inghinidhe na hÉireann, first annual report (National Library Ireland (hereafter NLI), Ir 94109).

55 *Ibid.*

56 Maria Perolz, witness statement (MA BMH, WS 246), p. 1.

57 *Ibid.*

58 *Ibid.,* pp. 5–6.

59 Inghinidhe na hÉireann, first annual report (NLI), December 1901.

60 Helena Molony witness statement (MA BMH, WS 391), p. 2.

61 *Ibid.*

62 *Ibid.*

63 Maria Perolz witness statement (MA BMH, WS 246), p. 2.

64 Arthur Swinson, *A register of the Regiments and Corps of the British Army,* p. 67.

65 Helena Molony witness statement (MA BMH, WS 391), pp. 2–8.

66 Seán O'Casey, *Autobiographies 1,* p. 236.

67 Helena Molony witness statement (MA BMH, WS 391), p. 3.

68 *Ibid.*

69 Margaret H. Keogh (née Quinn) witness statement (MA BMH, WS 273), p. 3. She is known in all the primary sources as Máire Quinn, but called herself Margaret in her witness statement.

70 Helena Molony witness statement (MA BMH, WS 391), p. 8.

71 *Ibid.,* p. 8.

72 Mary Hamilton, *The Silver Road,* p. 137.

CHAPTER 3

1   Helena Molony witness statement (Kilmainham Gaol Museum

(KGM)), p. 59.

2   Rosemary Cullen Owens, 'Votes for Ladies votes for women', p. 3.

3   Myrtle Hill, *Women in Ireland: A Century of Change*, p. 55.

4   Rosemary Cullen Owens, *A social history of Women in Ireland 1870–1970*, p. 84.

5   *Bean na hÉireann*, vol. 14, pp. 13–14.

6   RIC Files, Sinn Féin League, 1906 (PRO, CO 904/23, p/64/70).

7   *Bean na hÉireann*, vol. 14, pp. 13–14.

8   *Ibid.*

9   *Ibid.*, vol. 16, p. 14.

10 Helena Molony witness statement (MA BMH, WS 391 & Kilmainham Gaol Museum), p. 7.

11 *Ibid.*

12 George Moore, *A Drama in Muslin*, p. 175.

13 *Ibid.*, *Hail and Farewell*, p. 699.

14 Diary of Constance Gore Booth, 1 March 1892 (National Museum Dublin, EW 892).

15 Lady Fingall, *Seventy Years Young*, p. 192.

16 Henry William Gore Booth, last will and testament, 1900, Somerset House, London.

17 Tony Farmer, *Ordinary Lives*, p. 25.

18 *The Irish Times,* 30 October 1881.

19 *Thom's Directory* (Dublin, 1902), p. 1436.

20 *Ibid.*

21 Seán O'Casey, *Autobiographies 1*, pp. 596–7.

22 *Ibid.*

23 Seán O'Faolain, *Constance Markievicz*, p. 25; Charles Townshend, *Easter 1916: the Irish Rebellion*, p. 21.

24 Countess de Markievicz, *Women: ideals and the nation*, p. 16.

25 Helena Molony witness statement (MA BMH, WS 391), p. 64.

26 Mary McLoughlin witness statement (MA BMH, WS 934), p. 1.

27 Helena Molony witness statement (MA BMH, WS 391), p. 68.

28 *Ibid.*, p. 68.

29 *Éire, the Irish Nation*, 16 June 1923.

30 *Ibid.*

31 Seán O'Casey, *Autobiographies 1*, pp. 596–7.

32 RIC police report, 6 August 1911 (PRO, CO 904/210–305).

33 *Ibid.*

34 *Ibid.*

35 C. Desmond Greaves, *The Life and Times of James Connolly*, p. 253.

36 Brian O'Higgins, *Wolfe Tone Annual* (Dublin, 1950), p. 40.

37 Dublin Municipal Council, annual report, vol. 1, no. 95, 1912.

38 *Irish Citizen*, 13 Oct. 1913.

39 Dublin Municipal Council, annual report, vol. 1, no. 95, 1912.

40 Helena Molony witness statement (Kilmainham Gaol Museum), p. 8.

41 *Ibid.*

42 Audrey Woods, *Dublin Outsiders*, pp. 172–3.

43 Kathleen Lynn witness statement (Allen Library Dublin (henceforth ALD), no. 60118, box 106), p. 3.

44 *Ibid.*

45 One of the most interesting aspects of this paper was that while the IWFL confined its membership to women, the editors of its newspaper were male. They were Francis Sheehy Skeffington and James Cousins who were the husbands of the co-founders of the IWFL, Hanna Sheehy Skeffington and Margaret Cousins.

46 R.M. Fox, *History of the Irish Citizen Army*, pp. 3–4.

47 Nora Connolly, *Unbroken Tradition*, pp. 3–4.

48 Seán O'Casey, *Autobiographies 1*, pp. 596–7.

49 Pádraig Yeates, *Lockout: Dublin 1913*, p. 331.

50 Seán O'Casey, *The Story of the Irish Citizen Army*, p. 9.

CHAPTER 4

1 Áine Ceannt witness statement (MA BMH, WS 264), p. 9.

2 *Ibid.*

3   Seán O'Casey, *The Story of the Irish Citizen Army*, p. 14.

4   *Ibid.*

5   *Ibid.*, p. 16.

6   *The Irish Times*, 3 April 1914.

7   *Ibid.*

8   *Ibid.*

9   RIC police report, 23 June 1915 (PRO, CO 904/205).

10 Jack McCann, 'Margaret Dobbs' in *The Glynns*, vol. ii (1983), pp. 41–6.

11 Elizabeth Bloxham witness statement (MA BMH, WS 632), p. 1.

12 *Ibid.*

13 *Ibid.*

14 Nancy Wyse witness statement (MA BMH, WS 541), pp. 11–12.

15 *The Irish Times*, 7 April 1914.

16 *Irish Citizen*, 2 May 1914.

17 *Ibid.*

18 *Ibid.*

19 *Ibid.*

20 Sydney Gifford Czira, *The Years Flew By*, p. 57.

21 *Irish Press*, 4 Feb. 1936.

22 *Irish Citizen*, 21 May 1914.

23 *Ibid.*

24 Lady Gordon, *The Winds of Time*, pp. 165–6.

25 Siobhán Lankford, *The Hope and the Sadness*, pp. 78–9.

26 *The Irish Times*, 5 May 1914.

27 *Irish Volunteer*, 9 May 1914.

28 *The Irish Times*, 8 May 1914.

29 Inghinidhe na hÉireann meeting, 23 May 1914 (UCDAD, Sighle Humphreys papers (henceforth Humphreys papers (p106/1165 (1)).

30 Seán O'Casey, *The Story of the Irish Citizen Army*, p. 46.

31 Elizabeth Bloxham witness statement (MA BMH, WS 632), pp. 5–6.

32 Cumann na mBan manifesto, 8 August 1914 (UCDAD, MacSwiney papers, P48a/20).

33 *Irish Volunteer*, 23 May 1914, p. 1.

34 RIC police report, 3 April 1915 (PRO, CO 904/215–412).

35 *Ibid.*

36 Siobhán Lankford, *The Hope and the Sadness*, p. 101.

37 Seán O'Casey, *The Story of the Irish Citizen Army*, p. 34.

38 William O'Brien, Contemporaneous Documents (MA, CD 119/31).

39 Report by the Joint War Committee, 1921.

40 *The Irish Times*, 13 August 1914.

41 Lord and Lady Aberdeen, *We Twa*, p. 230.

42 RIC police report, 21 January 1915 (PRO, CO 904/215–412).

43 *The Irish Times*, 17 October 1914, p. 6.

44 *Ibid.*

45 *Leabhar na mBan* pamphlet published by Cumann na mBan in 1919, p. 5.

46 Kathleen Clarke, *Revolutionary Woman*, p. 49.

47 Cumann na mBan manifesto, 8 August 1914 (UCDAD, MacSwiney papers, P48a/20).

48 Cumann na mBan manifesto, 5 October 1914 (NLI Ir 94108), p. 48.

49 Mary McLoughlin witness statement (MA BMH, WS 934), p. 1.

50 *Irish Volunteer*, 21 August 1915.

51 Elizabeth Bloxham witness statement (MA BMH, WS 632), pp. 31–2.

52 *Ibid.*

53 Lil Conlon, *Cumann na mBan and the women of Ireland*, p. 16.

54 *Ibid.*

55 K. O'Doherty witness statement (MA BMH, WS 355), p. 3.

56 Eilís Bean Uí Chonaill (Ní Riain), witness statement (MA BMH, WS 568), p. 2.

57 *Irish Volunteer*, 16 October 1915.

58 *Ibid.*

59 Margaret Kennedy, Witness Statement (MA BMH, WS 185), p. 2.

60 *Irish Volunteer*, 8 Jan. 1916.

61 *Ibid.*

62 *Ibid.*

63 Margaret Skinnider, *Doing My Bit for Ireland*, p. 9.

64 *Irish Volunteer*, 27 Nov. 1915.

65 *Ibid.*

66 *Ibid.*

67 *Ibid.*, 11 March 1915.

68 *Irish Worker*, 6 February 1916.

69 Seamus Robinson personal account (undated) (UCDAD, Coyle papers, p61/13).

70 *Ibid.*

71 Eilís Bean Uí Chonaill (Ní Riain), witness statement (MA BMH, WS 568), p. 6.

72 *Ibid.*

73 Kathleen Lynn witness statement (ALD, no. 60118, box 106), p. 3.

74 Helena Molony witness statement (KGM), p. 34.

75 William O'Brien, CD documents (MA BMH, CD 191).

76 *Irish Volunteer*, 15 April 1916.

77 Kitty O'Doherty witness statement (MA BMH, WS 355), p. 24.

78 Nancy Wyse Power witness statement (MA BMH, WS 541), p. 17.

79 Kathleen Lynn witness statement (ALD, no. 60118, box 106), p. 3.

80 William O'Brien, *Forth the Banners go*, p. 287.

81 Kathleen Lynn witness statement (ALD, no. 60118, box 106), p. 3.

CHAPTER 5

1 Seamus Robinson personal account (UCDAD, Coyle papers, p61/13 (14)).

2 Rose McNamara witness statement (MA BMH, WS 482), p. 5.

3 Eilís Bean Uí Chonaill (Ní Riain), witness statement (MA BMH, WS 568), p. 6.

4 Seán Byrne witness statement (MA BMH, WS 422) pp. 7–8.

5   Josephine Purfield Wall, personal recollection (UCDAD, Coyle papers, p61/4 (44)).

6   Seamus Robinson, personal account of the rebellion (UCDAD, Coyle papers p61/13 (16)).

7   R.M. Fox, *Green Banners*, p. 288.

8   British Military authority, report on the rebellion, 26 April 1916 (PRO, War Office papers (henceforth WO), 40/35–69).

9   Mrs Tom Barry (Leslie Price) witness statement (MA BMH, WS 1754), p. 11.

10   Kathleen Lynn witness statement (ALD, no. 60118 box 106), p. 5.

11   *Ibid.*, p. 5.

12   Helena Molony witness statement (Kilmainham Gaol Museum), p. 37.

13   Kathleen Lynn witness statement (ALD, 60118 box 106), p. 4.

14   Nora O'Daly, 'The Women of Easter week', p. 4.

15   *Ibid.*

16   *Ibid.*

17   *Ibid.*

18   Jill Liddington & Jill Norris, *One hand tied behind us*, p. 13.

19   Elizabeth Bowen, *History of the Shelbourne hotel*, p. 156.

20   Geraldine Fitzgerald, extract from her personal diary, 24 April 1916 (WO 35/207).

21   *Ibid.*

22   *Ibid.*

23   May McLoughlin witness statement (MA BMH, WS 934), p. 2.

24   *Ibid.*

25   Lily O'Brennan, 'We Surrender', pp. 303–8.

26   *Ibid.*

27   *Ibid.*

28   Rose McNamara witness statement (MA BMH, WS 482), p. 5.

29   Eilís Bean Uí Chonaill (Ní Riain), witness statement (MA BMH, WS 568), p. 9.

30   www.icrc.org.

31 Áine Heron witness statement (MA BMH, WS 293), p. 5.

32 R.M. Fox, *Green Banners*, p. 293.

33 May McLoughlin witness statement (MA BMH, WS 934), p. 2.

34 Eilís Bean Uí Chonaill (Ní Riain), witness statement (MA BMH, WS 568), p. 9.

35 *Ibid*, p. 11.

36 Peter O'Dwyer, *Towards a History of Irish spirituality*, p. 241.

37 Gertie Colly Murphy, personal account of 1916 (Kilmainham Gaol Museum), p. 4.

38 *Ibid*.

39 Louise Gavan Duffy witness statement (MA BMH, WS 216), p. 10.

40 *Ibid*.

41 Molly Reynolds witness statement (MA BMH, WS 195), p. 7.

42 Leslie Price witness statement (MA BMH, WS 216), p. 12.

43 Joe Good, *Enchanted by Dreams*, pp. 56–7.

44 *Ibid*, p. 58.

45 *Ibid*.

46 *Ibid*.

47 Elizabeth O'Farrell, 'Events of Easter week', p. 267.

48 *Ibid*., p. 268.

49 Bureau Military History, Brother Allen (MA Contemporaneous documents, CD 75/1/4).

50 Julia Grennan, 'Account of Easter week, undated', p. 396.

51 Elizabeth O'Farrell, 'Events of Easter week', p. 330.

52 *Ibid*.

53 *Ibid*.

54 *Ibid*.

55 Fr Aloysius witness statement (Military Bureau WS 200), p. 6; Fr Augustine (WS 920), p. 11.

56 *Ibid*.

57 RIC police report, 19 May 1916 (PRO, WO BMH, WO 35/69).

58 Annie Mannion witness statement (MA BMH, WS 297), p. 4.

59   *Ibid.*

60   Áine Ceannt witness statement (MA BMH, WS 264), p. 29.

61   *Ibid.*, p. 28.

62   Joe McGallogly witness statement (MA BMH, WS 244), p. 12.

63   *Ibid.*

64   Countess de Markievicz, Court Martial, 4 May 1916 (PRO, WO 35–207–127).

65   *Ibid.*

66   *Ibid.*

67   *Ibid.*

68   William W. Wylie, manuscript of his autobiography (PRO, 30–89/2), p. 6; Charles Townshend, *Easter 1916: The Irish Rebellion*, p. 286.

69   William W. Wylie, *ibid.*, p. 30.

70   Brigid Martin (née Foley) witness statement (MA BMH, WS 398), p. 15.

71   Grace Gifford Plunkett witness statement (MA BMH, WS 257), p. 1.

72   *Ibid.*

73   *Ibid.*, p. 10.

74   *Ibid.*, p. 12

75   Geraldine Plunkett Dillon, *All in the blood*, p. 247.

76   Charles Townshend, *Easter 1916: The Irish Rebellion*, p. 283.

77   Lily O'Brennan, 'We Surrender', p. 305.

78   *Ibid.*, pp. 306–7.

79   *Ibid.*

80   Kathleen Lynn witness statement (ALD, no. 60118, box 106), pp. 1–2.

81   Helena Molony witness statement (Kilmainham Gaol Museum), p. 46.

82   Kathleen Lynn, witness statement (ALD, no. 60118, box 106), pp. 1–2.

83   *Ibid.*

84   *Ibid.*

85   Matron E.W. Sharp, prison matron, Holloway, 6 September 1916 (PRO, CO 904/209–297), p. 74.

86 Kathleen Lynn, witness statement (ALD, no. 60118, box 106, part 2), p. 1.

87 Winifred Carney, 21 June 1916 (PRO, HO 144/1457–314179).

88 *The Irish Times 1916 Rebellion handbook* (Dublin, 1916), p. 67.

89 Maria Perolz witness statement (MA BMH, WS 246), p. 5.

90 DMP report (PRO, CO 904/209–297).

91 RIC police report (PRO, CO 904/213).

92 Winifred Carney, 8 November 1916 (PRO, HO 144/1457–31479).

93 Nancy Wyse Power witness statement (MA BMH, WS 587), p. 5.

94 *Leabhar na mBan*, pamphlet published by Cumann na mBan in 1919, p. 3.

95 Kathleen Clarke, *Revolutionary Woman*, p. 133.

96 *Ibid.*

Chapter 6

1 Irish National Aid Association (hereafter INAA) constitution, May 1916 in INAAVDF (NLI, MS 24341), p. 1.

2 *Ibid.*

3 Irish National Aid Association Volunteer and Dependents' Fund accounts (NLI, (henceforth INAAVDF), MS 24,345).

4 *Ibid.*

5 *Ibid.*

6 *Ibid.*

7 INAAVDF financial report in *Catholic Bulletin*, ix, no. 8 (1919), p. 428.

8 *Ibid.*

9 *Ibid.*

10 RIC police report, 9 June 1916 (PRO, CO 904/215–408–249).

11 *Ibid.*

12 *Ibid.*

13 RIC police report, 9 September 1916 (PRO, CO 904/215–408).

14 RIC police report, 26 September 1916 (PRO, CO 904/213).

15 *Ibid.*

16 RIC police report, 20 January 1917 (PRO, CO 904/213).

17 *Ibid.*

18 Joanne Mooney Eichacker, *Irish Republican Women in America*, p. 63.

19 *Ibid.*

20 John J. Splain, 'The Irish movement in the United States since 1911' in William G. Fitzgerald (ed.), *The Voice of Ireland*, p. 231.

21 RIC police report, 18 January 1917 (PRO, CO 904/210–305).

22 John J. Splain, 'The Irish movement in the United States since 1911' in William G. Fitzgerald (ed.), *The Voice of Ireland*, p. 231.

23 INAAVDF accounts (NLI, INAAVDF papers, MS/23,468–473, and MS/24,320–501).

24 *Ibid.*

25 *Ibid.*

26 *Ibid.*

27 INAAVDF financial report in *Catholic Bulletin*, ix, no. 8 (1919), p. 412.

28 INAAVDF accounts (NLI, INAAVDF papers, MS/23,468–473, and MS/24,320–501).

29 *Ibid.*

30 INAAVDF financial report in *Catholic Bulletin*, ix no. 8 (1919), p. 424.

31 *Ibid.*

32 *Ibid.*

33 *Ibid.*

Chapter 7

1 RIC files Count and Countess Plunkett 15 Jan. 1917 (PRO, CO 213/359), p. 48.

2 *Ibid.*

3 Mrs J. McGuinness, invitation card to the meeting of the 'Irish

assembly' (ALD, miscellaneous files).

4   F.S.L. Lyons, *Ireland Since the Famine*, p. 389.

5   Michael Laffan, *The Resurrection of Ireland, The Sinn Féin Party 1916–1923*, p. 93.

6   Arthur Mitchell & Pádraig Ó Snodaigh (eds), *Irish Political Documents 1916–1948*, p. 32.

7   Minute book a conference of Women Delegates to the all Ireland Conference (WDIC), 12 May 1917 (NLI MS 21 194 /47).

8   *Ibid.*

9   *Ibid.*

10   *Ibid.*

11   *Ibid.*

12   Áine Ceannt witness statement (MA BMH, WS 264), p. 51.

13   *Ibid.*

14   Esther Roper, *Prison Letters of Countess Markievicz*, p. 137.

15   John MacDonagh, invitation to reception at the Mansion House, June 1917 (NLI, INAAVDF papers, MS 24 352).

16   Minute book WDIC, 23 July 1917.

17   Oliver Snoddy, 'Three by-elections of 1917', p. 343.

18   Pádraig O'Keeffe letter to Eamon de Valera (MA BMH, WS 1725).

19   *Ibid.*

20   RIC police report, 24 July 1917 (PRO, CO 904/23).

21   *Ibid.*, 15 September 1917 (PRO, CO 904/23).

22   *Daily Mail*, 1 October 1917.

23   Minute book WDIC, 23 July 1917.

24   *Ibid.*

25   *Ibid.*, 25 September 1917.

26   *Ibid.*, 2 October 1917.

27   *Ibid.*, 25 September 1917.

28   *Ibid.*, 16 October 1917.

29   Cumann na mBan convention report, 28/29 September 1918 (UCDAD, Humphreys papers, p106/1128), p. 1.

30   RIC police Files Proceedings of the Sinn Féin Convention (hereafter

Sinn Féin Convention), 25/26 October 1917 (PRO, CO 904/23), pp. 7–8.

31   *Ibid.*

32   *Ibid.*

33   *Ibid.*

34   *Ibid.*, p. 19.

35   Patrick O'Keeffe witness statement (MA BMH, WS 1275).

36   RIC police files, Sinn Féin Convention, 25/26 October 1917 (PRO, CO 904/23), p. 21.

37   *Ibid.*

38   *Ibid.*, p. 22.

39   *Ibid.* The term 'will be under the bed' refers to a colloquial expression for cowardice that came into use after the rebellion in 1916, and it origins can be traced to families living in the centre of the chaos of the conflict who placed their children under their beds to protect them from gunfire.

40   *Ibid.*

41   *Ibid.*, p. 23.

42   *Ibid.*, p. 24.

43   *Ibid.*

44   *Ibid.*

45   *Ibid.*, p. 25.

46   *Ibid.*, p. 26.

47   *Ibid.*

48   Minute book WDIC, 17 September 1917.

49   Sinn Féin Convention, 25/26 October 1917 (PRO, CO 904/23), p. 28.

50   *Ibid.*, p. 75.

51   *Ibid.*, p. 77.

52   *Ibid.*, p. 33.

53   *Ibid.*, pp. 36–7.

54   *Ibid.*, p. 33.

55   *Ibid.*, p. 35–6 .

56   *Ibid.*

57 *Ibid.*, p. 37.

58 *Ibid.*

59 Kathleen Clarke, *Revolutionary Woman*, p. 148.

60 Áine Ceannt witness statement (MA BMH, WS 264), p. 32.

61 Sinn Féin Convention, 25/26 October 1917 (PRO, CO 904/23), p. 75.

62 *Ibid.*, p. 43.

63 *Ibid.*

64 *Ibid.*

65 *Ibid.*, pp. 43–4.

66 *Ibid.*

67 Ernie O'Malley, *On Another Man's Wound*, p. 63.

68 Minute book WDIC, 29 October 1917.

69 *Ibid.*

70 *Ibid.*

71 *Ibid.*, 27 November 1917 (NLI, MS 21 194 /47).

72 *Ibid.*

73 Ernie O'Malley, *On Another Man's Wound*, p. 63.

74 Áine Ceannt witness statement (MA BMH, WS 264), p. 52.

75 Minute book WDIC, 15 January 1918.

76 Áine Ceannt witness statement (MA BMH, WS 264), p. 52.

CHAPTER 8

1 RIC Police files, Sinn Féin, Circular, February 1918 (PRO, CO Papers, CO 904/207–256), p. 1.

2 *Ibid.*

3 *Ibid.*

4 *Ibid.*

5 *Ibid.*, p. 4.

6 *Ibid.*, pp. 1–2.

7 Municipal Council of the City of Dublin, minutes, 12 March 1918 (DCA, Minute Book 44), p. 53.

8   Diarmaid Ferriter, *Lovers of Liberty*, pp. 28–9.

9   Municipal Council of the City of Dublin, minutes, 12 March 1918 (DCA, Minute Book 44), p. 53.

10   *Ibid.*

11   *Ibid.*

12   Minute book WDIC, 26 February 1918.

13   *Ibid.*

14   Génna Fiodoyne was some kind of cultural nationalist organisation, but I cannot find any more information about them.

15   Irish Society for the Combating of the Spread of Venereal Disease (ISCVD), St Ultans Hospital committee minute book 1, 10 April 1918 (College of Physicians archive) (hereafter CPA, St Ultans Hospital committee).

16   *Ibid.*

17   Annual report, Women's National Health Association, 1921, p. 4.

18   *Ibid.*, p. 26.

19   Minute book WDIC, 26 March 1918.

20   *Ibid.*

21   *Ibid.*

22   *Irish Citizen*, 7 April 1918.

23   *Ibid.*

24   *Ibid.*

25   ISCVD minutes, 19 April 1918.

26   *Ibid.*

27   *Ibid.*

28   *Ibid.*

29   *Ibid.*

30   *Ibid,* May 1918.

31   *Ibid.*, 9 May 1918.

32   *Ibid.*, 13 May 1918.

33   *Ibid.*

34   *Ibid.*, 1 June 1918.

35   Arthur Mitchell & Pádraig Ó Snodaigh (eds),*Irish Political Documents*

1916–1948, pp. 41–2.

36 *Ibid.*

37 F.S.L. Lyons, *Ireland since the Famine*, p. 396.

38 Kathleen Lynn witness statement (MA BMH, WS 357), p. 5.

39 RIC police report, Kathleen Lynn, 17 May 1918 (PRO, CO 904/207–238).

40 Sinn Féin Funds case, 20 May 1918 (NAI, book 119), p. 33.

41 Cumann na mBan convention, 28/29 September 1918 (UCDAD, Humphreys papers, p106/1128), p. 5.

42 Alice Stopford Green, Municipal Council Dublin, minutes (DCA, p 326).

43 Nancy Wyse Power witness statement (MA BMH, WS 732), p. 5.

44 *Ibid.*

45 *Ibid.*

46 *Ibid.*

47 Eithne Coyle memoir (UCDAD, Coyle papers, p61/2 (2)), p. 6.

48 *Ibid.*

49 *The Gaelic American*, 13 July 1918.

50 *Ibid.*

51 Sinn Féin Funds case, 23 May 1918 (NAI, book 119), p. 37.

52 Máire Comerford memoir, 'Dangerous Ground' (UCDAD, Máire Comerford papers, LA18).

53 Madeleine Ffrench Mullen to Hanna Sheehy Skeffington, 27 August 1918 (NLI, Sheehy Skeffington papers, MS 22,682).

54 CPIVD minutes, 11 July 1918.

55 Letter from Madeleine Ffrench Mullen to Hanna Sheehy Skeffington, 27 August 1918 (NLI, MS 22,682).

56 *Ibid.*

57 CPIVD minutes, 5 September 1918.

58 RIC Police files, Letter Joseph Flood town clerk to Edward Shortt, Chief Secretary for Ireland, 28 October 1918 (PRO, CO 904/207–238).

59 RIC Police files, Dr Charles Cameron to Edward Shortt, 31 October

1918 (PRO, CO 904/207–238).

60 *Ibid.*

61 Sinn Féin Ard Fheis, 1918 (PRO, CO 904/203).

62 *Ibid.*

63 CPIVD minutes, 26 September 1918.

64 Kathleen Lynn witness statement (MA BMH, WS 357), p. 6.

65 CPIVD minutes, 7 November 1918.

66 Kathleen Lynn witness statement (MA BMH, WS 357), p. 6.

67 CPIVD minutes, 9 November 1918.

68 Kathleen Clarke, *Revolutionary Woman*, pp. 160–1.

69 *Ibid.*

70 Dublin Metropolitan Police (DMP) report, 14 April 1918 (PRO, CO 904/24).

71 Kathleen Clarke, *Revolutionary Woman*, p. 155.

72 *Ibid.*, pp. 155–6.

73 Holloway Prison, governor's report, 13 July 1918 (PRO, CO 904/209–208).

74 *Ibid.*, 20 August 1918 (PRO, CO 904/209–297).

75 *Ibid.*

76 *Ibid.*, 28 August 1918.

77 Esther Roper (ed.), *Prison Letters of Countess Markievicz*, p. 185.

78 *Ibid.*

79 Countess de Markievicz to Madge Daly, November 1918 (NUI Limerick, Madge Daly papers (henceforth cited Daly papers), box 1 folder 18).

80 Maud Gonne MacBride to British Home Office, 4 July 1918 (PRO, HO 144/1465).

81 Holloway Prison, governor's report, 6 July 1918 (PRO, CO 904/208).

82 *Ibid.*, 11 September 1918 (PRO, HO 144/1465).

83 *Ibid.*, 13 September 1918 (PRO, CO 904/208).

84 *Ibid.*, 14 September 1918 (PRO, CO 904/208).

85 *Ibid.*

86 *Ibid.*

87 Holloway Prison, governor's report, 24 September 1918 (PRO, CO 904/208).

88 *Ibid.*, 22 October 1918.

89 Holloway Prison, governor's report, medical report on Maud Gonne MacBride, 24 October 1918 (PRO, HO 144/1465).

90 *Ibid.*

91 *Daily News,* 10 November 1918, p. 2.

92 *Ibid.*

93 W. Sutcliffe, MD, Ipswich Sanatorium to F. Coutts, 8 November 1918 (PRO, CO 904/209–297).

94 Chief Secretary, Dublin Castle, Edward Shortt, 28 November 1918 (PRO, CO 904/208, 41241).

95 RIC police report, 10 July 1918 (PRO, CO 904/215–203).

96 *Ibid.*

97 *Ibid.*

98 RIC police report, 11 September 1918 (PRO, CO 904/215–408).

99 Nancy Wyse Power witness statement (MA BMH, WS 732), p. 5.

100 Cumann na mBan convention, 28/29 September 1918 (UCDAD, Humphreys papers, p106/1128), p. 2.

101 *Ibid.*

102 *Ibid.*

103 Eilís Bean Uí Chonaill (Ní Riain) witness statement (MA BMH, WS 568), p. 12.

104 *Ibid.*

105 Cumann na mBan convention, 28/29 September 1918 (UCDAD, Humphreys papers, p106/1128), p. 2.

106 *Ibid.*

107 *Ibid.*

108 Sinn Féin Árd Chomhairle first annual report 20 August 1918 (PRO. CO 904/203-172).

109 Robert Barton Contemporaneous Documents Bureau of Military History (MA CD 264.5.3–3.1).

110 Sinn Féin Funds case, 25 November 1918 (NAI, Book 119), p. 77.

111 Jennie Wyse Power 'The political influence of women in modern Ireland' in William G. Fitzgerald (ed.) *The Voice of Ireland*, p. 160.

CHAPTER 9

1   F.S.L. Lyons, *Ireland Since the Famine*, p. 400.

2   Arthur Mitchell & Pádraig Ó Snodaigh (eds), *Irish Political Documents 1916–1948*, pp. 55.

3   *Ibid.*

4   WDIC minute book, 30 January 1919.

5   *Ibid.*

6   Dáil Éireann, parliamentary debates, 1 April 1919 (http://www.oireachtas-debates.gov.ie).

7   *Ibid.*

8   *Ibid.*, 2 April 1919.

9   *Ibid.*, 10 April 1919.

10   *Weekly Observer*, 27 September 1919.

11   *Ibid.*

12   Eithne Coyle, personal memoir (undated) (UCDAD, Coyle papers, p61/4).

13   Ignatius Phayre, 'From the terror to the truce', in William G. Fitzgerald (ed.) *The Voice of Ireland*, p. 27.

14   John J. Splain, 'The Irish Movement in the United States since 1911', in William G. Fitzgerald (ed.) *The Voice of Ireland*, pp. 227–8.

15   John J. Splain, 'Under which King', in William G. Fitzgerald (ed.) *The Voice of Ireland*, p. 251.

16   *Ibid.*

17   Dáil Éireann, parliamentary debates, 10 April 1919 (http://www.oireachtas-debates.gov.ie).

18   *Ibid.*, 20 August 1919.

19   *Ibid.*

20   *Ibid.*

21 *Ibid.*

22 Esther Roper (ed.), *Prison Letters of Countess Markievicz*, pp. 223–4.

23 Report of General Prison Board of Ireland, 22 July 1919 (PRO, CO 904/209–297).

24 *Ibid.*

25 Countess de Markievicz to Madge Daly, June–September 1919 (Daly papers, box 1 folder 18).

26 RIC police report, 18 October 1920 (PRO, CO 904/209–297).

27 *Ibid.*

28 *Ibid.*

29 *Ibid.*

30 Nancy Wyse Power witness statement (MA BMH, WS 587), p. 13.

31 RIC police report, 18 October 1920 (PRO, CO 904/209–297).

32 *Ibid.*

33 *Ibid.*

34 D.J. Hickey, J.E. Doherty (eds), *A New Dictionary of Irish History from 1800*, p. 35.

35 J.J. Lee, *Ireland 1912–1985: Politics and Society*, p. 43.

36 Joost Augusteijn, *From Public Defiance to Guerrilla Warfare*, p. 124.

37 Eilís Bean Uí Chonaill (Ní Riain) witness statement (MA BMH, WS 568).

38 Annie Murphy, personal statement, undated (UCDAD, Coyle papers, p61/4 (62–64)).

39 Margaret Connory, report to the executive committee Irish White Cross, 2 June 1922 (MA, Dublin) .

40 Cumann na mBan convention report, 28 September 1918 (UCDAD, Humphreys papers p106/1128/1–(7)).

41 Sighle Hartnett, personal statement, undated (UCDAD, Coyle papers, p61/4 (85)).

42 Annie Murphy, personal statement, undated (UCDAD, Coyle papers, p61/4 (62–64)).

43 Charlotte Dempsey (née Heney), personal statement, undated (UCDAD, Coyle papers, p61/4 (22)).

44 Cumann na mBan convention report, 22 October 1921 (Kilmainham Gaol Museum), p. 3.

45 *Ibid.*

46 Margaret Broderick Nicholson witness statement (MA BMH, WS 1682), p. 4.

47 *Ibid.*

48 *Ibid.*

49 *Ibid.*

50 Joost Augusteijn, *From Public Defiance to Guerrilla Warfare*, p. 144.

51 John Healy, *Nineteen Acres*, p. 54.

52 RIC police Divisional Commissioner's report, Westmeath, 19 Oct. 1921 (CO 904/156a).

53 Esther Roper, *Prison Letters of Countess Markievicz*, p. 266.

54 Sinn Féin Funds case, 20 November 1919 (NAI Book 20), pp. 44–45.

55 F.S.L. Lyons, *Ireland since the Famine*, p. 407.

56 *Ibid.*

57 Minutes of the Municipal Council of the City of Dublin, 6 September 1920 (DCA, no. 44, p. 53).

58 *Ibid.*

59 John J. Splain, 'Under which King?', in William G. Fitzgerald (ed.) *The Voice of Ireland*, p. 252.

60 J. Anthony Gaughan (ed.), *Memoir: Senator James G. Douglas*, p. 169.

61 RIC police report, documents captured at Glenvar, 22 June 1921 (PRO, CO 904/23–7), p. 58.

62 *Ibid.*

63 J. Anthony Gaughan (ed.), *Memoir: Senator James G. Douglas*, p. 62

64 Bernadette Whelan, *United States Foreign Policy and Ireland*, p. 343.

65 Irish White Cross report (undated), p. 34.

66 J. Anthony Gaughan (ed.), *Memoir: Senator James G. Douglas*, p. 62.

67 Irish White Cross report (undated), p. 63.

68 *Ibid.*, p. 35.

69 *Ibid.*, p. 66.

70 *Ibid.*, p. 114.

71 J. Anthony Gaughan (ed.), *Memoir: Senator James G. Douglas,* p. 169.

72 RIC police report, documents captured at Glenvar, 22 June 1921 (PRO, CO 904/23–7), p. 58.

73 Irish White Cross report (undated), p. 110.

74 *Ibid.*

75 *Ibid.*, p. 111.

76 *Ibid.*, p. 139.

77 Eilis Uí Chonaill (née Ní Riain) witness statement (MA BMH, WS 568), p. 55.

78 *Ibid.*

79 Lil Conlon, *Cumann na mBan and the Women of Ireland*, p. 178.

80 *Ibid.*

81 *Ibid.*

82 *Ibid.*

83 *Ibid.*

84 *Ibid.*

85 *Ibid.*, p. 230.

86 Sighle Rigney, personal statement, undated (UCDAD, Humphreys papers, pp. 106–1408).

87 Lil Conlon, *Cumann na mBan and the Women of Ireland*, p. 183.

88 Countess de Markievicz, court martial, 2 December 1920 (PRO, WO papers, WO/35–133), p. 237.

89 Sighle Rigney, personal statement, undated (UCDAD Humphreys papers, p106–1408).

90 *Ibid.*

91 *Ibid.*

92 *Ibid.*

93 *Ibid.*

94 *Ibid.*

95 *Ibid.*

CHAPTER 10

1   J.J. Lee, *Ireland 1912–1985*, p. 43.

2   House of Commons debates, 21 Feb. 1921 (vol. 18 cc624–73): www.parliment.uk/hansard.

3   American Commission on Conditions in Ireland, p. 86.

4   Hanna Sheehy Skeffington, Statement of Atrocities against Women (NLI ILB 330,) p. 3.

5   *Ibid.*

6   *Irish Exile*, April 1921.

7   Margaret K. Connory, report to the executive Irish White Cross, 4 June 1922 (MA), p. 1.

8   British Labour Party, Commission to Ireland (henceforth BLPCI) (London, 1921), p. 58.

9   *Ibid.*, p. 54.

10 *Ibid.*, p. 13.

11 *Ibid.*, p. 29.

12 Daniel J. Murphy, *The Journals of Lady Gregory*, books 1–29, pp. 196–7.

13 BLPCI, p. 29.

14 Hanna Sheehy Skeffington, Statement on Atrocities against Women in Ireland (NLI ILB 300), p. 3.

15 *Ibid.*

16 Fintan Murphy, Bureau Military History (MA, CD 227/29/2).

17 *Ibid.*

18 *Ibid.*

19 BLPCI, p. 19.

20 Hanna Sheehy Skeffington, Statement on Atrocities against Women in Ireland (NLI ILB 300), p. 3.

21 BLPCI, p. 80.

22 *Ibid.*

23 *Ibid.*

24 *Ibid.*

25 *Ibid.*, p. 81.

26 *Ibid.*; Oscar Traynor Collection (MA, CD 120/1/4).

27 *Ibid.*

28 BLPCI, p. 80.

29 *Ibid.*, p. 81.

30 DMP reports, Oscar Traynor Collection, Bureau of Military History CD 120/1–4.

31 The terror in Ireland, 1919–1921 (pamphlet, NLI Ir. 94109), p. 34.

32 Richard Willis & John Bolster (BMH contemporaneous documents, CD 240/1/1).

33 *Ibid.*

34 *Irish Exile*, July 1921.

35 *Ibid.*

36 *Ibid.*

37 Margaret K. Connory, report to the executive IWC (MA, Dublin).

38 *Ibid.*

39 *Ibid.*

40 Hanna Sheehy Skeffington, Statement on Atrocities against Women in Ireland (NLI ILB 300), p. 3.

41 *Ibid.*

42 RIC police report, documents captured at Glenvar, 22 June 1921 (PRO, CO 904/23), p. 5.

43 WDIC, leaflet in minute book, undated (NLI, MS 21 194 /47) .

44 RIC police report, documents captured at Glenvar, 22 June 1921 (PRO, CO 904/23), p. 29.

45 *Ibid.*, p. 31.

46 *Ibid.*

CHAPTER 11

1 Rossa F. Downing, 'Men, women, and memories' in William G. Fitzgerald (ed.), *The Voice of Ireland*, p. 221.

2 RIC police report, documents captured at Glenvar, 22 June 1921 (PRO, CO 904–23), p. 57.

3   Rossa F. Downing, 'Men, women, and memories' in William G. Fitzgerald (ed.), *The Voice of Ireland*, p. 221.

4   RIC police report, documents captured at Glenvar, 22 June 1921 (PRO, CO papers CO 904/23), p. 75.

5   Seán Harling witness statement (MA BMH, WS 935), p. 7.

6   *Ibid.*

7   RIC police report, 22 June 1921 (PRO, CO 904–23).

8   Seán Harling witness statement (MA BMH, WS 935), p. 7.

9   *Ibid.*

10 *Ibid.*, p. 8.

11 Dáil Éireann, official correspondence relating to the peace negotiations June–September 1921 (Dublin, 1921), p. 4.

12 *Ibid.*

13 Irish White Cross report (undated), p. 60.

14 *Ibid.*

15 Jennie Wyse Power to Nancy Wyse Power, 9 October 1921 (UCDAD, Humphreys papers, p106/726).

16 *Ibid.*

17 Michael Laffan, *The Resurrection of Ireland*, p. 346.

18 *Ibid.*, p. 347.

19 *Ibid.*

20 Jennie Wyse Power to Nancy Wyse Power, 9 October 1921 (UCDAD, Humphreys papers, p106/726).

21 Cumann na mBan report, annual convention, 22–23 October 1921 (Kilmainham Gaol Museum), p. 2.

22 *Ibid.*, p. 1.

23 *Ibid.*, pp. 1–2.

24 Sinn Féin Funds case, 15 November 1921 (NAI Book 20), p. 97.

25 RIC police report, 31 July 1921 (PRO, CO 904/24).

26 *Ibid.*

27 Jennie Wyse Power to Nancy Wyse Power, 7 December 1921 (UCDAD, Humphreys papers, p106/734).

28 *Ibid*, 11 December 1921 (UCDAD, Humphreys papers, p106/735).

29 *Ibid.*

30 *Ibid.*

31 *Ibid.*

32 *Ibid.*

33 Fionán Lynch, Dáil Éireann parliamentary debates, 20 December 1921 (www.oireachtas-debates.gov.ie).

34 Kathleen O'Callaghan, Dáil Éireann parliamentary debates, 20 December 1921.

35 *Ibid.*

36 *Ibid.*

37 *Ibid.*

38 Mary MacSwiney, Dáil Éireann parliamentary debates, 21 December 1921.

39 *Ibid.*

40 *Ibid.*

41 *Ibid.*

42 F.S.L. Lyons, *Ireland since the Famine*, p. 442.

43 J.J. Lee, *Ireland 1912–1985*, p. 51.

44 *Ibid.*

45 Mary MacSwiney, Dáil Éireann parliamentary debates, 21 December 1921.

46 *Ibid.*

47 *Ibid.*

48 *Ibid.*

49 Michael Colivet, Dáil Éireann parliamentary debates, 21 December 1921.

50 Jennie Wyse Power to Nancy Wyse Power, 22 December 1921 (UCDAD, Humphreys papers, p106/736).

51 *Ibid.*

52 *Ibid.*

53 Kathleen Clarke, Dáil Éireann parliamentary debates, 22 December 1921.

54 *Ibid.*

55 *Ibid.*

56 Jennie Wyse Power to Nancy Wyse Power, 22 December 1921 (UCDAD, Humphreys papers, p106/736).

57 Countess de Markievicz, Dáil Éireann parliamentary debates, 3 January 1922.

58 *Ibid.*

59 *Ibid.*

60 *Ibid.*

61 *Ibid.*

62 *Ibid.*

63 *Ibid.*

64 Michael Collins, Dáil Éireann parliamentary debates, 3 January 1922.

65 Margaret Pearse, Dáil Éireann parliamentary debates, 4 January 1922.

66 *Ibid.*

67 *Ibid.*

68 *Ibid.*

69 Letter from Jennie Wyse Power to Nancy Wyse Power, 7 January 1922 (UCDAD, Humphreys 106/721/937).

70 *Ibid.*, 12 February 1922 (UCDAD, Humphreys 106/721/721).

CHAPTER 12

1 *Poblacht na hÉireann*, 3 January 1922.

2 *Ibid.*, 17 January 1922.

3 Peter Pyne, 'The third Sinn Féin party 1923–1926', in *Economic and Social Review*, vol. 1, no. 1 (1969), pp. 29–30.

4 Sinn Féin Funds case, 17 January 1922 (NAI Book 20), p. 101.

5 *Ibid.*, p. 104.

6 *Ibid.*

7 *Cumann na Poblachta*, leaflet, 19 January 1922 (UCDAD, MacSwiney papers, 48/a (38) (3)).

8   Letter from Jennie Wyse Power to Nancy Wyse Power, 15 January 1922 (UCDAD, Humphreys papers, p106/740).

9   Letter from Seán T. O'Kelly to Sinn Féin membership, 19 January 1922 (UCDAD, MacSwiney papers, 48/a (38) (4)).

10 *Poblacht na hÉireann*, 22 March 1922.

11 F.S.L. Lyons, *Ireland since the Famine*, pp. 353–4.

12 Letter from Jennie Wyse Power, to Nancy Wyse Power, 24 February 1922 (UCDAD, Humphreys papers, p106/744).

13 *Ibid.*, 8 January 1922 (UCDAD, Humphreys papers, p106/738). The plan to send de Markievicz to the USA was set in motion in early January by the anti-Treaty faction before they formed Cumann na Poblachta.

14 J.J. Ó Ceallaigh (Sceilg), 23 April 1948 (NAI, SFFC papers, 2b/82/118, book 39), p. 6.

15 *Ibid.*

16 Letter from Jennie Wyse Power to Nancy Wyse Power, 15 January 1922 (UCDAD, Humphreys papers, p106/740).

17 *Ibid.*

18 Mary MacSwiney to Cumann na mBan in Cork, 15 January 1922 (UCDAD, MacSwiney papers p48a/38 (1)).

19 Jennie Wyse Power to Nancy Wyse Power, 29 January 1922 (UCDAD, Humphreys papers, p106/742).

20 Mary MacSwiney to Cumann na mBan in Cork, 15 January 1922 (UCDAD, MacSwiney papers p48a/38 (1)).

21 *Ibid.*

22 *Cork Examiner*, 31 January 1922.

23 *Ibid.*

24 *Ibid.*, 2 February 1922.

25 *Ibid.*, 5 February 1922.

26 *Ibid.*, 3 February 1922.

27 *Irish Independent*, 6 February 1922.

28 Florence O'Donoghue, *No Other Law*, p. 231.

29 F.S.L. Lyons, *Ireland since the Famine*, p. 455.

30 Jennie Wyse Power to Nancy Wyse Power, 7 February 1922 (UCDAD, Humphreys papers, p106/743).

31 *Ibid.*

32 *The Irish Times*, 6 February 1922; *Irish Independent*, 6 Feb. 1922.

33 *Irish Independent*, 6 Feb. 1922.

34 *Ibid.*

35 *The Irish Times*, 6 February 1922.

36 *Ibid.*

37 *Ibid.*

38 *Ibid.*

39 *Ibid.*

40 *Irish Independent*, 6 February 1922.

41 *Ibid.*

42 *Ibid.*

43 Cumann na mBan, captured documents, 7 February 1923 (MA, Captured Papers, lot no 51).

44 *The Irish Times*, 6 February 1922.

45 Jennie Wyse Power, 'The political influence of Women in Ireland' in William G. Fitzgerald (ed.), *The Voice of Ireland*, p. 161.

46 *Ibid.*

47 *The Irish Times*, 6 February 1922.

48 Lil Conlon, *Cumann na mBan and the Women of Ireland*, pp. 267–8.

49 *Ibid.*

50 Cumann na Saoirse, CID notes, undated (MA, Captured Papers, lot 223).

51 Cumann na Saoirse, 20 July 1922 (NAI, Dept of Taoiseach files, S1–575).

52 *Cork Examiner*, 6 March 1922.

53 *Ibid.*

54 Mary MacSwiney to executive Cumann na mBan, 12 March 1922 (UCDAD, MacSwiney papers, 48/a (9)).

55 *Ibid.*

56 *Ibid.*

57 *Ibid.*

58 Sinn Féin Funds case, 3 March 1922 (NAI, Book 20), p. 108.

59 Jennie Wyse Power to Nancy Wyse Power, 24 February 1922 (UCDAD, Humphreys papers, p106/744).

60 *Ibid.*

61 *Ibid.*

62 *Poblacht na hÉireann*, 22 March 1922.

63 Florence O'Donoghue, *No Other Law*, p. 224–5.

64 *Ibid.*

65 Cumann na mBan newspaper, *Cumann na mBan*, May 1922.

BIBLIOGRAPHY

PRIMARY SOURCES

MANUSCRIPTS AND PAPERS

Cork
Cork Archives Institute: Siobhán Lankford papers

Dublin
Allen Library: Kathleen Lynn papers; Elizabeth O'Farrell papers
College of Physicians: Kathleen Lynn papers
Dáil Éireann: Official Correspondence Relating to the Peace
　　Negotiations, June–September 1921
Kilmainham Gaol Museum: Civil War female prisoner autograph
　　books; Helena Molony papers

Military Archives
Bureau of Military History papers
Captured papers collection
Con Costello papers
Civil War general internment ledgers
Civil War internment location ledgers
Civil War prison parcels ledgers
Free State Ceremonial Commemorations papers

National Archives
Dáil Éireann cabinet papers
Sinn Féin papers
1901 Census household returns
1911 Census household returns
Wills

National Library

Hanna Sheehy Skeffington papers

Irish National Aid Association

Irish National Aid Association Volunteer and Dependents' fund

Irish National Aid Volunteer Dependants' fund

Chrissie O'Reilly papers

Republican Pamphlets collection

Royal Commission, The conditions of women's work in Ireland 1893-
  1894

WDIC and Cumann na dTeachtaire minute book

Society of Friends Archive

Senator James G.Douglas papers

University College Dublin, Archive Department

Elizabeth Bloxham papers

Marie Comerford papers

Eithne Coyle O'Donnell papers

Fianna Fáil archive

Sheila Humphreys O'Donovan papers

Seán McEntee papers

Mary MacSwiney papers

Limerick University Library

Madge Daly Papers

London, Public Record Office

British army records

Colonial Office papers for Ireland (CO)

Home Office papers for Ireland (HO)

Register of births deaths and marriages

Somerset House wills and probate

War Office papers for Ireland (WO)

SECONDARY SOURCES

Abbott, Richard, *Police Casualties in Ireland 1919–1921* (Mercier Press, Cork, 2000)

Aberdeen, Lord and Lady, *We Twa*, Vol. 2 (W. Collins and Sons, London, 1925)

Andrews, C.S., *Dublin made me: an autobiography* (Mercier, Cork, 1979)

Augusteijn, Joost, *From Public Defiance to Guerrilla Warfare* (Irish Academic Press, Dublin, 1996)

Balliett, Conrad A., 'The Lives – and Lies – of Maud Gonne', *Eire-Ireland*, vol. 14, no. 3, Autumn 1979

Barlett, Thomas, & Keith, Jeffery, *A Military History of Ireland* (Cambridge University Press, 1996)

Barton, Brian, *From behind a closed door: secret court martial records of the Easter Rising* (Blackstaff Press, Belfast, 2002)

Beckett J.C., *The Making of Modern Ireland* (Faber, London, 1966)

Behan, Kathleen, *Mother of all the Behans* (Poolbeg, Dublin, 1984)

Berresford Ellis, P., *A History of the Irish Working Class* (Victor Gollancz, London, 1972)

Bigallet, Fanny, 'Saint Ultan's Hospital: The first decade 1919–1932' (unpublished MA National University Ireland Maynooth, 1998)

Bock, Gisela, 'Women's history and gender history, aspects of an international debate', *Gender & History* I (1989), pp. 7–30

Bourke, Marcus, *John O'Leary: a study in Irish Separatism* (Anvil Books, Kerry, 1967)

Bowen, Elizabeth, *History of the Shelbourne Hotel* (Harrap, London, 1951)

Bowyer Bell, J., *The secret army: a history of the IRA 1916–1970* (Sphere Books, London, 1972)

Boylan, Henry, *A dictionary of Irish biography* (3rd ed., Gill & Macmillan, Dublin, 1998)

Breathnach, Eileen, 'Women in Higher education 1879–1914', *Crane Bag*, iv (1980), pp. 47–54

Brennan, John, *The years flew by: recollections of Sydney Gifford Czira* (Arlen House, Galway, 1974)

Brennan, Patricia, 'Inghinidhe na hÉireann and nationalism in the Irish Dramatic Movement' (unpublished thesis University College Dublin, 1974)

Byrne, Patrick, *The Irish Republican Congress revisited* (Dublin, 1993)

Cardozo, Nancy, *Lucky Eyes and a High Heart: the Life of Maud Gonne* (Bobbs-Merril, New York, 1978)

Caulfield, Max, *The Easter Rebellion* (Gill & Macmillan, Dublin, 1995)

Ceannt, Áine, *The story of the White Cross* (Three Candles, Dublin, 1948)

Clarke, Kathleen, *Revolutionary Woman: An autobiography 1878–1972* (O'Brien Press, Dublin, 1991)

Clarke, Pyne Olga, *She came of decent people* (Pelham Books, London, 1985)

Collis Ramsey, Dr, *In Castle and Court House* (T. Werner Laurie, London, undated)

Colum, Mary, *Life and the dream* (Dolmen Press, Dublin, 1966)

Conditions in Ireland Interim report (American Commission on Conditions in Ireland, New York, 1921)

Conlon, Lil, *Cumann na mBan and the women of Ireland* (Kilkenny people, Kilkenny, 1969)

Connolly Heron, Ina, 'James Connolly', *Liberty* (Mar. 1966-Oct. 1966)

Connolly, Nora, *Unbroken Tradition* (Boni & Liveright, New York, 1918)

Constantine, Stephen, Kirby, Maurice W. & Rose, Mary B. (eds), *The First World War in British History* (Edward Arnold, London, 1995)

Coolahan, John, *Irish Education: history and structure* (Institute of Public Administration, Dublin, 1981)

Coogan, Tim Pat, *Michael Collins* (Arrow, London, 1990)

— *De Valera: Long Fellow, Long shadow* (Hutchinson, London, 1993)

Coxhead, Elizabeth, *Lady Gregory: a literary portrait* (Macmillan & Company, London, 1961)

— *Daughters of Erin* (Colin Smyth, London, 1979)

Cronin, Seán, *The McGarrity papers* (Clann na Gael, Kerry, 1973)

— *Frank Ryan: the search for the Republic* (Repsol Publishing, Dublin, 1980)

Cullen, Mary (ed.), *Girls don't do Honours: Irish Women in Education in the*

19th and 20th Century (Women's Education Bureau, Dublin, 1987)

Czira, Sydney Gifford, *The Years Flew By: the recollections of Madame Sydney Czira* (Gifford and Craven, Dublin, 1974)

Daly, Mary, E., 'The Interaction between economics and ideology' in *Journal of Women's History*, xi (Winter/Spring 1995), pp. 101–115

— 'Women in the Irish workforce from pre-industrial to modern times' in *Saothar* 7 (1983), pp. 74–81

de Burca, Séamus, 'Growing up in Dublin' in *Dublin Historical Record*, xxix (Dec. 1975–Sept. 1976), pp. 82–99

de Markievicz Constance, *What Republicans stand for* (Forward, Glasgow, 1923)

— *Women ideals and the nation* (Bean na hÉireann, Dublin, 1909)

Dillon, Geraldine Plunkett, *All in the blood: A memoir of the Plunkett family, the 1916 Rising and the War of Independence* (edited by Honor O'Brolchain, A&A Farmar, Dublin, 2006)

Dirrane, Brigid, *A Woman of Aran* (Blackwater Press, Dublin 1997)

Dooley, Terence, *The Decline of the Big House in Ireland* (Wolfhound Press, Dublin, 2001)

Dunlevy, Mairead, *Dress in Ireland: a history* (Collins Press, Cork, 1999)

Dunphy, Richard, 'Review article: Gender and sexuality in Ireland', *Irish Historical Studies* xxvi (Nov. 1999), pp. 549–557

English, Richard, *Prisoners: the civil war letters of Ernie O'Malley* (Dublin, 1991)

Fanning, Ronan (ed.), *Documents on Irish Foreign Policy*, Vol. 1 (Dublin, 1998)

Farmar, Tony, *Ordinary Lives: the private lives of three generations of Ireland's professional classes* (Gill & Macmillan, Dublin, 1995)

Ferriter, Diarmaid, *'Lovers of Liberty?' Local government in twentieth century Ireland* (National Archives of Ireland, Dublin, 2001)

Fingall Countess, *Seventy Years Young* (Lilliput Press, Dublin, 1995)

Fitzgerald, William G. (ed.), *The Voice of Ireland, A Memoir of Freedom's day by its foremost leader* (Virtue and Company London 1925)

Fitzpatrick, David, *Politics and Irish Life 1913–1921, provincial experience of war and revolution* (Cork University Press, Cork, 1998)

— *Harry Boland's Irish Revolution* (Cork University Press, Cork, 2003)

Fitzsimon, Christopher, 'The Dublin Theatre: during the years leading up to the opening of the Abbey Theatre' in *Dublin Historical Record*, xxix (Dec. 1975–Sept. 1976), pp. 83–99

Fortescue, J.W., *History of the 17th Lancers* (Macmillan & Co., London, 1895)

Foster, R.F., *W.B. Yeats: A life* (Oxford University Press, New York, 1997)

Fox, R.M., *Green Banners: the story of the Irish Struggle* (Secker & Warburg, London, 1938)

— *Rebel Irishwomen* (Talbot Press, Dublin, 1938)

— *History of the Irish Citizen Army* (Duffy, Dublin, 1943)

— *Louie Bennet: Her Life and Times* (Talbot Press, Dublin, 1957)

Frazier, Adrian, *Behind the scenes: Yeats, Horniman and the struggle for the Abbey Theatre* (University of California Press, 1990)

Gallagher, Michael (ed.), *Irish Elections 1922–44* (PASI, Limerick, 1993)

Gaughan, Anthony A.J. (ed.), *Memoir: Senator James G. Douglas* (UCD Press, Dublin, 1998)

Gilmore, George, *Labour and the Republican Movement* (Dublin, 1966)

Glenavy, Lady Beatrice, *Today We Will Only Gossip* (Constable, London, 1964)

Good, Joe, *Enchanted by Dreams* (Brandon, 1996)

Gordon, Lady Edith, *The Winds of Time* (John Murray, London, 1934)

Graef, Hilda, *A History of Doctrine and Devotion* (Sheed & Ward, New York, 1965)

Greaves, C. Desmond, *Liam Mellows and the Irish Revolution* (Lawrence & Wishart, London, 1971)

— *The Life and Times of James Connolly* (Lawrence & Wishart, London, 1986)

Grennan, Julia, 'Account of Easter week, undated' in *Catholic Bulletin*, vii, no. 6 (April 1917)

— 'Julia Grennan's story of the surrender', *The Catholic Bulletin*, vii (June 1917), pp. 396–398

Griffin, Susan, *The Book of Courtesans* (Broadway Books, New York, 2001)

Hamilton, Mary, *The Silver Road* (Alcuin Press, London, 1947)

Hart, Peter, *The IRA and its Enemies* (Clarendon Press, Oxford, 1998)

Haverty, Anne, *Constance Markievicz: Irish Revolutionary* (Pandora, London, 1988)

Hayes, Alan & Urguart Diane (eds), *Irish Women's History Reader* (Irish Academic Press, London, 2001)

Healy, John, *Nineteen Acres* (Kenny's Bookshop, Galway, 1978)

Hearn, Mona, *Below Stairs: Domestic Service Remembered in Dublin and Beyond 1880–1922* (Lilliput Press, Dublin, 1993)

Hickman, Katie, *Courtesans: Money, Sex and Fame in the Nineteenth Century* (Perennial, London, 2003)

Hickey, D.J. & Doherty, J.E., *A New Dictionary of Irish History from 1800* (Gill & Macmillan, Dublin, 2003)

Hill, Myrtle, *Women in Ireland: A Century of Change* (Blackstaff, Belfast, 2003)

Hobson, Bulmer, *Ireland yesterday and today* (Anvil Books, Kerry, 1968)

Hogan, R. & Kilroy, J., *The Abbey Theatre: the Years of Synge 1905–1909* (Colin Smyth, Dublin, 1978)

Hogan, Robert, & O'Neill Michael J. (eds), *Joseph Holloway: a Selection from his Unpublished Journal Impressions of a Dublin Playgoer* (South Illinois University Press, 1967)

Holmes, Janice & Urguart, Diane (eds), *Coming into the light: the work politics and religion of women in Ulster 1840–1940* (The Institute of Studies Belfast, 1994)

Hopkinson, Michael, *The Irish War of Independence* (Gill & Macmillan, Dublin, 2002)

Hunt, Hugh, *The Abbey: Ireland's National Theatre 1904–1979* (Gill & Macmillan, Dublin, 1979)

INAAVDF, 'Report of the Irish National Aid and Volunteer Dependents' Fund', *The Catholic Bulletin*, ix (August 1919), pp. 410–436

Irish White Cross, *Irish White Cross report* (Dublin, 1922)

Johnson, Turner Sheila, *Alice: a life of Alice Milligan* (Colourpoint Press, Omagh, 1994)

Jones, Greta & Malcolm, Elizabeth, *Medicine Disease and the State in Ireland 1650–1940* (Cork University Press, Cork, 1999)

Jones, Mary (ed.), *These Obstreperous Lassies: a history of the Irish Women Workers' Union* (Gill & Macmillan, Dublin, 1988)

Jordan, Anthony J., *Willie Yeats and the Gonne-MacBrides* (self published, Dublin, 1997)

Keane, Maureen, *Ishbel, Lady Aberdeen in Ireland* (Colourpoint, Newtownards, 1999)

Keogh, Dermot, *Twentieth-Century Ireland: Nation and State* (Gill & Macmillan, Dublin, 1994)

Kerryman, the, *Dublin's Fighting story 1913–21* (Kerry, undated)

Kerryman, the, *Limerick's Fighting story 1913–21* (Kerry, undated)

Kiberd, Declan (ed.), *1916 Rebellion Handbook* (Mourne River Press, Dublin, 1998)

Knirck, Jason, *Women of the Dáil: Gender, Republicanism and the Anglo-Irish Treaty* (Irish Academic Press, Dublin, 2006)

— 'Ghosts and Realities: Female TDs and the Treaty debate' in *Éire-Ireland*, xxxii (1996), pp. 170–190

Laffan, Michael, *The Resurrection of Ireland: The Sinn Féin Party 1916–1923* (Cambridge University Press, Cambridge, 1999)

Lane, Fintan, *The Origins of Modern Irish Socialism 1881–1896* (Cork University Press, 1997)

Lankford Siobhán, *The Hope and the Sadness* (Tower Books, Cork, 1980)

Ledger, Sally & Luckhurst, Roger, *The fin de siecle: A reader in cultural history 1880–1900* (Oxford University Press, Oxford, 2000)

Lee, J.J., *Ireland 1912–1985: Politics and Society* (Cambridge University Press, Cambridge, 1989)

Lehne, Sylke, 'Fenianism – A Male Business: a case study of Mary Jane O'Donovan Rossa 1845–1916' (unpublished MA thesis, National University Ireland Maynooth, 1995)

Lerner, Gerda, *Why History Matters: Life and Thought* (Oxford University Press, Oxford, 1998)

Levenson, Leah & Natterstad, Jerry H., *Hanna Sheehy Skeffington, Irish Feminist* (Syracuse University Press, New York, 1986)

Levenson, Samuel, *Maud Gonne: a biography of Yeats' beloved* (Cassell, London, New York, 1977)

Lewis, Gifford, *Eva Gore Booth and Esther Roper: a biography* (Pandora,

London, 1988)

Liddington, Jill & Norris, Jill, *One hand tied behind us: Rise of the women's suffrage movement* (2nd edition, Duckworth, London, 2000)

Luddy, Maria, *Women in Ireland 1800–1918* (Cork University Press, Cork, 1995)

Luddy, Maria & Murphy, Cliona (eds), *Women surviving* (Poolbeg, Dublin, 1990)

Lurie, Alison, *The Language of Clothes* (with illustrations assembled by Doris Palca, Bloomsbury, London, 1992)

Lynch, Diarmuid, (edited by Florence O'Donoghue) *The IRB and the 1916 Insurrection* (Mercier Press, Cork, 1957)

Lyons, F.S.L., *Ireland since the Famine* (Revised edition, Collins/Fontana, London, 1982)

Lyons, J.B., *Brief lives of Irish doctors* (Blackwater Press, Dublin, 1978)

Macardle, Dorothy, *The Irish Republic* (Corgi Books, London, 1968)

— *Tragedies of Kerry* (Kerry, undated)

MacBride, Maud Gonne, *A servant of the Queen: Her own story* (Golden Eagle books, Dublin, 1938)

MacBride White, Anna & Jeffares, Norman (eds), *The Gonne–Yeats letters 1893–1938* (Hutchinson, London, 1992)

MacThomáis, Éamonn, *Down Dublin Streets 1916* (Dublin, 1965)

Maguire, Martin, *Servants to the public: A history of local government and public services union 1901–1990* (Institute of Public Administration, Dublin, 1998)

Maher, Michael (ed.), *Irish Spirituality* (Veritas Publications, Dublin, 1981)

Marreco, Anne, *The Rebel Countess: The life and times of Constance Markievicz* (Corgi Books, London, 1967)

Martin, F.X. (ed.), *The Irish Volunteers: recollections and documents 1913–1919 Dublin* (Duffy, Dublin, 1963)

— (ed.), *The Howth gun running 1914* (Brown & Nolan, Dublin, 1964)

— *Leaders and men of the Easter Rising* (Methuen, London, 1967)

Maume, Patrick, *The Long Gestation: Irish Nationalist life 1891–1918* (Gill Macmillan, Dublin 1999)

Maye, Brian, *Arthur Griffith* (Griffith College Publications, Dublin,

1997)

McCann, Jack, 'Margaret Dobbs' in *The Glynns*, vol ii, (1983), pp. 41–46

McCarthy, Cal, *Cumann na mBan and the Irish Revolution* (Collins Press, Cork, 2007)

McCarthy, M.J.F., *Five years in Ireland* (Hodges & Figgis, London, 1901)

McCoole Sinead, *Guns and Chiffon* (Government publications, Stationary Office Dublin 1997)

— *Hazel Lavery: a life 1880–1935* (Lilliput Press, Dublin, 1996)

— *No Ordinary Women: Irish female Activists in the Revolutionary years 1900–1923* (O'Brien Press, Dublin 2003)

McCracken, Donal P., *MacBride's Brigade: Irish commandos in the Anglo-Boer War* (Four Courts Press, Dublin, 1999)

McDowell, R.B., *Alice Stopford Green: a passionate historian* (Allen Figgis & Co., Dublin, 1967)

McHugh, Roger (ed.), *Dublin 1916* (Arlington Books, London, 1966)

Merriman, John, *A History of Modern Europe* (2 vols) (W.W. Norton & Company, London, 1996)

Mikhail, E.H. (ed.), *The Abbey Theatre: interviews and recollections* (Macmillan, Basingstoke, 1988)

Mitchell, Arthur & Ó Snodaigh, Pádraig (eds), *Irish Political Documents 1916–1948* (Irish Academic Press, Dublin, 1985)

Mooney Eichacker, Joanne, *Irish Republican Women in America: lecture tours, 1916–1925* (Irish Academic Press, Dublin, 2003)

Moore, George, *Hail and Farewell* (edited by Richard Cave, Colin Smyth, Bucks 1976)

— *A Drama in Muslin* (reprint, Colin Smyth, London, 1981)

Morgan, Austen, *James Connolly: a political biography* (Pluto Press, Manchester, 1988)

Mulcahy, Risteárd, *Richard Mulcahy: A family memoir 1886–1971* (Aurelian Press, Dublin, 1999)

Mulvihill, Margaret, *Charlotte Desparde: a biography* (Pandora, London, 1989)

Murphy, Daniel J. (ed.), *The Journals of Lady Gregory* (Colin Smyth, London, 1978)

Murray, Peter, 'Irish Culture nationalism in the United Kingdom state: Politics and the Gaelic League 1900–18', *Irish Political Studies*, 8 (1993), pp. 55–72

Ní Shiublaigh, Máire, *The splendid years: recollections as told to Edward Kenny* (James Duffy, Dublin, 1955)

Norman, Diane, *Terrible Beauty: a life of Constance Markievicz* (Poolbeg, Dublin, 1988)

O'Brennan, Lily, 'We Surrender' in *An Cosantóir* vii, no 6 (June 1947), pp. 303–15

O'Brien Connolly, Nora, *Portrait of a Rebel Father* (Talbot Press, Dublin, 1935)

O'Brien, William, *Forth the Banners Go* (Three Candles, Dublin, 1969)

Ó Broin, León, *Dublin Castle and the 1916 Rising* (Helicon Press, Dublin, 1966)

— *Revolutionary Underground: the story of the IRB, 1858–1924* (Gill & Macmillan, Dublin, 1976)

— *Frank Duff: a biography* (Gill & Macmillan, Dublin, 1982)

— *Protestant nationalists in revolutionary Ireland. The Stopford Connection* (Gill & Macmillan, Dublin, 1985)

— *W.E. Wylie and the Irish Revolution 1916–1921* (Gill & Macmillan, Dublin, 1989)

O'Casey, Seán, *The Story of the Irish Citizen Army* (Dublin, 1919)

— 'Drums Under the Window' in *Autobiographies 1* (Papermac, London, 1963)

Ó Céirín, Kit & Cyril, *Women of Ireland: a biographic dictionary* (Tireolas, Galway, 1996)

O'Connor, Emmet, *A Labour History of Ireland 1824–1960* (Gill & Macmillan, Dublin, 1992)

O'Daly, Nora, 'The Women of Easter week' in *An t-Oglách* 29 (April 1926), pp. 3–6

O'Donnell, Ruan (ed.), *The impact of the 1916 Rising: Among the nations* (Irish Academic Press, Dublin, 2008)

O'Donoghue, Florence, *No Other Law: the story of Liam Lynch and the Irish Republican Army* (Irish Press, Dublin, 1954)

O'Dowd, Mary & Wichert, Sabine (eds), *Chattel, Servant or Citizen:*

Women's Status in Church, State, and Society (UCD Press, Dublin, 1995)

Ó Duibhir, Ciarán, *Sinn Féin: the first election 1908* (Drumlin Publications, Manorhamilton, 1993)

O'Dwyer, Peter, *Towards a History of Irish Spirituality* (The Columba Press, Dublin, 1995)

O'Faolain, Séan, *Constance Markievicz* (Jonathan Cape, London, 1934)

O'Farrell, Elizabeth, 'Events of Easter week' in *Catholic Bulletin*, vii, no. 4 (April 1917)

— 'Miss Elizabeth O'Farrell's story of the surrender' in *The Catholic Bulletin*, vii (May 1917), pp. 265–270, 329–334

O'Farrell, Padraic, *Who's Who, in the war of independence and Civil War 1916–23* (Lilliput Press, Dublin, 1997)

O'Grady, John, *The Life and Work of Sarah Purser* (Four Courts, Dublin, 1996)

O'Leary, Cornelius, *Irish Elections 1918–1977: parties' voters and proportional representation* (Gill & Macmillan Dublin, 1979)

O'Mahony, Seán, *Frongoch: University of Revolution* (FDR Teoranta, Dublin, 1987)

Ó Maitiú, Séamus, *W&R Jacob: Celebrating 150 years of Irish Biscuit Making* (Woodfield Press, Dublin, 2001)

O'Malley, Ernie, *On Another Man's Wound* (Anvil, Dublin, 2002)

O'Neill, Máire, 'The Dublin Women's suffrage association and its successors' in *The Dublin Historical record*, xxxviii (Sept. 1985), pp. 126–140

— *Jennie Wyse Power 1858–1941* (Blackwater Press, Dublin, 1991)

— *Grace Gifford Plunkett: and Irish Freedom* (Irish Academic Press, Dublin, 2000)

O'Riordan, John, J., *Irish Catholic Spirituality* (The Columba Press, Dublin, 1998)

O'Sullivan, Michael, *Seán Lemass* (Blackwater Press, Dublin, 1994)

Ó Tuama, Seán (ed.), *The Gaelic League Idea* (Mercier Press, Cork, 1972)

Owens, Rosemary Cullen, 'Votes for Ladies votes for women' in *Saothar*, 9, (1983) pp. 32–47

— *Smashing times: A history of Irish Women's Suffrage Movement, 1889–*

1922 (Attic Press, Dublin, 1984)

— *Louie Bennett* (Cork University Press, 2001)

— *A social history of Women in Ireland* 1870–1970 (Gill Macmillan, Dublin, 2005)

Parnell, Anna, *The tale of a great sham* (Arlen House, Galway, 1986)

Pašeta, Senia, *Before the Revolution: Nationalism, Social Change and Ireland's Catholic elite, 1979–1922* (Cork University Press, 1999)

— 'Nationalist responses to two royal visits to Ireland, 1900 and 1903' in *Irish Historical Studies* xxxi (Nov. 1999), pp. 489–504

Prunty, Jacinta, *Dublin Slums 1800-1925: A study in urban geography* (Irish Academic Press, Dublin, 1998)

Pyle, Hilary, *Susan L. Mitchell, Red-Headed Rebel: poet and mystic of the Irish Cultural Renaissance* (Woodfield Press, Dublin, 1998)

Pyne, Peter, 'The Third Sinn Féin Party 1923–26' in *Economic and Social Journal* (Oct. 1969), pp. 29–50, 229–256

Red Cross and Order of St John, *Reports of Joint War Committee of the Red Cross and the Order of St John* (1921; Reprinted by the Imperial War Museum, London, 2009)

Report of the Labour Commission to Ireland (Labour Party, London, 1921)

Reynolds, M., 'Cumann na mBan in the GPO', *An t-Oglách* 29 (March 1926), pp. 3–5

Ring, Jim, *Erskine Childers* (John Murray, London, 1996)

Robbins, Frank, *Under the starry plough: Recollections of the Irish Citizen Army* (The Academy Press, Dublin, 1977)

Robertson, Nora, *The Crowned Harp* (Allen Figgis, Dublin, 1960)

Roper, Esther, *Prison letters of Countess Markievicz* (Longmans Green, London, 1934)

Rowbotham, Sheila, *Women's consciousness, Man's world* (Penguin Books, London, 1973)

Saddlemeyer, Ann & Smith, Colin (eds), *Lady Gregory: fifty years after* (Colin Smyth, Buckinghamshire, 1987)

Sandford, Jeremy (ed.), *Mary Carbery's West Cork Journal 1898–1901* (Lilliput Press, Dublin, 1998)

Sanger, W.W., MD, *The History of Prostitution: its extent, causes, and effects throughout the world* (Medical publishing Co., New York, 1897)

Sharp, John, *Reapers of the harvest: The Redemptorists in Great Britain and Ireland 1843–1898* (Veritas Publications, Dublin, 1989)

Simonton, Deborah, *A history of European women's work: 1700 to the present* (Routledge, London, 1998)

Skinnider, Margaret, *Doing My Bit for Ireland* (Century, New York, 1917)

Snoddy, Oliver, 'Three by-elections of 1917' in *The Capuchin Annual* (Dublin, 1968), pp. 341–347

Stephens, James, *The Insurrection in Dublin* (Colin Smyth, London 1992)

Swinson, Arthur, *A Register of the Regiments and Corps of the British Army* (Archive Press, London, 1972)

Taaffe, Michael, *Those days are gone away* (Hutchinson, London, 1959)

Taillon, Ruth, *The women of 1916: when history was made* (Beyond the Pale publications, Dublin, 1996)

Taylor, Lawrence, *Occasions of Faith: an Anthropology of Irish Catholics* (Lilliput Press, Dublin, 1997)

TeBrake, Janet, K., 'Irish peasant women in revolt: the Land League years', *Irish Historical Studies,* xxviii (May 1992), pp. 63–80

Thurman, Judith, *A Life of Colette* (Bloomsbury, London, 1999)

Tombs, Robert (ed.), *Nationhood and nationalism in France* (Harper Collins, London, 1991)

Townshend, Charles, *Easter 1916: The Irish Rebellion* (Allen Lane & Penquin Books, London, 2005)

Tynan, Katharine, *Twenty-Five Years: Reminiscences,* London (J. Murray, London, 1913)

— *A little book of manners* (Dublin, 1918)

— *Memories* (Eveleigh Nash & Grayson, Edinburgh, 1924)

Valiulis Gialanella, Maryann, *General Richard Mulcahy: and the founding of the Irish Free State* (Irish Academic Press, Dublin, 1992)

— 'Power and gender in the Irish Free State', *Journal of Women's History,* xi (Winter/Spring 1995), pp. 117–135

— & O'Dowd, Mary (eds), *Women & Irish History* (Wolfhound Press, Dublin, 1997)

Van Voris, Jacqueline, *Constance de Markievicz: in the Cause of Ireland*

(Massachusetts University Press, 1967)

Walker, Brian M., *Parliamentary election results in Ireland 1918–90* (Royal Irish Academy, Dublin, 1993)

Ward, Margaret, *Unmanageable Revolutionaries: Women and Irish Nationalism* (Brandon Press, Kerry, 1983)

— *Maud Gonne: a life* (Pandora, London, 1990)

— *Hanna Sheehy Skeffington: a life* (Attic Press, Cork, 1997)

Warner, Marina, *Joan of Arc: The Image of a Female Legend* (Weidenfeld & Nicolson, New York, 1981)

Whelan, Bernadette, *United States Foreign Policy and Ireland: From Empire to Independence 1913-1929* (Four Courts Press Dublin 2006)

Wilmot, Irwin, *Betrayal in Ireland* (Belfast, undated)

Woods, Audrey, *Dublin Outsiders: a History of the Mendicity Institution, 1818–1998* (A & A Farmer, Dublin, 1998)

Wyse Power, Senator, 'My recollections of Anna Parnell' in *Dublin Metropolitan Magazine* (March DATE), pp. 15–17

Yeates, Pádraig, *Lockout: Dublin 1913* (Gill & Macmillan, Dublin, 2000)

Yeats, W.B., *Autobiographies* (Macmillan Press, London, 1980)

INDEX

W

Walker, Marie (see also Máire Ní
    Shiublaigh) 59
Walker, Mrs 107
Walsh, Anna 284
Walsh, J.J. 149
Walsh, Miss 109
Walsh, Miss M.T. 190
Walsh, Rev. Dr William 163, 256
Waterford 82, 120, 194, 209, 224,
    231, 239, 268
Wexford 82, 216, 231, 249, 260, 261,
    271, 328
White, Jack 83, 84, 90, 91, 334
White, Miss 333
White, Miss S. 31, 35
White, P. 53
Wicklow 93, 232, 235
Wigham, Joseph T. 256, 257
Williams, Miss 201
Willis, Richard 270
Wilson, Mrs 201
Wolfe Tone Memorial Committee
    58, 104, 186
Women's Auxiliary Corps 107
Women's Day 218
Women's International League for
    Peace and Freedom (WILPF)
    280, 281, 351
Women's National Health Associa-
    tion (WNHA) 78, 106, 174,
    208, 209
Women Delegates to the All Ireland
    Conference (WDIC) 11, 180,
    181, 187, 188, 189, 194, 200,
    349
Woods, Sir Robert 286
Wyse Power, Jennie 10, 15, 31, 32,
    33, 34, 35, 57, 93, 95, 96, 99,
    102, 109, 110, 119, 121, 158,
    163, 187, 188, 189, 190, 194,
    200, 201, 202, 217, 232, 237,
    253, 257, 260, 271, 288, 289,
    292, 293, 294, 299, 300, 301,
    302, 306, 307, 310, 311, 312,
    313, 316, 317, 318, 321, 322,
    326, 349

Wyse Power, Nancy 96, 120, 158,
    171, 215, 217, 218, 231, 260,
    284, 289, 293, 294, 299, 300,
    311, 326, 333, 342

Y

Yeats, Elizabeth 23, 24, 72
Yeats, Jack 26, 72
Yeats, Lily 23, 24, 72
Yeats, W.B. 26, 28, 52, 59, 65, 72, 229
Young, Ellen 58
Young, May 58

Z

Zola, Emile 55